International Logistics

Second Edition

Donald F. Wood
San Francisco State University

Anthony P. Barone
Independent Consultant

Paul R. Murphy
John Carroll University

Daniel L. Wardlow
San Francisco State University

AMACOM
American Management Association
New York • Atlanta • Brussels • Buenos Aires • Chicago • London • Mexico City
San Francisco • Shanghai • Tokyo • Toronto • Washington, D.C.

This publication is designed to provide accurate and authoritative information in regard to the subject matter covered. It is sold with the understanding that the publisher is not engaged in rendering legal, accounting, or other professional service. If legal advice or other expert assistance is required, the services of a competent professional person should be sought.

Library of Congress Cataloging-in-Publication Data

International logistics / Donald F. Wood . . . [et al.]—2nd ed.
    p. cm.
Includes bibliographical references and index.
    ISBN 0-8144-0666-1
    1. Physical distribution of goods—Management.   2. Business logistics.
3. International trade.   I. Wood, Donald F., 1935-
    HF5415.7 .I553 2002
    658.7—dc21

                                                                2002004267

Printing number

10   9   8   7   6   5   4   3   2   1

Contents

Preface

In preparing this second edition, we toyed briefly with changing its title. The change we considered was to use *supply chain* in place of *logistics*. We chose not to, mainly because supply chains are umbrellas that cover much more than logistics. We believe that logistics is that part of the supply chain responsible for the physical movement of materials and, sometimes, people.

A number of people and organizations helped us, and their assistance should be recognized. They include: Robert L. Argentieri, Eunice Coleman, Patricia J. Daugherty, Robert Derbin, Efstahios Efstathiou, Robert Hannus, Gary Hunter, Arne Jensen, Gothenburg University, Ken Knox, Brian Law, California Maritime Academy, Douglas Long, Eugene Magad, Nathan Muhlethaler, Dale S. Rogers, Robert Rouse, John Silvey, and Clyde Kenneth Walter.

This book is intended for use in both the business world and in classrooms. A separate *Instructor's Manual* is available from the publisher and may be requested on school letterhead.

Preface to the First Edition

Both academia and the real world are showing a vastly increased interest in international logistics. Although this book covers the entire topic, it may not contain sufficient detail to answer all questions. The topic—and the challenge—is much larger than any single book can cover!

A number of people helped us, and their assistance should be recognized. They include Robert L. Argentieri, Eunice Coleman, Patricia J. Daugherty, Robert Derbin, Robert Hannus, Ken Knox, Douglas Long, Eugene L. Magad, Dale S. Rogers, Robert Rouse, John Silvey, and Clyde Kenneth Walter.

This book is designed for both the business world and the classroom. A separate *Instructor's Manual* has been prepared and may be requested on school letterhead.

1

Overview

Introduction

This book is about international logistics and the role of international logistics systems in global supply chain management. *International* means that it will deal with transactions involving individuals or firms in more than one nation. *Logistics* means the organized movement of goods, services, and, sometimes, people. Logistics was originally a military term encompassing the processes to supply combat and troop support. In trade, logistics handles the physical movement of products between one or more participants in the supply chain. When we speak of international logistics systems, we mean the complex web of carriers, forwarders, bankers, information and communication companies, traders, and so on that facilitate international transactions, trades, and movements of goods and services. *Global supply chain management* refers to the complex integration of processes necessary to manage materials from their point of origin through manufacturing and shipment to the final consumer (or beyond, in the case of recycling).

While the book deals mainly with the flow of goods, it also mentions movements of people. They are important for several reasons. In the case of airlines, the movement of people often dictates the movement of aircraft that happen to have space for carrying cargo as well. Business travel is important. We also see movements of people across borders in search of better employment opportunities. Also, while we usually think in terms of moving goods to people, people also move toward goods. In towns along peaceful borders anywhere in the world, large numbers of daytime visitors cross into neighboring nations in search of bargains unavailable at home.

Many factors influence the flow of goods and people between nations. Political situations are very important. Trade between the U.S. and Iraq has been limited to humanitarian relief supplies since the Persian Gulf War of 1990 because the U.S. currently embargoes trade with the Iraqi political regime now in power in Baghdad. We now see rapidly evolving consumer economies in Russia and China, and these will have many impacts on trade and travel volumes and patterns. Friendly nations negotiate treaties to increase the flow of commerce between them. Examples of such comprehensive trade treaties include the North American Free Trade Agreement (NAFTA) and the trade union of the European Community. On the other hand, wars, boycotts, and terrorism have a dampening effect. Consider the 10 percent decline in gross domestic product (GDP) in Israel and the 40 percent decline in Palestinian GDP due to unrest in 2000 and 2001. Consumer confidence was shaken and a mild recession intensified in the United States by the terrorist attacks on the World Trade Center and the Pentagon in 2001.

The tragic events of September 11, 2001, are still too close to us to be fully evaluated, or even understood. The principal target of the terrorists, the World Trade Center in New York City was, among other things, a symbol of the ever increasing importance of world commerce. (What is believed to be the same group of terrorists exploded a bomb in the structure a few years ago.) At the risk of appearing to ignore the senseless loss of several thousand innocent people, we should point out the tragedy also has impacted upon international logistics.

On the morning of September 11, 2001, the Port of New York and New Jersey, one of the world's busiest ports, shut down. In the port area long lines of truckers, either hauling containers to docks or on their way to pick up loaded containers, stood motionless. These lines of trucks stretched for miles, blocking streets and snarling traffic. In the same day the nation's airlines were grounded and incoming international flights were diverted to Canada. Planes destined for the United States were held in Paris, London, and Tokyo. There was no sound of jet aircraft taking off from the region's several airports. Transport workers throughout the area stood idle, and looked from a distance at the black and gray smoke pouring out of the cavity at ground zero. Almost immediately all bridges and tunnels in the area were also closed, tying up traffic in the several hundred mile stretch between Boston and northern Virginia. In short, almost all traffic came to a halt and some communication networks were not functioning.

Day two was not much better. Then, gradually, the transportation arteries were open and goods again began to flow. Carriers and forwarders had to make many adjustments. That would make another story. Our point is that the terrorist attack brought commerce through a major hub to a halt and caused interruptions that took weeks and months to repair. Our international supply chains are vulnerable to attack. Security, or lack of security, are now topics of vital importance. Today's supply chain manager must now recognize that the international logistics system is susceptible to terrorist attacks. New security requirements add to the costs of doing business and new elements of risk have been added to the logistics equations.

Economic conditions and relative economic strengths also influence trade patterns. Changes in relative values of two nations' currencies influence amounts and directions of trade and tourism between them. Also, they influence the carrier's cost of doing business since the firm's revenues and costs are in several fluctuating currencies. Some U.S. airlines have stopped serving certain developing countries because they can't use the local currency earned there. The carrier fears being paid in declining currencies while accruing charges that must be paid in a currency that is gathering strength. Shifting currency values add an element of uncertainty to all international transactions.

Since the mid-1970s, petroleum and its price have had a significant impact upon international logistics. Petroleum is the single largest commodity to move by sea, and the demand for tankers has repercussions throughout all international shipping markets. Oil spills from tankers are a matter of continual concern. Movements of coal depend upon the price of oil, although to most users, coal is a less desirable fuel. Fuel represents a major cost item for both sea and air carriers. In times of high fuel prices, air and sea carriers often add a fuel surcharge to their freight rates, and this impacts shippers as an added cost of moving along the supply chain.

Technological improvements also influence international logistics. The most pronounced one as we enter a new century has been the revolution in information management in international logistics. The Internet has provided access to a host of facilitating tools for managing global supply chains. Managers today are able to control information about inventory in transit in the same ways that managers once controlled actual inventory stocks. Global logistics systems have become quite predictable and reliable due to this enhanced information flow, and thus have become more manageable and precise. We are now seeing the beginnings of routinized logistics in space. The Italian government has contributed three containerized space freight modules to the development of the international Space Station Alpha. Looking to the not-too-distant future, space logistics opens up logistical opportunities and challenges of its own.

Environmental protection issues are also having an impact. Many nations are enacting more stringent packaging regulations in an effort to increase resource recycling. Aircraft engine noise restrictions are forcing airlines to retire aircraft from some markets (although they still can be used in some parts of the world). Double hull tankers are now being required in U.S. ports to reduce the likelihood of oil spills. However, as some nations enact stricter environmental and worker safety measures, manufacturing is sometimes shifted to those nations with less restrictive standards or lax enforcement. One recent problem has been the dumping of toxic wastes in nations willing to import those wastes for a fee.

International logistics is more difficult to manage than domestic logistics because the assumptions made by managers may not be as reliable, situations are generally less stable, the geography is much broader, and monitoring logistics processes is more complex. Business practices and standards differ from nation to nation. Consider the problems of a global paint manufacturer. Many pigments and other paint ingredients have regulatory limitations regarding products with which they may or may not be used. ClearCross, an international trade software firm, is developing global regulatory information systems to streamline the global operations of firms with such complex supply chain problems.[1]

Cultural differences also play major roles in selling and establishing ongoing relationships. The hard sell may be effective on the streets of Brooklyn but totally futile in Japan. The German businessman may be very direct and precise in price negotiations, while the Italian may be very deliberately and expertly coy. The American may want everything in writing, in contract form, whereas personal relationships will count for everything with the Saudi. Indeed, insisting too much on legalisms may be offensive to a foreign businessman and cause the deal to collapse.

Systems of jurisprudence vary also. Contract law and the uniform commercial code as known in the United States are not universal. Firing a distributor in Venezuela, Argentina, or Saudi Arabia is not like firing a distributor in Hong Kong. Indeed, it may be very difficult to impossible to fire a distributor in certain countries.

Furthermore, enforcement of existing laws may be spotty. A number of African ports are plagued by blatantly illegal practices, supported by corrupt port officials. Take, for example, the case of a two-month nightmare faced by a Maltese-flagged ship in the port of Conakry, Ghana:

> It was supposed to be a simple delivery of bagged rice. . . . During that time, the ship was repeatedly pilfered by local labor, attacked by armed bandits, and faced hostile, corrupt port officials. After nearly two months of being stuck in port, the bunker to power the vessel was running out. The captain took a big risk and ordered the ship to sail full steam from Conakry, even though port officials still held the vessel's certificates.[2]

---

[1]Biederman, David (2001), "Across Borders and Beyond," *Journal of Commerce Week,* March 26–April 1, 2001, p. 31.

[2]Timlen, Thomas (2000), "Troubled Waters," *American Shipper,* October 2000, p. 26.

The ship was eventually issued new certificates by the government of Malta and changed its name.

International logistics is clearly more challenging and costly than domestic logistics. Significant cost differences exist for the increased inventory needed due to the length of international transportation times. The tradeoffs between inventory cost and transportation cost become magnified in international logistics, rendering some domestic solutions to those tradeoffs irrelevant to global movement of goods. A second category of increased cost is the complex documentation that is generally required in international trade but is nearly absent in domestic trade.

International Logistics for the Firm

There are many definitions of logistics. The U.S.-based Council of Logistics Management defines logistics as the process of "planning, implementing, and controlling the physical and information flows concerned with materials and final goods from point of origin to point of usage."[3] Most professional literature today states that the following are logistics functions, although many firms do not include all of them under their logistics umbrella:

> customer service; demand forecasting; documentation flow; handling returns; inter-plant movements; inventory management (inbound, plant, and outbound); parts/service support; materials handling; order processing; plant and warehouse site selection; production scheduling; protective packaging; purchasing; salvage scrap disposal; traffic management; and warehouse and distribution center management.[4]

All of these functions will be covered in this book, sometimes from more than one viewpoint. Also inherent in logistics are the information, communications, control, and management mechanisms necessary to effectively manage a logistics system. Most of the discussion in the book will deal with private-sector transactions, although in international transactions, sometimes a government is a buying or selling party, or both. The discussion of all these different activities is scattered throughout the book. In part because many concepts of international logistics are new, they and the relationships between and among them are not universally agreed upon. In some instances the reader, the practitioner, or the supply chain manager will have to determine the proper ways of integrating them.

In international logistics, there are many different participants: the buyers, the sellers, the carriers, the intermediaries or middlemen, and, sometimes, the

---

[3]Council of Logistics Management website: *http://www.clml.org*

[4]*Encyclopedia Britannica* (1993), Chicago, Encyclopedia Britannica, Inc., Vol. 28, pp. 878–882.

government. It will be hard to know whose viewpoint is being taken. Traditionally, the viewpoint taken is that of the exporter, although importing is equally important. The following diagram shows the general flow of goods from a supply chain management perspective:

> sourcing raw materials > components or sub-assemblies > production line > wholesaler > retailer > customer

A slightly different grouping of these activities as seen from different perspectives would be: 1) procurement (the relationship between the firm and its suppliers); 2) conversion management (what the firm does with inputs); and 3) physical distribution management (the relationship between the firm and its customers).

While the general flow of goods appears straightforward, its implementation can be complex and roundabout. For example, Levi Strauss, an American clothing manufacturer headquartered in San Francisco, manufactures goods worldwide. Tracking its U.S. production of "Slates" (dressy slacks for men and women) gives an interesting example of implementation complexity. The fabric for the pants is manufactured in both the U.S. and Mexico and travels by truck to Miami, Florida. In Miami, the fabric is cut according to design patterns and matched up with required ancillary materials such as labels, buttons, and zippers (also manufactured in the U.S. and shipped by truck to Miami). The cut sets are then shipped by ocean container freight to a manufacturing-in-bond trade zone in the Dominican Republic. The cut sets are sewn together there and returned by ocean container freight to Miami. As the goods enter and leave the manufacturing-in-bond trade zone in the Dominican Republic duty free, they are subject to examination by customs authorities in both the United States and the Dominican Republic. Once the goods are returned to Miami, they are shipped by truck to a Levi's distribution center in Little Rock, Arkansas where they are sorted and stored for reshipment (usually by truck, but sometimes by air) to Levi's retail store customers.

Levi's takes advantage of lower labor costs in the Dominican Republic for the time-consuming assembly of the pants. Because the goods are held in a foreign trade zone within the Dominican Republic at all times, Levi's can state their Slates are "Made in the U.S.A." The goods have never really "entered" the Dominican Republic, since their assembly step takes place in the foreign trade zone. To complicate the logistics just a bit more, occasionally orders are rushed, with the substitution of air freight to and from the Dominican Republic special trade zone.

Once such complex systems are established, their operations become routine. But even the routine has exceptions, which require the intervention of logistics managers. Levi's once lost an entire aircraft full of Slates cut sets when the plane crashed on takeoff from Miami en route to the Dominican Republic. Levi's has also lost whole container loads of cut sets and finished Slates when the containers fell into the ocean off containerships encountering rough seas.[5] As a result, there are probably a number of very well-dressed sharks swimming in the Bermuda Triangle today!

However, more than goods flow in international logistics. The payment must go from the buyer to the seller; and there is a flow in both directions of "paperwork" (documents may be on paper, or increasingly in electronic form). To explain the various flows one can use the concept of channels.

Channels are networks and have been used to explain the functioning of marketing arrangements. The transaction channel handles contracting and trading, while the distribution channel deals with the physical movement of product. The channels are separated from each other, that is, a firm may locate sales offices in a different set of cities from where it locates distribution warehouses. However, the two channels are linked to the extent that sales or payments "trigger" release of goods to the buyer. This book adapts and expands this approach in an attempt to better understand international logistics operations. For our purposes, three channels will be discussed: the *transaction channel,* which handles the buying, selling and collection of payment; the *distribution channel,* through which the good moves physically; and the *documentation/communications* channel.

The book shall discuss also the intermediaries, whose role is to help the channels operate more smoothly. Shippers and carriers have varying involvement in foreign transactions and need these intermediaries to help in all, or at least some, situations. The facilitating role of intermediaries is important. Advice to a firm thinking of its first export or import shipment remains the same: "Contact a freight forwarder."

One consultant suggested four evolutionary stages for the shipper's involvement in international logistics:

Stage 1—we focus on today because of a crisis. Our effectiveness measure is actual cost versus sales, and examples of our activities would be arranging to receive containers or to work with foreign freight forwarders.

Stage 2—we focus on this month because of budget pressure. Our effectiveness measure is actual cost versus budget, and examples of our activities would be arranging export shipments, or negotiating with overseas suppliers of transportation services.

---

[5]Author interview with Debbie Gross, Levi Strauss and Company, July 3, 2001.

Stage 3—we focus on this year because of an improvement program. Our effectiveness measure is actual versus annual goals, and examples of our activities would be setting up overseas distribution, setting up just-in-time (JIT) suppliers; or production scheduling.

Stage 4—we focus on the long term because we want to gain strategic advantage. Our effectiveness measure is world competition, and examples of our activities would be integrating operations planning and control worldwide or participating in strategic decisions worldwide.[6]

Within logistics channels, the concept of cost trade-offs is used. The manager may pay more for one element of service in order to save an even larger amount on a different element. Here's an example of trade-offs related to the shipment of museum-quality works of art:

> Identifying the risks and developing techniques to minimize them is the work of transport managers from museums and auction houses, forwarders specializing in art, and the chosen carriers. Developing transportation strategies based on mode of transport, packing requirements, supervision, and insurance, and determining how they inter-relate can be compared to the techniques used by commercial and industrial risk management firms. Thus higher packing costs may be balanced out by lower supervision expenses; using an escort or courier may lower insurance premiums and packing costs; shipping by air freight, the rates of which are based on volume as opposed to weight, may provide further savings.[7]

Logistics also serves as an integrating function in supply chain management. Because of the long distances and lead times involved with global sourcing and distribution, top quality logistics systems development and management are essential to minimize costs and maximize customer service in global supply chains. Most modern logistics and supply chain thought also includes the development of "partnerships" with longtime suppliers or customers. International logistics helps to integrate different parties in the various logistics channels throughout the world.

Outline for This Book

This book is divided into four parts. The introductory part consists of Chapters 1 through 3. Chapter 2 deals with government's interest in international trade and transportation, and includes such topics as: earning foreign exchange; issues of

---

[6]*Distribution,* October 1987, p. 14. Material based on an A.T. Kearney presentation.

[7]KLM Cargovision, "Packing up the Pieces," 12 (January/February 1990).

national defense including civilian reserve capability; flags of convenience; government subsidies for international carriers; cargo preference; air route allocation; boycotts; dumping; and export administration regulations and controls. Chapter 3 deals with logistics and transportation in different parts of the world. Compared with the United States, there are differences in units of measure; value of time; capital/labor trade-offs; and suitability of Western equipment. Developing nations often have hard currency shortages, and use pre-shipment inspections to protect their limited hard currency supply. The organization of groups of nations into trade blocs is also described.

Part 2 of the book covers the international transportation system, and consists of six chapters. Chapter 4 is about ocean vessels and discusses types and sizes of ships. There are bulk carriers: tankers, dry cargo carriers, and LNG ships, and there are break-bulk carriers, container, LASH and Ro/Ro ships. Chapter 5 deals with the charter market for bulk ocean carriers and covers both voyage charters and time charters. There is discussion of the supply of and demand for ships, and the relationship between tramp and liner markets. Chapter 6 handles the ocean liner system, which is the method by which liner companies operating in the same market control competition. The book will cover capacity restriction/sharing agreements; rate making; shippers' associations; and service contracts.

Chapter 7 is about international air carriers. It starts with a discussion of the development of international aviation and the Chicago and Bermuda conferences held during the 1940s that determined how airline markets should be allocated. Also discussed are bilateral agreements, passenger airlines (both scheduled and chartered), all cargo carriers, overnight parcel services, and air freight forwarders. Chapter 8 covers surface transportation to and from U.S. ports and to and from Canada and Mexico. Included are discussions of containerization and land bridges. Chapter 9 deals with seaports, airports, and canals, focusing on port and airport functions and markets. Chapter 9 also covers canals, bridges, tunnels, and their influences on the flow of trade.

Part 3 of this book is about international logistics activities other than transportation. Chapter 10 discusses logistics functions and lists and describes many of the intermediaries who help the channels function. Examples of intermediaries are freight forwarders, export packers, and customs house brokers. Chapter 11 covers the sales transaction and includes terms of sales, handling of payments, letters of credit, and risks of payment. Chapter 12 handles documentation and insurance in more detail, covering various documents used, cargo insurance, risks and perils (damage, loss, fraud), loss prevention, and claims settlement.

Chapter 13 discusses the logistics of product movement and includes inventories, warehousing, facility site location, protective packaging, transportation management, hazardous materials, and customer service. Chapter 14 covers international sourcing and interplant logistics. This discussion includes importing, interfirm/interplant logistics, and related party transactions.

Part 4 concludes the book and attempts to pull its various sections together, in the same manner that logistics can pull a firm together. Chapter 15 provides a unique application of international logistics concepts to famine relief problems. Chapter 16 looks at international logistics as an integrating tool for global supply chain management and it covers logistics partnerships. Chapter 17 covers future issues in international—and space—transportation and logistics.

Summary

International logistics deals with goods transactions involving parties in two or more nations. The word *logistics* was originally used for military applications but today covers commercial activities as well. Goods move through channels, as do orders, payments, and documents. The book will discuss these three channels and how they are integrated. In addition, it will discuss intermediaries and how they ensure that the channels function relatively smoothly.

International logistics must take into account difference in cultures, currency, and transportation systems. According to most accounts, this makes international logistics more difficult than domestic logistics. The relationships between and among many logistical activities are not standardized; they still are determined on a case-by-case basis.

End-of-Chapter Questions

1. Describe logistics as a business process.
2. What is global supply chain management? What is the role of international logistics in global supply chain management?
3. Make a list of logistics activities and participants in global supply chains.
4. What are channels? Give examples of different channel flows.
5. What are channel intermediaries? Give examples of different types of intermediaries.
6. What is a cost trade-off? Give an example from international logistics practice.

CASE • *WWE: Emergency Response to Terrorism*

Julie McDonald had just arrived at her desk at World Wide Express (WWE) headquarters in Louisville, Kentucky. It was a beautiful, sunny, and warm September morning, and Julie's view of the WWE plane-loading ramp was quiet. All WWE flights had departed hours ago from the massive sorting facility at Louisville International Airport, and the planes were in cities all over the world awaiting that day's cargo. She watched the sun glint off the tail of a giant WWE MD-11 as it sat in the maintenance hangar a few thousand feet down the ramp.

Julie had worked for WWE for eight years, during a time of rapid international expansion. She had spent time working in France and Japan for WWE, and now was a manager responsible for balancing loads on WWE's international flights that connected with the Louisville domestic hub. Her job was a very "hands-on" position that involved constantly solving fast-changing puzzles of numbers of flights, aircraft capacity, flight times, and parcel volumes.

Just a couple minutes before 8 A.M., Julie walked out of her office into the hallway to grab her first cup of coffee of the day. From a conference room down the hall, she heard a very loud discussion competing with sound from a television set. She walked into the conference room to see five of her fellow WWE colleagues transfixed by the events unfolding on television. To her horror, she saw CNN reporting that an office tower at the World Trade Center had been hit by a plane. She thought to herself: surely only a small plane, it couldn't have been a jet. But as she watched the live CNN feed from New York, a second plane, clearly a very large jetliner, plowed into the second tower of the World Trade Center with horrible explosive force. The WWE employees were stunned speechless; they couldn't move their eyes from the television screen.

Nancy Bourget, a French WWE manager now stationed in Louisville, was the first to break the silence. "Mon Dieu! This is terrorism. Oh, the people at work in New York!" Then the gray faces in the room blanched as Julie said "Whose planes were those?"

Julie ran from the conference room back to her office and called the WWE flight operations center. "Bob, flight ops" was the answer on the phone. "Bob, Julie McDonald in load management. Whose planes were those?"

"We don't know; we're on the phone to the FAA right now. We think they were passenger planes, not freight. We're also contacting the few planes we have up right now. I'll call you back when I know something." Click.

Julie pointed her Web browser to ABCnews.com, which was sending a live video of the disaster in New York City. She didn't know what to do. All she could think about were the thousands of people who work in the World Trade Center. Did they have a way to escape? Was there time for them to get out safely? As she stared at the monitor, the most surreal horror unfolded before her. A tower in flames collapsed as if it imploded. Julie's phone rang once, twice, three times, four times before she realized her phone was ringing. "Julie, load management."

"Bob in flight ops. Our planes are OK. The FAA is telling us to hold a line open for an urgent set of flight operations orders."

"Bob. One of the towers just collapsed. I can't believe I'm seeing this." She heard confused discussion on the other end of the line.

"Gotta go," and Bob hung up the phone. Julie returned to the conference room to find a dozen colleagues. Several were crying. One had become violently ill and ran to a restroom. Julie announced that they weren't WWE planes. Her announcement met with blank stares. Nancy said, "Both towers are gone."

Julie's mind wandered beyond the incomprehensible events unfolding before her. Something inside was reminding her that this disaster would have immediate consequences for WWE and its customers. She had to return to work. There was no alternative.

As she reached her office, the phone rang again. "It's Bob, Julie. The FAA has immediately grounded all U.S. airspace. Everything has got to land immediately. We just turned around our early flight out of Germany and sent it back. The flight from Japan is gonna land in the next hour in Anchorage. We have no idea how long this is going to last, but the FAA has never cleared all airspace over the whole country before. This is serious. You need to get your service interruption contingency plan going."

"Right. Just got the email from Ron here too . . . did you get it? Meeting in the first floor conference room in 15 minutes."

"Um, yeah . . . I'll be there."

Julie knew the contingency plan by heart. She'd written the section on load management. But they had never anticipated grounding their entire U.S. flight operations! She grabbed her contingency plan manual and a notepad and headed to the conference room.

The room was tense, and small conversations were hushed. Bob stood to begin the meeting. "This is unbelievable. But we have to focus here. They weren't WWE planes, and the FAA is shutting down all domestic airspace, including international arrivals. We've contacted all our planes, they're OK, and we've returned them to base wherever possible. We've had a couple of landings where we shouldn't be . . . got a flight from London just set down in Gander, as in Gander Newfoundland. The FAA said to expect 24 to 72 hours. Just unbelievable."

Julie began to think of the WWE customers. Surely they would understand this service interruption was extraordinary. But how could WWE continue to function if no flights were moving?

Questions for *WWE: Emergency Response to Terrorism*

1. WWE offers several delivery time options, including next-day, two-day, and three-day shipping. What are the consequences of a disruption of 24 hours for each of those categories of service?

2. What are the consequences of a disruption of 72 hours for each of those categories of service? What consideration should be given to WWE service guarantees to their customers?

3. WWE operates its flight services on a "hub and spoke" system where packages are flown to an intermediate destination, sorted, and then flown to their final destination city. With the Louisville hub out of service, should all international hubs also be shut down? Should WWE flight operations worldwide be halted?

4. If the flight disruption lasts longer than 24 hours, what are some alternatives WWE could use to keep parcels moving?

5. If the flight disruption lasts longer than 24 hours, how might you modify the "hub and spoke" system temporarily?

6. What would you do with the packages on board the London-to-Louisville flight that had landed in Gander?

2

Governments' Interest and Involvement in International Logistics

Introduction

All nations support international trade for a number of reasons. Most of the reasons deal with promoting their own economies. A second set of reasons relates to national defense. This chapter will cover both topics. It will also look at many other ways that policies of individual or collective governments influence flows within the supply chain.

Economic Importance

All governments of the world are interested in both international trade and international transportation. This is for many reasons. It is generally believed that each country produces what it can best, and then is able to trade some of its surpluses for goods or services that other nations have to offer. All nations would like to export more than they import, in order to generate a positive balance of trade, which helps bolster both the country's currency and its employment.

Conversely, nations attempt to limit imports by assessing duties on them, or establishing quotas, although sometimes the purpose of these controls is to protect local producers. There are also many "hidden" tariff barriers that discourage the importation and flow of foreign goods. Logistics systems must be designed to take them into account.

There are several costs associated with international logistics, and they are in addition to the price of the product. If a good is either exported or imported, there are costs of transport and insurance. If these services are provided by the exporting nation's firms, then the importing nation must import the goods, then provide the transportation for carrying the goods to the port of entry and the insurance for the movement. If the importing nation can provide the transportation and insurance, then they are "importing" only the goods. For example, "British exporters have been encouraged by government agencies to sell on a delivered price basis for two reasons. The customer, it is said, wants a price he can compare locally and the British exporter selling delivered is more likely to nominate a British forwarder or carrier."[1] Later chapters will deal with terms of sale; they are of significance to more than merely the buyer and the seller.

The examples given so far deal only with importing and exporting nations, as though there were only two. Actually, there are more. The term *cross-trader* applies to a nation whose firms carry or facilitate the movement of goods between two other nations. An example would be nation A's vessels carrying commerce between nations B and C. Norway is a good example; they operate many more ships than are needed for their own exports and imports.

To give an example of the importance of these international transport payments, here are U.S. foreign trade figures for 2000 (in billions of dollars)[2]:

Exports of goods, services & income receipts	1,418
Merchandise	772
Travel	82
Passenger fares	20
Other transportation	30
Imports of goods, services & income	−1,809
Merchandise	−1,441
Travel	−64
Passenger fares	−24
Other transportation	−41

Expenditures for travel, passenger fares, and other transportation paid to U.S.-based firms by foreigners show up as exports, while those that U.S. citizens and firms pay to foreign firms (including cross-traders) show up as imports. Expenditures by U.S. citizens paid to U.S. firms—for example, buying an airline ticket on United Airlines from New York to Rome—would not show up in this tally. Exports of transportation equipment are also important and help contribute to the nation's balance of payments. Boeing is one of the largest exporters in the U.S.

Another way to earn foreign exchange is to supply laborers to work in other

---

[1]G. J. Davies, "The International Logistics Concept," *International Journal of Physical Distribution and Materials Management* (vol. 17, no. 2, 1987), p. 23.

[2]U. S. Bureau of Economic Analysis website, July 16, 2001.

nations and send part of their earnings home. Some nations supply merchant sea-men, the Philippines being a frequently-cited example. "Bangladesh, one of the world's poorest places, gratefully receives $1.25 billion a year from its 200,000 or so working in the Persian Gulf, Malaysia and South Korea."[3]

Handling foreign trade also creates jobs with carriers, in the handling of export/import shipments, and in servicing overseas transportation. This chapter deals almost entirely with government involvement with international transportation. Remember that international transportation is but one cost component of international logistics, and, in turn, international logistics is but one cost component of international trade.

National Defense Concerns

In the late 1980s, the Cold War was declared dead, and the U.S. government's concerns for national defense assumed a lower priority. Had this book been written two decades ago, it's likely that an entire chapter or two would have been devoted to issues related to international transportation and the nation's defense. Many U.S. policies still in effect were drawn up with grander defense concerns in mind.

As the United States decides how to react to the terrorist attacks on the World Trade Center and the Pentagon, there will be renewed thought given to national defense. What roles will transportation play? Only a few years ago novelist Tom Clancy gave readers a preview of what World War III (a conventional war) might have been like. Interestingly, much of Clancy's war was dependent upon the United States' ability to resupply its NATO allies across the North Atlantic. In one scene, Ed Morris, captain of a U.S. Navy frigate used for convoy escort duty, was watching the assembly of a fleet of merchant vessels at the mouth of the Delaware River. He noted:

> The military Airlift Command's huge aircraft could ferry the troops across to Germany where they would be mated with their pre-positioned equipment, but when their unit loads of munitions ran out, the resupply would have to be ferried across the way it always had been, in ugly, fat, slow merchant ships—targets. Maybe the merchies weren't so slow any more, and were larger than before, but there were fewer of them. During his naval career, the American merchant fleet had fallen sharply, even supplemented by these federally funded vessels. Now a submarine could sink one ship and get the benefit it would have achieved in World War II by sinking four or five.[4]

---

[3]*The Journal of Commerce* (December 26, 1996), p. 1A.

[4]Tom Clancy, *Red Storm Rising,* (New York: G. P. Putnam's Sons, 1986), p. 151.

For many years there was a close relationship between cargo ships and armed vessels. Countries used their navy to protect their merchant fleets. During the War of 1812, the U.S. commissioned over 500 privateers to attack British shipping. The U.S. Army Corps of Engineers today is responsible for dredging harbors and navigation channels. This involvement of the Corps in navigation projects dates to the 1820s, after it had been found that during the War of 1812 the U.S. couldn't move a defending army fast enough to keep up with an enemy army that could move along the coast by sea. The Corps became involved in developing a series of inland canals that could be used to move a defending army.

Admiral Alfred T. Mahan wrote *The Influence of Sea Power upon History, 1660–1783* in 1890; this book influenced President Theodore Roosevelt to decide that the U.S. must become a world naval power, which it did. Events during both World Wars I and II took a terrible toll on U.S. merchant shipping and, at various times during both wars, lack of merchant shipping capability sharply limited the military's ability to move. In both the Spanish American War and World War I, the U.S. had many problems of port congestion. During World War I, the government had to take over U.S. railroads because of congestion at East Coast ports. Early in both World Wars, the U.S., while still neutral, sided with Britain and sent it supplies. German submarines attacked the U.S. vessels, and this helped lead the U.S. into war. Rights of neutrals at sea are questionable even today—an example in the late 1980s being the Iran–Iraq war.

There are also questions of producing ships and airplanes. As mentioned above, in both World Wars the U.S. had tremendous need for shipping capacity. In World War II, it wasn't until 1943 that the U.S. was building merchant tonnage faster than it was being sunk. However, in World War I, not a single warplane built in the U.S. reached Europe before the war's end and only 500 of the 3,000 ships built in the U.S. were done before the end of the war. Interestingly, after both wars there was a glut of tonnage remaining and this made it hard for the commercial shipbuilding industry to sell new ships. At the end of World War II there was a glut of DC-3 airplanes, and many were destroyed outright on the ground.

Initially in war, civilian equipment is drawn into military use. In the early days of World War II, U.S. airline aircraft carried troops to the Aleutians, which were believed in danger of invasion; and commercial inter- and intracoastal freighters were called into government service and used to sail around Africa in order to supply the British defending the Suez Canal. (At war's end, these freighters were unable to recapture their domestic markets.) Figure 2–1 is from World War II and shows troops and their equipment stored on the deck of a freighter in the Pacific.

In the post-World War II era, the U.S. used aircraft to supply Berlin during the Soviet blockade. The U.S. Interstate system (whose correct title is "The National System of Interstate and Defense Highways") was justified, in part, by its

Figure 2–1 World War II troops and their equipment on the deck of a freighter in the Pacific. Photo courtesy U.S. Coast Guard.

possible value during wartime. At the signing of the bill authorizing the system, President Eisenhower recalled how the German Autobahn was virtually impossible to destroy by bombing (except at bridges), while railroads were easy to disrupt. Clearances above the U.S. Interstate roads were dictated by the heights needed to move a trailer-borne missile of the 1950s era.

The U.S. blockade of Cuba in the early 1960s forced the Soviets to back down because they lacked military seapower. After that setback, Russia began expanding its navy and merchant marine to a point where it was equal to that of the U.S. The Soviet merchant fleet functioned as a cross-trader earning hard western currencies. It was very active in U.S.–Pacific trades until it became the target of boycotts following the Soviet invasion of Afghanistan in 1979.

One of the more interesting examples of the relationship between commercial and military transport comes from the British experience in the Falklands. At the beginning of hostilities, Britain converted the QEII and six cargo ships so they could be used to support military operations. (Plans already existed for making the conversions; the appropriate vessels nearest to Britain were requisitioned first.) The British used a 100-ship task force, including nine 25,000-ton tankers from BP (British Petroleum, a private company). They refueled warships at sea. (In the 1970s BP and the Ministry of Defense had agreed on outfitting some commercial tankers so that they could refuel combat ships at sea.) Technically, the British Government chartered these vessels; they could have requisitioned them. The tankers were positioned along the South Atlantic and relied on satellite navigation to keep their position.[5] From a logistics standpoint, the Falklands' location was probably about the worst location for the British to have to fight. The challenges of supply were probably greater than the challenges of battle.

The U.S. military maintains several "fast-deployment" vessels throughout the world. They contain all the heavy equipment that would be required by, say, a division of army troops. U.S. response to a situation where military force was needed would be to fly the troops and have them met by a fast-deployment ship that carries the tanks, artillery, etc. that they need. Some of the current fast-deployment vessels were originally built for Sea Land in the early 1970s. They were designated as "SL-7s" and fell into disuse when fuel prices rose in the mid-1970s. Eventually, Sea Land sold them to the Navy, which converted them to fast-deployment vessels.

> In the war against Iraq that took place in late 1990 and early 1991, the U.S. government relied heavily on foreign-flag vessels.
>
> One of the lessons learned as a result of Desert Storm and Desert Shield was the need for faster sealift. Airlift support worked quite well and during the first week the Air Force had deployed ten squadrons of F-15 and F-16 aircraft with support personnel and their equipment. . . . Sealift, however, did not go as smoothly. The Navy's Fast Ship class, capable of thirty knots or better, encountered mechanical problems. The most serious breakdown was one ship lost its boiler and had to be towed to Spain for repairs. Other problems included delays with the activation of the Ready Reserve Fleet, which is kept in different stages of readiness, and problems with the sourcing of commercial ships to be chartered by the Military Sealift Command. Mechanical problems delayed shipments by as much as three weeks or more in the initial stages of the buildup of forces in the Gulf. In the end, 213 conventional ships using 91 foreign flag vessels were used during the Gulf War.[6]

---

[5]Operation "Corporate" BP Shipping Ltd's. Involvement in the Falkland Island Crisis, 1982, published by BP, ca. 1983, p. 9.

[6]M. Theodore Farris II and Don Welch, "High-Speed Ship Technology: Maritime Vessels for the 21st Century," *Transportation Journal* (Fall 1998), p. 125.

The services also rely on private-sector contractors to carry some of their loads. Commercial ocean and air carriers with military contracts have a provision that they will place a certain percent of their capacity under military control, if needed.[7] One merchant marine contract clause was that 50 percent of a line's U.S.-flag (that is, registered in the United States) tonnage would be made available, half (25 percent) available in 30 days, and the second half (25 percent) in 60 days. "Mothball" fleets on both coasts have old merchant ships that could be restored to service. They are equipped with devices that slow electric current to retard rust (cathodic protection), and work orders for bringing them up to operating condition are updated periodically. During the Vietnam War, 101 ships were taken out of the mothball fleet for carrying military supplies. In the more recent difficulties with Iraq, the age and condition of vessels in the reserve fleet limited their utilization, and the U.S. government found it easier to charter vessels flying other flags.

An issue involving use of private-sector ships during war is: To how much danger may or should civilian employees be exposed? Can they be ordered into combat areas? (In World War II, British merchant sailors had more casualties per capita than did servicemen in the British armed forces.)

There are many technology transfers between commercial and military applications. A few examples are radar, satellite navigation (the same grid to be used by intercontinental ballistic missiles is used by commercial Global Positioning Systems), helicopters, hovercraft, all-wheel drive trucks, the jeep, and intermodal containers. At various times in the development of aviation some bombers and transport aircraft appeared to be first cousins. Or, look at the Douglas DC-3, first introduced as a commercial aircraft in 1935. A large number were built for the military during World War II (it's one of the top ten models still, in terms of units produced). During the Normandy invasion, they carried paratroopers, and then supplies the next day. In Vietnam, DC-3s were used as slow-moving gunships to strafe the sides of hills.

A book dealing with U. S. government policy toward the merchant marine or toward international airlines would be a better forum for addressing issues regarding the adequacy of programs in terms of meeting defense transportation needs. A few topics worth mentioning are:

The use of commercial carriers for espionage purposes. For example, Soviets used airline aircraft for espionage, and they were not allowed to fly over

---

[7]See: Ira Lewis and Daniel Y. Coulter, "The Voluntary Intermodal Sealift Agreement: Strategic Transportation for National Defense," *The Transportation Journal* (Fall 2000), pp. 26–33.

locations such as Groton, Connecticut, site of a major U.S. submarine installation. The U.S. CIA also has operated an airline as a front for some of its operations.

In peacetime, how much cargo and passengers should move on civilian and how much on military carriers?

Inter-service rivalry hurts, often with respect to development of equipment.

Keeping hardware suppliers alive during peacetime.

What is "effective control" over U.S.-owned vessels flying a foreign flag?

How adaptable is equipment being adopted for commercial uses for military purposes?

U.S. has too little sea or airlift capability for any major military operation overseas.

U.S. has little commercial shipbuilding capacity.

U.S. dependence on oil imports means it must be able to protect the sea lanes carrying the oil.

Is the U.S. training enough people to design, build, operate, and maintain all the transport and logistics equipment that it might need in wartime? (Many reserve vessels activated for supplying Desert Shield were steam-powered, while most contemporary vessels are powered by diesel. "The demand for engineers with experience on steam plants prompted the enlistment of several older mariners, including an 82-year old second mate. . . ."[8])

If conventional war is not a current threat, what about terrorism?

Export Controls on Strategic Materials

The previous section dealt with national defense concerns as they impacted international transportation systems. Another aspect of defense thinking deals with controls on the exports of specific materials to nations that are not the closest of allies, known as strategic controls. (This distinction made more sense during the Cold War.) There are also stringent controls on the export of materials related to nuclear energy.

Strategic controls seek to control what was once referred to as the "hemorrhaging" of American technological know-how. Strategic controls over high-technology products and technical data have as their objective denying enemies and potential enemies the hardware and know-how that might later be used

---

[8]*American Shipper,* April, 1991, p. 33.

against the U.S. Espionage, both military and commercial, is a serious international problem. In 1996, McDonnell Douglas executives in China rejected charges they were slow to prevent machine tools supplied to a Chinese aircraft factory from being diverted to military production.[9]

Export controls pursuant to foreign policy objectives can affect any commodity and can arise at any time. In these instances, they are of foreign policy rather than direct military significance. For example, controls were placed on exports to Argentina when that country went to war with England over the Falklands. Similarly, limits were placed on grain exports to the Soviets when they invaded Afghanistan. However, note that exporters who are not in sympathy with the government's controls may attempt to evade them by using elaborate and circuitous routings of documentation, payments, and goods.

Companies involved in the manufacture of goods with potentially hostile applications need to consider not only the intended use of the commodity (the use the manufacturer intends) but also potential uses. For example, technology used in the peaceful activity of measuring seismic waves in the oil exploration industry has been adapted for use in underground nuclear weapons testing. Medical CAT scan technology has been adapted for use in submarine and anti-submarine warfare. Simple fiber-optic technology used in novelty lamps has found its way into night-vision armaments.

These controls apply not only to tangible articles but also to technical information. Export controls apply to blueprints, drawings, technical documents, photographs, facility tours, and even discussion of technology. Controls extend to foreign affiliates of U.S. persons as well and to the re-export of American goods and goods made from American components from foreign jurisdictions. U.S. export regulations require that one of three "diversion control" statements be printed on export documentation. On government export documents one reads:

> These commodities licensed by the United States
> for ultimate destination [country name].
> Diversion contrary to U.S. law prohibited.

The manner by which controls are exercised is by requiring that all exports from the United States be licensed. Most non-strategic commodities move under a general license that is a published authorization to export without submission of an export license application. Thus, if one is not required to obtain a "validated license" one is licensed to ship under a general license. How does an exporter know whether a license is necessary? Having an intuitive clue may be a

---

[9]*The Journal of Commerce,* November 6, 1996, p. 4A.

good start. But the definitive statement must come through reference to the Export Administration regulations. Commodities are controlled on the basis of what they are and where they are ultimately going.

The first step is to determine how the merchandise or technology is classified. This is done by referring to the "Commodity Control List" (CCL) section of the regulations. Often, commodities are categorized by what they do, by describing them rather than naming them. For example, an item may read: "equipment for measuring pressures of 100 Torr or less having corrosion resistant sensing elements of nickel . . . ."

Having found the appropriate classification, the regulations will indicate which controls apply to what nation. Control types indicate the type of material being controlled and the countries to which the controls apply. One should then consult the Bureau of Export Administration web pages. They will state which commodity and country groups regulations apply and under what conditions validated licenses will be required.

A number of different license types exist to facilitate the needs of commerce. Individual Validated Licenses are good for one ultimate consignee for up to one year and up to a specified quantity. Multiple shipments can be made against the one license. Project licenses are single licenses, good for one year, replacing at least 25 individual licenses. Project licenses permit export of a variety of different articles to a large scale project such as construction of a refinery. Other types of licenses exist with other specific purposes. These include "distribution licenses" for multiple approved consignees; and "service and supply licenses" covering replacement parts, and so on. Companies exporting restricted commodities should visit the Department of Commerce websites.

The issue of export controls is important in the concept of international logistics channels since the physical delivery of the goods cannot be made without addressing the export license requirement issue. The U.S. State Department maintains lists of groups whose assets are being frozen. Since 9-11, there has been an increase in restrictions on trade with certain countries and certain parties.

Boycotts and Antiboycotts

A complicated issue for those involved in buying and selling abroad deals with boycotts. Boycotts take many forms; most of us are familiar with consumer-level boycotts, such as those against tuna-processing firms that destroy porpoises as they net tuna, or firms that oversell infant formula in developing nations. Boycotts such as these are international in scope. In addition, governments sometime boycott other governments. The target of most U.S. boycotts was South Africa; and in the summer of 1990, one of Nelson Mandela's messages as he toured the

U.S. was to "keep the pressure on" with regards to U.S. sanctions against South Africa. In short, businesses that might be subject to boycott regulations should check to determine whether any specific laws apply. As a practical matter, the firm should also be aware of public relations consequences; they might be targets of consumer-level boycotts in domestic markets. Potential violence and terrorism are also possible consequences. The United States has restricted travel and trade with Cuba for many decades although, in late 2001, some shipments of U.S. grain were delivered to Cuban ports.

Since 1990, the UN Security Council has had economic sanctions in place against Iraq, and this has included a maritime blockade that eventually was lifted to the extent that some Iraqi oil could be exported if the money earned was used to pay for food, medicine, and humanitarian supplies. "On February 3, 2000, U.S. warships participating in the multinational maritime interdiction force stopped, then boarded by helicopter, and finally diverted to Oman, a Russian tanker just outside the Persian Gulf. . . ."[10] After chemical tests determined that the oil came from Iraq, it was seized and sold, with the money received placed in an escrow account maintained by the UN.

The United States is not the only nation that uses boycotts. The best-known boycott in the world today is that of some Arab states against Israel. Since the U.S. disagrees with the aims of this boycott, it has laws that make it illegal for a U.S. company or its affiliates to participate 1) in the economic boycott of a country friendly to the United States, or 2) in the discrimination of any U.S. citizen on the basis of race, creed, religion, sex or ethnic background pursuant to the request of a foreign power. Moreover, requests from foreign parties for such compliance must be reported to the U.S. Department of Commerce. It is not the intention of the United States to restrict the power of any sovereign government to impose a boycott, but rather to prevent U.S. companies and persons from being coerced into becoming instruments of that foreign power's policy. In fact, while some sales may have been lost as a result of American sellers' noncompliance with boycott requests, the prohibition against compliance is well known to trading partners.

The Arab boycott of Israel has had some impact on transportation. International carriers cannot have routes that go directly between Arab States and Israel. Israeli immigration agents do not stamp passports of international business travelers, which reduces the number of questions the businessmen have to answer the next time they attempt to enter an Arab state.

---

[10]*The American Journal of International Law,* vol. 94, July, 2000, p. 540.

Controls on Imports

Individual governments place restrictions on certain imports. These controls will either alter or halt the flow. Sometimes a tariff duty is charged to the product; this raises its price to the consumer and usually reduces the actual quantity of the product that is imported. This is known as a tariff barrier.

A nontariff barrier also restricts the flow of imports. Some are outright quotas that place an upper limit on the amount of a product that will be imported from another nation within a given period of time. Other nontariff barriers are requirements that, one way or another, hinder the flow of an imported product, often by raising its final price. Here's a brief discussion of one nontariff barrier in Hungary:

> Imports of cars more than four years old are prohibited, on environmental and safety grounds. An exception involves specialized old vehicles, which may be imported, provided they pass a specialized technical test. Unfortunately, such a prohibition combined with high tariffs on imports of new cars (with large engines) from nonpreferential sources and the global quota on new and relatively new cars tends to curb competition. The resulting increase in the prices of such cars is likely to reduce the pace of replacements of old cars, which are usually more polluting and embody lower safety standards than new or relatively new cars. Consequently, this prohibition in combination with other tariff and nontariff border measures may be counterproductive from the standpoint of environmental protection and safety.[11]

Local content requirements state that a certain percentage of a product's final value must be added in the nation where it is being sold. This poses a challenge to the supply chain designer since work on the product must occur at more than one site. Usually this means finishing the final product near the delivery site, although it is also possible to meet this goal by purchasing many components from the nation where the product is to be finally sold.

Imports are also regulated because of the interest in protecting consumers or the environment. In the year 2001, there was considerable consternation regarding mad-cow and foot-and-mouth diseases and the possibility of their spreading.

Government Support for Its International Carriers

All governments support their international ocean and air carriers. Often the reason they do so is that others do it. Today an agenda item as world leaders get

---

[11]Michael Daly and Hiroaki Kuwahara, "Tariffs and non-tariff barriers to trade in Hungary," *Economics of Transition* vol. 7, no. 3, 1999, p. 732.

together to discuss international economic problems is to have all nations cut back on these sorts of subsidies. Nonetheless, the subsidies exist, and for a variety of reasons.

There are a number of additional reasons for government support of international carriers. Developing nations want to use their own carriers as a rate equalizer to make certain that they are not exploited by the more developed nations. Furthermore, nations want to use transportation to develop trade ties in desirable directions; indeed, an old reason had been to develop colonies. Finally, some nations simply want to keep abreast of transport technology.

Cargo preference relates to restricting the flow of certain traffic to a nation's own flag vessels. For the United States, this is usually interpreted that 50 percent of shipments of products supported in one way or another by federal funds have to move on U.S. bottoms. Starting in 1989, three-fourths of "Food for Peace" crops and grain sold under the Agriculture Department's export promotion programs were to be shipped on U.S.-flag vessels. Cargoes funded by the U.S. Department of Defense are supposed to move on U.S.-flag vessels. U.S. cargo preference rules also apply to imports, as some U.S. cities discovered as they imported foreign-built buses and rail transit vehicles, purchased with subsidies from the Federal Transit Administration.

Preference rules sometimes work in funny ways. In 1985, a U.S. citizen noticed that there was no U.S.-flag service to Iceland, so he formed a small shipping company, hoping to carry U.S. Navy cargo because of cargo preference.

> As the only American-flag operator on the route, he could be assured of [the U.S.] Navy's business because of cargo preference laws. . . . [The firm] published the same tariff rates as the small Icelandic ships which had monopolized the business for years . . . [and the firm] was on its way to making a fortune when it became apparent he had stepped on several toes—those of the Navy and the Icelandic government, which threatened to throw the Navy off the island unless it went back to using Icelandic ships.[12]

The Navy then began flying in the cargo, apparently to force the U.S.-flag carrier out of business. The issue apparently was decided in late 1986. The U.S.-flag line got 35 percent of the cargo, even though under U.S. law, it was entitled to carry 100 percent.[13] However, this did not end the dispute; it has continued to the present. An article in a 2000 shipping journal had the headline "U.S., Iceland embroiled over NATO cargo," and recounted the disagreement that started in the mid-1980s and apparently has yet to be resolved.[14]

---

[12]*American Shipper,* October, 1986, p. 20.

[13]*American Shipper,* November, 1986, p. 12.

[14]*American Shipper,* June, 2000, p. 80.

Other nations also have cargo preference rules. For example, in 1988, Korea tried to enforce regulations calling for carriage of 100 percent of its steel exports on Korean-flag vessels. The U.S. objected, and Korea lowered the limit to 70 percent.[15] Some other nations exercise cargo preference through restricting the use of port terminals to their own flag carriers.

Cargo preference can also be achieved by bilateral agreements, with the U.S. agreement with Brazil being a good example. Beginning in 1970, Brazil and the U.S. signed agreements giving each nation's fleet half of the trade. One item in the 1986 agreement said neither government would "adopt or pursue measures which would interfere with the development of intermodal rates and services within the territory of the other party."[16] This was desired by the U.S. since its carriers were more containerized. In early 1990 was an announcement that the agreement had been renewed once again; apparently the 40/40/20 split, with 20 percent carried by cross-traders. Specific lines were listed for carrying each of the three shares of traffic.

Reference was just made to the "40/40/20 split." That is in reference to a liner code, adopted by most nations of the world that, if enforced, reserves liner traffic between nations A and B in the following manner: 40 percent moves on vessels of nation A; 40 percent moves on vessels of nation B; and 20 percent moves on vessels from any other nation. (Liners offer scheduled service and carry cargo that is more valuable than do bulk carriers.) This code was adopted by UNCTAD (the United Nations Conference on Trade and Development) with the strong backing of developing nations since they were often excluded from carrying cargo to and from their own ports. In the early days of the 40/40/20 rule, developing nations using it found their rates went up since they didn't have the tonnage to carry that much traffic. There are several other reasons why developing nations had trouble with code. Developing nation liner trade routes that are nearly exclusively with developed countries are usually highly imbalanced with an average import/export balance of 7:1 by volume and nearly 9:1 by value.[17] So the code, adopted in the early 1980s, still has not had much impact. However, in 1988, it was reported that: "Nigerian officials want to use their right to carry 40 percent, not to actually fill Nigerian ships but to sell that right to other carriers. They would, in effect, put their Liner Code share on the open market for bidding by shipping companies."[18]

---

[15]*American Shipper,* September, 1988, p. 32.

[16]*American Shipper,* February, 1986, p. 14.

[17]Ernest G. Frankel, "Restrictive Shipping Practices: Boom or Blight for developing countries?" a lecture delivered in Seattle on November 20, 1984, (Seattle: University of Washington Sea Grant Program, 1985), p. 6.

[18]*American Shipper,* November, 1988, p. 20.

Cargo preference also applies to airlines. An article regarding imported flowers said:

> Air carrier monopoly is the greatest problem flower importers face, according to Christine Martindale, Esprit-Miami's president. 'For a long time, the Columbians wouldn't grant landing rights to U.S. airlines unless they paid a landing fee of $10,000. Avianca Airlines, the national air carrier of Columbia, had a monopoly on carrying flowers. Anytime it got upset with the flower growers, its planes would suddenly "break down" 10 days before Valentine's Day, for example. . . . To counter the Avianca monopoly, Martindale imported flowers on smaller airlines owned or leased by Columbians living in Miami. They could avoid the landing fee because they were Columbians.[19]

Cargo preference has been discussed at some length because of its importance to international logistics: it often controls the choice of a carrier's flag and, in reality, the shipper may find only one available carrier flying that flag. In early 1994, as the Japanese reluctantly began importing rice, they were insisting that it be carried on Japanese-flag vessels.[20]

Shipbuilding subsidies are another form of aiding a merchant marine. For many years, the U.S. used construction differential subsidies to offset the higher labor costs associated with using U.S. shipyards. These programs were cut back sharply in the mid-1980s. The Jones Act requires ships used in U.S. domestic trades to be built in the U.S.

The United States does not subsidize its commercial airline aircraft building industry directly. On the other hand, the Airbus, built by a consortium of several European nations, is subsidized by those governments (French, German, British, and Spanish). These four nations contend that the U.S. government subsidizes Boeing through defense contracts.

The United States also subsidized liner operations with a program of operating differential subsidies. In 1997, the United States began a ten-year program that provided subsidies of about $2,100,000 per year to the operators of 47 U.S. flag merchant vessels carrying foreign trade. These subsidized carriers must maintain agreements with the Department of Defense to make the vessels and related equipment available in times of national emergency. The 47 subsidized vessels in 1997 consisted of 36 container ships, five LASH vessels, three combination container and Ro/Ro vessels, and three truck/auto carriers.

The U.S. Federal Maritime Commission (FMC) protects carriers serving U.S. ports by monitoring rates charged by foreign state carriers. A controlled carrier's

---

[19]*Inbound Logistics,* January, 1987, p. 29.

[20]*The Journal of Commerce,* February 17, 1994, p. 1B.

assets are directly or indirectly controlled by the government under whose registry the vessels of the carrier operate. The FMC may suspend these lines' rates if they are below a level that is just or reasonable. This was aimed at Soviet practices of the late 1970s, when they undercut rates in order to earn hard currencies. In 1998 two U.S. carriers filed complaints that were aimed at practices of the Chinese government and two of its state-controlled carriers. Apparently the issue was "predatory" pricing and, as of mid-2001, has yet to be resolved.[21] Also pending were complaints against Japan and some of its port policies that allegedly discriminate against U.S. ship lines.

Several other U.S. programs that aid its merchant marine include a federal and several federally supported maritime academies that train merchant marine officers, the dredging of ports and harbors, the Coast Guard, and limited research and development.

All nations, acting individually and together, have programs that ensure the safety of international carriers, their passengers, and freight. Many of the programs apply to both domestic and international operations. The U.S. Coast Guard, just mentioned, has a wide range of responsibilities. In the United States, the Federal Aviation Administration is concerned with aviation safety. Nations that endure long winters have special programs that deal with winter navigation. Sometimes certain routes, such as the St. Lawrence Seaway, close during the winter. Other routes are kept open with ice breakers.

Cabotage technically does not involve international trade but it should be mentioned. It is a worldwide practice and it means that each nation reserves for its own carriers the exclusive rights to carry domestic traffic. Thus, water traffic between Seattle and Long Beach or air traffic between Los Angeles and Hawaii must move on U.S.-flag carriers. The Jones Act controls most the U.S. merchant marine cabotage regulations. For example, a few years ago, it was reported that:

> Between December 21, 1989 and January 3, 1990, one of the coldest winter periods in New England, shippers—on six occasions—asked for Jones Act waivers to carry fuel oil. Three were approved because there were no U.S.-flag vessels available; three were denied.[22]

Feeder services that would carry containers from smaller U.S. feeder ports to a major U.S. hub port would have to rely on U.S.-flag carriers.

The European Union is phasing out cabotage practices. Greece managed to

---

[21]*JofC Week,* July 2–8, 2001, pp. 16–17.

[22]*American Shipper,* March 1990, p. 32. One of the granted waivers was not used because the foreign-flag vessel left port with a cargo for Europe.

hang on to cabotage protection until the year 2004. This was demanded because of the political strength of its local maritime unions and the nation's large number of islands (over 300). European airlines are now free to fly anywhere within Europe.

Port State Control and Flags of Convenience

There are relatively few controls on international shipping. Each nation claims territorial control for some distance from its shores, and vessels operating within those territorial waters are subject to the nation's rules. A vessel visiting a port is subject to *port state control,* meaning that a nation may apply its own rules to visitors. Port state control deals with operational matters and equipment. In 1995, for example, about 200 foreign ships were ordered to remain in U. K. ports until deficiencies were remedied. Port state inspections are associated primarily with Western European, U.S., and Canadian authorities. Inspections concentrate on safety and operational matters such as the condition of life-saving equipment. Selection of vessels for inspection depends upon their nation of registry and age. "When safety inspectors boarded the bulk carrier *Cathy* last August, they uncovered a number of deficiencies ranging from a shortage of medical equipment to defective life rafts and fire-fighting equipment, broken emergency lighting and a damaged hull. The Cypriot-registered vessel was ordered to remain in the Belgian port of Ghent until more than two dozen faults were rectified."[23] Vessels are also subject to the laws of the nation where they are registered and, in a sense, the vessel is a part of that nation; this is known as "flag state control."

A commonly discussed topic in international transportation involves flags of convenience. While previous discussion has focused on the role of U.S.-flag carriers, there are instances where the U.S. firm prefers not to fly the U.S. flag, but instead registers them in another nation. When the owner who lives in one nation chooses to register his vessels in a second nation and have them fly that second nation's flag, he is said to be flying a "flag of convenience." The usual reason today that U.S. firms do this is that they can avoid paying high U.S. labor costs associated with U.S.-flag vessels. Other Western nations also use flags of convenience. In 1998, the range of ship captains' wages ranged by a factor of seven, that is, the highest-paid captain earned seven times the lowest-paid captain. For able-bodied seamen, the factor was 25. These differences are often based on the flag of the vessel and the nationality of the officer and crew. As examples, in 1998, a vessel captain from Norway earned four times more than a

---

[23]*The Journal of Commerce* (November 7, 1996), p. 2B.

captain from the Philippines; an able-bodied seaman from the United Kingdom earned 24 times more than an able-bodied seaman from Bangladesh.[24]

Seafarers' unions object to flags-of-convenience vessels because of their alleged harsh working conditions, unsafe vessels, and low pay. In 2000, they listed the following as flag-of-convenience nations: Antigua and Barbuda, Aruba (Netherlands), Bahamas, Belize, Bermuda (UK), Burma, Cambodia, Canary Islands (Spain), Cayman Islands (UK), Cook Islands (New Zealand), Cyprus, Gibraltar (UK), Honduras, Lebanon, Liberia, Luxembourg, Malta, Marshall Islands (USA), Mauritius, Netherlands Antilles, Panama, St. Vincent, Sri Lanka, Tuvalu, and Vanuatu. According to the International Transport Workers Federation, in 1998, the worst ten flags in terms of numbers of vessels lost were Panama, Belize, Bahamas, St. Vincent, Cyprus, Russia, Malta, China, Turkey, and Antigua and Barbuda.[25]

Flags of convenience have been used for centuries. Prior to World War II, the Neutrality Acts prohibited U.S.-flag vessels from carrying arms to Britain. (These Acts were adopted after World War I since it was felt that the U.S. had been drawn into World War I because of German submarine attacks on U.S. ships supplying Britain.) After World War II, flags of convenience were used by Greek shipowners when it was feared that Communists would take over the Greek government and nationalize the Greek merchant fleet.

Two news items from the late 1980s illustrate how flags of convenience are used in awkward political situations. One item dealt with the importation of South African lobster tails into the United States despite the fact that imports of that sort were banned by the United States. The importer "said his firm is not violating sanctions imposed by Congress because the lobsters are caught from Cayman Islands-registered ships. The country of origin of seafood is technically determined by the flag of the ship that catches or processes it rather than by the ownership of the cargo or the vessel."[26] The second item said: "CBS reported Monday that $75,000 . . . was used by Marine Lieutenant Colonel Oliver North . . . to charter a Danish freighter to deliver a load of Soviet bloc rifles and other weapons to the Contras in the spring of 1985, at a time when Congress had prohibited U.S. military aid to the rebels."[27]

---

[24]International Transport Workers' Federation website, 2000.

[25]International Transport Workers' Federation website, 2000. Also on the list is the German International Ship Register, which is German controlled but not exactly the same as being German-flagged.

[26]*San Francisco Chronicle,* February 25, 1987.

[27]*San Francisco Chronicle,* April 22, 1987, p. 1.

During the Iran–Iraq War U.S. flags were placed on foreign tankers operating in the Persian Gulf, in order to justify their protection by the U.S. Navy.

When a flag-of-convenience is used, the vessel is said to be *flagged out.* The concept is not restricted to ships. In early 2000, Danish truck owners reregistered some of their trucks in Luxembourg where registration fees and taxes are lower.[28]

Controls on International Aviation

Despite what has been said about cargo preference, it is possible for merchant ships to sail to and from virtually any port in the world. This does not necessarily mean that they can carry cargo in profitable amounts, but the freedom to sail is there. International aviation is much more restrictive. It is believed that, following World War I, nations did not want to open up their skies for fear of letting potential enemies observe military installations. Hence, international flying has been more restricted. Up until World War II, nations used bilateral agreements to exchange air service with each other.

Bilateral agreements allow traffic to move back and forth between two nations. During the World War II period, as aircraft range increased, it became clear that round-the-world service would be technologically feasible. However, this would involve stops at many nations along the way. The Allied nations (those joined to fight Germany, Japan, and Italy) met in Chicago in 1944 in an attempt to set up a framework for controlling post-World War II international airline aviation. The Chicago convention was attended by 55 nations; Soviet envoys had planned to attend, but turned around en route and returned to U.S.S.R. The Chicago convention

> can be described with reasonable accuracy as an attempt by the United States to capitalize on its overwhelmingly strong bargaining position in international aviation by securing for itself a near-monopoly of long-haul air transport. . . . As Charles M. Sackery put it, the United States position was "similar to that taken by the proverbial elephant, who, while he danced through the chicken yard, cried: Everyone for himself."[29]

In essence, the United States argued for freedom of the skies, and wanted virtually no restrictions on postwar airline aviation. Britain wanted: 1) bilateral ne-

---

[28]*The Journal of Commerce* (January 10, 2000), p. 3. Truckers were also installing larger fuel tanks that would allow them to buy fuel in low-tax areas and operate in high-tax areas without needing to refuel.

[29]Robert L. Thornton, *International Airlines and Politics,* (Ann Arbor: University of Michigan, 1970), p. 22.

gotiations on a route-by-route basis, which she would benefit from since only she had territories as part of the British Commonwealth that could be used for 'round the world routes; and 2) to delay portions of the conference until after the war, when other powers would be stronger and less dependent upon the United States.

At the Chicago convention, it was agreed to form the International Civil Aviation Organization (ICAO), to which individual nations would belong and which would handle matters of international air navigation and safety. (The ICAO later became a part of the United Nations, which was created in 1945.) At the Chicago convention it was also decided that bilateral agreements were to be used to establish routes and four freedoms were established. They were:

Freedom 1. To fly over foreign territory with advance permission. (This is sometimes revoked, examples being conflicts involving India–Pakistan, South Africa, Israel.) Some nations allow airline aircraft to pass through their air space, but they charge overflight fees. In 1997, Canada earned approximately US$125 million from overflight fees.[30]

Freedom 2. To stop in foreign nation for fuel and repairs.

Freedom 3. To carry passengers and cargo from an airline's home country to a foreign country.

Freedom 4. To carry passengers and cargo from another country to the airline's home country

Note that the set of freedoms is incomplete. For round-the-world service an airliner from nation A might have to fly a route A-B-C-D-E-F-G-A. None of the four freedoms gave it the right to carry passengers between, say, D and E. So, in 1946 the nations met again, this time in Bermuda (and this convention is now referred to as Bermuda I). They agreed on a fifth freedom:

Freedom 5. To carry passengers and cargo from an airline's home country to one foreign nation and to pick up passengers and cargo going to another foreign nation.

In addition, the Bermuda Conference decided that after the routes and the number of flights had been agreed upon by various nations, the actual rates and quality of service would be determined by the International Air Transport Association (IATA), a cartel to which individual airlines belonged.

---

[30]*The Journal of Commerce,* (May 1, 1997), p. 1B.

Here are some examples of early Australian agreements with other nations.

Canada, 1946, Australian route via specified intermediate points to Vancouver; a Canadian route to Sydney.

USA, 1946, Australian routes to Honolulu and San Francisco and beyond to (a) Vancouver and (b) to New York, the British Isles, Europe and beyond; US routes via intermediate points to Darwin, Sydney, Melbourne and Perth and beyond (South Pacific); and to Sydney and Melbourne (North Pacific).

India, 1949, Australian route via specified points to Calcutta or Dehli and any other points in India to be agreed upon and beyond; Indian route to Sydney and Melbourne and/or any other point in Australia to be agreed upon and beyond.

Italy, 1960, Australian route via specified intermediate points to Rome and beyond to London; an Italian route via specified intermediate points to Sydney and Melbourne.[31]

Note two factors. First, there is a mirror-like quality; that is, the other nation asks for the opposite. This resulted in double-tracking of routes; some markets would go from zero to two airlines. Secondly, the country is usually attempting to develop the option of flying beyond and using fifth-freedom rights to carry passengers and cargo between other nations, rather than having to return home. This is an issue today, in that Japanese airlines flying to the U.S. West Coast want to fly beyond to Latin America; conversely, U.S. airlines flying to Tokyo want to fly beyond to other Asian nations.

There are a number of reasons for establishing international airline routes. Many foreign airlines were owned in total or part by their respective governments, so the government determined that it was in their national interest to develop certain routes. Types of routes are:

Business travel—say, to Zurich, Tokyo, Hong Kong;

Personal travel—as tourists, or for ethnic or religious reasons;

Gateway—between major areas, an example being London and New York;[32]

Diplomatic—to Brasilia or Washington, D.C.;

---

[31]Commonwealth of Australia, *Civil Aviation, 1969–1970,* (Canberra, 1970), p. 111.

[32]As aircraft ranges increase, gateways change. "Interestingly airlines no longer view things in terms of West Coast U.S. gateways. The longer range transports, particularly the Boeing 747s of now and the future, are making gateway thinking obsolete." *Air Transport World,* April, 1986, p. 2.

Poor surface accessibility—Berlin (prior to 1990);

Strategic policy—U.S. to Latin America before World War II or Aeroflot to Africa or Cuba;

Prestige—Concorde;

Military—PanAm routes to Saigon in the 1960s, or Aeroflot flights to Hanoi;

Colonial—maintain ties.[33]

Note that some of the reasons for routes may reflect goals different from airline profitability. Many international airlines outside the U.S. have been government-owned, and not subject to business-like goals of profitability.

During President Clinton's administration the United States pushed for "open skies" and tried to do away with bilateral agreements. By the close of the Clinton administration, the U.S. had entered into open-skies agreements with about 30 nations. These agreements took the place of existing bilateral treaties. The open skies agreements had two components. One removed limits on the number of flights between the two nations (although in some markets there are airport capacity constraints). The second provides reciprocal fifth-freedom rights. Some agreements have added **sixth-freedom** and **seventh-freedom** rights. The sixth freedom comes from a three-nation arrangement: X, Y, and Z using third and fourth freedoms between X and Y, and third and fourth freedoms between Y and Z. An example would be New York–Brussels–Tel Aviv service. It benefits an airline since it feeds into itself, and may also help in smaller markets. The **seventh freedom** allows an airline to carry traffic between two points, neither of which is the airline's home.[34]

Labor Unions

Labor unions exist in most countries of the world. Individual governments are aware of their political clout. To the extent unions represent workers in different countries, they have some limited power to exercise their "muscle" in an international arena. For example, on January 20, 1997, dock workers on the U.S. West Coast, along with dockworkers in most western European nations, Australia, and Japan engaged in a one-day walkout in sympathy to dockworkers in Liverpool

---

[33]Gidwitz, pp. 161–167.

[34]In early days, a developing nation would allow an airline of former colonial power to provide service. The eighth freedom is cabotage traffic. In 1979 foreign airlines were allowed to fly from Honolulu and California because of a U.S. airline strike and the DC-10 grounding.

who had been laid off in a downsizing operation in 1994. "The action showed how powerless shipowners are to prevent work stoppages. . . . Even though the West Coast employer group, the Pacific Maritime Association, obtained an arbitrator's ruling in advance of Monday's action declaring it illegal, dockworkers walked off anyway."[35] Some vessel owners who used Liverpool facilities targeted by the union encountered difficulties in having their ships loaded in other parts of the world. "For example, in 1996 Australian dockers in Sydney deliberately delayed ABC shipping, who normally shipped 600–700 containers through Liverpool per trip. Likewise, one of Liverpool's biggest users, the shipping company ACL, faced short-term action by dockers on the U.S. East Coast and elsewhere."[36] Figure 2–2 shows a sign of support for laid-off Liverpool dockworkers.

United Parcel Service (UPS), a large integrated parcel service headquartered in the U.S., has operations in many countries. Unions representing more than 200,000 UPS employees in 11 countries are establishing a permanent body to negotiate labor issues with UPS. The International Transport Workers' Federation is orchestrating the movement, and receiving the full support of the Teamsters, which represents 180,000 UPS employees in the U.S.[37]

Because of their political stature, unions have the ability to influence governmental policies in their respective nations. As workers they also fear losing their jobs to those willing to work for less. "Bay Area iron workers are suing a Shanghai firm that delivered four gigantic cranes across the Pacific Ocean and to the Port of Oakland, contending that the firm paid workers from China as little as $4 a day to unload and install the steel behemoths. The Shanghai Zhenhua Port Machinery Co., Ltd. . . . ignored agreements to use union workers in the Bay Area and instead employed its own workers, who came over on temporary work visas, the suit alleges."[38]

Environmental Issues

Most governments today profess their interest in preventing further degradation of the earth's environment. Environmentalists, often working through the Green movement, have gained considerable influence in several countries. Any number

---

[35]*The Journal of Commerce* (January 22, 1997), p. 1A.

[36]Noel Castree, "Geographic Scale and Grass-Roots Internationalism: The Liverpool Dock Dispute, 1995–1998," *Economic Geography* Vol. 76, no. 2, July 2000, p. 282.

[37]*The Journal of Commerce* (February 13, 1997), p. 23.

[38]*San Francisco Chronicle* (January 12, 2001), p. A22.

Figure 2–2   Picture of a sign stenciled on a concrete wall in Switzerland, showing support for the Liverpool dockworkers who were laid off when the docks were privatized.

of pro-environmental polices have been adopted, although often the government (and the public) soon lose interest. Nonetheless, the environmental protection policies have considerable influence on logistics systems, whether it be choice of vehicle, hours of operation, or type of packaging. Consider this news item from 1995:

> Rotterdam—A Swedish-owned supertanker is the first ship to pay lower harbor dues in Rotterdam as a reward for its superior safety standards. The 285,700 deadweight-ton Liberian-registered Ambon won a Green Award Certificate that entitled it to a six percent discount on Rotterdam's port charges. . . . The award is dependent on the vessel's design, as well as management and crewing

standards. . . . The six percent discount is on top of a 17 percent discount in harbor dues for tankers fitted with segregated ballast tanks.[39]

Multigovernment Programs

To this point, the text has spoken of controls by single governments. In many instances governments work together, and carriers and shippers are also bound by multigovernment agreements and treaties. Many commercial practices on the Great Lakes, for example, are controlled by treaties between the U.S. and Canada. The two nations have a joint commission to decide these matters, such as the minimum size vessel sailing between Lakes Huron and Erie for which a pilot should be required.

Within the past century, international conferences have drawn up sets of rules—often called "conventions"—which often come near to being laws (although adoption and enforcement are not uniform). As early as 1899, 37 nations met to draw up rules of navigation in an attempt to reduce the number of collisions at sea. Throughout the 20th century, there were a series of conventions dealing with the safety of life at sea. Within the past few decades, emphasis has switched to issues related to oil spills. Many proposed conventions are controversial. Consider this:

> In 1969 the first International Convention on Tonnage Measurement was adopted. This became a rather controversial convention dealing with sensitive issues. The idea behind the convention was to establish cleared rules for measurements of a ship's gross tonnage. This is important to ship owners because most port charges and canal dues are based on this measurement. This creates an incentive to manipulate the designs to get a lower gross tonnage, without getting lower cargo carrying capacity. Occasionally this was at the expense of stability and thus safety. It took 13 years before the convention had the required number of acceptances, so it was not until 1982 that the convention came into force.[40]

Under the UN there are several groups concerned with navigation. The International Maritime Organization discusses and prepares drafts of conventions for possible adoption. The International Labour Organization (ILO) "has been instrumental in bringing about important conventions dealing with working conditions onboard ships. These include provisions on manning, hours of work, pen-

---

[39]*The Journal of Commerce* (February 13, 1995), p. 18.

[40]Niko Wijnolst and Tor Wergeland, *Shipping* (Delft: Delft Univ. Press, 1997), page 430.

sion, vacation, sick pay and minimum wages."[41] The UN Conference on Trade and Development (UNCTAD) concerns itself with improving the economic interests of developing countries.

Mention has already been made of the International Civil Aviation Organization (ICAO), formed by the Chicago Convention in 1944. It is an organization of governments with its headquarters in Montreal. The ICAO has developed standardized air navigation practices, rules of the air, navigation charts, communications, etc. They run training programs for people interested in air traffic control and communications, and they provide technical assistance to developing nations. There are regional branches of ICAO serving various areas in the world.

The Universal Postal Union is affiliated with the United Nations and headquartered at Bern, Switzerland. This is one of the oldest worldwide organizations, dating to 1874. It unites all nations into a single postal territory, with each nation agreeing to deliver mail from other members by the best available means. International postal rates are set by this group. Parcel post is also handled on an international basis, somewhat dependent upon agreements between specific nations. The postal service provides the largest distribution network in the world, and can reach places that commercial carriers choose not to serve.

In addition to government and multigovernment controls, there are other institutions that have considerable influence on international trade and transport. They include the groups that determine the adequacy of hulls for carrying cargoes and that insure carriers' equipment and freight; the international banking industry; and cartels that control—or attempt to control—various worldwide economic activities. While these organizations generally are not government-owned or operated, they are not completely independent of the governments of their respective members.

Summary

Governments are involved in international transportation for several reasons. One is to earn foreign exchange and another is based on the relationship between transportation and a nation's defense. Each nation, in its own way, supports its own international carriers.

Ocean shipping is less regulated than air transport. Governments control most routes flown by airlines. There are several worldwide organizations that help create a sense of structure and order for the international logistics system.

---

[41]Niko Wijnolst and Tor Wergeland, *Shipping,* (Delft: Delft Univ. Press, 1997), page 428.

End-of-Chapter Questions

1. What are some of the economic reasons causing nations to support their international carriers?

2. What are some of the national defense concerns that cause nations to support their international carriers?

3. Why do countries control the export of some products to certain other nations?

4. What are nontariff barriers? What impacts do they have?

5. What are cargo preference rules? Do you agree with the concept? Why or why not?

6. What is cabotage?

7. What are flags-of-convenience? Why are they used?

8. Why are international airline routes more closely controlled than routes used by merchant vessels?

9. Who is responsible for the safety of international transportation?

10. What are some multinational groups that have an impact on international logistics?

CASE • *Port of Short Beach*

Eric Raff's small office on the fourth floor of the Port of Short Beach office building was in the rear, and its single window looked out over a railroad switching yard. Gathered with Raff on this February morning were Wyndham Young, who worked for Wyoming Minerals and had flown in from Denver, and Loretta Brown, from the Short Beach City Attorney's office. Raff and Young were to work out some details of a contract between the Port and Wyoming Minerals. Ms. Brown was there to provide legal advice, since her office had to approve the legal format of any contract entered into by a city agency, such as the board of port commissioners. Ms. Brown said, "Eric, tell me a little about the proposal."

Raff responded: "Wyoming Minerals is about to sign a ten-year contract to sell coal to Japan, between two and three million tons per year. They will pay us, the port, 10–12 cents per ton per year for the first million tons and 8–10 cents for any tons over a million. Since they will be tying up the Van Huntley site, they've also guaranteed us a minimum of $200,000 per year for ten years. At this point they have tentative agreements with the Japanese buyer, the railroad, and with us. They have to negotiate some final points in each contract, including ours."

Raff then served coffee, and after a brief discussion of ski conditions throughout the Pacific Northwest, he suggested that they get down to business. "For starters," he said, "I don't think we're here to talk about money, but rather to decide about everything else the contract must include. Some of them will cost us, the Port; others will cost Wyoming Minerals, the tenant. Later, our higher-ups will have to decide who will be responsible for what and whether that should influence the rate of rental."

"How will the responsibilities be divided between the Port and the tenant?" asked Ms. Brown. "Who does what?"

"Ideally," responded Raff, "we provide the land and collect the rent checks. . . ."

"Ho-ho-ho," interjected Young. "Most contracts entered into by West Coast ports are in the public record and most of them show that the ports do more than that."

"Port Director Langtree's memo mentioned a legal description of the land involved," said Ms. Brown. "Will there be any problems there?"

"Negative," said Raff. "We have clear title and no property line or water rights disputes. Port policy only requires that it be used for 'navigationally related' purposes, which this is. We've already sent maps and drawings to Wyoming's engineers, who need them for their talks with the railroad."

"We appreciated your sending them promptly," said Young. "Also, let me mention something not in Mr. Langtree's memo, but agreed to, and that is that we will build the coal loading/unloading facility on your land. It will be able to handle incoming unit trains of 100 cars each. Each car will be unloaded by being swiveled 170 degrees inside the unloading shed. Then it will be returned to the upright position, and the entire train will move ahead the length of one car. A new car will be in place, turned over and dumped, turned upright, and so on. The coal will be stockpiled outside. At times, there may be as much as several hundred thousand tons stockpiled. Along the water's edge, we'll have a vessel loader, which is fed from a conveyor system running below the stockpile. We'll be able to load vessels at a rate of 3,000 to 4,000 tons per hour."

"What kind of money will that cost?" asked Ms. Brown.

"Between 25 and 40 million," responded Young. "Since you're a public agency, we want you to borrow the money for building the loading/unloading facility since interest on your obligations is exempt from federal income taxation. You can borrow for less, and you can lease the facility back to us for ten years, effective the minute it's completed. We'll pay you 20 percent of your costs the minute it goes into operation, and we'll pay the balance over six years at a rate of interest one percent higher than whatever you had to pay to borrow the money. That will be on top of the rent figures mentioned in Mr. Langtree's memo."

"Who owns the equipment after ten years?" asked Raff.

"You own it as soon as you pay the contractor," said Young. "We never own it. We just lease it from you for ten years—to coincide with our rental of the land."

Raff said, "That seems clear. Now, looking at other contracts we have, here are a few items we like to see in them. We want the tenant responsible for a private security system and for a fire sprinkler system inside any structures. You must maintain fire and related insurance on your structure and tenant liability insurance. You must agree to comply with all federal and state laws and local ordinances and building codes. The port engineer must approve plans for any structures placed on the property. You must agree to maintain all property. . . ."

"Hold on a minute, there," said Young, "I think you've just struck a nerve. The dock wall next to the water isn't in great shape right now. And, as you know, it will deteriorate naturally over ten years. I don't think we can blindly assume responsibility for maintaining the dock wall. It could cost several million to replace."

"Let's skip that for now," said Raff. "I'd better talk to our engineers before we pursue that issue further. Another standard item that I want to mention is that the tenant must collect and pass on to us the wharfage charges that all commercial vessels using our port facilities must pay. They're based on vessel length and run two dollars per foot of vessel length per twenty-four-hour day. We don't worry about cheating on this item, since it's pretty hard to hide a vessel. The last item, almost 'boilerplate' in nature, is that we agree to an arbitrator in case disagreements arise under this contract."

"Aside from maintaining the dock wall, how do the other standard items sound to you?" asked Raff.

"Oh, all right, I guess," Young replied. "Of course, our legal staff will have to approve them, but they're not obstacles."

"Well, that's good," said Raff. "Obviously, Langtree wants a contract you folks can live with."

"This meeting is going along more quickly than I anticipated," said Ms. Brown, as she accepted her second cup of coffee. "When are you going to mention the port director's favorite charity, Eric?" she said with a mischievous grin.

"Oh," exclaimed Raff, "I wish you hadn't mentioned that, Loretta!" Young looked up, surprised.

"Why not?" replied Ms. Brown. "He'll have to learn sooner or later."

"Well, what it is, is this," said Raff, speaking slowly. "It seems my boss, Mr. Langtree, thinks the city council and the board of port commissioners are both niggardly when it comes to funding his entertainment and travel budget. So, to overcome this deficiency, a number of port tenants show their appreciation for the good job he's doing by kicking into a 'special' port development fund that the director uses as he sees fit."

"That sounds accurate," said Ms. Brown, as Raff gave her a dirty look.

"Is this the only 'special accommodation' expected of us?" asked Young, who realized that the discussion had moved away from routine matters.

"As a matter of fact," said Ms. Brown, "the party in power, people like my boss, also like to know that port tenants appreciate them. . . ."

"Interesting as this is," said Young, "I don't think I'm authorized to make any commitments of this sort. We operate in a lot of foreign countries and, obviously, what you're saying to me isn't new. Tell you what, Eric," he continued, "the next time Mr. Langtree meets with my boss, he'd better lay this all out in front of him."

"Oh, Mr. Langtree would never say anything directly," responded Raff. "He relies on his staff for help in matters such a this."

"Look, and I'm repeating myself," said Young. "This is a matter outside my authority. If Langtree won't discuss it with Mr. Fulbright, the best I can do is mention it to Fulbright or whomever I talk with when I call in later today to discuss items you and I can't resolve. Now, let's move on."

"One thing I'd like to raise now is whether Wyoming would object to a clause in the contract that restricted you to handling only the outbound movement of coal. We don't like our tenants subleasing their facilities to handle other cargoes because they may then compete with our other tenants," said Raff.

"Well, then," responded Young, "would you agree not to lease any other lands for handling export coal during the period of our agreement?"

"I'd have to think about that," answered Raff.

"I think we'd like the right to handle other bulk materials, in case markets for them develop," said Young, "which leads me to think that some of them are denser than coal and—when loaded aboard a ship—would cause it to set deeper in the water. I understand that right now you've got 35 feet of water below low tide, alongside the property. . . ."

"That's right," said Raff, "and that's deep enough to handle the vessels you're likely to use for coal."

"But if we wanted it deeper?" probed Young

"I see two problems there," answered Raff. "First of all, why do you need it? Secondly, there are limits to the dock wall's strength. If we dredge more alongside it, the whole thing may give way and collapse into the water. . . ."

"That may be," interjected Young, "but for our investment and with the potential of the Japanese market for coal, we don't want to be limited right off the bat as to the size of ship we can use. What if the charter rates for larger ships drop? We won't be able to take advantage while some of our competitors will."

"We can guarantee that you'll have 35 feet of water along side," offered Raff.

"We may insist on 40," was Young's reply.

There was a long discussion as to the delays that could be caused by environmental protection reviews and by possible protests from individuals along the coal trains' proposed routes. It was agreed that there would be two contracts. The first would be a somewhat binding "letter of intent" indicating that the final contract would not become effective until the entire project had been approved by all governmental review bodies.

Young said they would want some provision specifying that the Port makes available at least one mile of rail trackage for possible use by a waiting unit train. While the parcel of land to be rented would accommodate the train being unloaded, there would be times when a second train would be waiting.

"Why can't you work this out with the railroad, in your contract with them?" asked Raff. "They've got lots of tracks."

"In the East, where coal-loading ports are congested, everybody's blaming everybody else for the problem," was Young's response. "We think you are in a better position to guarantee us a mile of vacant track, just where we'll need it; we don't want our 100-car train 'somewhere' on the BN system."

"One other thing," said Ms. Brown. "Will you have any heavy trucks moving in and out? In our other contracts, we need some provisions about that to protect our port's roads."

"Negative," was Young's answer. "It would only be in emergency situations."

"I'll look up how we've handled this in other contracts," said Raff. "We'll have to insert something about axle spacings and weights, and insist that trucks comply with state law. If they never left our property we could probably allow larger rigs. Think about that before we do the next draft of the contract."

It was now noon, and the trio went to a nearby waterfront seafood restaurant for lunch. Raff offered to pick up the check, adding that it was being paid out of the port director's special fund. As they were studying the menu, Young noted that the prices of his two favorite West Coast seafoods, salmon and crab, climbed each time he came to the Coast.

"You're so right," said Raff. "We follow the economics of fishing since some of our land is leased to commercial fishermen. Their prices are going up, just like everybody else's. Which reminds me, our contract with you has to have some adjustments in it so that the rents keep up with the cost of living."

"Will that cost of living clause cover everything in the contract?" asked Young.

"Yes," answered Raff.

"I don't think it should cover the purchase/leaseback of the materials-handling equipment," said Young. "We're reimbursing you for the interest rate you have to pay, plus one percent, and I think that the interest rate the market sets already reflects the rate of inflation."

"I hear you," answered Raff. "I'll have to run that one by my boss."

The meal was served and the three engaged in small talk, and walked back to

Raff's office quickly, because a rainstorm was threatening. As they sat down in Raff's office, the drops of rain started splashing on the window sill. Ms. Brown asked Young, "Will rainy weather affect your operation here?"

"Not really," was Young's answer. "We'll have a moat around our entire facility and the runoff from the coal piles will be collected, and the coal particles and dust removed, before the water is allowed to drain into the bay. Wet coal has slightly different handling characteristics but our equipment takes them in account. Of course, wet coal loads heavier into a ship."

"That raises a question," said Ms. Brown. " You're going to pay us by the ton. Is that a wet ton, a dry ton, or what? It seems to me that we should insist you drench your coal piles with thousands of gallons of water every day as a dust suppression measure. Then we'll collect more money as you load those heavy tons."

Young grinned and said "Coal is sold on a BTU-content basis. Our loading facility will have a tiny conveyor belt feeding off of the main conveyor belt that loads the ship. The tiny conveyor leads into a testing lab where a third party collects and analyzes the samples and then tells us the number of BTU's that were loaded on the ship."

"Who is the third party?" asked Ms. Brown.

"An independent testing lab that we and the Japanese coal buyer pay jointly," was Young's answer. "We'll use the lab figures to determine how much we owe you."

The next issue discussed was whether harbor pilots and tugs were necessary to dock the coal vessels. Raff said the Port felt they were, since if a vessel went aground because of mishandling, it might tie up vessel traffic and harm the business of other dock operators.

Young complained that the decision whether to use tugs and pilots should be left to the ship's captain. Requiring them for all vessels would add to Wyoming Mineral's overall costs. He said that an international firm such as Wyoming Minerals had to avoid being saddled with "useless" local work practices, which other ports where they also operated might try to impose. "The only wording we've accepted elsewhere deals with requiring pilots and tugs for vessels above a certain size," said Young.

The last items the three discussed were allowing the Port of Short Beach to audit Wyoming Mineral's records, insofar as was necessary to determine volumes of coal the dock handled; options for Wyoming Minerals to have first right of renewal of the contract at its expiration; and definitions of "Acts of God," embargoes, labor disputes, and so on to the extent that they would relieve one or both parties from fulfilling one or more parts of the contract.

One item the three could not resolve was who should pay for any additional environmental protection equipment that other government agencies might require during the ten-year contract period. "In the eighties and nineties," said

Young, "we were sometimes forced to add expensive dust suppression equipment even though our contract with the port in question had only one or two years to go. We feel that since ports are also government agencies they should bear those costs which their sister or brother governmental agencies suddenly decide are necessary."

Questions for *Port of Short Beach*

Questions 1 through 4 require you to draft proposed paragraphs of the contract under consideration. For your purposes, assume that the language must be as un-ambiguous as possible.

1. Assume you are Raff. From his (the Port's) standpoint, draft the paragraph dealing with maintenance of the dock wall and provision of thirty-five feet of water depth alongside. (Try to place the burden on the tenant.)

2. Assume you are Young. From Wyoming Mineral's point of view, draft the paragraph that deals with maintenance of the dock wall and the provision of forty feet of water depth alongside. (Try to place the burden on the Port.)

3. From the standpoint of either party, write a paragraph that incorporates use of the cost-of-living index into adjusting the dollar amounts of rental payments in future years.

4. From the standpoint of either party, write a paragraph that covers the purchase by the Port and lease back to Wyoming Minerals of the materials-handling equipment. Should this include additional language that takes into account the changing value of the dollar over time? Discuss.

5. The Port of Short Beach wants to be paid at a certain rate per ton of coal handled, but rain or dust suppression sprinklers will increase the weight of a given volume of coal. How might this be resolved?

6. Assume that you are Young's superior and he reports to you that Port tenants are apparently expected to make contributions to the port director's "special" fund. What, if anything, should you do? Why?

7. Assume that at some later date an environmental protection agency requires that additional, expensive pollution control devices be installed at the dock. Who should pay for them? Why?

8. Should the Port agree not to lease any other lands for handling export coal during the period of the lease? Why or why not?

3

Logistics in Different Parts of the World

Introduction

> "The world is truly getting smaller and the marketplace is getting bigger. Global logistics can help bridge the gap between service and efficiency, but it is not easy."[1]

In developed nations, businesses enjoy the best logistics and transportation professionals, systems, and infrastructure in the world. Managers take for granted such standards as advanced Internet-based technologies, high-capacity national highway systems, broad-band fiber-optic communications capabilities, seamless multimodal transportation, modern port facilities, high-density air traffic control, and a cadre of qualified, experienced logistics professionals and service agencies. What is experienced as the norm of logistics practice in the developed countries is often only an aspirational goal of logisticians in many other places in the world.

That said, one often perceives the world through a uniquely nationalist perspective. It's hard not to. "Self-referencing criteria"[2] force a frame of reference that is unique to one's business and professional experience. If one is not careful, it's easy to look down upon or criticize as inferior the state of logistics and transportation development in other countries. "It's sure not like the way we do it back home!" is a common comment from managers returning from their first

---

[1] PriceWaterhouseCoopers website: *http://www.supplychain.pwcglobal.com*

[2] Cateora, Philip and Susan Keaveney (1987), *Marketing: An International Perspective,* Homewood, IL: Irwin.

overseas business experience. A more informed perspective examines the differences among countries, and evaluates each based on strengths and weaknesses, and the appropriateness of the logistical system to the business and cultural environment. Understanding different expectations for logistics performance may turn initial perceptions of inferiority to an appreciation for other ways of accomplishing logistics objectives.

This chapter examines the nature of cultural differences and their impact on logistics practice and describes briefly the current state of logistics and transportation in the first world, emerging nations, and the third world. The chapter then discusses emergent regional trade blocs and their impact on strategic logistics practice.

Getting Started

For the firm making its first international shipment, an international freight forwarder should be retained to advise on matters such as terms of sale, transportation, and documentation. For imports, one would probably retain a customshouse broker to help the goods clear customs. Or one might rely entirely on the comprehensive global logistics services offered by "small parcel" carriers such as FedEx, UPS, or DHL (see *http://www.fedex.com* for an example of the services offered by one firm).

Very few business people would settle for a single international transaction. The world beckons both as a market and as a source of inputs. One soon learns that there are many global variations on "how things happen at home." Take holidays as an example. Looking at only a handful of major nations, Australia celebrates Australia Day, January 26; Anzac Day, April 25; and the Queen's Birthday, June 12. Brazil celebrates Independence Day on September 7. Canada celebrates Victoria Day on May 22 and Thanksgiving in early October. In France, Labor Day is on May 1; Armistice Day is on both May 8 and November 11; and Bastille Day is on July 14. Many nations celebrate various religious holidays. All this means that there will be extra charges or delays in having work done when the holidays occur; at the very least, the consignee's place of business may be closed and the delivery cannot be made.

Carriers hand out booklets that outline general facts that one must know when trading with countries where they provide service. Such information is typically available through a carrier's website as well. Common examples are lists of goods that cannot be exported into or taken out of certain countries, documentation requirements, and long lists of information about climate, clothing, and local customs. More specialized guides are available, including an extensive free set of country background notes and commercial guides from the U.S. State Department *(http://www.state.gov)*. Another guide, distributed by a maritime insurance company, described ports and how conditions at each port may affect the flow of cargo. Consider this description of Port Rashid, Dubai:

Transportation service—Truck only

Cargo storage—Covered space is marginal. Extensive, hard surfaces open storage areas are present.

Special cranes—Heavy lift capacity is 41 tons. Container, 3 with 80 ton capacity.

Air cargo—Dubai International Airport, 3.2 kilometers from port

Cargo handling—Port equipment is adequate to handle most normal cargo traffic. No pier-side cranes provided; vessels must use own gear. There are 3 Ro/Ro ramps.

General: Weather is hot with temperature extremes reaching 50°C in July and August. Rain is infrequent, but substantial when it falls. Special entrance permits are required. Arabic markings and use of international symbols help to ensure proper handling. . . .[3]

Again, one would probably consult with a forwarder and a carrier before attempting a shipment to such a port. However, with experience and help, a small firm can soon develop into a regular exporter and importer. One other item that the beginning exporter or importer should assess is the political stability of the area with which trade is being considered. Profits may appear to be high, until one factors in the political risks that reduce the chances of successfully completing the transaction.

At the other extreme from the firm that is venturing into foreign trade is the large firm already engaged in many international transactions and shipments, and attempting to be a true "global" firm. They face the task of establishing and maintaining global logistics functions. PriceWaterhouseCoopers suggests:

Development of a global logistics strategy to align all logistics initiatives on a global basis is essential . . . [and provides] the framework to move to the "best in class" level. The approach should understand that no two locations would have the same needs or be at the same level in their logistics development. Local conditions, needs, and customer expectations will make the requirements of each market very different. The global logistics strategy must take these

---

[3]CIGNA Ports of the World (1992), 15th ed., Philadephia, PA: CIGNA Companies, p. 41.

> differences into account and create tactics that are appropriate for each region to achieve significant benefits in changing the logistics paradigm.[4]

Both large and small firms must be aware of differences throughout the world as they establish a global presence.

Later in this chapter, nations will be grouped into three categories, according to their overall level of economic development. One reason that firms in the more developed countries locate some of their facilities in less developed countries is to take advantage of the much lower wage rates in the latter. U.S. Department of Labor data for average hourly manufacturing wages in 2000 (in U.S. dollars) showed the U.S. at $19.20. Germany was $26.18, Canada, $15.60, and Japan, $20.89. At the other end were Taiwan, $5.62, and Mexico, $2.12. (Useful statistics on international labor comparisons are available free from the U.S. Bureau of Labor Statistics at *http://www.bls.gov.*)

Understanding Cultural Differences

Culture has been described as the personality of a society, encompassing abstract ideas such as ethics and value systems as well as material objects. Professor Michael R. Solomon defines culture as "the accumulation of shared meanings, rituals, norms, and traditions among the members of a society."[5] There are three defining features that mark all cultures. First, culture is not inherited as some genetic trait, it is learned through a process of enculturation from the moment of birth. The unique expressions of family life, school, religion, and social interactions serve to teach a set of cultural standards of behavior and give a common context in which to lead one's life. Because it is learned from such an early age, it is difficult (if not impossible) to change one's enculturated context. Second, the sum total of this unique accumulation of enculturated knowledge, beliefs, values, customs, and behavior forms an integrated whole. Interrelationships are created between different aspects of a person's life, and the total of their experience in a culture leads to a defined cultural identity. Third, cultural traits are shared with other members in the society. These shared cultural traits form the basis for a set of unspoken guidelines or rules by which individual members of the society interact with each other and behave. With such a broad definition of culture, one can begin to see culture as the outcome of the process of encultur-

---

[4]From the PriceWaterhouseCoopers website: *http://www.supplychain.pwcglobal.com*

[5]Solomon, Michael R. (1998), *Consumer Behavior: Buying, Having, and Being,* Upper Saddle River, NJ: Prentice-Hall, p. 495.

ation. It is the result of a society's members' cumulative interactions and generations of behavior.

Given that culture is learned from a very early age, cultural experience forms such an integral part of a person's being, and sharing one's culture reinforces cultural boundaries, it is difficult for managers to escape their own enculturation and to acculturate to a new culture. Fortunately, such acculturation is not necessary for business success in a foreign country. But an awareness of one's own ethnocentric perspectives and a willingness to go beyond them and learn about a different cultural environment will help to minimize cultural problems one may encounter in foreign countries.

The Cultural Environment: Beliefs, Values, Customs

Beliefs refer to a person's knowledge about some thing (an object, a product, a person, a behavior). Beliefs generally take the form of a statement that begins with "I know that. . . ." In a sense, beliefs are knowledge of the particular, rather than of the general. For example, a logistics manager may believe that the key to increased system productivity is better management of bar code data within the firm. Beliefs are usually tied to one's experience, as seen through the mindset of a given culture. Beliefs may be shared among individuals, but only through the common context of cultural experience. Beliefs also change as an individual's knowledge set grows.

Values are similar to beliefs, differing in that values deal more with the general rather than the particular. Values guide culturally appropriate behavior, and thus are widely held among members of the society. Because they are widely held and deal with the general, they are enduring and not easily changed. For example, one widely held value of western logistics managers is efficiency, both as an objective performance norm as well as a personally held value that guides their own and their firm's behavior.

Both beliefs and values affect a person's attitudes. An understanding of a culture's beliefs and attitudes helps predict the way that an individual will respond to a particular situation. Knowledge of beliefs and values give hints at a cultural predisposition to behave in a certain way. Such knowledge also helps one to understand why her or his reactions to a given situation may be quite different from those of people from a different culture.

Customs are different from beliefs and values. Customs refer to actual behaviors that are shared among members of a society. These common behaviors are the culturally acceptable manner of behaving in specific situations. Most customs are tied to everyday behavior. Beliefs and values guide customs: they form the rules base from which behavior arises. For example, a cultural value may dictate respect for authority. An associated custom may be a rigorous adherence to a chain of command that exists in an organization.

Managing Differences with U.S. Cultural Values

One way to overcome cultural barriers in business is to have a thorough understanding of the core values held by people of the United States (hereafter Americans) and examine the way in which these core values relate to those of other cultures. Each culture has a distinctive set of values that guide its members. Americans hold some values in common with other cultures; the value of achievement and success is shared with the Japanese, for example. Other values are uniquely American. By studying where U.S. values are similar and where they differ from those in other cultures, one gains a deeper knowledge of one's self and a more informed perspective as to why things differ in other cultures.

Americans value achievement, success, and progress. There is a perennial optimism that dictates tomorrow will be better than today. Achievement as a value speaks to the internalized sense of accomplishment one feels when a task is successfully completed. Often coupled with that internal feeling is the external sense of success. Success speaks to recognition from peers. Achievement and success often go hand-in-hand. What enables achievement and success for many individuals is the belief that it is always possible to better one's self, that progress or improvement of one's position simply requires good hard work. One sees such values commonly expressed in the workplace and also in the output of the workplace.

These values of achievement, success, and progress also fuel technological change. American culture thrives on change, and attributes little value to old ways of doing things. A byproduct of this set of values may be the American emphasis on youthfulness, which excludes the elderly from most dynamic aspects of the U.S. culture. Consider how different Japanese culture is in its expression of the values of achievement, success, and progress. Japanese tend to view achievement, success, and progress in a broader social context than people in the United States. While Americans adopt such values and hold them dear as individuals, a more altruistic tone characterizes the Japanese manifestation of the same values. The good of the whole is valued more than the good of the individual, leading to some rather different expressions of common cultural values. The elderly are honored in Japan in part due to religious differences, but also due to a recognition of their significant place in history and the changes brought about by one's forefathers. Elderly people are seen as knowledgeable, experienced individuals who have a unique perspective on progress and who can assist in avoiding a headlong plunge into progress for progress' sake.

Cultural values of efficiency, punctuality, and practicality guide the American work ethos. In the quest for efficiency, one seeks out any technology that saves time and effort. Related to that quest is a desire for practicality—a search for anything that makes problem solving easier or facilitates the completion of any task. Underlying both efficiency and practicality is an American desire for punctuality. One logistical expression of these American values has been the headlong rush of U.S. industry to adopt just-in-time systems for inventory and production savings. One tends to view time as a scarce resource which can be allocated and utilized; in many respects, time—or the ability to save time—for American business is similar in importance to the traditional economic inputs of land, labor, and capital. Time is viewed as linear and can be allocated, used, or wasted.

Contrast this American cultural perception of time with two other views. In some cultures, particularly those where seasonal change is minimal, time is viewed as a circular rather than linear construct. Today is perceived to be not that different from yesterday, nor will it likely be much different from tomorrow. The utility of time under such cultural perceptions is greatly diminished. Tasks which are not accomplished today may just as easily be accomplished tomorrow, and tasks held over from yesterday may just as easily be held again until tomorrow. A circular notion of time seems alien to American managers, and has been the source of much frustration in negotiation with counterparts from other cultures. Yet such a conceptualization of time works perfectly well within its cultural context—it is a value that dictates customary behaviors.

Yet another view of time is seen in cultures that spring from agrarian roots. Time there may be perceived as procedural rather than linear. Certain auspices must combine to indicate that the time is right for any given behavior. One cannot plant until the spring floodwaters have receded, nor harvest until after the first frost. Thus, the allocation of time as a resource is meaningless to members of such cultures. No event can take place before its auspicious time, nor could it take place afterwards. Ritual and procedure dictate the timing of events, not some arbitrary division of time as kept by a clock. Thus, in such a culture, offense may be taken as eager American managers seem to wish to circumvent ritual and tradition in an effort to gain efficiency or time savings. When saving time is a meaningless idea, an obsession with punctuality is often viewed as rudeness or as a personal flaw such as impatience. Imagine how one might go about explaining the importance of just-in-time systems to a counterpart from another culture that places no utility on time itself!

Other uniquely American cultural values that impact business behavior include individualism, freedom of choice, and conformity. Americans pride themselves on individual expression through freedom of choice. They believe that they are free to be whomever they want to be, and that they have the right to make choices for themselves. This American focus on individualism may be related to a disdain for dependency. Americans are taught to be self-reliant, and with that self-reliance they accept responsibility for their choices. There is an inherent conflict between these two cultural values and the value of conformity. Americans also desire to "fit in" to the rest of society. Nonconformists are frowned upon and often labeled as eccentrics, loners, or deviants. The contradiction in American life between this desire for individualism and freedom of choice and the opposing value of conformity is puzzling to many outsiders. The gregarious nature of many Americans is often a manifestation of the desire for individualism, yet the consensus managerial style is tied to the desire for conformity.

Language Differences

One obvious difference between cultures is language. Language refers to the common set of symbols used to exchange ideas through communication between individuals. As such, language includes not only the written and spoken use of these symbols, but also the gestural and other nonverbal components of communication. Language often presents the most immediate barrier to understanding another culture. As language is the common means of expression within a culture, it is inherently laden with meaning that will be obscure to the cultural outsider.

Marketing literature is rife with anecdotal evidence of how language differences lead to business miscommunication. Imagine the problems American consumers might have with the Japanese coffee creamer "Creap," or the Scandinavian product which unfreezes car locks called "Super Piss."[6] The automobile industry has had its own problems with language: Rolls-Royce's "Silver Mist" translated into German as "Silver Manure;" Ford's "Fiera" truck shared the slang meaning "ugly old woman" in Spanish; in Mexican Spanish, Ford's "Caliente" was understood to be a streetwalker; and in Brazil, the "Pinto" was Portuguese slang for "small male appendage."[7]

But how does one manage these nuances of meaning one-on-one in the context of day-to-day business activity? One way is through learning the language of the other culture. Because languages are heavy with idiomatic meaning, learning another language with any fluency inevitably leads to a greater understanding of that language's cultural antecedents. Often one hears that certain ideas or

---

[6]Rivkin, Steve (1996), "The Name Game Heats Up," *Marketing News* (April 22, 1996), p. 8.

[7]Rivkin, Steve (1996).

concepts are not translatable. This usually means that one culture's experience or world-view is dissimilar to that of another culture. For example, in English there are very few words to describe frozen precipitation in weather (snow, sleet, hail). In Inuit, where cold weather is a daily fact of life and survival depends on accurate depiction of weather, there are some seventeen words to describe frozen precipitate.

Some languages are highly dependent on the context in which words are presented, others less so. English, for example, is considered to be a "low-context" language where meaning is carried largely by individual words. Japanese on the other hand, is a high-context language. Words used in certain combinations often hold very different meanings, and when used in different situations convey very different ideas. Thus, the manner in which a person is addressed in Japanese is highly significant; in English, only address mannerisms or a sarcastic tone that are obviously disrespectful carry differing meaning.

Written communications present a challenge across cultures. It is insufficient to merely translate from one language to another. A second translation back to the original language is necessary to compare with the original text. Errors in translation occur not only through poor work but also through a lack of shared conceptualization between languages. It is good advice to translate from English to the second language, and use a different translator to "back translate" to English again from the secondary text. Differences between the English versions often must be reconciled by use of more illustrative or concise language that parallels similar constructs in the second language. Another strategy for clear translations is to avoid the use of idiomatic language.

Cultural differences are many. Beliefs, values, customs, language—all impact the way one interacts with business counterparts. Differences can get in the way of the simplest of business activities. Yet a few steps toward understanding cultural differences and sharing one's own culture go a long way toward smoothing relationships across cultural boundaries. It is important to be aware of those self-referencing criteria that are brought to bear because of enculturation and not allow them to become barriers to successful business activity.

Logistical Development in Different Nations

This following section will profile logistics activities and standards by looking at three categories of nations: the first world, the emerging economies, and the third world. In each section, we present the typical conditions managers should expect to find and point out some similarities and differences with logistical practices in countries such as the United States.

It is possible to measure different levels of logistics achievement, despite differences in national accounting standards and practices. The Global Logistics Research Team at Michigan State University developed a model for firm-level logistical excellence, and a set of standards by which to benchmark any firm's logistics performance. They measured strategies, organizational development, logistics performance, the use of information technology, and strategic alliances.[8]

However, it is much more difficult to measure a nation's logistics performance. Any firm's logistical performance will necessarily be limited by the political, social, and economic aspects of its national environment. In the United States, for example, over 90 percent of the roadways are paved surface. But in Zimbabwe, only 19 percent of the roadways are paved surface, and 35 percent of the roadways are unimproved dirt.[9] Clearly, one working with logistics systems involving these two nations would have to adjust his or her expectations as to the "normal" truck transportation time and reliability.

The First World: An Evolved Logistics Infrastructure

In the past 20 years, we have come to see a world of interlinked economies, where corporations span national boundaries and render the concept of a nation-state secondary to corporate activity. This interlinked economic world consists largely of three distinct geographical clusters of nations: Japan, the United States and Canada, and the members of the European Union.

In this "first world" of logistics, companies have become more important than nation states as their power transcends national borders. The national identity of any of these companies begins to blur. In a sense, what really is the national identity of a company like Toyota? While many of Toyota's stockholders may be Japanese, Toyota's most important markets are the United States and Europe, and a high percentage of Toyota cars sold in the United States and Europe are made locally in Toyota-owned plants. The national identity of Toyota is blurred, but its market identity is clear as a manufacturer of several lines of quality automobiles and trucks and industrial construction and materials handling equipment.

This blurring of the lines between nations and corporate identities has a profound impact on the practice of logistics. We have seen rapid dissemination across national boundaries of new logistics concepts and practices by corporations themselves. The corporate trend toward globalization has forced the spread of advanced management practices across cultural boundaries in the quest for

---

[8]Global Logistics Research Team at Michigan State University (1995), *World Class Logistics: The Challenge of Managing Continuous Change,* Oak Brook, IL: Council of Logistics Management.

[9]Addus, Abdussalam A. and Anwar S. Khan (2000), "Air Transportation in Sub-Saharan Africa," *Transportation Quarterly,* 54 (4), p. 47–58.

competitive advantage. Take, for example, the Japanese *kanban* relationship be-tween a corporation and its suppliers. From a managerial standpoint, the em-phasis is on full disclosure and cooperation between buyer and seller to create seamless vertical integration. The creation of such *kanban* systems in the 1970s enabled major Japanese corporations to develop tremendous economies of scale and scope, giving them a significant competitive edge.

One now sees that cooperation between buyer and seller in marketing chan-nels has largely replaced competition between buyer and seller as an American business norm. The logistics manifestation of the *kanban* system is just-in-time inventory and production. And the *kanban* strategy is now nearly universally ac-cepted business practice among globally proficient firms.

In a similar way, American logistics practice during the 1980s in the area of outsourcing was influenced by the European experience. In Europe, there is a long history of outsourcing logistics functions. Outsourcing was more difficult to achieve in the United States prior to carrier deregulation that took place in 1980. The tradition of using logistics outsourcing developed a strategic advan-tage for European companies serving more than one national marketplace. The advantages of outsourcing certain functions were realized by American compa-nies that faced increasing competition from their European counterparts. Thus outsourcing migrated to America in the 1980s and 1990s.

Today we see the global diffusion of advanced logistics information tech-nologies and management practices, spearheaded by mostly American innova-tion in Internet-based technology and communications. In the coming decades, we envision the broad diffusion of advanced applications in transportation, in-ventory management, customer service, and procurement functions throughout firms in the first world of logistics. The ultimate goal is the seamless integration of information management throughout an enterprise's supply chain. Much progress remains to be made in this regard. A recent survey of U.S. firms finds only 25 percent of them consider they have achieved any degree of such logis-tics information integration.[10]

The globalization drive has brought down cultural barriers to the way busi-nesses behave in first-world logistics. Companies have melded the best aspects from global business practice in an effort to remain competitive with their sim-ilarly global competitors. Simply put, to successfully do business today one must study and implement excellent logistics practices, learning from the best prac-tices of companies world-wide.

---

[10]Gibson, Brian J., Craig M. Gustin, and Stephen M. Rutner (2000), "The Use of Logistics In-formation Systems Throughout the Supply Chain," *Annual Conference Proceedings of the Council of Logistics Management,* Oak Brook, IL: Council of Logistics Management, pp. 159–172.

When examining the similarities and differences in practice within the logistics first world, one sees more similarities going forward. The global competitive drive dictates that similarity in business practice is the only way for a global corporation to succeed. More standardization of logistics practice is the trend inside first world logistics.

Infrastructure

In first-world logistics, one sees highly developed infrastructures. Japan, the United States and Canada, and the European Union nations all have highly developed national highway systems, port facilities, state-of-the-art air freight handling, sophisticated information systems, advanced communications facilities, elaborate rail, and multimodal transportation. While all of the logistics infrastructures can be said to be highly evolved, certain differences remain due to historical development and geography. For example, highways through much of Europe are narrower than in the United States. This minor infrastructure variation dictates that goods transport equipment be designed slightly differently. Advances in the use of multimodal transportation and containerization standards have largely rendered these minor roadway differences moot. Containers move easily from Japanese trailers to American container ships, and to European rail. The importance of serving this integrated market has forced standards which work in all of the evolved infrastructure environments.

One significant trend of the 1990s continues to remain relevant in the new century: environmentalism. Respect for the natural environment has led to additional infrastructure concerns. Many urban areas now face vehicular gridlock during certain hours each day. In Japan and the United States, the just-in-time delivery system is being threatened by this congestion since carefully scheduled trucks get stuck in nearly endless traffic jams. In the United States, only one new major airport went into service in the past decade, despite a near doubling of commercial passenger traffic and a similar increase in air freight. Concerns about air, water, land, noise, and visual pollution now influence the way in which infrastructures are developed, maintained, and improved. For example, the construction of a much-needed advanced technology runway at San Francisco International Airport has been on hold for years due to environmental concerns regarding San Francisco Bay. These infrastructure concerns have impacted logistics practice in the short term by changing logistics behavior (for example, limiting urban deliveries to non-peak hours, reducing permissible vehicle size and loads, forcing expanded use of less-than-optimal air terminal facilities), and will impact the future practice of logistics as infrastructures are both constrained and rebuilt with tomorrow's needs in mind.

Environmental protection practices and standards are similarly high in these countries. Japan, for example, recycles a higher percentage of many materials than most nations. Germany has very stringent packaging recycling requirements. Return packaging channels have been established in most of these countries at both consumer and channel intermediary levels.

Performance

Logistics operating standards have similarly spread through the first world because of the globalization of business practice. Business customers have very similar expectations for logistics system performance, regardless of where in the first world they're operating. These advances in logistics performance expectations have been fueled by increasing similarity in consumer markets. Thus overnight air freight, the instantaneous tracking of goods in transit, electronic data interchange, just-in-time, materials resource planning, distribution resource planning, and enterprise resource planning have transcended buzzwords to become norms of logistics operating practice. The state-of-the-art moves rapidly across national boundaries as companies take concepts and behaviors proven in one country to facilities that they own or manage in other countries.

Information Systems

Advances in computer technology and communications capabilities spread at the same rate throughout the logistics first world. Inventory managers in Spain have similar access to retail store point-of-sale (POS) data as U.S. managers do. With the spread of such advanced technology tools as bar coding, automated materials handling equipment, POS systems, desktop and mobile computing in networked environments connected to the Internet, electronic data interchange, and expert systems, logistics information professionals would be at home anywhere in these nations. Increased expectations in the consumer marketplace have demanded that logistics information systems keep up in order to meet exacting service standards.

While the information technology transfer has been complete in the logistics first world, different information standards remain a barrier to seamless logistics practice. In the United States, for example, there are uniform standards for product bar coding (the UPC, or Universal Product Code) that enable precision inventory control at manufacturer, wholesaler, and retail levels. In the European Union, bar coding also has been embraced as a means to better inventory control. Yet the EU nations have adopted a similar, though different set of bar code standards to identify products than that used in the U.S. While the required hardware can read any bar code, software has to be written to make EU bar codes translate to U.S. equivalents (and vice versa). We anticipate a global consolidation in the next decade around new ISO three-dimensional code standards.

Human Resources

Logistics managers have also become increasingly sophisticated as the level of demand for better logistics performance has increased. Logistics managers are increasingly called upon for their professional inputs into corporate and marketing strategies and are expected to manage increasing loads of ever-more detailed information more efficiently. As managers have learned to balance inventory needs against information needs, logistics professionals have increasingly become information specialists. Cultural differences aside, a logistics manager from Japan would be functionally at home in a counterpart's position in America. Similar technical and managerial skills are required for both positions, and logistics professionals continue to rise in the corporate hierarchy in relation to the relative importance of logistics as a strategically manipulated variable.

One encouraging trend has been the spread of logistics professional education and training programs throughout the first world. European and Japanese business schools are now offering specialized study in logistics and transportation management. The U.S. Council of Logistics Management and the Canadian Association for Logistics Management both have active professional development programs which engage logistics professionals from the United States, Canada, Japan, and the European Union.

Strategic and Financial Resources

One driving strategy that has shaped logistics practice is the change from a company-centered view to a consumer-centered view. Companies today are pitted against each other in a battle for market share. In the global marketplace with very large economies of scale and scope, it was easy for companies to narrow their focus too much and fall into the company-centric trap. A renewed focus on meeting the customer's needs so uniquely as to remove competitors from the customer's mindset has become a dominant way of thinking in corporate strategy. The drive to get to know the customer better has also brought about increased prominence for logistics as a strategic means of increasing customer satisfaction. Logistics managers are now very aware of customer service standards, managing exceptional order requirements, and custom tailoring their system performance to the needs of customers.

This new strategic thrust has brought considerably more financial resources to bear in the development of advanced, customer-driven logistics systems. Corporate trends such as sole-sourcing have forced many companies to spend additional capital resources to develop their logistics systems and human resources. We expect that this renewed interest in the customer and the strategic shift toward cooperation in an attempt to build vertical channel integration will continue in the coming decades, forcing the development of even more sophisticated logistics resources.

From a logistics manager's point of view, all seems harmonious and well in the first world. Expectations are rarely off the mark when comparing logistics systems development and performance. While cultural and historical differences remain in the practice of logistics, the trend has clearly been toward systems integration and standardization. As long as the final consumer markets continue to make such high level demands of manufacturers, wholesalers, and retailers in the logistics first world, our logistics systems will increase in similarity rather than diverge.

The Emerging Nations

In this grouping for discussion of emerging nations are such countries as Russia, Thailand, Indonesia, Taiwan, China, Brazil, and the new market economies in Eastern Europe. Each enjoys a rapid pace of industrialization, high levels of literacy and training, but comparatively low (though quickly rising) per-capita incomes. One continues to see countries where exports of raw materials and finished goods exceed the imports of consumer goods. National industrial policy often has focused on rapid industrialization at the expense of an advanced consumer marketplace.

One could argue that it is the absence of an advanced consumer marketplace that has inhibited the development of advanced logistics performance in the emerging nations. Companies operating in such countries' consumer marketplaces often are still engaged in a parallel striving strategy: a company-centered perspective. Companies often focus on zero-sum games of beating the competition. While logistics performance can play a crucial role in such games, one most often sees logistics relegated to the category of a necessary expense rather than as a strategic tool.

The development of advanced logistics has also often been held back by the lack of an appropriate logistics infrastructure. In some emerging nations, the logistics infrastructure has been built around the export of raw materials. A People's Republic of China transportation booklet says, "Most of the railroads in old

China were built to suit the needs of the imperialists who intended to dominate China at that time."[11] This national one-way infrastructure flow design inhibits reverse, or importing, logistics flows. One sees uneven levels of development across transportation modes, for example. A country that focuses on the export of raw materials may have fairly advanced rail systems leading to bulk-loading port export facilities. Such transportation infrastructures require considerable re-working and redesign to be made appropriate for advanced logistics practice.

Consider the transportation infrastructure of China. There are over one million kilometers of roads in China, but only 2 percent of those roads are considered first or second grade. Over half of the roads in China are unimproved dirt, and impassable on rainy days. Over one-third of the villages in China have no road access. Fifteen major coastal ports are currently operating at 16 percent over-capacity, resulting in a typical 500 ships per day waiting to load or unload. Some ships linger in port for as long as two months at a time, with serious and costly implications for inventory management.[12]

It is difficult to implement the strategic options possible in advanced multi-modal transportation systems in a country that does not have an adequate high-way system, regardless of the level of development of its rail, port, or air facili-ties. In China, multimodal transportation companies are a relatively new phenomenon and have very limited operating capacity at this time. The tradi-tional system of rail, road, waterway, and aviation are managed independently by different government departments, and have no inherent incentives to coop-erate in providing transportation services across modes. Complicating this lack of coordination is the relative scarcity of containerized operations within China. Just over 7 percent of transportation facilities are equipped to handle container-ized freight, and there is a national shortage of freight containers.[13]

Emphasis on Infrastructure Renewal and Development

Many emerging nations have a coordinated national industrial policy to encour-age the renewal and development of their business infrastructures. Particularly since the demise of economic central planning, the emerging nations have looked toward the first-world nations for a vision of the future of economic develop-ment. Their aspirational goals have begun to focus on the development of more

---

[11]Traffic and Transportation in China, Beijing: Foreign Languages Printing House (1986), p. 14.

[12]Zhang, Hong (1999), "Logistics in China," (presentation at San Francisco State University), Chinese Academy of Social Sciences: Institute of Finance and Trade Economics.

[13]Zhang, Hong (1999), "Logistics in China," (presentation at San Francisco State University), Chinese Academy of Social Sciences: Institute of Finance and Trade Economics.

advanced consumer economies. This change in economic development emphasis will gradually bring about the necessary infrastructure to support advanced logistics performance.

In some respects, many of the emerging nations are in a position to leapfrog the triad nations in infrastructure technology. Consider the situation of Hungary, which is replacing its entire telecommunications system. The Hungarian telephone system was formerly a mishmash of 1920s German switching and line technology combined with 1950s era Soviet instrumentation. If it is necessary to rewire and reswitch an entire communications network, did it not make sense to adopt the highest level state-of-the-art equipment available? Why rewire the country with copper wire if fiber-optics are more cost-effective and clearly the direction communications technology is heading? Today Hungary is building what is arguably a more sophisticated communications system than the hybrid technology systems now operating in the United States. Alexander Gerschenkron's theories of economic development, popular at mid-century, dealt with the "advantages of backwardness." Less-developed (then called "backward") nations, when they developed, had the advantage of choosing the very latest of available technologies, jumping ahead of other economies that had been less recently "developed."

Even environmentally-correct leapfrogging may be possible. In Western Europe, where highways are overcrowded, "most planners have decided Easterners should rebuild their economies around rail transport. Some experts have even claimed that Eastern Europe has been given a unique opportunity to avoid the mistake the West has made in building its economies around the road infrastructure."[14] This trend toward technological leapfrogging is by no means uniform in the emerging nations, as some nations continue to neglect infrastructure development. China, for example, proposed to spend only half of the World Bank's recommended levels for transportation infrastructure improvements in its most recent five-year plan.[15]

In this rush toward advancing the state of national economies, logistics managers face a variety of challenges in the emerging nations. Technologies that work perfectly well in the logistics first world are not even a possibility in many emerging nations. Consider the simple use of an established technology such as point-of-sale information systems by retailers. In Russia, with the telecommunications system in the midst of massive reconstruction, telephone lines are often

---

[14]*Transport Topics,* March 22, 1993, p. 12.

[15]Zhang, Hong (1999), "Logistics in China," (presentation at San Francisco State University), Chinese Academy of Social Sciences: Institute of Finance and Trade Economics.

unreliable and not uniformly capable of handling high-speed data communications. Interlinking retail stores with distribution facilities and manufacturers (a standard practice in the first-world countries) becomes a logistics nightmare at best.

Influence of Firms versus Government

Depending on the particulars of national industrial policies, one sees an intricate balance and dance occurring between firms and the governments of the emerging nations. Large, global corporations are often operating in the emerging nations. Frequently they use these countries as sources of raw materials, subassemblies, finished goods, or low-cost labor, and occasionally they see these countries as developing markets for consumer products. Such firms often exert considerable influence over government, especially when government may be courting foreign direct investment.

These firms are in a position to direct the development of logistics infrastructures through their influence. One sees the development of port facilities, laying of rail and communications backbone, and airport reconstruction that benefits particular companies. This gives involved companies a direct strategic advantage as the emerging nations develop into advanced consumer economies. For example, General Motors, DaimlerChrysler, Volkswagen, and Toyota have all collaborated to influence the development of transportation and telecommunications infrastructure in China, where each of the firms has located assembly plants.

Economic "Stepchild" or Financial Spheres of Influence

Many emerging nations find their economies and resultant logistics systems tied to neighboring first-world nations through exactly such influences. Eighty percent of the foreign direct investment in the Czech Republic has been supplied by German companies. The net outcome of this form of national renewal is likely to be an economic satellite state of the German Republic. The Czech economy is linked by financial ties, management structures, and logistics systems to established German firms and markets, and through them to world markets.

Such economic stepchild development is a mixed blessing. Seemingly inevitable, it brings rapid modernization to these emerging nations and can jump-start a consumer economy, but at the cost of closely tied economic destinies. But we know that advanced logistics systems cannot function in outdated, inadequate national infrastructures. Indeed, infrastructure and other logistics systems are needed to support logistics systems. Truckers, for example, need regular access to parts and to fuel. To the extent that these advanced infrastructures are necessary conditions for the emergence of consumer economies, the economic stepchild model is one strategy for rapid development.

The state of logistics development and sophistication in the emerging countries is highly varied. Logistics managers are likely to encounter operating, functional logistics systems that seem hopelessly antiquated by first-world logistics standards. However, considering the level of sophistication of the resident consumer economies, many of these existent logistics systems function in an acceptable manner. When the systems do work, one often sees very high levels of inventory supporting them. As the cushion in the system, inventory is an expensive means of making inefficient logistics systems work. Again, it's a chicken-and-egg problem: Advanced logistics systems will develop to support advanced consumer economies. But the development of those economies will be inhibited by the absence of advanced logistical systems.

The Third World

In contrast to the logistics first world and the emerging economies, third-world countries are defined by low levels of industrialization, literacy, and per-capita income. Included in this group of countries, for example, would be the Sudan, Afghanistan, Haiti, and Ethiopia. The national economies of the third world focus on subsistence and maintenance, and are often agrarian-based or have large nomadic populations. Consumer markets are primitive even in the major cities of the third world, with most consumption geared toward meeting subsistence needs such as food, clothing, and housing. First world nation-style consumer economies are almost completely unknown, or exist on a very small scale to cater to the needs of the small upper class of the country.

Most third-world countries have limited import/export activity by first-world standards. Many of these nations see that developed nations control the world's shipping, airlines, and cargo insurance. For example, many African nations found that their transportation infrastructures were developed to feed into the major European nations' carrier routes by sea and air. As onetime colonies, they were used to the practice of having the transport price added to the price of goods they bought, and subtracted from the price of goods they sold. Third-world countries often export natural resources, agricultural products, or other raw materials. Imports tend to be limited to essential manufactured goods, often due to negative balance of trade standings. In 1998, the World Bank reported that 60 percent of African exports were raw materials (compared to 33 percent for all developing countries), and only 19 percent of all African exports were manufactured goods (compared to 54 percent for all developing countries).[16]

Infrastructure Insufficiency

The logistics infrastructure in many third-world countries reflects a legacy of early industrial development, often at the direction of a colonial power. Again, these infrastructures were frequently constructed with one-way logistics in mind—exporting the country's principal natural resource or agricultural product. The history and structure of the railroads in the Sudan provides an example of this development.

The Sudan is a country of almost a million square miles in area, located in eastern Africa. The northern part of the country is largely desert with an Islamic population, and the south is fertile farmland with a mostly Christian and Animist population. Some 20 million people live in the Sudan, though Khartoum is the largest city with about 400,000 people. The British colonized the Sudan heavily during the 18th and 19th centuries, and designed and built the Sudan's transportation infrastructure. Exports from the Sudan to Britain included millet, sorghum, cotton, chromium, and asbestos. Port Sudan on the Red Sea was built by the British to handle export traffic. A main rail line was constructed to connect Port Sudan (which is in the arid northeast) with Khartoum, the administrative capital in central Sudan. Agriculture and mining activities take place largely in the south, and a number of feeder lines extend southward from Khartoum along the upper Nile river to the southern part of the country. Rail was chosen as the preferred transportation mode due to the long distances required to move commodities from production to export. Highway development was not emphasized, as railroads were the only mode that was practical for heavy goods.

Since the population is largely agrarian and widely dispersed, there was no need to move people from area to area within the country, so highway development came quite late in the colonial era. Before the country became independent in 1956, the British completed a skeletal system of paved two-lane roads and telephone lines that link major cities. With Soviet help, Sudan built a national airline (Air Sudan) during the 1960s and 70s that connected major cities in the Sudan with neighboring countries in east Africa.

Since the end of the colonial era, there has been little additional investment made in the national infrastructure of the Sudan. Maintenance has been deferred, and highway conditions today are significantly deteriorated. Aging British and

---

[16]Addus, Abdussalam A. and Anwar S. Khan (2000), "Air Transportation in Sub-Saharan Africa," *Transportation Quarterly*, 54 (4), pp. 47–58.

Soviet-made rail stock ply a barely passable rail system, and Air Sudan's fleet flies only intermittently as parts and fuel availability remains problematic. The government of the Sudan continues to be occupied by a civil war that divides the Islamic north from the remainder of the nation, and the national economy is in disarray. In the 1990s, the average transit time for rail shipments between Khartoum and Wau (600 air miles) was 10 to 12 days. Passage by road could take over two weeks, depending on war activities, local weather, and flooding conditions. Communications between Khartoum and Wau by telephone were often impossible, and shortwave radio and radiotelephone were considered more reliable.

Transportation

The logistics and transportation infrastructure that does exist in many third-world countries is inadequate to support advanced business logistics and is poorly maintained and operated. The governments of these countries are woefully aware of the infrastructure insufficiencies, but lack the capital and expertise to make major improvements. Figure 3–1, while old, is a photograph of a truck

Figure 3–1 Truck loading-unloading facility achieved by digging a hole to place truck bed at ground level. Photo courtesy of Organization of American States, Columbus Memorial Library, Photograph Collection.

loading/unloading facility built in a country where labor was very cheap; apparently it was easiest to have labor dig out a hole so that the truck's bed would be at ground level, rather than building a raised loading/unloading dock. Often the governments also lack the impetus for expanded development due to the subsistence nature of their economies.

> In attempting to secure direct overseas shipping services, most [South-West Pacific] island governments are faced with the prospect of upgrading their ports to a standard, and at a cost, which is not warranted by their small volume of trade. However, to lag behind in port development clearly risks being bypassed by international carriers for whom rapid turnaround and efficient unitized cargo-handling are essential for profitable operation. Thus, governments effectively have no choice but to embark on costly port-upgrading schemes and to risk the probable consequences of over investment and underutilization.[17]

A difficult problem for these governments is to decide whether transportation investment should be linked to developing direct exports or to strengthening the local economy. Politically, the second alternative is often better because it ties the nation together.

Highway transport is most beneficial to the largest number of people in a developing country. Some can merely walk or walk a bicycle laden with goods along a path. Also, small-scale entrepreneurs will spring up, to fix bikes or trucks or to sell fuel. From a study in Malaya, "after the highway was usable, traders came daily from as far as 10 miles by bicycle or motorcycle to buy fish and other items, and returned home in the late afternoon for the opening of their own local market. Before this, fresh fish was a rarity, even though the sea was only 10 miles away."[18] The same study of five roads in Malaya showed social development followed in "the form of increased attendance at schools, greater use of medical facilities, increased reading of newspapers, use of governmental services and facilities, and introduction to the other amenities of modern life."[19]

In the case of Africa, where varied and difficult topography and politics isolate a good portion of the population from world trade, Abdussalam and Khan make a persuasive case for the use of low-cost, short-haul, light aircraft to stim-

---

[17]Dunbar-Nobes, A.C. (1984), "Port Problems and Small Island Economies: The Case of the South-West Pacific," in *Seaport Systems and Spatial Change,* B.S. Hoyle and D. Hilling (eds.), New York: John Wiley, p. 87.

[18]Hughes, William (1969), "Social Benefits Through Improved Transport in Malaya," in Transport and Economic Goals, Edwin Haefele (ed.), Washington: The Brookings Institution, p. 120.

[19]Hughes, William (1969), "Social Benefits Through Improved Transport in Malaya," in Transport and Economic Goals, Edwin Haefele (ed.), Washington: The Brookings Institution, p. 121.

ulate local economic development.[20] Such aircraft have relatively inexpensive infrastructure requirements, and thus seem a route to more rapid development than conventional rail or heavy aircraft facilities.

The legacy of colonialism's emphasis on the export of raw materials and agricultural goods can been seen in the development of transportation systems in many third-world countries. Given their origin as bulk-loading commodity facilities, ports often have inadequate or lack entirely modern container loading/unloading facilities. Some third-world ports suffer from port congestion, and multimodalism remains rare. Equipment available in-country is highly variable, and maintenance can be problematic from the standpoint of finding parts supplies and qualified mechanics and operators. The ownership of transportation modes is also highly variable, with many countries owning and operating rail, port, and air facilities while allowing privately owned trucking or waterway transportation.

Warehousing/Inventories/Customer Service

Finding appropriate warehousing and storage space in third-world countries can also be problematic. Often, major warehouse facilities exist only at ports of entry and were designed as export inventory holding areas. As with the transportation system, one can expect a combination of government and private ownership of warehousing depending on the economic and developmental history of the country. Advanced materials handling equipment is often not available, though exceptions are notable. In Jamaica, for example, an automated bauxite loading facility is available as a legacy of Alcoa's export activities there in the 1960s and 70s.

Inventory management is also difficult. Sudden government actions may close borders, turning off—for an indeterminate time—pipelines through which goods were flowing. Because local currencies fluctuate wildly, it may be unrealistic to attempt to value inventories in local terms. "Preferential exchange rates are sometimes established to affect the nature and timing of imports. These actions may be good for business—inducing bulk shipments—but disastrous for inventory levels."[21]

While first-world logistics executives like to describe their systems as customer-driven, the concept is nearly meaningless in most third-world countries. There are many shortages, and it is almost always a sellers' market. Popular customer service measures, as used in the first world, such as "in-stock

---

[20]Addus, Abdussalam A. and Anwar S. Khan (2000), "Air Transportation in Sub-Saharan Africa," *Transportation Quarterly,* 54 (4), pp. 47–58.

[21]Wakefield, Victor (1992), "Managing Global Inventories," *Global Connections,* 10 (Fall 1992).

availability, speed of service and service consistency would be irrelevant; given this situation the firm has little control over the timing and availability of inventory. The chronic shortage of foreign exchange and its rationing implies that replenishment rates are nearly always less than optimal."[22]

Information

Information management technology in some third-world countries often dates to the paper-and-pen era of the 1950s. While personal computers are now widely available, the absence of reliable and high quality communications systems tends to limit their usefulness in business logistics settings. Such advanced technologies as bar coding, automatic inventory replenishment and reorder systems, and EDI are not possible to implement. One additional problem often faced by logistics professionals in the third world is the lack of reliable data concerning business activity. Private sources of market-based data do not exist, and government monitoring of the private sector is often unreliable. Thus important information about population demographic shifts that would be useful for demand and inventory forecasting is quite often unavailable.

Communications are poor and many companies engage in inventory overstocking as a cautionary measure. In Coca-Cola's new bottling facility in Luanda, Angola, for example, 220 metric tons of sugar are routinely stockpiled, an amount far exceeding immediate production requirements. Coca-Cola also maintains a substantial inventory of new empty bottles imported from the United Arab Emirates. The company faces delays averaging 49 days for goods to clear customs at Angolan ports.[23]

Human Resources

While it is possible to find skilled labor in third world countries that is appropriate to the level of logistics technology available, it can be difficult to find native logistics professionals who have a grasp of contemporary strategic logistics management. This problem is not unique to the third-world nations. Many emerging nations also face a shortage of logistics personnel. As always, the training of needed human resources is high on the list of improvements required to implement advanced logistics systems.

---

[22]Dadzie, Kofi Q. (1990), "Transfer of Logistics Knowledge to Third World Countries," *International Journal of Physical Distribution and Logistics Management,* 20 (9), pp. 56–68.

[23]*New York Times* (2001), "Braving War and Graft, Coke Goes Back To Angola," April 22, 2001, p. 3-1.

Trade Issues

Shortages of hard currency are common in third-world countries. Many of these nations are saddled with enormous debt burdens and simply lack reserves of currency for trade purposes. Countertrade or bartering is sometimes the only way international commerce can be maintained, and such arrangements often create challenging problems for logistics professionals. Consider Boeing's trade of jet aircraft to the government of Poland in exchange for canned hams during the 1980s. While logistics professionals at Boeing were certainly quite capable of handling the export from the United States, the land-based warehousing functions and surface transportation of the agricultural goods bartered required different types of logistics expertise. Such barter arrangements make for creative logistics problem solving.

Pre-shipment inspections (PSIs) are imposed by about 40 third-world nations who are short of hard currency and have problems with illegal flights of currency. Inspection companies, paid by the importer or the importing government, physically inspect goods in order to test their quality and perform price comparisons in order to assure the integrity of invoiced price. U.S. exporters complain for two reasons:

1. An outside agent is commenting upon the price of the goods. "Celanese decided to yank a shipment of fiber off of a freighter in Miami and ship the goods back to South Carolina rather than lower its prices by 9 percent, as the [pre-inspection] agent demanded."[24]

2. The whole process takes more time: "You'd better add $500 to your quote and five weeks more lead time if you're shipping to a country that employs a pre-inspection service."[25]

The most important benefit claimed by these companies is the prevention of fraud. "Over"- and "under"-invoicing is believed to be a major source of illegal capital flight from less developed countries. PSI's are contracted, as quasi-customs authorities, by the central banks of these countries, in order to detect and dissuade the practice.

Over-invoicing is the practice of billing a price unjustifiably higher than fair market or higher than is actually payable by the importer. In both cases the aim is to get dollars out of the importing country. If the buyer and seller are related

---

[24]*The Christian Science Monitor,* April 20, 1987, p. 6.

[25]*Distribution,* March 1987, p. 11.

parties, overinvoicing may simply serve the purpose of extracting capital in circumvention of exchange restrictions. In some cases, the importer and exporter enter into agreements whereby the exporter then fraudulently invoices more than the agreed price and deposits the balance in a bank outside the importer's country for the account of the importer. Overinvoicing may have other purposes as well, such as increasing the cost of goods of the importing company and thereby reducing its income tax liability. When the importing company is a subsidiary of the exporter, this may be the aim.

Under-invoicing is the practice of invoicing less than is actually payable. Under invoicing serves to reduce the dutiable value of the imported goods and thereby avoid the payment of duties and taxes on imports.

Whenever a country is denied the full value of the goods it exports, that country is robbed of earnings. Developing countries cannot afford the theft of resources. Thus, theoretically, the functions performed by PSIs are noble and just. However, the potential abuses are considerable. For example, it is exceedingly difficult to differentiate a high price from a fraudulent price. A high price may simply result from the particular commercial arrangement, special packaging, terms of sale, or other factors.

Governmental Stability

For a variety of reasons that are political, cultural, and economic, many third-world nations suffer from governmental instability. In addition to the obvious uncertainty such instability adds to the profit concerns of a firm, logistics operations can be severely impaired. Systems that operated relatively well under one government can change dramatically under a new government. Government and private institutions often change hands, and the old agreements and procedures suddenly no longer apply. Infrastructure deteriorates: "In Angola and Mozambique, they had quite a developed road and rail infrastructure, but it's been damaged by civil war" said a manager of a major shipping line.[26]

Governmental instability in one nation can sometimes spread to neighboring countries, throwing whole regions into chaos for years at a time. Consider the upheaval in the central African nations of The Congo, Rwanda, Burundi, Uganda, and Zambia. Disputes and a high degree of instability in this region continue as of the writing of this book. Yet despite such chaos, governments, firms, and individuals within such countries continue to have needs, and those needs in-

---

[26]Knee, Richard (1999), "Shipping to Africa," *World Trade,* January 1999, pp. 88–89.

evitably require logistics as part of their solution. A high degree of awareness, cultural and political sensitivity, and quick-footed flexibility seem to be valuable skills for logistics managers facing such an operating environment.

Ethical Considerations

Many third-world countries are weak both politically and economically. They frequently are exploited. A number of issues should be discussed here.

Dumping is the sale of goods for export at prices below those set in the producer's market. Dumping helps to prop up domestic prices in the exporter's country while assuring the utilization of excess manufacturing/producing capacity. Sometimes dumping is used simply to gain or retain a foothold in a foreign market. Both dumping and subsidized exports are considered unfair trade competition. Third-world nations allege that dumping is used to keep their home industries from developing.

The word *dumping* has another connotation as well. It is sometimes used in connection with the export of product that is banned for sale in the exporting country. Outdated food, pharmaceutical, agricultural, and veterinary products which cannot be sold domestically might be dumped in the export market. Toys banned because of the hazard they present to children, pesticides and herbicides found damaging to the environment, and other substandard or banned products are sometimes purchased by unscrupulous individuals and sold for export.

Such practices are not only immoral, unethical and often illegal, they are clearly bad business as well. They damage the reputation of manufacturers and their distributors and open the doors to product liability suits.

To combat this many countries require affidavits from exporters certifying that the goods being exported are both free from defect and sold freely in the country of exportation. Often, exporters must obtain local chamber of commerce certifications attesting to the fact the exporter is who he says he is. These documents, sometimes called *certificates of free sale,* are often required before the importer can clear his merchandise.

In recent years, a third form of "dumping" has been that of toxic wastes. Call it a toxic memorial, a monument to loose laws and fast money. On a rural Haitian beach stand rows upon rows of barrels filled with 3,000 tons of municipal incinerator ash from Philadelphia, dumped one night by a barge called the *Khian Sea.* The boat had entered port with a permit to unload fertilizer. . . . A hundred workers began unloading the ash building a heap only yards from incoming waves. They unloaded 3,000 tons out of more than 13,000 on board before the Haitian government intervened, ordering the ash back onto the barge. Under the cover of darkness, the *Khian Sea* disappeared. Six Haitian governments have come and gone since that night in 1988, but the ash remains, although some has washed out with the tides or blown off with the winds.[27]

As some nations enact more stringent antipollution measures, it becomes profitable for unscrupulous individuals to scheme to merely move the waste, rather than dispose of it. A related problem is the location or relocation of industries to countries where there are few or no pollution or worker safety controls. Sometimes hazardous wastes are "dumped" in countries willing to accept them for a fee. In early 2001, Russia, for example, proposed to accept spent radioactive nuclear power plant fuel for permanent storage for a fee of $1,600 per kilogram.

Another issue is bribery. In many nations around the world (and not just in third-world countries), the payment of small bribes is customary and is useful in speeding goods through port facilities, warehouses, import and export document clearance, customs, and on/off of transportation systems. Coca-Cola encountered demands for bribes on its re-entry into the Angolan market. As Mr. Islay Rhind, managing director of Coca-Cola Bottling (Luanda) put it:

> "We bring with us a very rigid code of conduct, which isn't necessarily very popular in a place like Angola, which has this reputation for corruption. But that's who we are, that's what we are, that's the way we do business. It was very difficult to get people to understand that that's what we do and why. We don't pay bribes. We don't take bribes. It's a hard road but that's the way it is. Once the community knows who you are, what you are, it ceases to become an issue. Everyone knows we won't pay to have our telephones reconnected, we won't pay policemen to let our trucks through, so we don't have to bribe anybody."[28]

Mr. Rhind's position in Angola may be bolstered by a local understanding that Coca-Cola's investment of $40 million in bottling plants has brought many new jobs, including those at businesses which have opened to serve Coca-Cola's local needs. Contrast Coca-Cola Bottling (Luanda)'s position on bribery with that of a manager for Phyto-Riker Pharmaceuticals. Commenting on operations in Ghana:

---

[27]Chepesiuk, Ron (1991), "From Ash to Ash, the International Trade in Toxic Waste," *E. Magazine,* 32 (July/August 1991).

[28]*New York Times* (2001), "Braving War and Graft, Coke Goes Back To Angola," April 22, 2001, p. 3-1.

"... you have to be prepared to grease a few palms.' Agents for customs and other regulatory units are 'highly bureaucratic and underpaid,' and they don't miss a chance to make a few extra dollars where they can ..."[29]

The payment of bribes is often customary within the society and is not viewed locally as a corrupt or illegal practice. In fact, such payments are sometimes considered part of the normal compensation such employees receive on their job and payment is almost mandatory. The U.S. government has attempted to legislate how U.S. businesses must conduct their transactions overseas through the Foreign Corrupt Practices Act and other laws. These laws do not recognize cultural differences, and to one way of thinking, constitute the imposition of self-referencing criteria on another culture. The international logistics professional may be confronted with an ethical dilemma in such situations when U.S. law conflicts with local custom. Such professionals should air these concerns within their companies to achieve corporate norms for business practice under these conditions. In most countries, outright theft, graft, and large-scale bribery or corruption are illegal. Such situations can generally be resolved through local law enforcement and legal channels.

Certain types of logistics fraud flourish in these areas of the world where it is impossible to have the same levels of controls that might be in place in more developed parts of the world. Even shiploads of cargo disappear. Some ships have met diverse fates. Some have been scuttled after their cargo was surreptitiously unloaded at an unscheduled port. Some have vanished only to reappear under a new name and a new flag, with the old name faintly visible under the old paint. Some are diverted to a different port, where the cargo is sold to the highest bidder while the original purchaser waits in vain.

The challenges facing logistics professionals operating in the third world are many and varied. Situations arise quickly and resources may be scarce, forcing creative solutions to seemingly unsolvable problems. Logisticians operating in such environments learn quickly to be comfortable under conditions of ambiguity and manage to make do and adapt resources at hand to the problems faced.

Trade Blocs

A major global political (and business) trend for the past 20 years has been the simplification or elimination of trade barriers and restrictions among neighboring countries. The creation of such free-trade zones or trade blocs is a recognition that barriers to trade among neighbors is not conducive for business and for

---

[29]Knee, Richard 1999, "Shipping to Africa," *World Trade,* January 1999, pp. 88–89.

national economic development. The economic logic underpinning the establishment of such new, broader trade zones recognizes the specialization of land, labor, and capital resources among the members of the trade bloc. For example: One nation may have an abundance of raw materials, though lack the human resources or production facilities to efficiently develop these resources. A second nation may have human resources and advanced production capabilities, but lack its own raw materials. By allowing companies in each of the nations unrestricted access to needed resources, finished goods may be supplied to both countries at substantially reduced cost, benefiting consumers in both countries.

While the logic seems simple, the negotiation and implementation of free trade zones is quite difficult and fraught with nationalism and protectionist sentiments. To create a true free-trade zone, all markets of member countries must be equally accessible to companies from anywhere inside the trade zone. This creates problems when member nations desire to protect nascent industrial development or highly profitable national industries or agriculture. Levying of protectionist tariffs is contradictory within a free-trade zone, and the inevitable result of dismantling trade barriers is a shifting of industries within the trade bloc to locations that make economic sense (that is, where costs are minimized). The attendant social upheaval can be traumatic.

At the same time that trade barriers vanish within a trade bloc, protectionist barriers can be raised between trade blocs themselves. The infamous "Banana War" between the United States (and implicitly NAFTA) and the European Community (EC) during 1997–2000 is an excellent example of such bloc protectionism. U.S. firms demanded greater access to the EC for bananas grown in certain Central American countries. For largely political and protectionist reasons related to former colonies of European nations, the EC imposed high tariffs on bananas from U.S. firms. In retaliation, the U.S. government imposed outrageously high tariffs (in some cases exceeding 100 percent of the good's value) on French cheeses and a number of luxury goods made exclusively in the EC.

Two developed-nation trade blocs bear consideration from a logistics management perspective. The economic unification of the fifteen member nations of the European Community took place in 1992 and today represents a formidable force in global trade. The North American Free Trade Agreement (NAFTA) deals with the U.S./Canadian/Mexican free-trade zone established by treaty in 1990. Also described are three regional trade blocs of emerging nations: ASEAN, MERCOSUR, and CARICOM.

The European Community

The European Community's 12 member nations decided during the 1980s to extend the notion of the original common market to a full deregulated business environment across national boundaries by the year 1992. This involved a renegotiation of all aspects of trade rules among the original 12 (now 15) countries. The impetus for such a development was clear. The EC faced substantial trade disadvantages with the United States and Japan and was battling these disadvantages from an internally divisive base. The EC member countries were individually relatively small economically and at a power disadvantage vis-a-vis American or Japanese trade. But by banding together to present a unified front to American and Japanese trade interests, the EC would wield substantial economic power and face its trade adversaries on more equal footing.

Additional advantages were seen in the synergy of a unified market representing some 300 million consumers. Manufacturers would have coordinated access to this new large market and would be able to reap economies of scale and scope that were simply not possible in a divided Europe. The prospect of a large common consumer base coupled with the possibility of raising unified trade barriers to external threats caused the common market to push forward toward an eventual economic unification of 15 countries. Negotiations aimed at implementing the first stages of this unification by January 1, 1992 were well underway during the late 1980s, and most of those provisions have now been implemented by the member nations. This represents the creation of an important new trade bloc. In effect, a new marketplace with a population greater than that of the United States came into being.

While a number of provisions have remained problematic (for example, the rollout of a common currency, the Euro, in 2002 was not accepted by Great Britain, which retained its own currency), many logistical concerns were among those to be resolved in the first stages of implementation of the 1992 accords. Prior to the unification of this market, each country had different import and export regulations, transportation laws, communications standards, inventory valuation and accounting methods, and product storage standards. Furthermore, each country had retained some protective tariffs that were governed by a crazy quilt of regulations peculiar to each trading dyad and product category.

As a result of this trade confusion, the cross-border transport of goods was cumbersome. Truck and rail freight shipments often faced days of delay at border crossings as paperwork was filed and checked and rechecked. Shipping goods across multiple borders within the community was a headache. Transportation systems, while technically highly evolved, were burdened with inefficient operations as goods massed at national boundaries. Differing communications standards inhibited the high-speed transmission of data, and multiple standards created compatibility problems. Differences in accounting standards for inventory valuation caused massive seasonal shifting of inventory across borders to avoid taxation and the de facto ineffective forward positioning of inventory relative to final consumption markets. Clearly, the economic benefits from creating a more efficient flow of goods and information was a driving force behind economic unification.

The simple act of dropping tariffs and simplifying import/export regulation was sufficient to improve the efficiency of transportation throughout the community. Border delays are now nearly nonexistent as shipments are no longer inspected and paperwork processed at national frontiers. In early 1993, a Milan-based trucker who specialized in carrying race horses said that twelve hours had been shaved off the time it took to ship a breeding mare from Italy to Ireland and back, saving $700 on the round trip. "A dozen export-import forms were eliminated, and veterinary checks now take place only at the destination."[30] Not all transportation barriers are being removed. Neighboring nations still enforce their own regulations regarding truck dimensions and hours of operations. Environmentalists prefer that trucking throughout Europe be discouraged so that freight traffic will be shifted to rail and water, which are less damaging to the environment. This has become a significant issue in Switzerland; while not a member of the EU, the country is an important transportation nexus for all of Europe.

Other changes mandated by economic unification are being implemented more slowly. Changing the technical standards for telecommunications must be considered carefully, and downward compatibility with existing communications infrastructure is an important problem. The gradual upgrade of the EC's telecommunications network will make this transition easier as time goes on; the adoption of a common mobile telephone standard for Europe is an example of the progress possible. Changes in accounting practices have caused some disruption in the way business information is reported as many firms take onetime charges to earnings during the changeover. This has been especially the case with the shift to the Euro as a common currency.

The substantial reduction in regulation also has freed competitive forces within the EC.[31] Roadway haulage has been deregulated, opening up formerly protected national markets to competition from other EC nations and potentially from companies outside the EC nations. The EC has mandated the development of high-speed rail for both passenger and freight by the year 2015, which is intended to change the balance of freight moved by air, rail, and highway. Air cargo has also been deregulated, and freight rates across modes have fallen as a result. The use of multimodal transportation is now more common. Logistics

---

[30]*Time,* March 1, 1993, p. 41.

[31]Straetz, Bob (1991), "EC Single Market in Transportation Creates Openings for U.S. Firms," *Business Week,* October 21, 1991, pp. 13–16.

management has become increasingly important in the post-1992 EC, as managers now have the opportunity to manipulate logistics variables in ways heretofore impossible.[32]

The strategic implications of a unified market should be apparent to the American logistics manager. The 15 member nations operate in a similar fashion to the 50 American states. Procedures, laws, and technology are largely being standardized and logistics practices have become more uniform as the integration is completed. These changes have made it possible to site manufacturing facilities, distribution networks, and transportation systems according to market needs rather than according to national boundaries. Logistics managers operating within the EC have redesigned logistics systems to conform with the needs of the larger, unified market. As businesses are now free to treat the marketplace as a whole and without international political considerations, we expect that logistics systems costs will decline and throughput efficiency will improve. For example, Mondavi Wineries used to print 13 different labels for wine that it exported to the EC area. "Under European Community rules, a winemaker can sell product throughout the continent with a single label, as long as the wine is distributed from one location within the EC. So Mondavi began acting as its own importer, using Rotterdam as a central distribution point. . . . The only requirement is that the wine pass through Rotterdam first."[33]

A comprehensive website dealing with the European Community can be found at *http://europa.eu.int* (European Union On-Line). Contemporary issues regarding the admission of new nations from southern and eastern Europe are important to monitor for logistics professionals.

NAFTA

The U.S./Canada Free Trade Agreement was negotiated between the United States and Canada during the 1980s, and took effect January 1, 1989. Mexico joined NAFTA as a full member in 1995. NAFTA sought to bring about many of the benefits seen in the economic unification of Europe, but without the complete economic integration of the three nations. Simply put, the United States, Canada, and Mexico desired to create a common market where tariffs and other trade barriers would be substantially reduced or eliminated to permit the free flow of goods and services across the border.

---

[32]Poist, Richard F. and Carl Scheraga (1991), "Perspectives of Logistics Executives on the Post-1992 European Environment," *Transportation Journal,* 31 (1), pp. 36–44.

[33]*World Trade,* April 1992, p. 66.

The United States and Canada have long enjoyed special trade relations. Trading across the world's longest undefended border, each nation has long been the other's largest trading partner. Many firms of Canadian and U.S. ownership operate on both sides of the border, daily shipping raw materials, work-in-process, and finished goods to markets in both the U.S. and Canada. The friendly nature of the relations between the two countries and the long history of close business ties facilitated the negotiation of the treaty. Similarly, many U.S. companies developed trade relationships with Mexican firms in the 1970s and 80s, and heavily invested in U.S.-owned manufacturing plants along the Mexican-U.S. border. The implementation of NAFTA in the U.S. and Canada has been facilitated by the two nations sharing many technical standards, similar levels of logistics infrastructure development, and similarities in markets. Since joining NAFTA, Mexico's standards and infrastructure are developing to fit into established U.S.-Canadian systems.

While NAFTA has simplified the movement of goods across the border between markets, it has not achieved the type of full economic integration seen in Europe. Labor, for example, remains the province of each respective nation and does not move freely across borders. Limitations remain on cross-border capital investment as well. NAFTA focused on facilitating exchange of goods. In that sense, the changes for logistics managers have perhaps been more dramatic than for consumers. It is now possible to site distribution facilities and manufacturing plants closer to markets and without regard to national boundaries. The resulting efficiencies improve both profits and service to different markets. As Canada continues its efforts to deregulate transportation services, competition from the freed U.S. service providers has caused additional drops in freight costs. Since 1989, cross-border sourcing and freight movements have increased substantially.

The addition of Mexico to NAFTA was not without controversy. Business practice, accounting standards, transportation system design, manufacturing standards, and communications standards differed dramatically between Mexico and the two northern nations. The level of economic development is also very different, resulting in wildly different costs of labor. Proponents argued that adding Mexico would open a very large market to U.S. and Canadian companies. Opponents focused on the loss of skilled high-paying jobs in manufacturing to lower cost Mexican labor. In the near future, it is expected that Mexican truck freight firms will have expanded access to the U.S. market as well. Allowing Mexican trucking firms equal access to the U.S. market has been opposed by organized labor in the U.S. under the guise of highway safety issues. The Teamsters union in the United States capitalized on the relatively high failure rate of Mexican short-haul trucks in U.S. safety inspections (37 percent) versus

U.S. carriers combined long- and short-haul fleets (24 percent), though some highway safety experts have disputed these comparisons.[34]

At the writing of this book, the inclusion of Mexico into NAFTA seems to have had more benefit than cost to U.S. firms. U.S. exports to Mexico in 2000 were up 170 percent from the 1993 level, while overall U.S. exports had risen 68 percent. During that same time, Mexican exports to the U.S. grew 241 percent. The U.S. has also achieved a more balanced trade with Mexico (the 2000 trade deficit was 10 percent), as compared to its trade with the European Community (14 percent), Japan (38 percent), or China (72 percent).[35] The strategic implications of NAFTA should be apparent: open-market access, freedom to design manufacturing and logistics systems according to market demands, and decreased logistics costs with improved system productivity.

There are a number of NAFTA websites. Among the most useful starting points for NAFTA information on the Web are U.S. Department of Commerce sites *(http://www.mac.doc.gov/nafta, http://www.ito.doc.gov/cscanada, http://uscommerce.org.mx).*

ASEAN

The Association of Southeast Asian Nations includes Brunei Darussalam, Cambodia, Indonesia, Laos, Malaysia, Myanmar, Philippines, Singapore, Thailand, and Vietnam. Unlike some regional trade blocs, ASEAN has focused in the past decade on expanding member nations' trade reach outside the bloc. This seems a logical focus for ASEAN's emerging and third-world members, given that many large global firms already operate simultaneously in several ASEAN nations and export the products of those endeavors outside the ASEAN bloc. The U.S.–ASEAN Business Council maintains a comprehensive website on ASEAN trade at *http://www.us-asean.org.*

MERCOSUR

The Southern Cone Common Market was created by the Treaty of Asuncion, signed in 1991 by Argentina, Brazil, Uruguay, and Paraguay. This regional trade bloc was formed to create:

---

[34]*New York Times* (2001), "Teamsters May Stall Bush Goals For Mexican Trucks and Trade," July 30, 2001, p. A1.

[35]*Business Week* (2001), "NAFTA's Scorecard: So Far, So Good," July 9, 2001, pp. 54–56.

an external common tariff and a commercial common policy regarding other states or group of states and the coordination of positions in international and regional commercial economic forums.

the coordination of macroeconomic policies from different sectors among member States: foreign trade, agricultural, industrial, fiscal, currency, foreign exchange and capitals, services, customs, transports and communications policies and others to be agreed upon in order to assure adequate competition conditions among member states.

the member States commitment to harmonizing their legislation in the pertinent areas so as to strengthen the integration process.[36]

Chile and Bolivia negotiated free-trade agreements with MERCOSUR in 1996 and 1997, and are effectively members. An interregional agreement of cooperation was signed with the European Union in 1995 and with the Centro American Common Market in 1998. MERCOSUR has not fully achieved its goals of reducing internal tariffs and simultaneously raising external tariffs, though they have made substantial progress in that regard and in adopting uniform trade standards among the member nations. MERCOSUR is currently negotiating a Free Trade Area of the Americas (ALCA) with 30 nations in North and South America, which is expected to take effect in 2005.

A comprehensive website dealing with MERCOSUR, including trade statistics, can be found at *http://www.mercosur.org,* and a website devoted to building interfirm trade relationships can be found at *http://www.mercosur.com.*

CARICOM

The Caribbean Community and Common Market (CARICOM) was established by the Treaty of Chaguaramas, which was signed by Barbados, Jamaica, Guyana, and Trinidad & Tobago, and went into effect in 1973. Subsequently, 11 more Caribbean nations have joined CARICOM, including Antigua, Belize, Dominica, Grenada, Saint Lucia, Montserrat, St. Kitts/Nevis/Anguilla and St. Vincent, The Bahamas, Suriname, British Virgin Islands, and the Turks and Caicos Islands. From inception, CARICOM has focused on the integration of the economies of the member states, as well as the larger political functions of a common foreign policy and social and humanitarian programs.

The national economies of CARICOM are tiny by global standards, and many are underdeveloped with existing economic institutions in many of the nations having horizons limited by the legacies of colonialism. While many of the

---

[36]From "Historic Brief," *http://www.mercosur.org*

CARICOM nations export natural resources and agricultural goods, tourism has emerged as the most important industry in the Caribbean. As this book was written, CARICOM was engaged in continued study of the effects of NAFTA on Caribbean trade and existing trade agreements (such as the Caribbean–Canada Trade Agreement), building active trade relationships with Venezuela and Columbia, and furthering economic integration within the CARICOM bloc.

CARICOM maintains a comprehensive website dealing with trade and political issues, as well as useful trade statistics at *http://www.caricom.org.*

On the Horizon

At the 2001 Summit of the Americas meeting of the leaders of 34 nations in the Western Hemisphere, a Free Trade Area of the Americas (FTAA) was proposed for implementation sometime after 2005. Drafts of such a comprehensive free-trade-zone agreement have been completed and are under discussion as this book is written. The FTAA would create a free-trade zone extending from Canada down through the Americas to Argentina and Chile. Such a wide-sweeping revision of international trade will undoubtably be controversial from a number of perspectives. We recommend you check the FTAA website for current developments: *http://www.ftaa-alca.org.*

Summary

Logistics systems and business practices are not uniform throughout the world. That is because the world itself is not uniform and there are many cultural differences that must be bridged for effective business communications and transactions to take place.

For purposes of discussion, nations of the world were placed into three categories with respect to the development of their logistics systems. Not surprisingly, the sophistication of a nation's logistics infrastructure is closely correlated to its overall level of economic development. Brief mention was also made of regional trading blocs: the EC, NAFTA, ASEAN, MERCOSUR and CARICOM.

End-of-Chapter Questions

1. Explain the concept of self-referencing criteria. Give an example of how logistics practices in your country could invoke self-referencing criteria and affect your decision making.

2. As a consultant to a small businessperson who is interested in

beginning to export goods, what kind of advice would you give? Give three websites you might find useful as references in your advice.

3. Define culture and give three examples of how culture affects logistics practice.

4. Define beliefs, values, and customs. Give examples to help explain how differences in each affect logistics practices.

5. Describe the first world of logistics practice. Be sure to comment on infrastructure, performance, information systems, human resources, and strategic and financial resources.

6. Describe the emerging nations in terms of their logistics practice. Be sure to comment on infrastructure, performance, information systems, human resources, and strategic and financial resources.

7. How do the roles of government differ between first-world logistics nations and those in the emerging world?

8. Explain the concept of an economic-stepchild nation and what the implications of such a trade arrangement might be for logistics in that country.

9. Describe the third world in terms of their logistics practice. Be sure to comment on infrastructure, performance, information systems, human resources, and strategic and financial resources.

10. How do third-world nation trade issues affect the practice of logistics between a third-world nation and a first-world nation?

11. Describe the logistics problems associated with governmental instability in third-world nations.

12. What is the role of inventory when dealing with logistics in the third world?

13. Give three ethical issues involved with logistics in third-world nations and illustrate with examples from the current press.

14. What are the advantages and disadvantages for logistics practitioners operating within a single trade bloc?

15. What are the advantages and disadvantages for logistics practitioners operating among multiple trade blocs?

16. From a logistics perspective, what are the essential differences between NAFTA and the European Union?

17. How will the newly developing trade blocs (such as the FTAA) affect logistics practice in the future?

CASE • *Minex Phosphates*

Minex Phosphates is a chemical importing firm located in Port Arthur, Texas. They specialize in the global commodity market for phosphates, which are salts of phosphoric acid, a common ingredient in agricultural fertilizers. Phosphates are found in many nations as a naturally occurring mineral salt and are of relatively low value on a per-ton basis.

John Stryker is a buyer for Minex and has worked in the global mineral commodities business ever since he completed his MBA at Michigan State University in the 1990s. He's built up an extensive network of contacts and often travels overseas in search of potential suppliers.

On Monday morning, John arrives at the office to find a voicemail message from Hassan Abdullah, calling from Amman, Jordan. John looks through his Palm Pilot, trying to remember if he'd ever met Mr. Abdullah on a trip to the Middle East. An entry in the Palm Pilot reads:

> Dr. Hassan Abdullah
> Assistant Managing Director
> Jordanian National Mineral Exchange
> 12 al-Hambra St.
> Amman, Jordan

Along with a telephone and fax number, John finds his own note: "Met him at a U.S. trade mission hospitality suite in Cairo, September 1999. Possible phosphate source, though price currently too high."

John picked up the phone, dialed 011-962, and Dr. Abdullah's phone number. Instead of an immediate answer, the phone rang and rang. Just as John was about to hang up, the phone was picked up by a man who quite apparently spoke very little English. Yes, this appeared to be Dr. Abdullah's office, and no, Dr. Abdullah was not in the office. John attempted to leave a message, but uncertain it would be delivered, John hung up, wishing he spoke Arabic!

With no reply awaiting him on Tuesday morning, John decided to fax a note to Dr. Abdullah instead of leaving a voice message. The short fax was informal:

> Dear Hassan:
> It is a real pleasure to hear from you after our meeting in Cairo in 1999. Our company continues to be interested in Jordanian phosphates, and I am eager to speak with you regarding the global market for phosphates and a possible business relationship between Minex and the Jordanian National Mineral Exchange. Please call or fax with a good time for us to begin our discussions.
> Warm Regards,
> John Stryker

John thought the tone just right to demonstrate interest but no commitment at this stage. He was curious as to what Dr. Abdullah had on his mind.

Wednesday morning, John received a call at 8:00 A.M. from a man named Hamid, who was Dr. Abdullah's secretary. Hamid was friendly enough, but indicated that Dr. Abdullah was not at all sure who Mr. Stryker was, and most certainly did not have a close friend by that name. Dr. Abdullah was interested in discussing business arrangements, but wanted Hamid to find out more about this Mr. Stryker who appeared to be mistaken about their prior friendship.

John immediately realized he'd broached some sort of Jordanian business protocol. He apologized to Hamid for his too-informal tone, and told Hamid that he had indeed met Dr. Abdullah in Cairo in 1999. Hamid asked John to hold.

While on hold, John thought to himself: "this is a fine way to start a new business contact! What did I do wrong?" Just then another voice came on the line and said "Mr. Stryker? This is Dr. Abdullah. I am pleased we finally have the opportunity to speak to each other."

John breathed a sigh of relief, and began small talk to connect with Dr. Abdullah over their 1999 Cairo meeting. "Yes, yes, I do remember you, and I had your business card, so I called you when I found the world commodity price for phosphates rising, with perhaps the idea that your company in the United States would again be interested in Jordanian minerals." John thought . . . so he does remember me!

"Mr. Stryker, we propose to sell you 50,000 tons of Grade B mixed phosphates at a price of 45 U.S. dollars per ton delivered to the port of Aqaba. Do you have a need for such?"

John briefly considered the commodity price for that grade, the market trend upward, his customers' needs, and realized he was being offered a great deal. "Yes. I think we would be most interested in that quantity, although we may not want to receive all 50,000 tons in a single shipment. Would it be possible to break the shipment into three portions, delivered 30 days apart?"

"Well, yes, of course, anything is possible. We would be shipping from northern Jordan to Aqaba by train, and our freight costs would be higher for rail if we don't ship the entire 50,000 tons on a single train. But we could consider such if you would pay the difference in our rail freight costs within Jordan."

Faced with a more complex transportation solution, and one that relied on some knowledge of Jordanian rail freight rates, John countered: "Perhaps we could take all 50,000 tons at one time if the price were a bit lower to reflect our costs in holding the inventory for our customers."

"Ah. It is a pity we are speaking by telephone, Mr. Stryker. I am sure we would understand each other if we could just see each other face to face. If you were here in Amman, we would go to my home and share a meal."

John wavered. He didn't know how to respond to that statement. "Yes, that would be very nice indeed." He paused.

"Good. Then when can I expect you to visit Amman so that we may discuss not just one transaction, but establishing the healthy relationship as friends which we need to go further together?"

John hesitated. He knew that his boss would approve a trip to Jordan if it meant opening up a good new source for phosphates. But he wondered why Dr. Abdullah was not willing to negotiate by telephone. "I can be there a week from tomorrow, that would be Thursday next week. I will call Hamid with my arrival times and my hotel arrangements."

"Good, good, Mr. Stryker. I look forward to renewing our friendship."

Early the next morning, John called Hamid to tell him he would be arriving in Amman the following Thursday at about 2 P.M., and would be staying at the Hilton. "This is good, and is convenient for us to meet at our offices in Amman" said Hamid. "Dr. Abdullah would like to meet you for dinner on Thursday evening. And we will be meeting on Saturday morning at our office, yes? At 10 A.M., yes?"

"Saturday?" John didn't need a day to adjust for time differences, and he was arriving Thursday. "Could we meet on Friday?"

There was a very long pause before Hamid spoke. "Mr. Stryker, surely you know that Friday is a day of worship in Jordan, and we do not conduct business in any form on Fridays. I cannot ask Dr. Abdullah to meet to discuss business on a Friday."

John gulped . . . another gaffe in protocol. "Yes, that is true, so we will meet Thursday evening and again on Saturday morning. I will call your office on my arrival at the Hilton."

Over the next week, John contacted a number of Minex's customers for phosphates to discuss possible orders. He found that he could likely sell all 50,000 tons of phosphates over the next six months, and could take advance orders at a variety of prices and delivery dates. If he could deliver 10,000 tons within a month, he could sell to a single customer at a price of $105/ton. Two months out, he had customers who were willing to pay $95/ton, and could reliably be expected to accept another 20,000 tons. Beyond that, the prices seemed more speculative, with some smaller customers saying they would pay over $105/ton, and others chiming in with large orders just below $95/ton. Of course, there was also the possibility that John would find another mineral importer/wholesaler who would be willing to take a good portion of this 50,000 tons immediately, though not through Port Arthur. He also knew that bulk freight rates for 50,000 tons in a single shipment were going to be around $20/ton, though if he had to ship smaller quantities, the per-ton price would be higher.

As John left Houston for Amman, he felt like he had a number of possibilities with U.S. customers and a decent opportunity to make an excellent profit for his firm. But he was unsure what he would face in negotiations with Dr. Abdullah once he arrived in Amman.

Questions for *Minex Phosphates*

1. Make a list of all of John's mistakes in protocol in his dealings with Dr. Abdullah thus far. What advice would you have for John for his first face-to-face meeting?

2. When is a ton not a ton? Could there be a discrepancy between the U.S. and Jordanian measures? If so, what is the true cost per ton?

3. John consults tramp steamer availability and finds he can charter two ships from Aqaba, one which holds 30,000 tons and another which holds 20,000 tons. He knows he has demand from his customers for 30,000 tons, but has been able to find only one competing wholesaler who will take 10,000 tons through Port Everglades (Florida), and that at a price of $80/ton. What can John afford to pay for ocean freight on a per-ton basis to these tramp steamer companies and still make a 15 percent return on investment for his company?

4. Dr. Abdullah is willing to negotiate on phased deliveries to Aqaba. He is willing to sell the phosphates F.O.B. Es Salt, which is the rail center nearest the mining area, for a price of $30/ton. Es Salt is in northern Jordan, and is closer to Israel, Syria, and Lebanon than it is to Aqaba. What are some alternative geographic routings that John should consider for shipping the phosphate by rail to a port? To what extent will Middle Eastern politics enter into the decision to use an alternative rail route and port? What land-based transportation price differential will make such a decision feasible?

5. Phosphates are a bulk commodity, but must be protected from adverse conditions (including rain) while in transit. What would John want to know about port facilities at Aqaba or an alternative loading port? And what should he know about Jordanian seasonal weather?

6. Construct three different scenarios for Minex's customers, incorporating shipping arrangements (both land and ocean), cost price(s) and retail price(s). How would John use these scenarios in planning his negotiations with Dr. Abdullah?

4

Ocean Ships and Shipping

Introduction

There are three basic types of ocean carriers: 1) private fleets; 2) tramps (chartered or leased vessels); and 3) liner carriers. Private fleets are owned by merchants or manufacturers themselves in order to carry their own goods. Oil companies and lumber companies often own and operate large fleets of specialized ships. They do so in order to control both the availability of carriage and the cost thereof and also to insure that the right kind of ship is available to meet their special needs. Their ships are the size and type of vessel these companies need, and they have the particular operating characteristics required to support the business of the owners.

Most trading companies do not have the need on an ongoing basis to economically warrant ownership and operation of their own ships. These traders fall into the category of shipload lot size shippers or less than shipload size shippers. Shipload shippers—and reference here is to companies that ship thousands of tons of cargo at a time, such as chemicals—avail themselves of "tramp" shipping services, chartering vessels as they need them. Shippers of smaller quantities utilize liner services.

This is the first of three chapters that deal with ocean shipping. This chapter deals with the various types of ships that are in use by both shippers who own them and firms that own them for others to use. Chapter 5 deals with bulk carriers and charter arrangements that are used when a shipper has sufficient cargo to justify utilizing an entire vessel. Chapter 6 deals with movements of smaller quantities, more valuable per unit of weight, that move on regularly scheduled liner vessels.

Many terms will be introduced in this chapter that will require further explanation or definition. An attempt will be made to define new words and phrases as they occur.

Cargo Types

One way to classify vessels is by the type or types of cargo they carry. This classification is also useful in determining whether they will be chartered by a single user or be used to carry smaller shipments tendered by many shippers.

Bulk cargo is loaded by shovel, pump, bucket, or scoop, is in free form, and must be contained. Here is a definition: "*Cargo* is said to be stowed in bulk when it is stowed loose instead of being first packed in containers."[1] (With this definition, one is uncertain whether containers means retail-size packages or seagoing containers that are usually 8 x 8 x 20–40 feet. Often the only way to load any cargo aboard a containership is to load it into a container first. Special containers exist with leak-proof plastic linings. Bulk cargo, for example, raw sugar, would be loaded into the container, and becomes "containerized" cargo.)

Common examples of bulk cargoes are petroleum, grain, coal, iron ore, scrap iron, phosphates, and sulfur. Sometimes a portion of bulk cargo may be packaged: bagged rice, for example, is placed on top of bulk rice to give the entire load stability. Bulk cargo moves by weight. Sometimes the weight carried is determined by measuring the change in the vessel's depth in the water. For each vessel, one can determine how much water is being displaced as the vessel rides lower. The weight of this displaced water is equivalent to the weight of the cargo being loaded.

When coal is loaded for export it may have been rained upon several times between when it was mined, moved on rail cars, and stacked outside waiting to be loaded. This rain increases the coal's moisture content but adds nothing to its usefulness to the ultimate customer. Hence, at the loading dock, the coal's buyer and seller hire a neutral third party to continuously collect a small sample of coal (utilizing a tiny conveyor belt that moves off the major conveyor). The small sample is analyzed for BTU (British Thermal Units—a measure of energy content) per unit of weight. Hence, when the vessel is full, the weight of the coal is calculated, and then its BTU content, and the purchaser pays for the number of BTUs in the load.

Break-bulk is the other type of cargo, also called general, or packaged, cargo. It has high value per unit of weight, is usually manufactured or processed, and

---

[1]The Harper Group, *International Shipper's Atlas,* (San Francisco: Joseph DeGrace, 1968), p. 32.

moves by number or count. This moves in smaller quantities than bulk cargo, and usually on liner vessels that travel on regularly scheduled routes between ports. This cargo is loaded and unloaded on a piece-by-piece basis, although today it may be unitized or palletized by the shipper, meaning that it was built up into loads approximately 40 x 48 x 48 inches, covered by shrink wrap (to protect it from moisture and dust and to make it easier to detect pilferage), and held by steel straps. The cargo may also be containerized either at the shipper's place of business or at a consolidator's; this means the cargo was loaded into an 8 x 8 x 20–40-foot long container and tendered to the vessel line as a full container. Or, the vessel line itself may have loaded the cargo, along with cargo from other shippers, into containers so that it could be loaded.

Steel often moves as break-bulk cargo. This is because it is too heavy for conventional containers to handle. It's also too heavy for some piers to accommodate. Often it is transferred to rail cars or barges that are located next to the ocean vessel.

In container shipping circles another set of terms used is *CL,* standing for containerload, and *LCL,* standing for less-than containerload.[2] A containerload fills a container, and the container moves through the system as a filled container. A less-than containerload shipment is some fraction of a containerload and will be matched with other fractional loads, possibly owned by other parties, so as to fill a container that can be loaded on and off of the vessel. At the other end of the trip, the container is "devanned," or opened and its contents separated back into fractional loads. Figure 4–1 shows a hatchless containership, consisting of high racks placed inside a hull.

However, it is important to realize that not all liner cargo is containerized. Containerized shipping is very important in routes between Asia and Europe, in the North Atlantic between the United States and Europe; and the Pacific between the United States and Asia. In 2000, five of the world's six top container-handling ports were in Asia: Hong Kong, Singapore, Kaoshiung, Pusan, and Shanghai. In other trading regions, especially those south of the Equator, containers are less important.

Neo-bulk cargo has some characteristics of bulk and some characteristics of

---

[2]Sometimes, instead of CL, FCL is used, and it stands for Full Container Load. In rail shipments, CL and LCL stand for carload and less-than-carload. In freight classifications for each type of product shipped, a minimum weight is required to qualify for a carload rate, which is less per pound than the less-than-carload rate. Almost no U.S. railroads currently accept LCL shipments; however, they can be tendered to forwarders who consolidate them into rail carloads. In trucking, the terms TL and LTL stand for truckload and less-than-truckload. At present, U.S. motor carriers specialize in either TL or LTL traffic.

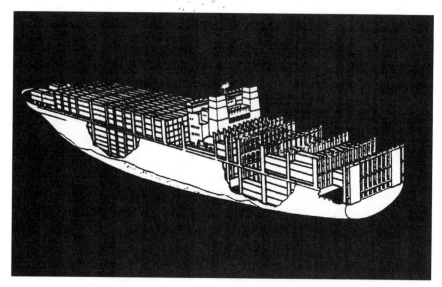

Figure 4–1 Drawing of a hatchless containership. Courtesy CIGNA Corporation, *Ports of the World,* 15th edition.

break-bulk cargo. It is usually worth more on a per-kilo basis and it often moves on specialized ocean vessels. The two best-known examples are new automobiles and logs. These movements often are a little off the routes of major shipping lanes. Logs, for example, originate in logging ports and move on either specialized vessels or in open-top containers. Autos are carried to auto terminals, often some distance from major port facilities. Auto-carrying ships require less water depth because their load is not dense. Facilities on shore tend to consume large acreages of land, since they are little more than parking lots holding inventories of thousands of new autos. Because of these land-intensive needs, the facility must be some distance from major port facilities where high cargo turnover is more important. Figure 4–2 shows the front of a cross-section of an auto-carrying ship, the deck levels of which can be adjusted. Autos and logs also move as break-bulk or containerized cargo. There are special auto-rack containers that can be contorted into different shapes to accommodate batches of autos with varying dimensions.

It is difficult to construct categories into which one can carefully classify all cargoes. Bulk cargo, for example, is carried on liner vessels that are scheduled to sail, but have not been able to fill up with more lucrative cargo. The term "topping off" is used, and a common cargo for this purpose is baled hay. The rate per ton charged for that haul is close to that paid for moving hay by the vessel

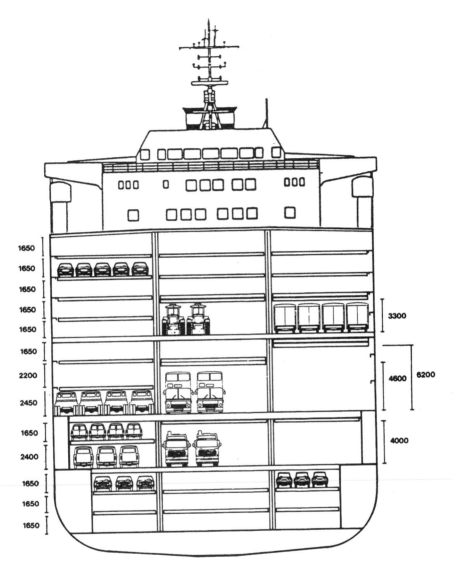

Figure 4–2 Cross-section view of an auto-carrying vessel. Courtesy of Wallenius Lines North America, Inc.

load. At the other extreme, a vessel might be loaded with a bulk cargo and would take on a partial load of oversize cargo that would ride on top of the deck. This is known as "deck" cargo. A common example is school buses or rail transit vehicles.

Another term that has come into use describing cargo is *project* cargo. That is not a specific type of item but related cargo needed for a single, certain purpose. Hence, if a contractor were rebuilding a structure in Kuwait or a portion of a major pipeline, the various materials that were to be obtained from outside the local area would be scheduled, purchased, consolidated at various ports, and shipped as needed. Often, project cargo is spread out over a number of voyages. Sometimes, project cargo is oversized and requires special transportation equipment and handling on both land and sea.

In summary, here is still another set of definitions for most noncontainerized cargo:

Noncontainerized cargo consists of bulk, neobulk, and break-bulk cargoes.

Bulk cargoes are those that can be air-blown, pumped, conveyored, belted, or generally handled in bulk rather than in discrete units. They include petroleum products, grain, sand, gravel, dry chemicals, and bulk liquids.

Break-bulk cargoes are generally cargoes that are conventionally stevedored and stowed as opposed to bulk, unitized and containerized cargoes. Examples are peas, beans, lentils, machinery, yachts and some wood products such as newsprint, pulp and linerboard.

Neo-bulk cargoes, though historically classified as general cargoes, move in volume, usually on specialized or dedicated vessels. Examples include autos, steel, logs, and livestock.

In the mid-1990s, it was estimated that about 3.2 billion metric tons of international oceanborne commerce was carried annually. The tonnage, expressed in metric tons, and ton-mileage (using nautical miles with one metric ton carried one nautical mile equaling a ton-mile), and average lengths of haul in nautical miles are shown in Table 4–1.

Table 4–1   *Worldwide Oceanborne Cargoes, ca 1995*

	Million of tons	Billion of ton-miles	Average length of haul
Crude oil	998	4,393	4,401
Oil products	309	1,090	3,527
Iron ore	306	1,676	5,477
Coal	279	1,480	5,304
Grain	162	860	5,308
Other commodities	1,218	4,037	3,314

Source: derived from figures in Niko Wijnolst and Tor Wergeland, *Shipping,* (Delft, Delft Univ. Press, 1997), pp. 13–15. Using a somewhat different base, UNCTAD figures showed a six percent increase in ton-miles of all ocean traffic between 1995 and 2000.

Vessels and Vessel Characteristics

> Once upon a time . . . , there was basically only one type of general-cargo ship at sea. This ship was narrow in proportion to its length and had from one to several holds with small hatches, each serviced by derricks which could lift loaded slings in and out and over the side onto a wharf or into lighters. . . . It was not greatly different in days of sail, when men hauling on ropes, rather than on donkey-engines powered the derricks. [With] the introduction of steam . . . , engine-powered vessels could operate handily in small and difficult places where large wind-powered vessels were at a disadvantage. Ships designed to handle cargo in this way could go almost anywhere there was water to float them . . .[3]

Today, one thinks of vessels as being specialized, usually in terms of cargo they are designed to haul or markets they are intended to serve. Vessel size can be expressed in exterior dimensions; however, a more common measure is tonnage. The most frequently used measure is *deadweight tonnage* (dwt); this is tons of cargo, stores, and fuel a vessel can carry. *Gross tonnage* is defined as the number of units of 100 cubic feet of permanently enclosed space in the ship, leaving out "exempted spaces" like double-bottom and peak tanks. *Net tonnage* is gross tonnage less spaces that cannot earn revenue, such as the engine room.[4] Gross tonnage applies to vessels, and is often used to compare the relative sizes of various nation's fleets.

Commercial ships are becoming larger. During World War II, the common U.S. tanker was referred to as a "T-2." The T-2 was rated at 16,500 dwt. Tankers exist today that can carry 30 times as much. Table 4–2 is the record of seagoing vessels, by number and gross tonnage, calling at the Port of Antwerp during the period 1965-2000, with the column on the right showing how the average size has increased.

The size of commercial vessels differs, and it is difficult to generalize what they are or should be. Most sizes fit the trades they happen to serve. One of the coauthors of this book was touring the Port of Lisbon, Portugal, whose main trade was conducted with Africa. The port was very busy; but the difference between that port and major U.S. ports was that the scale of all the vessels was

---

[3]H. C. Brookfield, "Boxes, Ports, and Places without Ports," in *Seaport Systems and Spatial Change,* edited by B. S. Hoyle and D. Hilling (New York: John Wiley & Sons, 1984), pp. 61–62.

[4]R. O. Goss, *Studies in Maritime Economics* (Cambridge, England: University Press, 1968), p. 158n. Another form of ton, unique to shipping, is called the measurement ton. That term applies to liner cargo and is a rule stating that cargo should also be measured to determine its cube, and every cubic meter should be counted as one ton, and if the vessel may collect more revenue using this rule, it will. This rule has considerable influence on product and packaging design.

Table 4–2   *Vessels Calling at Antwerp, 1965–2000*

Year	Number of vessels	Total gross registered tonnage (1000s)	Average tonnage
1965	18,065	55,383	3,066
1970	19,150	67,894	3,545
1975	17,376	60,986	3,510
1980	17,151	102,696	5,988
1985	16,646	120,644	7,248
1990	16,762	140,831	8,401
1995	15,223	167,858	11,026
2000	16,105	203,064	12,609

Source: Excerpted from *Annex to Hinterland,* published by the Port of Antwerp, Dec. 1992, page 3. Figures for 1995 and 2000 from port's website, *www.portofantwerp.be,* July 11, 2001.

much smaller. Cargo-carrying vessels operating in the Caribbean are also smaller than those operating in more major trades.

One also tends to think of vessels as having the same shape, that is, as size increases, all dimensions increase proportionately. This is generally so, although there are some exceptions. In Australia, wider shallow-draft ships are being built because of lack of harbor dredging. One is the Iron Pacific, a 231,850 dwt iron-ore carrier operating between Australia, Japan, and Korea. A conventionally proportioned ship of the same draft would be about 140,000 dwt.[5]

The actual volume of cargo that a vessel may carry is limited by its cubic capacity and its weight capacity. The same vessel loaded with iron ore will ride much deeper than if it were carrying grain. (When a vessel's weight capacity is reached, even though there is available space, this is known as "weighing out." If all the space is filled, even though the ship is not very low in the water, this is known as "cubing out.")

Along each side of a vessel one will see a symbol that looks like the one shown here:

---

[5]*The Pacific Maritime Magazine,* November, 1987, p. 6.

```
TF  _____
     I
F   _____  I
     I
     I _____ T
     I
     I
     I _____ S
     I
     I
     I _____ W
     I
     I
     I _____ WNA
```

This is known as the *Plimsoll mark.* Plimsoll marks,[6] also known as load lines, were originated by Samuel Plimsoll in 1876, although the Hanseatic League had regulated load lines as early as the 1100s. Depending on the season of year and the location where the vessel is sailing, these lines indicate the maximum draft that the vessel can be submerged. To load deeper is a violation of many nations' laws and of the insurance agreements covering the vessel and cargo. The initial purpose of the lines had been for the safety of sailors, because many had perished as overloaded vessels had sunk at sea. The lines for each vessel are determined by *classification societies,* which are neutral bodies in most maritime nations charged with examining both ships under construction as well as existing vessels for matters concerning vessel safety.

Classification societies have many duties. They prepare and enforce rules dealing with vessel design, alteration, and construction. They perform on-site inspections while vessels are being built or converted. They also inspect and certify the cargo-handling equipment that is carried aboard the vessel. They keep maintenance records of vessels under their supervision. Insurers of vessels and vessel cargo, bankers, and governments rely on their work. Vessel owners and shipyards are required to share all information with their respective classification society. Worldwide, there are about 40 classification societies. The major classification societies and the number of vessels under their respective supervision

---

[6]"The Evolution of the Load Line," *Surveyor* [American Bureau of Shipping], May, 1976, pp. 7–13. Here is what the letters stand for: TF = tropical freshwater allowance; F = fresh water allowance; T = tropical load line; S = summer load line; W = winter load line; and WNA = winter, North Atlantic load line.

are: American Bureau of Shipping, 11,794; Bureau Veritas, 7,068; China Classification Society, 1,717; Det Norske Veritas, 4,263; Germanisher Lloyd, 4,409; Korean Register of Shipping, 1,193; Lloyd's Register of Shipping, 6,600; Nippon Kaiji Kyokai, 6,156; Polish Register of Shipping, 1,030; Registro Italiano Navale, 3,319; and Russian Maritime Register, 7,790.[7]

How are ships powered? Most vessels built today are powered by diesels rather than steam turbines. Over the past decade, many steam vessels were retrofitted with diesel. In the early 1970s, one major U.S. container line introduced a fleet of vessels with a faster propulsion system, in an attempt to cut one sailing day off the trans-Pacific market. After the oil "crises" of the mid- and late-1970s, these vessels became very expensive to operate (and eventually were purchased by the U.S. Navy and converted to "fast deployment" military supply ships). When petroleum prices escalated, there was some interest shown in wind-powered sailing ships. A number were built and had computer-controlled sails and auxiliary power units to assist in case there were no winds and to improve maneuvering in ports. At present, some of these "sailing" ships are used for passenger cruise ships.

One aspect of vessel propulsion that is somewhat unique to water transportation is that the fuel efficiency of a conventional hulled vessel moving through the water drops as the speed increases. That is, fuel consumption increases more than speed does. While the numbers differ for each ship, an example would be that at one given speed, an increase in speed of 10 percent would increase fuel consumption by 15 percent; and at a much higher given speed, an increase in speed by ten percent would increase fuel consumption by 35 percent. Hence, speed is an important variable when determining the economic scheduling of ships. Also related to economics of scheduling is the time spent in port and the time at sea. While vessels must call at ports to find and discharge cargo, they are generally considered to be in a "productive" state when they are at sea.

Vessel Types

Table 4–3 shows the world's commercial fleet in 1998, in terms of vessel type, total gross tonnage, and average age (in years) of each vessel type.

Vessels tend to be categorized by the type of cargoes they haul. However, many vessels fit into more than one category. They shift cargo types from voyage to voyage or over the course of their lives. Many are built to have more than one purpose. Dry-bulk freighters today are often built with holds and hatch cov-

---

[7]Niko Wijnolst and Tor Wergeland, *Shipping*, (Delft, Delft Univ. Press, 1997), p. 378. Figures are for 1996.

Table 4–3   Commercial Vessels in the World, 1998

Vessel type	Number of vessels	Gross tonnage (Millions)	Age (Years)
Oil tankers	6,960	151	18
Bulk, dry	4,939	139	14
General cargo	16,824	56	20
Container	2,382	53	9
Ro/ro cargo	1,769	23	16
LNG	1,065	17	14
Chemical	2,363	15	13
Passenger/Ro/ro cargo	2,496	13	20
Bulk dry/oil (combi)	224	10	16
Refrigerated cargo	1,441	7	17
Other bulk dry	1,089	7	15
Passenger (cruise)	337	6	24
Self unloading dry bulk	161	3	26
Other dry cargo	271	2	23
Passenger ship	2,550	1	19
Other liquids	347	1	22
Passenger/general cargo	340	1	31

Source: International Transport Workers' Federation website, 2000.

ers at least 40 feet long so they could, if necessary, accommodate 40-foot containers.

Tankers

Tankers are the most important ship, measured in shares of the world's gross registered tonnage. As might be expected, they consist of a number of tank compartments, fitted with baffles inside to control the movements of cargo in rough seas. They have pumps and pipes, and are recognizable by the collection of piping on top of their top deck. Tanker discharge pumps are geared to be powered by the vessel's main engines. One tanker productivity or capacity baseline for many years was known as the "T-2 equivalent," that is, a 16,500 dwt tanker traveling at 14.5 knots. More recently, the tanker baseline is referred to as "worldscale" with charter rates being tied to that. In early 1989, a new worldwide tanker nominal freight scale was based on a tanker with standard vessel capacity of 75,000 metric tons of cargo, plus stores, water, and bunkers (fuel); with an average speed or 14.5 knots; bunker consumption: 55 metric tons per day for steaming, 100 tons for purposes other than steaming, and five metric tons for each port stay; port time: four days between port pairs, and 12 hours for each extra port; fixed hire rate: $12,000 per day; bunker (fuel) price: $74.50 per bunker ton; and canal transit times: Panama—24 hours, Suez—30 hours.[8]

The largest tankers carry crude oil. Smaller tankers, known as "product" tankers, carry refined petroleum products. They have a large number of tanks and can carry several products simultaneously. Some have heating systems to warm the products, making them easier to discharge.

Tankers are also the largest vessels in use. After the Suez closure of some decades ago, it became economical to build very large ships to carry oil from the Middle East to Europe by sailing around the southern tip of Africa. Classifications of large tankers include Very Large Crude Carrier (VLCC) as a vessel of 150,000 to 299,999 dwt; and Ultra Large Crude Carrier (ULCC) for tankers larger than that. As the price of petroleum increased, the demand for the large tankers declined. Many were tied up and used for oil storage. In December 1990, for example, 60 large tankers with a deadweight tonnage totaling 12.6 million (average 200,000 tons each) were used for oil storage. Environmental groups have been very critical of large tankers because of fears that any oil spills they might cause would be so large as to overwhelm the affected area. The Exxon Valdez disaster validated this fear, and the United States is requiring that tankers making future deliveries to U.S. ports be equipped with double hulls. "Current thinking is that the double-hull requirement will not spread to other countries. Vessels delivering oil from other countries to the U.S. will bring it to within about 100 miles of the U.S. shore in single-hull tankers. At that point out at sea it will be lightered (transferred at sea) to double-hull tankers that will deliver it to U.S. ports."[9]

There are also vessels known as "parcel tankers," such as those operated by Stolt-Nielsen. The newest Stolt-Nielsen vessels have 58 different tanks ranging from 350 to 2,200 cubic meters. Each is loaded/unloaded through a separate piping system. These vessels go on "round the world" voyages and they carry palm oil, coconut oil, chemicals, and refined petroleum products. Tanks need different types of coatings, and some are temperature-controlled. Stolt-Nielsen's spokesperson, Robert F. Matthes, said: ". . . we have a loosely-defined liner service."[10]

---

[8]*American Shipper,* February 1989, p. 52.

[9]Robert Thomas Hoffman and Donald F. Wood, "Impacts of U.S. Environmental Controls Upon Ocean Tankers," *Journal of Transportation Management,* Fall, 1996, page 39.

[10]*American Shipper,* May 1986, p. 78.

LNG (Liquefied Natural Gas) Carriers

LNG is a valuable byproduct in the oil industry and is most economically transported when it can be compressed to 1/630 of its gaseous volume, at which point it becomes liquid. LNG carriers are easily recognizable because they usually carry four huge spheres for holding their product. Temperatures within the spherical tanks are maintained at -260 degrees F, which would make steel brittle, so they are constructed of nickel steel or aluminum alloys and require special welding techniques.[11]

Ore and Bulk Carriers

These carriers are also called dry-bulk carriers. These ships have large compartments for carrying loads of ore, grain, or coal. Usually the entire ship is used for the same type of cargo, although the ship is divided into different compartments and could, in theory, carry a different cargo in each. Iron ore is the largest single tonnage of dry bulk cargo. Grain and coal follow, although their relative volumes change from year to year. Other bulk movements, much smaller in volume, are other forms of ore, rice, sugar, fertilizers, limestone, and scrap metals. Cement moves on dry-bulk vessels under moisture-proof conditions and is loaded and unloaded pneumatically.

An important distinction for dry-bulk carriers (and some other forms of vessels) is whether they carry equipment to load and unload cargoes. If they cannot, then they can be used only in ports where loading/discharge equipment is available. A geared bulk carrier has cargo-handling cranes and derricks installed on its main deck to load and unload cargo, while a gearless bulk carrier depends entirely on shoreside facilities for loading and unloading. A better use of capital resources is to have one shoreside material-handling facility serving the needs of all vessels on important trade routes rather than each vessel having its own infrequently used cargo handling facility.[12] In the ore trades, the vessels are usually not equipped with loading/unloading equipment because they perform repetitive back-and-forth movements between ore-loading docks and steel mills. In trades where origins and destinations continually change, it's necessary that the vessel be equipped to load or unload.

Dry-bulk carriers are not as large as tankers because tankers need not navigate

---

[11]Roy Nersesian, *Ships and Shipping,* (Tulsa: PennWell, 1981), p. 82.

[12]Roy Nersesian, *Ships and Shipping,* (Tulsa: PennWell, 1981), p. 48.

inside ports or next to dock facilities in order to load or discharge. Dry bulk carriers must dock next to land, and an expense to the shoreside operator is dredging the dock alongside his loading/unloading facility so that large vessels can moor there. In addition to dredging, the dock wall must be deepened, strengthened, and tied back so it does not collapse into the water. Because these costs limit the depths of berths, they also limit the size of vessel that can be used at these berths. Another limit on the size of dry bulk vessels is the dimensions of the Panama Canal. Most investors in vessels want a vessel that is able to transit the canal; otherwise the vessel will be foreclosed from many hauls. The term *Panamax* means a vessel that can pass through the Canal, and vessels that size can carry up to about 75,000 tons.

Bulk vessels too large to transit the Panama Canal are sometimes called *Capesize,* meaning that they have to sail around the cape of South America or South Africa. "A 'Handysize' bulk carrier has a maximum breadth of 23 meters and a length of 222.5 meters and is therefore able to sail the St. Lawrence Seaway to the Great Lakes of North America."[13]

In the early 1970s, a bulk slurry handling technique for iron ore known as "Marconaflo" was developed and installed on a fleet of vessels. The ore from the mine had water added and the mixture was agitated until it formed a thick, muddy substance that could be pumped. A flexible pipeline would lead offshore and the material would be pumped into a vessel that could be moored in deep water. After the vessel was loaded, the cargo would settle and most of the water would rise to the top of each hold. It would be decanted off and the vessel would set sail. At the destination port the vessel would moor off shore. At the bottom of each hold there was a washing machine agitator-like device and water would be introduced as the agitator was activated. This would form another slurry that could be pumped ashore using a flexible pipeline. A vessel with similar characteristics was once used for transporting wet wood pulp.

A specialized form of dry-bulk carrier, used on the Great Lakes for both domestic and international moves (U.S.–Canada), is called a "laker." Lakers are longer and narrower than ocean-going ships and would be unsafe to operate on oceans. Their principal cargoes are ore, coal, grain, salt, and limestone. Some lakers are equipped with self-unloading devices and their charter rates run about ten percent higher than lakers that are not similarly equipped. The largest lakers are "bottled up" in the upper four Great Lakes because they are too large to transit the Welland Canal that bypasses Niagara Falls. Some smaller lakers do sail down to the mouth of the St. Lawrence River, where they load with Labrador ore

---

[13]Niko Wijnolst and Tor Wergeland, *Shipping,* (Delft: Delft Univ. Press, 1997), page 71.

and take it back up into the Lakes. Some lakers also carry grain down to the Canadian elevators on the lower St. Lawrence, where it is subsequently loaded aboard ocean carriers.

Combination (Oil and Dry-Bulk) Carriers

A combination carrier usually means a bulk vessel that can carry either petroleum or dry cargo, built that way because the original owner/investor, at the time the vessel was being built, was uncertain whether the future markets over the vessel's life would favor dry or liquid bulk cargo. Such a vessel would have to visit a shipyard to be converted from a tanker to a dry-bulk vessel or vice versa.

The nickname "combi" is given to such vessel types, although the nickname has wider application to a vessel that either fits two definitions or has its cargo-carrying capacity split in some form. A combined Ro/Ro-containership is shown in Figure 4–3. As containerization was becoming popular, the term *combi* meant a ship that had both racks for carrying containers and conventional holds for traditional stevedore-stowed break-bulk cargoes.

Another very specialized vessel is called the container-oil-bulk carrier (COB). They are used in markets with regular cargo hauls going one way only. [An example is portions of Scandinavia ship forest products south and receive petroleum from the south.] Containers carry additional dry cargo moving in either direction. The Canadian Pacific ocean vessel line purchased a new fleet of what they refer to as "Con-Bulk ships" to haul steel products from Belgium to

Figure 4–3   Drawing of a combined container Ro/Ro vessel. Courtesy CIGNA Corporation, *Ports of the World,* 15th edition.

Quebec City, where they were off-loaded, with the then lighter ships going up to Montreal with the containers.[14]

General Cargo Vessels

The original general cargo carriers were called "break-bulk" and loaded on a piece-by-piece basis by stevedores. Palletization speeded up the process of handling loose freight. In the days before containerization, and continuing today in some of the non-containerized trades, carriers allowed shippers free carriage of the pallets themselves (the weight and cube of the platform itself) because of the efficiencies they promoted. Many carriers even offered shippers discounts on freight that arrived and could be handled on pallets.

The need to speed up the process of loading and unloading and to minimize idle time spawned containerization technology. *Containerization,* the carriage of goods in large intermodal boxes or barges, was the logical extension of palletization. Containers vastly increased freight handling capability and greatly reduce idle port time.

Thus special container-carrying vessels have emerged and proliferated along with shoreside infrastructures to move them. The ships themselves have been redesigned to carry containers in cells aboard the ship, to be "rolled" or driven aboard, or to carry barges called lighters. (*Lighter* is an old term for barges and originally referred to barges that received cargo at the railheads in New Jersey, across from Manhattan, and carried it to moored ships on the Manhattan waterfront, which loaded it, using ship's tackle. Unloading or loading a vessel utilizing a smaller vessel to move to and from shore is called *lightering.*)

Containerships are specifically designed to carry containers in cells aboard the ship. They are also called *cellular* ships. Land chassis, the frame and wheels atop which containers ride, are not carried aboard these ships. An inventory of this equipment must be maintained on both discharge and loading ports. Containers are unloaded from the ship by huge cranes and placed on waiting land chassis. These vessels are standardized to carry 20- or 40-foot long containers.

Containerships come in all sizes, and size is measured according to the number of TEUs (20-foot equivalent containers) they can carry. In late 1986, American President Lines ordered five 4300 TEU vessels, which are too wide for transiting the Panama Canal. According to APL President Timothy J. Rhein's statement at that time, "These are the first ships to be designed specifically for

---

[14]Yann Alix, Brian Slack, and Claude Comtois, "Alliance of Acquisition? Strategies for growth in the container shipping industry, the case of CP ships," *Journal of Transport Geography* (1999), p. 205. The vessels would carry containerized traffic back to Europe.

trans-Pacific service. By removing the limitation on the ships' beam, we were able to increase their capacity, while optimizing their speed, fuel efficiency, and stability."[15] They are 896 feet long and have beams of 130 feet. Ports handling them have had to increase the sizes of their shoreside cranes, and today the vessels are referred to as "Post-Panamax" containerships. Since then, containerships have become much larger. Some Maersk containerships built in the late 1990s can carry 8,400 TEUs. Even larger containerships are on the drawing boards. A "Suez-max" could carry 12,000 TEUs and a "Malacca-max" could carry over 18,000 TEUs. The larger the containership, the less its voyage costs per container. Estimates are that to carry a TEU between Rotterdam and Singapore, the costs are $220 on a Panamax-size container ship; they drop to $150 per TEU on the Malacca-max. However, the Malacca-max could not transit the present Suez Canal, and it's unclear how extensive a feeder system of smaller container ships would be required to carry containers to and from the Rotterdam and Singapore hubs.[16]

Most of the new ships being built to carry general cargo are containerships. They are fast replacing conventional break-bulk carriers. In 1990, the total tonnage of break-bulk fleet and the container fleet were approximately equal. In 1999, the tonnage of container ships was over three times greater than that of break-bulk vessels.[17] The break-bulk vessels continue to find niche markets in areas without container facilities, project cargoes, steel, and newsprint. Some bulk cargoes are now moving in containers. Grain is one example: the container box is lined and the grain poured into the box. Examples of specialized grain movements are beans, lentils, peas, and sunflower seeds. "Exports now include specialized varieties such as low-saturated-fat soybeans and more easily digestible soybeans with altered carbohydrates. There are organically produced grains, and genetically altered grains. There's wheat with specific baking characterics and high protein corn. . . ."[18] Buyers of grains are becoming more specific in stating their needs.

Roll on–roll off, or *"Ro/Ro"* vessels, are not constrained by cell lengths. Rolling cargo such as tractors and automobiles, are simply driven aboard the vessel. Truck trailers are driven aboard and parked. Specialized wheeled equipment, such as flat racks and framed tank containers, permit the easy handling of almost of every type of cargo.

---

[15]*Port of Oakland Progress* (July/August, 1988), p. 3.

[16]*American Shipper,* February, 2001, p. 68. The vessel will draw 69 feet and Rotterdam and Singapore are about the only feasible choices with such depths.

[17]*The Journal of Commerce,* Oct. 4, 1999, p. 7C.

[18]*JoCWeek,* August 28–September 3, 2000, p. 50.

The term "Lo/Lo" is used in a few areas of the world. It apparently means that the vessel carries its own loading/unloading equipment. A trade journal said: "Maersk Sealand . . . has deployed loft on/lift off (Lo/Lo) vessels—which have cranes onboard—that have carrying capacities of 500 twenty-foot equivalent units (TEUs) to 1,100 TEUs."[19]

"*LASH*" vessels (*"Lighter Aboard SHip"*) carry very large containers: barges. Cargo is loaded at pierside into barges that are themselves loaded aboard the ship. The advantage of LASH shipping is twofold. First, because of the shallow draft of the barges, they can be loaded in shallow-water seaports where the mother vessel itself cannot be accommodated. They can also be loaded/unloaded at river ports away from the seacoast and be towed down or up river. Second, delays within a port resulting from congestion can be avoided altogether by the mother ship, which never needs to await berth space. These features make LASH vessels particularly attractive in less-developed countries. LASH barges are 10 x 20 x 60 feet, and there are vessels handling even larger barges known as *Seabees*.

Neo-bulk Carriers

Neo-bulk carriers are specialized ships for carrying high-value cargoes. The best example are new-car carriers used for autos. Many have adjustable decks so they can reduce waste space above the motor vehicles' roofs. In the late 1980s, a firm announced it would develop a monthly service between Portland and Japan, using Ro/Ro vessels, with autos going one way, lumber the other.[20] Some auto carriers are designed to carry bulk loads as well; for example, soybeans as the return haul to Japan. In the year 2000, a handful of companies controlled the new-car carrying business. The main player was Wallenius Wilhelmsen, which had 70 ships and carried 1.5 million cars and trucks that year.[21] In the late 1990s, several auto-carrying vessels had to increase the space between decks so that they could haul new SUVs.

Another large neobulk haul is logs. Since logs themselves float, some log-carrying vessels are designed to tip sideways at such a sharp angle that the logs will slide off into the water. This would occur inside an enclosed water area and, later, the logs would be lifted ashore, one by one.

Other specialized neobulk vessels have been designed for carrying newsprint and livestock. There have been tankers that were equipped to carry only bulk wine or orange juice.

---

[19]*Shipping Digest,* June 11, 2001, p. 4.

[20]*American Shipper,* February, 1988, p. 68.

[21]*The Journal of Commerce,* February 16, 2000, p. 19.

Combined Passenger/Cargo Ships

In trades between North and South America, several vessels are operated that carry about 100 passengers plus containerized freight. The nature of the freight business in that market results in stops at many ports along the coastline, which pleases tourists. A slight advantage to cargo shippers is that the passenger vessel receives priority in docking in case the port is congested.

Other Ocean Vessel Types

There are many specialized vessels, with some so specialized as to be considered one of a kind. *Refrigerated carriers (reefers)* carry produce. The best-known are the white "banana boats" one sees carrying bananas from Latin America. Another large movement today is grapes from Chile to the United States in fully refrigerated vessels. Livestock carriers have ramps and decks designed to accommodate movements of cattle and sheep. They also have ventilating systems to maintain air circulation.

Another specialized type is the heavy-lift vessel with side stabilizers used to counterbalance heavy loads as they are loaded or discharged. Ballast tanks on the side away from the pier are filled as the vessel's crane that extends over the pier starts to lift a heavy load. The weight of the water being added to the tanks equals that of the load. Once the load is lifted, as it is moved toward the vessel's center, water in the tank is discharged. Figure 4–4 shows three container cranes being delivered to the Port of Amsterdam on a heavy-lift ship.

Some heavy-lift vessels for lifting and moving offshore oil rigs are built so that they can partially submerge, move under the load, rise in the water, lifting the load with them, and move to another spot. On July 19, 1999, "New Orleans saw one of its biggest cargo moves ever as a 5,900-ton, 126-foot tall oil platform was loaded upon a specially built ship and floated down the Mississippi River. The platform, being transported to Venezuela, was placed onto a submersible ship. Ballast tanks were filled to lower the ship's midsection underwater so the platform could be floated onto the deck."[22]

Short Sea Shipping

Short sea shipping is ocean shipping, often along a region's coast or connecting with islands. It frequently is feeder service, connecting to a few major ports that

---

[22]*The Journal of Commerce,* supplement, September 8, 1999, p. 18.

Figure 4–4 A heavy-lift ship carrying three container cranes, each 112 meters high and with sufficient reach to handle containerships 22 containers across. (Courtesy Amsterdam Port Authority.)

serve as hubs. In Europe, short sea shipping is considered more environmentally friendly than trucks. "Antwerp is connected to 141 ports in Europe and the Mediterranean by this type of service."[23] Hong Kong and Singapore are hubs for numerous smaller Asian ports. Vessels in short-sea markets are equipped so they can load and discharge cargos quickly.

FastShips

In the mid-1990s, considerable interest developed in so-called *FastShips* that were to save three days on the cross-Atlantic sailing, saving one day in each port and one day at sea. The reduced transit times would reduce shippers' investment in inventory. The vessel would fill the gap between conventional ocean service and air.

---

[23]James C. Johnson, et al, *Contemporary Logistics,* 7th ed., (Upper Saddle River, NJ: Prentice Hall, 1999), pp. 404–405.

FastShips officials say the vessels would be able to cross the rugged North Atlantic in three-and-a-half days, and would provide shippers with a guaranteed door-to-door transit time seven days between the U.S. Midwest and Central Europe. The cost to shippers would be roughly 13 cents to 18 cents per pound, they say. By way of comparison, they cite costs of 4 cents to 8 cents per pound for ocean freight, which takes 14 to 28 days to arrive, and air-freight costs that start at 35 cents to 60 cents per pound for belly-cargo service and jump to as much as $1.50 per pound for express service.[24]

The vessels would operate between Philadelphia and Cherbourg. Their hulls would ride high in the water to reduce water friction that slows conventional hulls. Containers will be loaded and unloaded using rail systems, and this will reduce the FastShips' time in port to six hours. Financing of the project is still not complete.

Barges

In addition to conventional vessels there are *barges,* unmanned vessels pulled (or pushed) by a tugboat. "Pusher units" are preferred because of less wave resistance, and better control over the barge. The principal saving is in crew costs since the tug requires a much smaller crew, eight or nine, rather than 25–30 on a regular ship. In some situations there are savings in product inventory costs; that is, the firm owns more barges than tugs; and when the tug arrives with a loaded barge, it leaves it behind to be unloaded, and picks up a waiting empty barge. This results in saving on wages while in port, since the tug merely picks up another barge, while a conventional ship would sit and wait while it is being unloaded or loaded. In the 1980s, Matson built a self-loading/unloading barge for use in intra-Hawaii container trade. On the barge is mounted a stern-thruster, controlled by radio from the tug, to eliminate the need for a second tug while docking. The stern thruster is at right angles to the vessel, and it is used to push the bow next to the pier. The barge was designed to carry 216 containers and 1700 long-tons of molasses.[25]

Barges are also used for oversized cargoes, since clearances on water routes are greater than for rail or truck. Hence, if one were building a large structure for shipment to another nation, both the construction site and the destination site must be next to waterways. The structure would be towed across the ocean by barge. One form of this application is the movement of off-shore oil-drilling rigs.

---

[24]*JoCWeek,* June 26–July 2, 2000, p. 13.

[25]"McDermott Builds $6 Million Barge for Matson's Use in Hawaii," Port Reporter, the *Pacific Maritime Magazine,* November, 1983, p. 8.

In the late 1970s, a pulp plant was built in Japan for use at a site in the Amazon River Basin in Brazil. Two large barges were built in Japan, and on one the pulp plant was constructed, and on the other the accompanying power plant was built. Care was taken to design both plants so that, when on a floating barge, the weight distribution would be even. The two barges, with plants on top, were then towed to Brazil. The destination site, adjacent to the Jari River, had been dredged out and a dike was placed between the dredged area and the river. Water was pumped out and piles were driven at the sites where the mill and the power plant were to be located. When the barges arrived, the dike was removed and the area flooded. Each barge was positioned exactly above the piles, and the dike rebuilt. As the water was pumped out, both barges settled on to the pilings. "Windows were cut in the sides of the barges, and the barges became the lower floors of the pulp and power plants. It was estimated that construction costs were reduced by 20 percent and two years of time was saved by having the plant built in Japan and towed to Brazil rather than having it constructed at the Brazilian site."[26]

There are a small number of "floating factories," on either barges or conventional ships, that are mainly associated with the fishing industry. They process, freeze, and can the fish that are being caught, as they follow the fishing fleet.

Vessel Ownership by Nation

Each year the United Nations Conference on Trade and Development (UNCTAD) tallies the maritime tonnage owned and controlled by each nation. As of January 1, 2000, Greeks owned 752 vessels flying the Greek flag plus 2,495 vessels that fly flags of convenience. The deadweight tonnage of this combined fleet totaled 133,381,588, and this represented over 18 percent of the world's merchant fleet, measured in terms of deadweight tons.[27] In descending order were Japan, Norway, the United States, China, Hong Kong, Germany, Republic of Korea, Taiwan, and the United Kingdom. These ten nations controlled just over two-thirds of the world's merchant tonnage. In terms of number of vessels over 1000 dwt, they controlled 53 percent.

Shipbuilding

The demand for ships is, of course, related to the aggregate demand of shippers throughout the world who need to move goods that they desire to buy or sell.

---

[26]Donald F. Wood and James C. Johnson, *Contemporary Transportation,* 2d. ed. (Tulsa, OK: PennWell, 1983), p. 403.

[27]United Nations Conference on Trade and Development, *Review of Maritime Transport 2000* (Geneva, 2000), page 28. Vessels under 1,000 tons were excluded.

The supply of shipping comes from many sources, but mainly private investors who project a positive income stream over the life of a vessel built for their own use or for use by others. Shipbuilding is subsidized by some nations, and some nations even subsidize ship scrapping operations in order to reduce the supply of older vessels.

Here is a summary of orders for new ships in 1999, by type of ship. Crude oil tankers: up to Panamax, 4; Panamax to 149,999 dwt, 9; 150,000 to 249,999 dwt, 16; 250,000 dwt and up, 28. Product tankers: up to 9,999 dwt, 20; 10,000 to 29,999 dwt, 7; 30,000 to Panamax, 31; larger than Panamax, 8. Chemical tankers, 74. LNG and LPG tankers, 111. Bulk-ore and coal carriers: up to 19,999 dwt, 26; 20,000 to 49,999 dwt, 76; 50,000 to Panamax, 197; Panamax to 124,999, 6; 125,000 and over, 41. Container vessels: up to 999 TEUs, 28; 1,000 to 1,999 TEUs, 31; 2,000 to 3,999 TEUs, 55; and 4,000 and more TEUs, 50. Other dry-cargo vessels, 349. Ro/Ro and car carriers, 47. Reefers, 1.[28]

South Korea and Japan are the world's leading shipbuilding nations. In the year 2000, each delivered about 38 percent of the new tonnage. When the output of China and Taiwan is added, then Asia's share of new tonnage equaled 83 percent of the world's deliveries in 2000. European shipbuilding nations include Croatia, Denmark, Finland, France, Germany, Italy, Netherlands, Norway, Poland, Spain, Sweden, and the United Kingdom, and together in 2000 they produced 14 percent of the world's new tonnage.[29]

Summary

There are several ways of classifying vessels. One is by their cargoes, with emphasis on the cargo type and characteristics. A related factor is the quantities in which the cargo is usually shipped. Bulk cargoes are either liquid or dry, with liquid cargoes being shipped on tankers, and dry cargoes moving on dry-bulk carriers. Break-bulk cargo is of higher value per unit of weight, and is handled on a piece-by-piece basis; today, much of it moves within containers. Neobulk cargo has some characteristics of bulk and some characteristics of break-bulk cargo, and it often moves on specialized ocean vessels.

A number of vessel types were discussed, including tankers, LNG carriers, ore and bulk carriers, lakers, and general cargo vessels. Included with the general cargo vessels were containership, Ro/Ro, and LASH vessels. Also mentioned were neobulk carriers and barges.

Greek interests own and control the most ships. South Korea and Japan are the world's two major shipbuilding nations.

---

[28]Website *www.chamber-of-shipping.org.tr,* July 11, 2001.

[29]Website *www. coltoncompany.com,* July 11, 2001.

End-of-Chapter Questions

1. What is bulk cargo? Give some examples.
2. What is break-bulk cargo? Give some examples.
3. What is neobulk cargo? Give some examples.
4. What is a Plimsoll mark? Why are they used?
5. What are the advantages and disadvantages of a vessel's carrying its own loading and unloading equipment?
6. What are lakers? Where are they used?
7. What are LASH vessels? Where might their use be advantageous?
8. When are ocean-going barges used?
9. What is the FastShip proposal? How successful, if at all, do you think it will be? Why?
10. What kinds of ships are being built? Where is most of this shipbuilding taking place?

CASE • *Macao Wastebaskets*

At the end of the war in Vietnam, Michael Machado settled in Macao, near Hong Kong, where he soon became involved in the manufacture of metal wastebaskets. At present, the one style he makes is cylindrical and, when packaged, weighs 10 pounds and measures exactly 2 cubic feet in volume. The wastebaskets have sold well, mainly because of the unique silk-screened patterns on the sides.

One day Linda Hernandez, whose business card indicated that she was a buyer for a large U.S. and Canadian chain store, appeared at Machado's office and said her firm was interested in purchasing a large number of the wastebaskets. Because her firm distributes a nationwide catalog and sells through a website, they would need a large number in their initial order. Ms. Hernandez indicated that if a purchase order were offered, it would be for 10,000 wastebaskets, plus an option to buy an additional 10,000 at the same price within one year. She further indicated that her firm would like to select certain colors for the silk-screen application since the wastebaskets would be one part of a large home-furnishing promotion.

Machado took Ms. Hernandez on a tour of his plant, where he showed her how the circular bottoms are cut out and attached to the rectangular sheet of metal that becomes the side. "Rectangular?" asked Ms. Hernandez. "That means your baskets are cylinders and can't be placed inside each other."

"So?" said Machado. "I could have told you that when you walked in the door."

"If they can't be nested, they'll cost an arm and a leg to ship," said Ms. Hernandez, "and I doubt that we could price them competitively with all those shipping charges. What you should do is taper your wastebaskets so that when they're packed, one can be slipped inside another and so on. The tapering wouldn't affect the silk screen patterns, which are the feature we want. I need price quotes, CIF, alongside ship, in Vancouver, B.C. Customs charges, if any, will be my problem."

Machado agreed to make some cost calculations, and Ms. Hernandez said she had several days of business in nearby Hong Kong and would return to his office on Thursday. She left, and Machado called Cameron Wong, an overseas freight forwarder with whom Machado did business. Machado explained the problem to Wong, and Machado also asked Henry Ng, his plant supervisor, to make some cost calculations regarding the manufacture of conical, rather than cylindrical, wastebaskets.

At 9:00 A.M. Wednesday they met. Ng explained that the machinery could be modified to cut and assemble wastebaskets with three different amounts of taper, and he referred to them as Styles A, B, and C. Production costs would differ because of trim and fitting. For conventional, non-tapered wastebaskets, the costs of production are $10,000 for 10,000 units. (All cost figures in this case are given in U.S. dollars.) For Style A, they would be $11,500 for the same number of units; Style B, $14,000; and Style C, $15,000. All could be silk-screened. The conventional wastebaskets weigh 10 pounds each; Style A, nine pounds; Style B, nine pounds; and Style C, eight pounds. The amount of taper determined how many wrapped baskets could be placed inside each other. Shipping volume, in cubic feet per 100 wastebaskets, would be conventional, non-tapered, 200 cubic feet; Style A, 150 cubic feet; Style B, 100 cubic feet; and Style C, 90 cubic feet. Note that styles A, B, and C are tapered and nested inside each other when shipped.

Machado then turned to Wong and asked, "What about transport costs?"

Wong replied, "There are several components. First, you have to get the packed wastebaskets from here to port. The best rate I can find is from Joseph Wong, who will charge $50 per trip from your factory to the pier. His truck will carry 800 cubic feet each trip; in this instance we don't have to worry about weight. The ocean freight rate on wastebaskets such as yours is $111.00 per ton (2,000 pounds), except that if they can get more revenue by considering every 40 cubic feet a ton, they charge you that way."

"What do you mean?" asked Ng.

"It's called 'vessel option' and is intended to encourage denser cargo," answered Wong. "All cargo given to the vessel is measured in both linear and weight measures, and if counting 40 cubic feet—or a cubic meter, which is about the same—as weighing 2,000 pounds, that's what they will do. An old

Volkswagen bus, for example, might weigh only 3,000 pounds, but it if occupies, say, 300 cubic feet, it's charged as though it weighed 300/40, or 7.5 tons."

"Are there other charges?" inquired Machado.

"Only one," answered Wong, "Insurance. Add your costs of production, delivery to port, ocean transportation, and that is C & F. For CIF you have to add the costs of insurance from here to alongside ship in Vancouver. Right now, insurance charges are about one percent of C & F. Sorry I didn't make all these exact calculations before coming, but I needed to hear what Ng had to say."

"Okay," said Machado. "Now, let's figure out whether we can afford to taper 10,000 wastebaskets. Let's get some sharp pencils and go to work."

Questions for *Macao Wastebaskets*

1. Calculate the total costs of the cylindrical wastebaskets. Assume that all relevant costs—including allowance for profit—have been given, and that Machado is interested in the "delivered" cost of the goods to alongside ship in Vancouver, where Ms. Hernandez would want the goods shipped.

2. Do the same for Style A wastebaskets.

3. Do the same for Style B wastebaskets.

4. Do the same for Style C wastebaskets.

5. Packaging costs have not been mentioned here. How, if at all, might the use of the tapered design impact the cost of packaging?

6. The case uses U.S. dollars yet the shipment is bound for Canada. Note the buyer wants the option of ordering more within a year. Machado wonders whether he would be better off using Canadian dollars rather than U.S. dollars. Using the date you receive this assignment, check back for one, two, and three years and compare the stability of the U.S. dollar and the Canadian dollar. Which do you think Machado should use? Why?

7. What other real-world factors do you think would be involved in determining the total costs of this transaction?

5

Chartering Bulk Ocean Carriers

Introduction

For the firm that ships or receives extremely large quantities of product, entire ships are used. Large is the operational word; a dry-bulk freighter may carry 65,000 tons compared with 50 to 80 tons in a common railcar. Handling vessel-loads of goods requires extensive cargo-handling equipment, storage space, and funds to invest in large stockpiles of inventory.

This chapter is brief, but it is necessary to separate the discussion of chartering ships for entire vessel loads of cargo and using liners for smaller shipments in lot sizes one associates with domestic transport (which will be covered in the next chapter). The reason for the separate discussion of vessel chartering is two-fold: first, the characteristics of international markets for and movement of bulk materials are unique; and second, an entire vessel load of product represents a huge amount of inventory, and may even serve as an apparent exception to current logistics thought regarding inventory costs and time value. The savings in transportation from shipping in bulk are so great that they overcome the additional inventory holding costs.

To understand the functioning of the vessel charter market, one must also understand the functioning of markets for various raw materials and commodities. These markets are themselves interrelated, petroleum and coal being the best example, with one competing with the other. Coke, a form of coal, is used in the production of steel, so there is a positive correlation in shipments of coke and iron ore. Sophisticated worldwide markets exist for trading petroleum, iron ore, coal, and grain, as well as commodities that move in smaller total volumes.

Traders continually learn of present and future prices of commodities at various markets throughout the world. More importantly, they study the spread in prices of the commodity at two different locations, for example, New Orleans and Hong Kong. At the same time these traders follow the market for charter shipping, which also fluctuates on a daily, even hourly, basis, to determine the costs of chartering a vessel to carry, again, for example, grain from New Orleans to Hong Kong. If the costs of chartering the vessel are less than the spread in grain prices, the trader will make tentative commitments to buy the grain in New Orleans at a certain future date, sell the grain in Hong Kong at that date plus estimated transit time between New Orleans and Hong Kong, and charter a vessel. The tentative commitments become binding, the transaction is completed, and the shipment made.

Note that there are three numeric values that may be different, but their relationship must be the same: the price for shipping the commodity must be less than the spread of commodity prices at the two different ports. Hence, grain will move from New Orleans to Hong Kong only if the relationship between the three values holds. So, buyers and sellers of commodities follow the price of vessels closely, in the same way that owners of vessels follow commodity markets. There is also some overlap, as shippers of some bulk commodities own vessels to meet a portion of their needs and rely on charters to move the remainder.

Just as the value of commodities fluctuates, so does the value of shipping. Charter rates change with each new contract, and the value of a vessel or fleet can be determined at any one time by taking today's charter rate, extending over the life of the vessel as a projected revenue flow and then capitalizing its value. That value is also known as the resale value because the number represents the worth of the vessel to a new owner, given today's charter rates. For an example from some years ago, as charter rates dropped, the calculated value of a sample tanker fleet (totaling about 250 vessels) also dropped from $4.1 billion to $3.0 billion.[1]

In some instances, when charter rates are very low, commodity traders will move materials in advance of when needed in order to take advantage of low transport costs. Offhand, this would seem contrary to modern logistics thought that favors many small shipments with every party holding little or no inventory. Just-in-time thought does not apply to most bulk materials, with the two best examples being heating coal and grain. Steam coal is mined all year, although peak consumption in the northern hemisphere is in the winter. Secondly, much of it must be transported and stockpiled near the point of consumption prior to winter. (Heating coal must be stored near the point of consumption because severe

---

[1]*The Journal of Commerce*, July 24, 1992, p. 10B.

winter weather itself interferes with its transport and distribution.) Grain has the opposite pattern; it is harvested at the end of the growing season, and the grain is transported to various markets for a consumption period that is spread out to last until the next harvest.

Movement of one's materials by the shipload might also appear contrary to modern logistics thinkers' preference for small lots. In very general terms, one thinks of newer vessels as becoming both larger and faster. There is some evidence that bulk movements by sea are going at a quicker pace. Later discussion will show that vessel speed is a variable that can be negotiated in the charter arrangement.

For bulk commodities that have relatively low values per ton, the cost of transport has greater influence upon the selling and the transportation decisions.

This chapter gives some data on major patterns in world's bulk shipping, which can be interpreted loosely as being the demand for shipping. The next topic is the supply of shipping. Third, the interrelationships among various bulk trades and between bulk and liner trades are covered. Then the discussion turns to the two most common types of charter arrangements, voyage and time. Last is a listing of many of the provisions that go into a charter agreement.

This is an opportune point to introduce the term *tramp,* which, as used here, refers to neither a down-and-out hobo nor a female of questionable repute. As the term is used here, *tramp* refers to an irregular route, unscheduled ocean carrier. Tramps are not vagrant or beggarly ships. A tramp ship will go wherever there is profitable cargo to be carried for as long as that cargo can be had. Tramps are employed on a charter rental-like basis by shippers of large tonnages. Tramp vessels are also designed for various special applications. Ore carriers of different capacities and draft target the various ore markets. Oil and other bulk liquid tankers specialize in petroleum cargoes. General purpose vessels are built to carry general packaged commodities such as bagged coffee, drummed and palletized cargoes, baled waste paper, hides, and so on. These ships are equipped with their own winches and booms to load and unload cargo even in the absence of shoreside facilities. The flexibility of these conventional class vessels make them particularly useful in the charter trade because they can go anywhere and carry just about anything.

One cannot tell by looking at a vessel whether it is a tramp, as the term refers more to the ownership/ contractual status that controls a vessel's operations. For example, with regard to refrigerated ships (reefers), consider the following:

> ...two-thirds of all reefer ships are break-bulk. Typically, they operate as tramps rather than regularly scheduled liner services, switching cargo from

season to season like harvesters following crops. The design trend of these vessels is "pallet friendly," with flush-sided, squared-off holds served by wide hatchways. The most popular height between decks is 3.5 meters, directly related to the standard palletized configuration of produce.[2]

A tramp is a vessel, often—but not necessarily—designed for bulk or specialized cargo, spending its life on irregular routes, following available cargo. There are also tramp container ships that liner firms use to supplement their fleet's needs.

Another word, unique to the topic, is *fixture,* which is the completed charter agreement or contract. Trade publications that follow changes in charter rates say that they are reporting recent "charter fixtures." *Fairplay* reported about 1700 fixtures for the month of April 2001. About half the vessels were for carrying crude oil, but they represent two-thirds of tonnage capacity chartered that month.[3]

Patterns of the World's Bulk Shipping

As indicated, the major bulk movements are of petroleum, iron ore, coal and grain.

Petroleum

Crude petroleum movements are shown in Table 5–1, and they represent the largest movement of cargo in the world. About half the world's shipping capacity is used to carry oil and oil products.

Petroleum and petroleum products move on tankers. Oil companies own only a small fraction and charter the remainder. This allows them to keep their own fleet completely utilized and rely on others to supply the remainder of their needs. Tankers come in all sizes, with the largest ones unable to find mooring spots adjacent to shore when they are fully loaded. They moor offshore and lighter their cargo to and from smaller ships alongside, or to or from shore via a floating pipe connection that is tethered to the bottom of the sea.

The size of tankers has changed over the years, with most explanations for the change referring first to the closure of the Suez Canal in 1956. With the closure of the Suez, tankers had to take the long route around the Cape of Good Hope. To make such journeys as economical as possible, it made sense to build tankers as large as possible. Super tankers were built weighing 500,000 tons.

By the middle of the 1970s, however, things began to change. The Suez was

---

[2]*Port of New Orleans Record,* January/February 1989, pp. 11–13.

[3]*http://www.fairplay.co.uk/,* May 23, 2001.

Table 5–1   Crude oil movements in 1994, showing destinations, and the percents of the total receipts they received from each source.

From	To					
	NW Europe	Mediterranean	North America	Japan	Others	World total
Middle East	55	35	27	77	73	53
North Africa	9	28	2	—	4	7
West Africa	10	15	19	1	5	10
Caribbean	5	4	35	2	6	13
Southeast Asia	—	—	3	19	5	5
Others	21	18	15	1	7	12
Total	100	100	100	100	100	100

Source: Niko Wijnolst and Tor Wergeland, *Shipping,* (Delft, Delft Univ. Press, 1997), p. 25. The right-hand column shows the percent that each source contributed to the world's supply of oil that year. More current origins-destination data were not found. However, UNCTAD publications indicate that ton-miles of crude oil increase one percent between 1994 and 1999, and for petroleum products the increase was eight percent.

reopened. The demand for crude oil began to drop as the price soared, and at the same time the previously cheap bunkers—the fuel that is used for ship's engines—became expensive and the cost of operating a VLCC (Very Large Crude Carrier) rose.

The giant ships therefore began to make their way to breakers' yards in the Far East where they were sold for scrap, and the shipyards turned to building medium-sized, sophisticated ships of around 100,000 tons.

In the late 1980s, however, patterns have changed again and VLCCs have once more become the cheapest way of transporting crude oil. Those shipyards still capable of building the giant ships are now doing so again, though this time usually no larger than 300,000 tons.[4]

A survey in 1994 looked at the lot size carried by tankers worldwide. Of all crude shipments, 34 percent went in lot sizes (or tankers with capacities) of 50–100,000 tonnes, 19 percent in the 100–150,000 tonne range, three percent in the 150–200,000 tonne range, 35 percent in the 200–300,000 tonne range, and nine percent in the 300,000+ tonne size.[5]

In the petroleum markets, tankers are also used for storage. They can be moored for up to ten years and function as semipermanent storage tanks. In

---

[4]*Transportation of Oil* (London: BP International, ca. 1990), p. 7.

[5]Niko Wijnolst and Tor Wergeland, *Shipping,* (Delft: Delft Univ. Press, 1997), p. 28. A tonne weighs 2,204.6 pounds.

1990, about five percent of the world's tanker capacity was being used for oil storage. Usually this is an additional inventory buffer along the production pipeline, but storage can be for other reasons also. In the 1980s, "Rumor ha[d] it that before the United States bombed his country, Libyan ruler Moammar Khaddafy chartered a fleet of tankers and filled them with oil piped from tanks on Libyan soil because he feared that his country's refineries and reserves would be subject to an American attack."[6]

It is also possible to speed up or slow down a fleet, which has the same effect as adding or subtracting vessels from the fleet. As the demand for oil picks up, a fleet's manager can increase the speed of tankers and thus reduce the amount of oil in the pipeline. This phenomenon happens industrywide. Consider these figures from the time of one of the earlier oil crises: The annual free world oil consumption was about 20 billion barrels, and the oil in the "pipeline" between wells and the users was about 10 billion barrels. At any one time, there are 750 million barrels aboard ship. If the world tanker fleets' speed increased by one knot, there would be a decrease of 100 million barrels aboard the fleet. This saving equals 1/2 of one percent of the free world's annual consumption. This is also the equivalent of freeing 14 percent of the world's tanker tonnage.[7]

Oil spills are a major concern for shippers of petroleum. They are caused by collisions, vessel break-ups, fires and explosions, running aground, and hull cracks. Exxon continues to receive bad publicity for its oil spill in Alaska. Newer tankers are designed to have separate ballast tanks (used to take on water to weigh down an empty vessel) rather than carrying ballast water in the cargo holds. This way, when the ballast is discharged, it has not been in contact with the remainder of the petroleum cargo. Under new U.S. laws, tankers calling at U.S. ports will be expected to have double hulls, believed to be an additional means of lessening the likelihood of oil spill. They will be phased in over 20 years. Figure 5–1 is the schematic of a double-hull arrangement with U-shaped tanks for ballast enclosing the tanks for oil. Figure 5–2 are top and side views. Oil companies are liable for oil spills and they exercise caution when chartering vessels, attempting to avoid older vessels. At present, the oil tanker charter market has become two-tier, with rates for vessels used to haul oil to the U.S. being higher because of the higher costs associated with a potential oil spill. Older vessels are being phased out and "rust-bucket" tankers will disappear within a couple of years as the escalating cost of maintenance and insurance, plus public pressure on oil companies not to charter bad ships, finally forces out unseawor-

---

[6]*Inbound Logistics*, July, 1986, p. 22.

[7]*World Oil Inventories* (New York: Exxon Corp., 1981), pp. 3–8.

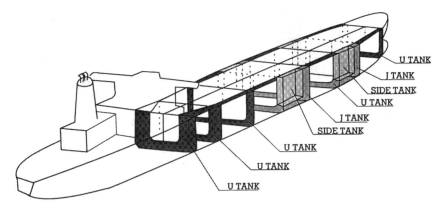

Figure 5–1 Schematic drawing of a double-hull arrangement with U-shape tanks for ballast enclosing the tanks for oil. Courtesy of Chevron Shipping Co.

thy ships. Tanker owners and operators also pay into insurance pools that cover environmental damage caused by oil spills.

It is difficult to judge the health of the tanker industry. Tanker owners perennially complain about the low rates that they must accept, while simultaneously ordering new vessels. Trade magazines continue to speak of the industry's ups and downs. In the year 2000 tanker rates climbed, with one example being the daily charge for a 200,000+ VLCC going from $27,000 to $41,000. The reason given in a trade journal was the December, 1999 breakup of the tanker *Erika* in the Bay of Biscay, spilling 8,000 tons of fuel oil on the beaches of France. The stricken vessel was 25 years old and this "caused many carriers to change their chartering policies and stop hiring vessels more than 20 years old."[8]

Iron Ore

The world's two fastest-growing steel producers are China and South Korea. Iron ore and coal represent two substantial movements in the world's waterborne commerce. In one sense they are linked because some coal is used in the steel-making process. Table 5–2 shows 1994 movements of iron ore and Table 5–3 shows similar data for coal. These two tables link origins and destinations. A survey in 1994 looked at the lot sizes of ore carried by vessels internationally. Of all iron ore shipments, seven percent went in lot sizes (or bulk vessels with capacities) of under 50,000 tonnes, 17 percent in the 50 to 100,000 tonne range,

---

[8]*JoCWeek* November 6–12, 2000, p. 24.

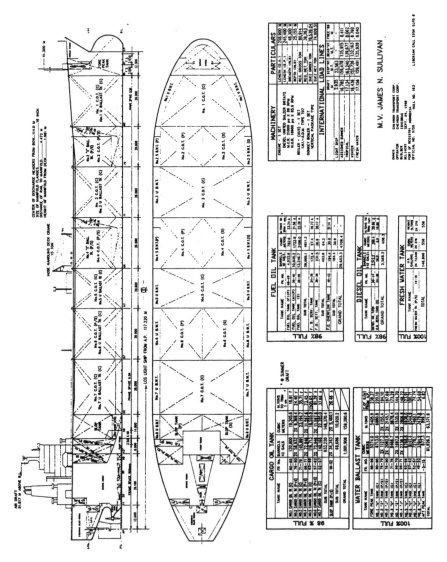

Figure 5–2 Top and side views of double-hull arrangement. Courtesy of Chevron Shipping Co.

Table 5–2   Major iron ore sources and markets 1994, in millions of tonnes

From	To UK/ continent	Mediterranean	Other Europe	U.S.	Japan	Other Far East	Others	World total
Scandinavia	14	—	2	—	—	1	1	21
Other Europe	2	—	2	—	—	—	—	4
West Africa	6	3	1	—	—	—	—	25
Other Africa	3	2	4	—	5	6	—	19
North America	15	1	1	7	1	1	—	27
South America (Atl.)	45	9	8	6	29	22	15	134
South America (Pac.)	1	—	—	—	4	7	1	13
Asia	1	2	1	—	20	8	1	33
Australia	19	3	2	1	57	41	2	124
Total	106	19	21	14	116	86	20	383

Source: Niko Wijnolst and Tor Wergeland, *Shipping,* (Delft, Delft Univ. Press, 1997), p. 29. Note that not all of this ore moves by sea. Totals do not match because of rounding. UNCTAD reports that ton miles of ore movements increased by two percent between 1994 and 1999.

Table 5–3   Major coal sources and markets 1994, in millions of tonnes

From	To UK/ continent	Mediterranean	Other Europe	South America	Japan	Other Far East	Others	Total
N. America	16	9	11	8	27	13	4	87
Australia	15	5	2	5	63	29	11	130
South Africa	14	4	12	2	6	12	5	54
South America	10	1	4	1	—	2	5	22
China	1	1	—	—	7	13	2	24
Former USSR	1	3	6	—	5	1	—	16
Other Eastern Europe	7	1	10	1	1	—	—	20
Western Europe	1	—	1	—	—	—	—	2
Others	5	—	2	—	10	11	1	29
Total	70	22	48	17	118	80	29	384

Source: Niko Wijnolst and Tor Wergeland, Shipping, (Delft: Delft Univ. Press, 1997), p. 32. UNCTAD reports show that ton miles of coal movements increased by 20 percent between 1994 and 1999.

31 percent in the 100 to 150,000 tonne range, 24 percent in the 150 to 200,000 tonne range, and 21 percent in 200,000+ tonne size lots.[9]

Coal

Coal has two major uses. Steam coal is used for heating, and in the United States that is principally for generating electric power. The other use for coal is in the steel-making process, and the material used there is known as coking coal. While there are two principal types of coal, there are many blends. Roberts Bank, near Vancouver, B.C. is a large coal exporting facility. As of 1990, they were stocking 20 to 25 different blends and grades of coal and one of their operational problems, familiar to many inventory managers, was that each additional blend they stocked cut into their overall storage capacity. That is, coal piles are not shaped like cubes, but like cones. "Every time you put another pile on the site, you lose about 50,000 tons of storage capacity," said the terminal's manager, although he noted that a coal outlet in Australia handled about 150 different products.[10] The most frequent lot size for shipping coal is 60 to 80,000 tonnes, the second most frequent is 100 to 150,000 tonnes, and the third most frequent lot size is under 50,000 tonnes.[11]

Some oceangoing vessels have self-unloading capability. This means that the consignee need not have unloading equipment at his dock. Such a vessel would charter for a higher rate; note, however, that it has less payload since it must forever carry the load of unloading equipment. One such vessel is the CSL *Innovator,* rebuilt for the Canadian Steamship Lines. It can unload at the rate of 4,500 metric tons per hour. The discharge boom is 200 feet long and can bend in the middle. It can be used to transfer cargo within the vessel. Conveyor belts move through the vessel and it is possible to blend cargoes from different holds. Lower cargo-contact surfaces are angled at 45 degrees, and are coated with a covering that has a low coefficient of friction. There's also a vibrating system to help shake cargo loose.[12]

Grain

Grain shipments move from three major growing areas: North America, South America, and Australia, and consist of wheat, maize, barley, oats, rye, sorghum, and soy beans. Grain movements for 1994 are shown in Table 5–4. Grain is a

---

[9]Niko Wijnolst and Tor Wergeland, *Shipping,* (Delft: Delft Univ. Press, 1997), page 32.

[10]*American Shipper,* July 1990, p. 75.

[11]Niko Wijnolst and Tor Wergeland, *Shipping,* (Delft: Delft Univ. Press, 1997), page 34. Figures are for 1994.

[12]*The Pacific Maritime Magazine,* July, 1989, p. 24.

Table 5–4   Grain movements, 1994 in millions of tonnes

From	To							
	Europe	Africa	America	Indian Ocean	Japan	Far East	Others	Total
U.S.A.	13	14	17	5	21	18	3	92
Canada	1	2	4	3	3	8	—	21
South America	7	1	7	—	2	2	—	19
Australia	1	1	1	4	2	7	1	17
Others	4	8	4	6	4	9	1	36
Totals	27	26	33	18	32	44	5	184

Source: Niko Wijnolst and Tor Wergeland, *Shipping,* (Delft: Delft Univ. Press, 1997), p. 35. UCTAD reports that ton-miles of grain movements increased by 17 percent between 1994 and 1999.

commodity with a strong futures market, meaning that some buying and selling is done with delivery dates somewhere in the future. A futures market for vessel chartering has also been developed, and it allows the party chartering the vessel to hedge on future charter costs in the same way he can hedge on future prices of commodities. Most of the transactions have been for grain movements, although there apparently have been insufficient futures transactions to establish a functioning market.

One U.S. government program generates considerable export tonnages of grain and similar food products, three quarters of which must move on U.S. flag vessels. Title II of the Agricultural Trade Development Act annually donates millions of metric tons of food overseas: bulgur (parched, cracked wheat), flour, corn-soy blend, cornmeal, and whole grains. The Agency for International Development in the State Department decides to which countries the food should go. Then voluntary agencies, such as Catholic Relief, Save the Children Federation, Church World Services, and so on, make specific program proposals for moving and distributing the food product.

Often smaller ships are used for grains because the destinations are ports in developing countries that have restricted drafts, berths, or unloading facilities. A spokesperson for the UN's World Food Program said his agency charters about 150 vessels a year and "if one divides that by the cargo we transport by sea, the average size would be about 11,000 tons. . . . One may say that we have orders ranging from 1,000 to 80,000 tons, and in my 25 years with the program, I recall having chartered vessels down to 500 tons deadweight and as high as a 120,000 tonner."[13] The most common parcel size for shipping grain in 1994 was under 50,000 tonnes.[14]

---

[13]*American Shipper,* November, 1991, p. 72.

[14]Niko Wijnolst and Tor Wergeland, *Shipping,* (Delft, Delft Univ. Press, 1997), page 36.

Other Bulk and Neo-bulk Cargoes

Other bulk cargoes include plastics in granular form, sugar, sulfur, salt, sand, gravel, bauxite, lignite, slag, cement, lime, gypsum, potash, rice, bone chips, talc, borax, scrap iron and steel (handled by magnets), and fertilizers. Some bulk cargo requires very special handling. An example is kaolin, often used in the making of paper. It must be kept perfectly clean; otherwise, it will smudge the new paper.

At receiving ports, the dockside facility bags the bulk product for distribution inland. Some bulk goods are also graded and sold at the port of import. Coffee beans often travel in burlap bags. The prospective buyer inserts a long tube into each bag and withdraws a few beans, using them to judge the quality of the bag's contents. Tobacco leaves are graded mainly on the basis of color and tobacco receiving sheds must have neutral lighting to make it easier to judge the product.

Millions of new automobiles and light trucks also move via ocean carrier. As with most shipping markets, one can argue that it is either stable or volatile. A number of Japanese and European car and truck manufacturers are locating assembly operations in the United States, and shipments of parts to them does not require use of car-carrying vessels. During Operations Desert Shield and Desert Storm, a number of car-carrying vessels were diverted from commercial business to carrying military equipment. Very recently, Eastern Europe has developed as a market for second-hand autos, originating mainly in Western Europe. Firms have sprouted up to buy, refurbish, transport and sell the autos. In many parts of the world there is also a lucrative trade in stolen automobiles.

The Supply of Shipping

A large supply of ships exists in the world, and only during wars do shortages occur. New ships are continually being added to the world's fleet and many—probably too many—nations heavily subsidize shipbuilding operations. New ships are always being built, and can be converted while under construction. During the Suez crises, hulls being built to carry dry cargo were all converted to tankers.

Newer vessels are often used in the more lucrative trades, and as they age they find themselves working in less demanding markets. Sometimes, when reading of a shipwreck, one will see that the vessel had led a long career and sailed in many different markets. Insurance rates increase for older vessels and operators, aware of this, keep their vessel away from markets where the exposure to possible liability is large.

Sometimes older vessels undergo major refurbishing. During the 1960s and

1970s many break-bulk cargo vessels were partially, then completely, converted to container-carrying ships. Often vessels are lengthened by being cut at right angles to the hull and having a new midsection inserted.

The U.S. maintains a large "mothball fleet" of old war ships and old cargo ships. These old ships are in near-retirement but have not yet been cut up for scrap. They are protected to some extent against the ravages of rust and time. Some are placed back into commercial service when needed.

Older vessels are eventually scrapped. Until recent years, Taiwan was a major center of vessel scrapping; now activity has moved to Pakistan and Bangladesh, nations with low-cost labor and few environmental controls. Sometimes the term "shipbreaking" is used. The amount of shipbreaking that occurs is dependent upon many factors, not the least of which is the market value of scrap metal.

Market Interrelationship

Some shippers who use liners also charter vessels to keep in better touch with vessel costs. "Volkswagen's transportation subsidiary has found it useful to employ a combination of time-chartered ships and liner services in its ocean transportation. Running time-chartered ships lets a company know what is going on in the market and how costs develop. It helps in negotiations with liner operators."[15] In mid-1993, major Swedish liner customers were upset by the surcharges that liner rate-making groups (conferences) were assessing on container traffic at Gothenburg, and were threatening to charter a ship of their own.[16]

Neo-bulk shipping has some characteristics of both bulk and general cargo, and involves fairly valuable cargoes moving by the vessel load. The shippers constantly trade off between or among liners, bulk carriers, or specialized vessels. To the extent they own vessels, they may charter them out to other parties for the return leg. Ro/Ro vessels are used for either liner service or for carrying new automobiles.

Mention has been made several times of "combis," vessels designed to function in several markets. Several years ago, the United States agreed to make available large tonnages of grain to the Russians. The lead headline in *The Journal of Commerce* said: "U.S. Tanker Firms Eye Russia Grain As Oil Market Sags," and the article indicated that tankers were often used to carry grain, and that of the grain shipped from the U.S. to Russia during the first quarter of 1993, "about one-third of those shipments moved on U.S.-flag tankers."[17]

---

[15]*American Shipper,* June, 1991, p. 95.

[16]*American Shipper,* May, 1993, p. 52.

[17]*The Journal of Commerce,* April 8, 1993, p. 1A.

Liner operators also charter vessels to supplement their scheduled fleet. There is an active market for tramp container ships mainly for use as feeder services connecting with cross-ocean movements. Some also perform inter-island carriage. Much of this activity is in Asia. In mid-1992, for example, a small (284 TEU-capacity) containership was chartered for a 12-month period at $4,300 per day by a small Chinese feeder line, and the trade press indicated that a number of small container ships, originally serving in other markets, had been chartered for use in Asia.

Shipping assets are very mobile and have no trouble following the market's demands. For example, if there is a major strike at Australian coal mines or docks that blocks all shipments, charter rates will drop in that part of the Pacific, but then vessel owners will move their vessels to other parts of the world where the market is better. From the standpoint of the logistics manager, it is important to realize that all these shipping services are highly interrelated and serve as substitutes for each other. There is considerable communication within the market and few well-kept secrets.

Types of Charter Arrangements

As indicated earlier, the international trader follows both spread in prices of bulk commodities in different areas of the world and the charter rates for carrying cargoes from locations where prices are low to where they are high. Whenever price spread is greater than chartering cost, a deal is made. This would be a one-shot arrangement and a voyage charter or trip charter would be made, covering only the specific move between the origin and destination, and within the time frame agreed to take possession of and deliver the commodity. The other widely used form of chartering is on the basis of a time charter, usually for a period of several months to a year. This would be used, for example, by a steel company that decided it needed to supplement its own fleet to the extent it could fully utilize another vessel for that specified period of time.

The term *bareboat charter* applies to a time charter in which the owner of the vessel supplies only the vessel and the user must provide the crew. This is also sometimes called a demise charter. Often these are used by individuals who see ships solely as an investment to be bought and sold; during the time they own the vessel they charter out to some user who assumes complete responsibility for the vessel's operation. There are, in fact, many variations of chartering agreements that are entered into. These agreements are influenced by tax laws or subsidies.

A contract of affreightment is a charter arrangement that commits the shipowner "to carry quantities of a specific cargo on a particular route or routes

Transportation News Ticker
The dry cargo and tanker fixtures listed herewith and compiled in London and New York, include the following information: voyage, loading date, ship's name, when obtainable, rates and other data, relating to the charter.

GLOSSARY

AR: American Tanker Rate Schedule Revised
RS: American Tanker Rate Schedule
Bends: Both ends
FIO: Free in and out
FIOS: Free in and out stowed
FIOT: Free in and out trimmed
Shex: Sunday-holidays excluded
Shinc: Sunday-holidays included
WS: Worldscale

GRAINS

Bahia Blanca to Novotallin, Apr. 1-10, 90,000 tons, heavy grains, soyas and sorghums. (POINT CLEAR). BTC re-let, Gr flag, built 1972, 113,826 dwt., $19,000. FIO, 8,000 tons load, custom of the port discharge.

Houston to Veracruz, Feb. 24-27, 20,000 tons, 10 percent, sorghums, (AYOGALUSENA), Pa flag, built 1972, $12.60. FIO, 15 days Shinc all purposes.

U.S. Gulf to Hodeida, early March, 32,000 tons, heavy grains, soyas and sorghums, (TO BE NAMED). $39.50, FIO, 5 days load, 2,000 tons discharge.

Mississippi River/Ghent-Hamburg range, Mar. 12-18, 57,000 deadweight cargo capacity, 3,115,670 grain cubic, any grains, (HYPHESTOS), Gr flag, built 1983, 75,466 dwt. bulk-oiler, $721,000 lump sum, equivalent to $12.95 basis heavy grains, soyas and sorghums (49 ft.) for Hamburg, FIO, 10 days.

U.S. Gulf to South Korea, Mar. 15-25, 50,000 tons, 5 percent, heavy grains, soyas and sorghums, (YU-KONG TONNAGE), $24.50, FIO, 10,000 tons load, 7,250-6,500 tons discharge, rptd.

U.S. Gulf to Taiwan, Apr. 26-May 8, 54,000 tons, 5 percent, heavy grains, soyas and sorghums, (KORE-AN TONNAGE), $24.50, FIO, 10,000 tons load, 4,000 tons Shex bends, rptd.

COAL

Baltimore to Sines, Mar. 5-14, 110,000 tons, coal, (EL DORADO), HK flag, built 1987, $4.75, FIO, 35,000 tons Shinc load, 25,000 tons Shinc discharge.

Hampton Roads and Richards Bay to Japan 16 meters, Mar. 20-30, 120,000 tons, 10 percent, coal, (TRICULA), lm flag, built 1981, $9.95, FIO, 30,000 tons Shinc-15,000 tons Shinc load/25,000 tons Shinc discharge.

TIMECHARTERS

Delivery Durban, trip via E.C. South America, redelivery E.C. Mexico, prompt, (FANIS), Cy flag, built 1977, 36,254 dwt., $6,500 daily, Pacnav.

Delivery Bin Qasim, trip via W.C. India, redelivery Japan, early March, (POSEIDON BREEZE), Sg flag, built 1982, 61,769 dwt., 13.8 knots ballast, 13 laden on 27 tons fuel oil plus 2.4 tons blended, $12,000 daily, Sanko.

Tanker Timecharter: Delivery U.S. Gulf, 3 days lighterage, prompt, (KENTUCKY), Pa flag, built 1980, 79,996 dwt., $29,000 daily, Skaugen.

Delivery dropping outbound pilot Ghent, trip about 30 days, redelivery Mediterranean, Feb. 25-28, (CA-MELLIA), Pa flag, built 1973, 24,812 dwt., 11 knots on 20 tons fuel oil plus 2 tons diesel oil, $11,000 daily, Shipping Corp. of Monrovia.

Delivery Avonmouth, trip, redelivery Far East, end Feb.-Mar., (ACHILLES II), Pa flag, built 1975, 37,389 dwt., Skaramanga type, $14,500 daily, Newco.

Delivery Taiwan, 12 months trading, prompt, (YEL-LOW AMBER), Cy flag, built 1978, 63,787 dwt., $9,800 daily, NSAC.

Figure 5–3 Excerpts from "Ship Fixture Breakdown" appearing in *The Journal of Commerce*. Reproduced courtesy of *The Journal of Commerce*.

over a given period of time using ships of his choice. . . ."[18] It is a form of multiple voyage charter and may extend over a period of years. The shipowner may deploy various vessels as they are needed to carry portions of the entire lot being shipped. Contracts of affreightment are "often used in LPG-gas, chemical and reefer shipping."[19]

Figure 5–3 is from *The Journal of Commerce* and it summarizes current chartering transactions, or fixtures. The grain and coal charters are for voyages; the

---

[18]Martin Stopford, *Maritime Economics* (London: Unwin Hyman, 1988), p. 22.

[19]Niko Wijnolst and Tor Wergeland, *Shipping,* (Delft: Delft Univ. Press, 1997), p. 390.

others are for time. Costs are expressed in various ways: some are per ton, some per day, and some a lump sum for the entire voyage. The summaries contain, in abbreviated form, sufficient information on each fixture so that those familiar with the market can determine both actual prices and trends. One would also have to make allowances for facts not given in the summaries. For example, there might be mechanical or dimensional constraints at either the port of loading or discharge that have an effect on the choice or scheduling of the vessel. Both the voyage and time charters also specify the location of the vessel at the beginning and the termination of the fixture; from the vessel owner's viewpoint, this is important because the availability of other charter customers in the vicinity is a consideration. By way of example, the owner of a dry cargo vessel would prefer to have a fixture terminate in New Orleans, where outbound movements of grain are always available, compared to the Middle East, where almost no dry bulk cargoes originate.

Several services track fixtures and report them to subscribers. Ship brokerage firms also report prices of their day's activities to their regular customers. Reference is sometimes made to the Baltic Freight Index. The index is a weighted average of each day's fixtures and is compared with the previous days. For April 30, 1993, the index was 1554, up from 1546 for the previous day.[20] Fifteen fixtures were included in that sample, including five time charters, and voyage charters for grain, coal, iron ore, and phosphate rock. The Baltic Freight Index is also used as the basis of future prices. One can charter a vessel for use in some "future" period and at some "future" price (tied to the Baltic Freight Index) and use this when making a commitment to some future delivery of a commodity. The Baltic Freight Index and the Freight Rate Futures for March 2, 1993 are shown in Figure 5–4. In a falling market the vessel owner may prefer a long-term time charter, while in a rising market the shipper may prefer the long-time commitment. Voyage charter rates fluctuate more dramatically. Charter rates always fluctuate. "The annual average rate for modern Capesize tonnage on the four major trade routes climbed dramatically by 67 percent, to $17,200 per day..., up from $10,300 per day in 1998, where rates had fallen by 41 percent from the 1997 level. For the Atlantic round voyage, the tonnage was employed at the average rate of $16,700 per day in 1999, whereas it was only paid at $8,600 per day in 1998."[21]

Chartering is handled through brokers, with one set representing vessel owners and the other vessel users (charterers). Some shippers work through a single

---

[20]*The Journal of Commerce,* May 4, 1993, p. 5B.

[21]United Nations Conference on Trade and Development, *Review of Maritime Transport 2000* (Geneva, 2000), pp. 58–59. Figures are for trip charters.

BALTIC FREIGHT INDEX

1369 (Mar. 2, 1993) Previous day — 1370

The Baltic International Freight Futures Market in London offers owners and charterers in the bulk shipping community a forum for futures trading of a freight rate index. The contracts are based on the Baltic Freight Index, announced daily, of 15 routes listed below.

Routes	Commodity	Weight	Dollars/ Metric Ton	Index
U.S. Gulf-North Continent	L. Grain	10%	13.742	1514
Trans-Atlantic Round	Time Charter	10%	9.642*	1472
U.S. Gulf-Japan	H. Grain	10%	24.625	1724
Skaw Passero-Taiwan-Japan	Time Charter	10%	13.458*	1817
U.S. North Pacific-Japan	H. Grain	7.5%	12.975	1406
Trans-Pacific Round	Time Charter	7.5%	9.442*	1404
U.S. Gulf-Venezuela	H. Grain	5%	21.042	1803
Skaw Passero-Far East	Time Charter	5%	14.242*	1782
Hampton Roads-Richards Bay-Japan	Coal	7.5%	10.083	0978
Hampton Roads-Rotterdam	Coal	5%	4.558	0936
Queensland-Rotterdam	Coal	5%	8.567	0779
Far East-Europe	Time Charter	5%	7.225*	0953
Tubarao-Rotterdam	Iron Ore	5%	4.592	0895
Casablanca-West Coast India	Phosrock	2.5%	30.792	0863
Aqaba-West Coast India	Phosrock	5%	15.808	1167

*Dollars per day.

FREIGHT RATE FUTURES

Mar. 2, 1993
Baltic International Freight Futures Market

	Close	High	Low	Vol.	Prev. Close
Mar.	1379	1375	1360	23	1355
Apr.	1380	1380	1360	93	1355
May	1342	1348	1330	84	1330
July	1195	1195	1190	4	1188
Oct.	1350	1350	1350	4	1335

Total sales, 208 contracts.

Figure 5–4 The Baltic Freight Index and Freight Rate Futures appearing in *The Journal of Commerce.* Reproduced courtesy of *The Journal of Commerce.*

broker exclusively, while others may contact several with their vessel needs and then favor the one who finds them the best arrangements. Shipowners also work through a single broker or let several bid for their business. Sometimes a third broker is used to facilitate the dealings between the shipper's broker and the owner's broker. A commission, say 2 and one-half percent of the total fixture, is split between the brokers handling the final transaction. Brokers specialize by vessel type, cargo type, and vessel size.

The shipper needing a vessel contacts his broker with specifications of the shipment; the shipper's broker then distributes this to a number of shipowners' brokers who specialize in the appropriate types of cargoes and vessels. One of them will then offer the vessel at a specified rate to the shipper's broker, and there will be a given time that the offer expires, say at the end of 24 hours. (The two brokers mentioned within this paragraph may have been given broad para-meters within which to bargain, or they may have to contact their principals every step of the way.) The shipper's broker then counters with a slightly lower bid that has an expiration time of, say, 12 hours on his counteroffer. The shipowner's broker counters with a shorter expiration time, and so on until one party or the other accepts or the deal falls apart. Neither side knows whether the other is going through a similar exercise with offers from competitors. One's main concern is that he has only one outstanding "live" offer at any one time; he must wait for the time to expire before he can make a live offer to a different party.

Note that the logistics manager may own both the commodity being shipped and the ship, and in a good shipping market the manager may consider chartering the vessel out to another party, since it can earn more for the company in that manner than it would moving the owner's own commodity. The terms of the charter would be such that the owner would have the vessel back at the time it was needed to haul his commodity. Note also that as the price of shipping rises, this increases the costs of inventories or stockpiles yet to be moved and the values of those that have been moved. When shipping rates become very high, some commodities will not move at all. The best examples of this are scrap paper and scrap metal, since transportation often accounts for two-thirds or more of their delivered costs. If one has stockpiles of a commodity or bulk product at different points worldwide, she or he would have to think very carefully about how fluctuating shipping rates influence the value of the inventories.

The Charter Agreement

Charter agreements are somewhat standardized by type of cargo, geographic market, or the exchange where brokers handling the transaction are headquartered, such as New York, Piraeus, or Hong Kong. Agreements are usually three to five pages long, with about half that space devoted to boilerplate and the other half with details specific to the fixture in question. Most of the following discussion is based on voyage charters.

Boilerplate is not to be ignored, since it is very much part of the contract. It is often printed in small type, and appears as separate sheets at the end of the agreement. Many contracts, for example, contain an "Ice" clause, which is about 500 words. This clause permits a vessel's captain to leave a port or area if he fears that his vessel will be trapped by forming ice, and then indicates how the two parties should reallocate responsibility for the voyage costs. Other boilerplate items include war risks, insurance, strike clauses, pollution, vessel and cargo cleanliness, relationship to third parties (stevedores, vessel pilots, port authorities), cancellation clauses, brokerage commissions, arbitration of disagreements, and certification that the vessel and cargo meet relevant international requirements as well as requirements of specific nations at which the vessel will call during its voyage. Sometimes, there is also a list of definitions or words and terms, including which form of ton is applicable. Sometimes there are specific prohibitions on the vessel or its master taking on additional cargo than that contracted. That is to keep the vessel's master from picking up additional money for his own pocket by selling unused space on the vessel, for example, by allowing others' cargo to be lashed to the vessel's deck.

Items specific to each fixture are the result of negotiations between the owner and charterer or their respective brokers. At this point the logistics manager, working for the shipper, may have to revise, or at least rethink, what he or she has learned as conventional wisdom. As mentioned earlier, many—but not all—bulk movements are spread over a season and consist of steadily moving a stockpile of materials from near the source to near the market. Investment in inventory may be less of an issue than seeing that the inventory is moved on a regular basis. The asset with the greater time value is the ship. The vessel owner, in a brisk market, wants to minimize the amount of time the vessel spends on each voyage, so it can be "turned" more quickly. This is analogous to a retailer or wholesaler's interest in generating a higher number of inventory turns to earn more revenues in a fixed facility.

Hence, the focus of the entire negotiation deals with allocating the vessel's time, and specific issues concern the costs of speeding up or slowing down various activities that impact the entire duration of the vessel's trip. If the charterer were concerned about the time value of the inventory being carried on the voyage, then both parties to the agreement would desire a speedy voyage. However, the charterer does not see things that way since often the items being negotiated increase the costs to him of moving the cargo more quickly, and most of these additional costs are not offset by other advantages of moving the inventory more quickly.

A ship owner, particularly one who has chartered his ship on a trip basis, on the other hand, is only making money while the ship is moving. He needs to drop the cargo quickly and move on to the next load. As rates go up, vessels will operate at higher speeds—owners will require them to. However, fuel consumption increases much more rapidly than does vessel speed. In a slow market, a vessel can be taken into a repair yard and tied up for leisurely repairs; in a brisk market, the repairs are deferred or, if they are performed, the work is done at a higher cost, and with a quicker turnaround. In addition to speeding up at sea, one can load and unload ships in ports at a faster rate.

The draft of the vessel may also determine its routing. Large tankers from the Middle East to Europe are too big to pass through the Suez Canal; however, they can pass through the Suez on the return voyage when they are light. This reduces the time for the return journey from 40 to 25 days. In mid-1992, as tanker rates climbed, some tankers started using the Suez for the return journey. However, industry leaders feared that the move to use the Suez would have an undesired effect of freeing up tonnage capacity and depressing tanker rates.[22] (This an equilibrium point of sorts; using the Suez to save on tanker rates reduces tanker rates to the point where the savings disappear.)

Items specific to the voyage include the name, age, and the country of registry of the vessel; names and addresses of parties to the agreement and their agents; types and amount of anticipated cargo; whether the cargo is hazardous; cleanliness of the vessel; calculation of payment; terms of payment; responsibility for canal tolls and port charges; and dates and places where the charterer accepts and relinquishes the vessel. Depending upon time of year and area of operation, the vessel's allowable draft is controlled by a seasonal load line, and the contract will often refer to the load line that controls the voyage being fixed. One must also take into account port charges on both ends of the voyage and canal dues, in case any are transited. The price of fuel for the vessel fluctuates and may also differ from port to port.

While the entire contract is of importance, there are a few clauses in each that have particular significance to the logistics manager. The description, density, and weight of the cargo are carefully defined when the charter rate is based on tonnage. One clause read "5,500 metric tons, 5 percent more or less at owner's option, pet[roleum] coke in bulk. Stowage about 54 cu. ft. per metric ton basis grain cubic of vessel."[23] In this case the ship's cubic capacity is known (this information is available in a number of trade guidebooks) and applying the density factor yielded the approximate weight. If the voyage fixture is for a lump sum, the weight is not specified but the charterer will, of course, load as much as possible. The starting date of the contract is specified, although there is some slack. "Laydays [when cargo is being loaded or unloaded] are not to commence before January 20, except with Charterers or their Agent's consent. Should vessel not be ready to load cargo hereunder by January 30, Charterers have the option of canceling this Charter." Charterers have varying needs for a clean vessel. "A recognized marine surveyor shall be employed to certify vessel as to cleanliness as to carriage of petroleum coke in bulk and fee for same shall be equally shared by Owners and charterers."

The using party must warrant "safe berths" on both ends of the trip. "Such berth shall have sufficient depth of water at all times and stages of water and tide

---

[22]*The Journal of Commerce,* October 9, 1992, p. 2A.

[23]This and other quotes are from actual fixtures.

to accommodate the vessel safely loaded with cargo. . ." or, "Charters guarantee 36′6″ salt water draft at discharge port." (Very large bulk carriers must move in and out of port with high tidal windows.) Usually the charterer is familiar with facilities at both port of loading and discharge. It is necessary to know the dimensions of the loading and unloading equipment as well as the dimensions of the ship, including the placement and sizes of hatch covers. Larger hatch openings allow larger buckets and faster operations. In fact, as part of the fixture, loading and unloading rates are specified. "Cargo is to be loaded at the average rate of 600 metric tons and discharged at the average rate of 400 metric tons, both per weather working day of 24 consecutive hours, Sundays and Holidays excepted." Rates of loading are usually faster than of unloading because loading is aided by gravity, and the fact that loading facilities in some trades are fewer in number than receiving facilities, hence are more likely to have higher capacity equipment. Many port laborers do not work on weekends, or else are paid at a much higher rate, hence there is always concern whether to wait for a weekday or pay the higher rate; and who should be responsible for absorbing the additional costs. (In most situations, it is also possible to speed the loading/ discharge by using additional equipment, working several holds at once. There are penalties that the charterer must pay if the guaranteed loading/discharge rates are not achieved, and the charge is known as *demurrage.* If the vessel is handled more quickly than agreed to, the shipowner credits the charterer and the credit is known as *despatch.* Usually, the despatch rate is one-half the demurrage rate.)

Relations with shoreside labor can be troublesome. One clause reads: "Vessel to supply whenever required the free use of winches and derricks in good working order with necessary motive power to drive them, also gear, runners, ropes and slings as on board and winchmen from Crew to work at the winches. However, if shore regulations do not allow Crew to work at the winches, winchmen from shore to be supplied and paid for by the Charterers."

Days at sea is an important issue. The vessel owner has daily costs of the vessel and its crew. Fuel costs are variable and will increase more, proportionately, than the speed of the ship. Hence there will be clauses saying: "Owners option to slow speed down to about 12 knots, weather permitting." That would be coupled with a clause saying: "[vessel] owner guarantees that if vessel loads by August 20, vessel will arrive Portland, Maine not later than September 22."

Charter contracts also have provisions for arbitration of disputes. Here are the reports of two arbitration cases.

In the M/V Carlita arbitration, a shipowner voyage chartered its vessel to carry pig iron from Sorel, Canada to Italy. The ship arrived at Sorel and tendered its notice of readiness. The berth was occupied and other ships were subsequently granted berthing priority by the cargo shipper. The Carlita then waited six days to berth.

The shipowner claimed $24,000 demurrage, which related to the priority berthing utilized at the facility. The shipowner alleged that the charterer failed to disclose the berthing arrangement when the contract was negotiated. The vessel owner argued that the charterer should not be permitted to rely on the charter laytime provision, which provided that time lost waiting for berth, if beyond the charterer's control, was not to count as laytime.

The charterer argued that the vessel loading rotation was outside of its control. Moreover, the priority arrangement was a matter of common knowledge. It had no obligation to advise the vessel owner of readily accessible facts.

The arbitrator agreed with the charterer's position.[24]

The second case dealt with the issue of paying to clean a vessel after it had carried a load of sulfur. The charter agreement said: "after discharge of cargo vessel's holds are to be thoroughly washed down with fresh water and cleaned as same are fully acceptable for loading grain cargo. Charterers to supply all labor, materials and fresh water for cleaning at their time and expense." The holds were cleaned and the vessel proceeded to Gibraltar where a surveyor determined that there was still sulfur residue and said that a second fresh water cleaning was required. Vessels are not allowed to wash their holds and discharge the residue into the Mediterranean, so the vessel had to buy fresh water in Gibraltar and then set sail for the Atlantic Ocean where the holds were again washed and the residue flushed. The vessel then returned to Gibraltar where it passed the surveyor's inspection. The arbitrators held that the charterers had to pay for the extra days the vessel went out into the Atlantic as well as for the bunkers consumed.[25]

Summary

The majority of the world's oceanborne commerce consists of bulk cargoes, such as petroleum, iron ore, coal, and grain that usually move by vessel load. The common way of hiring vessels for this purpose is through use of a charter agreement. Both the owner of the vessel and the charterer of the vessel operate through brokers to negotiate the arrangement.

Charter rates fluctuate and the commodities trader looks at prices of commodities in two separate markets and at the charter rates for vessels. If the charter rate is less than the spread in price between the two commodity markets, the

---

[24]*The Journal of Commerce*, May 6, 1993, p. 5B.

[25]*BIMCO Bulletin*, December, 1998, p. 54. The claim was settled for $58,000. Bunkers are marine fuel.

trader will simultaneously commit to 1) buy at the market where the price is low, 2) sell where the price is high, and 3) charter a vessel to move the goods between the two points.

Charter agreements are for a specific voyage or cover a period of time, usually between three months and a year. The market for chartering is very competitive, and the charter agreement is called a fixture.

End-of-Chapter Questions

1. What is a tramp vessel?
2. In maritime terms, what is a fixture?
3. Describe the general patterns in the international waterborne movements of petroleum.
4. How have environmental protection concerns impacted the market for chartering tankers?
5. Describe the general patterns in the international waterborne movements of coal.
6. What is a bareboat charter?
7. What is a contract of affreightment? When would it be used?
8. What various factors are taken into consideration in a time charter?
9. What various factors are taken into consideration in a voyage charter?
10. What determines the supply of and demand for shipping?

CASE • *Coals to Newcastle*

The Blizzard Steamship Company, headquartered in Hampton Roads, Virginia, had been asked to bid on a contract of affreightment for the carriage of several million tons of coal from Hampton Roads to an English port, where the coal would be unloaded and then move by rail to Newcastle. (Contracts of affreightment are used when a shipper has vast quantities of materials to move, often over a period of several years and requiring several vessels provided on a charter basis. The owners of the charter vessels, such as Blizzard, assign various vessels in their fleet to participate in the haulage.)

One of the vessels in Blizzard's fleet, the *Jennifer Young,* was ideally suited for this assignment, and Blizzard decided to determine first how much coal she could carry over a 12-month period, at which point he could decide which other vessel(s) to assign. There were no backhauls available so the vessel would sail light from England back to Hampton Roads.

The anticipated costs of operating the Jennifer Young follow. Days in port cost

Case Table One

Duration of round trip in days	Fuel carried (and consumed) in tons	Tons of coal carried
14	600	60,000
15	500	60,100
16	420	60,180
17	350	60,250
18	300	60,300
19	240	60,360
20	200	60,400

$1,000 each and days at sea cost $2,000 each. At sea there is also the cost of bunkers (fuel oil), which is expected to be $50 per ton. Fuel consumption per nautical mile of travel increases exponentially with the vessel's speed. All assumptions include a day in port at Hampton Roads for loading and two days at the English port for unloading. While the vessel is returning to the United States light, it is traveling against prevailing weather, so it takes the same number of days to cross in each direction.

The vessel, when loaded, is loaded as heavily as allowed by the insurer. If it carries less fuel it can carry more cargo. Hence, calculations for travel at slower speeds will show a slightly higher tonnage of coal carried per voyage. Case Table One shows the duration of a round trip (including three days in ports) and the load of coal and fuel carried.

Questions for *Coals to Newcastle*

1. How many round trips should the vessel make if the objective is to haul the most coal within one year? (The number of voyages can include a fraction since this would mean that a portion of the last voyage would be completed in the first days of the following year.)

2. How many round trips should the vessel make if the objective is to haul the coal at the lowest cost per ton within one year? (The number of voyages can include a fraction, since this would mean that a portion of the last voyage would be completed in the first days of the following year.)

3. Does it make a difference where the vessel is located before it is assigned to begin work on this haul?

4. Assume that the price of oil drops to $25 per ton. How, if at all, does this change your answer to one?

5. Assume that the price of oil drops to $10 per ton. How, if at all, does this change your answer to two?

6. Because of the volume of coal involved, Blizzard is considering purchasing some additional unloading equipment for the English port, which will reduce the *Jennifer Young's* stay in port from two days to one day. Assume it will be used only for unloading the *Jennifer Young*. How much would the additional unloading device be worth to Blizzard's firm in one year, assuming that the vessel's fuel costs $50 per ton?

6

The Ocean Liner Contract System

Introduction

Previous chapters have dealt with different types of vessels and with chartering bulk ocean carriers. This chapter deals with those vessels that operate on a scheduled basis, between major ports, and carry assortments of relatively high-value cargoes tendered by a multitude of shippers. Usually the products are manufactured or processed, and they move by number or count. These cargoes are sometimes called break-bulk or general cargo. Traditionally they were handled and stowed on a piece-by-piece basis by longshore labor. Today, in major sea lanes between Asia and Europe, the United States and Asia, and the United States and Europe, containerships carry the vast majority of this high-value traffic.

The relationship between buyers (shippers) and sellers (carriers) and groups of sellers (conferences or alliances) has changed dramatically over the last twenty years. This chapter will review how, in routes serving U.S. ports, this commercial relationship has moved from a tightly regulated environment to a largely unregulated environment wherein shippers and carriers are free to work out whatever commercial relationship best suits them in confidential contractual agreements. The United States' policies toward liner pricing differ from those in much of the remainder of the world. In 1999, a European journal said of the remainder of the world: "Liner shipping stands out in the world economy in being almost completely cartelized as far as pricing is concerned. Practically every trade route is covered by a separate coalition of liner conferences which fixes the freight rates."[1]

---

[1] *European Transport Law,* XXXIV, no. 6, 1999, p. 761.

Ocean Liner Conferences

A good place to start this review is to explore the institution of liner conferences. Liner conferences are organizations of vessel operators who serve similar markets. They form cartels to both regulate (some say, eliminate) competition among themselves and protect "their" market from outsiders. Today conferences in the American trades exist to facilitate cooperative relationships between carriers with the intent of reducing wasteful practices. Participation in conferences does not mean that members do not compete. Indeed, intense competition exists between conference members as they seek cargo.

Why does the U.S. government allow antitrust immunity in the maritime industry and not in other industries? Actually, the U.S. government does allow cartels in other industries. The examples known to most readers are professional football and baseball leagues. Competition among various team owners is strictly controlled. Ownership is profitable and it is almost impossible to establish a successful, competing league. Ocean liner service is another area where cartels, despite their disadvantages, are probably necessary. At present, the conference system in the United States is on the decline. The U.S. government has passed laws that have greatly weakened the power of conferences. Still, it has to be recognized that conferences do exist and that they remain popular outside the trades serving the United States.

The first ocean shipping conferences were formed in the trade between England and its colony India in the nineteenth century. The opening of the Suez Canal and the introduction of the steamship that was more productive than the sailing ship had produced an excess in vessel tonnage. Rates dropped below costs as owners engaged in cutthroat competition. Competitors would drop out of the trade and the irregularities in sailings upset many shippers who wanted stable service.

The initial conference agreement was brief, and the main body of text follows:

MEMORANDUM OF AGREEMENT

BETWEEN

STEAM SHIPOWNERS

ENGAGED IN THE TRADE BETWEEN

INDIA & THE UNITED KINGDOM,

FROM LONDON, LIVERPOOL, & GLASGOW

THIS AGREEMENT is for the purpose of working the Steam Shipping Trade with India, in the way most advantageous to the Trade and those engaged in it.

With this object it is intended to maintain a regular and sufficient supply of Steamship Tonnage, to meet the requirements for Calcutta, Madras, Colombo, Bombay, and Kurrachee; to distribute this Tonnage in such a way as to avoid waste; to regulate by tariff the rates of Freight and Passage-money, and the dates of departure; and generally to consider (with a desire to meet) the reasonable wishes of Government, Merchants, and Shippers, in the hope that they, equally with the parties to this Agreement, may find it to their interest to keep the business in its present channels; and to this end—

1.—The various Lines of Steamers to India, as set forth the Schedule annexed, are to be mutually respected, and no other Steamers are to be loaded on the berth without unanimous consent.

2.—Contracts for the conveyance of Coal and Railway material, taken with the consent of the parties to this Agreement, to be shared in the proportions as may be arranged hereafter.

N.B.—the object, however, being to protect the business of the Regular line steamers, rather that the absorption of the entire carrying trade, it is desirable to make arrangements with the Brokers who have hitherto been engaged in such contracts, in order to secure their co-operation.

3.—A preference being always given to the Steamers owned by the parties to this Agreement in chartering for Conference account, for berth, Coal, and Contract requirements at current rates.

4.—Any dispute arising out of this Agreement shall be submitted to the arbitration of Mr. Gray Hille.

Page three of the agreement was a table listing the ten lines and the number of annual sailings they could perform between specified ports in England and India. The only footnote to the table said: "The Anchor and Clan Lines are entitled to despatch one Steamer, alternately, every 28 days from Glasgow and Liverpool, for Colombo, Madras, and Calcutta, the quantity of Calcutta cargo by said steamers being limited to 750 freight tons, of which none to consist of fine goods, unless with the Consent of the Conference."

Page four listed 14 rules that dealt mainly with internal discipline. Rule 6 allowed members to: "reduce rates of freight to such extent as they may deem needful to meet such competition" (from nonmember vessels). The remainder of the document listed rates on specific products including pig iron, tinplate, boilers, window glass, carriages, wines and spirits, rope and wire, soap, thread, and saddlery. A column contained either a M or W for each item, and these stood for measurement (cubic) or weight measures and a note reading "Where W or M stated, that to be charged which is best for the vessel."

This, then, was the first conference agreement. Later ones were much longer and often were called "pooling" agreements. This meant that the vessel owners "pooled" or shared both their vessels and the earnings or profits at the year's end. It was necessary to pool the profits at the year's end in order to keep members sailing on schedule at times of the year when traffic was light.

Strong arguments have been made that the United States should not permit conferences to exist. Strong arguments in support of conferences have also been made. In the 1916 Shipping Act, Congress, following the advice of what was called the Alexander Report, allowed conferences to call at U.S. ports, although it placed some restrictions on their operations. This pattern has continued for many years. This was a compromise that recognizes both the need for shipping cartels and the potential evils associated with them.

Here's an example of how a conference might organize. Assume three lines, operating from Central America to Australia. Each has a ship and round trip takes three weeks. They would agree to have a ship sail each Monday, and not wait for more cargo. They would charge the same rates, and pay the same commissions to forwarders. At end of year, they would pool profits, meaning, for example, that each of the three would be guaranteed a minimum of, say, 25 percent of the three vessels' combined profits. In order to protect itself from outside competitors, the conference would give customers who agreed to use the conference exclusively a 15 percent rebate.

This discussion will continue by examining in more detail the relationships within the conference among its members; the conferences' relationship with outside vessels (non-conference, or independent, carriers); the conference relationship with shippers; and the conference's relationships with governments. The last two parts of the chapter will deal with conference rates, and with service contracts between conferences or liner operators and shippers.

Relationships Among Conference Members

Conferences exist throughout the world, although they are of varying strengths, and frequently reorganize or realign. The most usual grouping is vessels that sail between two port areas, for example, the U.S. Gulf ports and ports in the Western Mediterranean. Sometimes the conference covers shipments in both directions, sometimes only one. The reason is that some companies might have their vessels go back and forth, say, between the U.S. West Coast and Australia, while another line might sail from the United States to Australia, but then its vessel would sail to Japan, and then back to the West Coast. The first companies would probably belong to two conferences: the U.S. West Coast to Australia Conference and the Australia to U.S. West Coast Conference, while the last line might belong to three conferences: the U.S. West Coast to Australia Conference, the Australia to Japan Conference, and the Japan to U.S. West Coast Conference.

Often the same carrier belongs to several conferences, and sometimes these conferences compete with each other. An example would be that the same carrier might belong to a U.S. Gulf Coast to Baltic Conference and a U.S. North

Atlantic Ports to Baltic Conference. Both conferences would compete for a shipment, originating, say, in western Tennessee that could move through either Baltimore or New Orleans. Because the same lines belong to several conferences, this serves to limit competition between conferences. Indeed, different conferences often share the same office staff, and a single office door may have the names of a half dozen different conferences. Some conferences also act as trade associations, promoting trade between areas that they serve.

Conference members offer uniform, or near-uniform, service to shippers. They pay equal commissions to forwarders. Each member has a vote in rate and other matters (although sometimes votes are weighted), and the conference chair is its bargaining agent and spokesperson and is responsible for publishing the tariffs and classifications. Outside the United States, it may be common for traffic or profits to be pooled; at end of year for a three-line conference, for example, each member gets at least 25 percent but no more than 40 percent of the revenues, or the profits.

Experience has shown that conference members are not always honest with each other. Often they will allow a shipper to state a lower weight or lesser classification of his shipment in order to pay lower charges than the conference tariffs and classifications call for. A 1991 trade journal article said: "A Torrance, California-based fresh fruit exporter is suspected of having understated its cargo volumes in order to cut its freight bills. . . . Several bills of lading . . . showed lower numbers of containers than those indicated on other documents, such as export declarations and U.S. Department of Agriculture clearance certificates."[2] Hence, conferences hire outside policing agents to spot-check the members' honesty and reduce the problems of understating weights or underclassifying cargo. This is called self-policing.

When discussing membership of conferences, one needs also ask: is the conference open or closed? Closed conferences are more restrictive and do not allow outsiders to join. They are much more effective in monopolizing the trades that they serve. This raises the issue of how strong the controls are that a conference has over its member lines. This varies year by year and market by market. Some conferences exercise almost military control over the members and their members' practices, while in other conferences almost no member is charging the conference rates. A general observation is that when demand for shipping space is high, all members charge the published rates and discipline is good. As the market declines, some member lines get hungry and begin cutting rates, using a procedure known as "independent action." (One of the difficult tasks con-

---

[2] *American Shipper,* April, 1991, p. 20.

fronting a shipper's transportation manager is to determine how disciplined the conference is at any one time.)

In the Pacific trades, conferences, as one knew them, broke down in the early 1980s. A smaller number of conferences replaced them. These, in turn, were replaced by a superconference. Part of the rationale was that for container traffic, which was intermodal, the land bridge would give any carrier calling at one port the ability to reach all ports. "It was no longer essential, as in the 1920s or 30s, to have a set of ships or companies serving the west coast, or even in particular the northwest coast and the southwest coast; another set serving the Gulf coast; and still others serving the south Atlantic and the north Atlantic. Truly the conferences that reflected these groupings were made obsolete by the advent of containerization."[3]

A problem of growth in a conference's trade is that shippers want more ships in a trade, that is, more frequent sailings, while the liner operators would prefer to move to larger vessels. *Rationalization* is a term also applied to conference behavior, and it usually means reducing the capacity of an existing fleet to better fit a shrinking or level market. Sometimes, a conference member will be paid by other members to reduce or eliminate sailings. In 1990, conferences with some discipline agreed to reduce capacity-measured in terms of container slots. Carriers in similar container markets also can agree to charter container slots on each other's vessels. Sharing of terminal space and equipment can also be covered in an agreement.

In the mid-1990s another type of alliance began forming in the container trades. Carriers retain their individual identities but cooperate in the area of operations. Some things the lines do jointly are: agree whether to join conferences, coordinate sailings and data systems, interchange empty containers, manage container pools, operate feeder services, operate terminals, order new containers, purchase new ships, and practice reciprocal space chartering.[4] These alliances "now dominate the world's trade routes by providing global service. They are made up of the biggest container lines in the business."[5] As of January 2000, the world's leading container service operators were Maersk Sealand; Evergreen/Uniglory/Lloyd Triestino; P&O/Nedlloyd; Hinjin/DSR-Senator; Mediterranean Shipping; COSCO; NOL/APL; NYK Line; CMA/CGM/ANL;

[3]R. A. Velez, vice president, pricing, American President Lines, talk before National Maritime Council, Los Angeles, September 10, 1985, p. 6, typewritten.

[4]*American Shipper,* October, 1996, pp. 37–46.

[5]Yann Alix, Brian Slack, and Claude Comtois, "Alliance of Acquisition? Strategies for growth in the container shipping industry, the case of CP ships," *Journal of Transport Geography* (1999), p. 206.

and CP Ship Group. They controlled over 1,000 vessels and over half of the world's container carrying capacity.[6]

Why were alliances formed? Alix, Slack and Comtois explained: "Faced with the need to provide as extensive market coverage as possible while striving to fill the ever-growing capacities of the ships, nearly all the major container lines have responded by coming together in alliances. In this way they pool resources (ships, terminal facilities, etc.), and extend market coverage (enter markets that one company alone might not be capable of serving adequately). As in other sectors of the economy, strategic alliances enable firms to confront the challenges of uncertainty, allocation of resources, and market penetration."[7] So, while alliances are not conferences, their size allows them to exercise considerable clout in their dealings with shippers, port terminal operators, and connecting land carriers.

Conferences and Competition

An age-old problem of ocean liners has been that their lucrative traffic comes in an uneven flow. Valuable Christmas merchandise moves in a few months of the summer and autumn; desirable perishable fruits may have a brief season; and so on. The traditional problem is that some vessel operators, rather than serving a single market continuously, would follow the lucrative markets and be available only when there was great demand for service. This practice is known as "skimming the cream." Note, by the way, that one-time shippers have no objections to this practice. They benefit from having many vessels in port competing for their traffic.

However, another group of shippers move goods in an even flow. They want regular service and stable rates. The conference system serves their needs. In essence, they pay higher rates, but they get regular service. In some parts of the world, these shippers tie themselves to conferences by contracts (to be discussed later in this chapter), and these contracts make it difficult, although not impossible, for other non-conference lines to obtain these shippers' business.

At one time, when conferences were annoyed by a persistent competitor, they (the conference) subsidized a "fighting" ship. The fighting ship then followed the

---

[6]United Nations Conference on Trade and Development, *Review of Maritime Transport 2000* (Geneva, 2000), p. 50. Those listed as single firms had grown by outright acquisitions of other competing and complementary operators.

[7]Yann Alix, Brian Slack, and Claude Comtois, "Alliance of Acquisition? Strategies for growth in the container shipping industry, the case of CP ships," *Journal of Transport Geography* (1999), p. 206.

competitor from port to port, underselling the competitor until he decided to drop out of the market. (Fighting ships cannot be used by conferences serving U.S. ports.) However, and at the risk of confusing readers, the conferences do allow a limited amount of competition, usually offered by a firm that offers slightly poorer service at lower rates. This provides several advantages to the conference: one is political; they can deny that they are a monopoly. Second, the lone outside competitor performs a research or intelligence function for the conference; the outsider's business defines the fringe, or outer limits, of demand for transportation in a given market. To the outside observer, one is never certain how independent the "independent" vessel line is. In some markets, conference members and independents may enter into agreements on other matters, such as limiting the amount of available container slots.

In the 1970s, FESCO, a Soviet-flag and government-owned firm, operated liner service in the Pacific. Their goal was to earn foreign exchange; they even took on fuel from the U.S.S.R. at sea. They were non-conference, setting rates 40 percent below those charged by conferences. A number of prominent U.S. firms used FESCO and dropped their agreements to use the conference. (Then the U.S.S.R. invaded Afghanistan, and various boycotts cut into FESCO's business to the extent it stopped calling at U.S. ports.)

As mentioned above, some conferences compete with each other, although usually not very intensely, since often the same liner firm belongs to both conferences. The traditional pattern of conference competition resulted in rate equalization; that is, the combined rail/water rate from Nashville to Amsterdam was the same whether one used a Gulf port and Gulf-Western Europe Conference or an Atlantic port and another conference.

Conferences also compete with chartered vessels for vessel loads of traffic. Shippers' contracts with conferences allow them to charter vessels at no penalty. Hence, an alternative for conference shippers of large quantities is to charter a vessel. More important, because conference liners sail on regular schedules, they often are unable to fill their holds, or containers, with lucrative traffic. So they will fill up (*top off* is the maritime term meaning filling the tops of cargo holds) with less lucrative traffic, such as baled hay or grain or lumber. The rates they charge for this are the same as the current charter rates for similar cargo. For these commodities, the conference rates are said to be *open,* meaning that the conference member charges whatever he can. Open rates are often indications of a conference's recognized inability to control rates in their markets. Some years ago, major Pacific conferences declared all rates open, and soon thereafter the conferences collapsed.

It should always be kept in mind that shippers are not forced to deal with conferences. Shippers can, and do, negotiate with individual conference members.

This right is guaranteed by the so-called "right of independent action" provision of the Shipping Act. So conference members also compete with each other. In a typical scenario, a shipper will request proposals from all or most of the carriers, both in and out of conferences, with service to a particular market. While all ocean carriers may look the same on the surface, in fact they are all different. Ships may have different itineraries. Trade balances may be different. Some carriers need the business more than others. The result is that the shipper will receive multiple proposals from which to select and negotiate a final agreement. So, at least in the United States trades, conferences do not represent a substantial restraint of trade.

Conference Relationship with Shippers

The most common way for a conference, or carrier, to bind shippers is through use of a service contract. In the United States trades various reports indicate over ninety percent of all general cargoes move under service contract. In some markets (although not those involving U.S. ports) a system of deferred rebates is used with the shipper always having money due him on deposit with the conference. The rebates are calculated on the basis of 10 to 15 percent of what the shipper had paid in cargo rates over a six-month period. This amount is calculated and the shipper told of its amount. The funds are kept by the conference for another six months and will be paid to the shipper at that time, assuming he has not violated his contract with the conference. Of course by the time this amount is paid, another rebate has accrued and once again the shipper must wait for six months. The shipper knows the value of rebate due him and, if he decides to use a non-conference vessel, the forfeited deposit is a cost of making the change. This forfeited deposit is the shipper's immediate penalty for dropping use of the conference.

For conferences calling at U.S. ports, dual rates, with a 10–15 percent lower rate for firms signing an exclusive patronage contract, were used for many years. An excerpt from one contract read: "The Carriers agree that they will not provide contract rates to anyone not bound by a shippers rate agreement with the Carriers," and, "In the absence of an accomplished Agreement, the ordinary rate shall be 15 percent higher than the Contract (reduced) rate." Agreements involving dual rates are called "loyalty" contracts. In the United States, since carriers and conferences are free to negotiate any form of contract they wish, there has been some recent movement to reintroduce loyalty-type arrangements. In return for all of some fixed portion of the shipper's cargo, the conference or carrier will charge a reduced rate.

Service contracts also enable shippers to penalize carriers that do not have space when the shipper needs to book cargo. If the conference doesn't have a ship available, the shipper may reduce the number of containers committed under the contract, or even penalize the carrier with a further pricing reduction on containers that do move. Contracts proscribe what steps must be taken by the shipper to impose the penalty. Sometime this involves notifying the conference in addition to maintaining internal records.

There is considerable interaction between the conference and the shippers in terms of freight classifications and tariffs, which will be discussed below. There are procedures by which shippers, or groups of shippers (known as shippers associations), can request that classifications or tariff rates be changed. *Shippers associations* are groups of shippers who organize to negotiate with conferences as group. The best known example were the Australian wool growers, who had enough tonnage that they could charter their own ships, in case they felt that conference rates were unjustly high. Shippers Associations are new to the United States, being permitted by the Shipping Act of 1984. An example is East Coast liquor importers who were more concerned about service issues (mainly terms of payment) than with actual shipping rates.[8] Shippers associations may exist for the purpose of consolidating freight and negotiating service contracts. However, shippers may not band together for the purpose of fixing rates or boycotting carriers. These would subject the shippers to antitrust penalties.

Conference Relationships with Governments

Virtually all governments accept the principles of liner conferences as a necessary stabilizing element. So stabilizing, in fact, that some developing nations charge that the conference system makes it difficult for developing nations to break into the international markets. The discussion in chapter 2 of the 40/40/20 rule for liner cargo is an example of this concern. The rule still is not widely applied and there is considerable disagreement as to how it should be enforced and which nations can vote on amendments. The code presently applies only to liner conference traffic, but many developing nations want the code extended "to include multimodal transport, consortia, intermediaries such as freight forwarders and NVOCCs, and possibly non-liner cargo."[9]

Conferences have encountered some difficulties with other governments. A typical example was the Transatlantic Agreement (TAA), which became operational in 1993. It was an agreement by which the major shipping companies

---

[8]*American Shipper,* February, 1985, p. 27.

[9]*American Shipper,* June, 1991, p. 14.

wanted to gain tighter control of seriously loss-making shipping on the North Atlantic. They tried to achieve this by determining rates, capacity supply, and conditions of freight by mutual arrangement. Shippers, who were having difficulties securing loading capacity and could no longer negotiate terms with individual shipping companies, soon responded. In 1994, the TAA was banned by the European Commission on the basis of allegations of rate manipulation criticism of its capacity management, and the fact that cartel agreements also held for pre- and on-carriage over land. Also in 1994, the European Commission imposed fines on a group of 14 shipping companies—European and Asian members of the Far Eastern Freight Conference (FEFC)—for illegitimate price fixing and discriminatory practices.[10] Apparently, the European Commission still allows conferences to fix rates, but disallows collective exemptions from the rules of free competition for land transport.[11]

In the United States, in return for antitrust immunity, carriers agreed to some pro-shipper competitive features in a new law. These competitive features pacified the Department of Justice, a key player in maritime regulation, and temporarily satisfied shippers' objectives. The negotiated package known by some as "the shipper-carrier compromise" thereby won broad support and enough votes in the 1984 Congress to become law. However, that was not the end. Shippers continued to press for confidentiality in contracts. That objective was achieved with the passage of the Ocean Shipping Reform Act, known as OSRA, in 1998.

Some key provisions (including some carried forward from earlier laws) of interest to shippers include:

Conferences may negotiate confidential service contracts with shippers

Conferences shall be open (not closed)

Approved conferences have immunity from U.S. antitrust laws

Fighting ships prohibited

Conferences may fix rates and rationalize services

Conferences may publish intermodal rates

Conference members should negotiate inland transportation separately

---

[10]T. Heaver, H. Meersman, F. Moglia, and E. Van de Voorde, "Do Mergers and Alliances Influence European Shipping and Port Competition?" *Maritime Policy and Management* (October–December, 2000), p. 26.

[11]T. Heaver, H. Meersman, F. Moglia, and E. Van de Voorde, "Do Mergers and Alliances Influence European Shipping and Port Competition?" *Maritime Policy and Management* (October–December, 2000), p. 26.

Tariffs are no longer filed with the Federal Maritime Commission (FMC) but must be electronically accessible over the Internet at a reasonable charge

Members must be permitted to publish rates independently (This means a carrier can grant a shipper a rate in order to compete with independents. It also means a carrier can no longer tell shippers that a rate cannot be established because the conference will not allow it.)

Forwarders must be licensed and compensated

Non-vessel operators (NVOCCs or NVOs) are considered shippers to carriers

Non-vessel operators are considered carriers to shippers

Terminal operators may have agreements

Deferred rebates are illegal

Rates may vary with volume over time

Shippers may form shipper associations

The foregoing list is not comprehensive. The law, and the regulations published pursuant to it by the FMC, goes into considerable depth regarding such matters as the form of tariffs, time parameters which must be adhered to in the publishing of rates, content of service contracts, courts which shall have jurisdiction, requirements imposed on conferences, and so on. Note that this law applies only to conferences and ocean carriers serving U.S. ports. For shipments between ports elsewhere in the world, the rules may not be applicable. Figure 6–1 shows ship cords, used by carriers to advertise schedules. Note references to "conference service" and "independent" (non-conference) service.

The 1984 Act clarified the role of non-vessel operating common carriers (NVOCCs or NVOs). An NVO is a private company in the business of consolidating freight, usually small shipments, into containerload lots. NVOs came into existence soon after the containerization revolution of the 1960s. As "off pier" consolidators their labor costs were lower than "on pier" union labor. Today, NVOs handle most less-than-containerload cargo in the major trades and a considerable share of full-containerload traffic as well. The NVO issues its own bill of lading, assumes liability for loss or damage, and is bound by the rates and rules contained in its tariff of rules and rates.

NVOs with respect to steamship lines (vessel operators) are considered to be shippers. They even sign service contracts with carriers and conferences. When an NVO tenders cargo to a vessel operator, the vessel operator (VOCC) issues a bill of lading to the NVO as if he were the party having proprietary interest in the cargo (the shipper). With respect to the shipper itself, the NVO is a common carrier with common carrier liability. The NVO issues the shipper a bill of

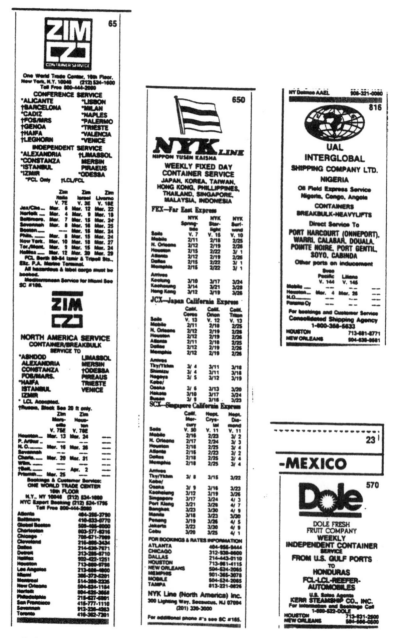

Figure 6–1 Ships' Cards from *The Journal of Commerce.* Courtesy of *The Journal of Commerce.*

lading as if it were the vessel operator itself. The law specifies that while NVOs may coload (consolidate with other NVOs), its bill of lading must so state and the rate it charges other NVOs may not be less than the commodity rate that would otherwise apply to any shipper of the same commodity. Regulation also require that NVOCCs be bonded and that tariffs be filed.

The law also covers ocean freight forwarders. Although not very different from the old law, the Act provides that forwarders must be licensed by the FMC in order to collect commissions from ocean carriers for cargo booked. The forwarder also provides the ocean carrier a service by preparing the ocean bill of lading. Forwarders are compensated for these services not only by the fee charged to the shipper, but also by the ocean carrier in the form of brokerage that is paid as percentage of the base freight bill on each shipment. Brokerage is an important source of revenue for forwarders. The Act reaffirms that it must be paid and sets a minimum of 1.25 percent. No maximum is set. NVOs also pay forwarders commissions. NVO commissions can range between five and 15 percent. The rate of brokerage must be published in the carrier's or conference's tariff. (Other nations do not require that brokerage be paid or brokerage rates published.)

Publishing Rates

Carriers of mixed freight have developed a method for charging that is applied almost universally. It relies on three different factors, all of which influence and determine the shipment's transportation charges. The first factor is classification, which looks at the handling characteristics of the freight. How easy or how difficult is it to handle? The second factor deals with the cargo's origin and destination. Usually the cost per mile drops over longer distances because the port costs (which are the same, irrespective of distance) can be spread over a greater number of sailing miles. The last factor deals with the size of the shipment; the carrier will charge less per unit of weight for a large shipment than for a small one. That is because the administrative costs to the carrier of handling 15 one-ton shipments are greater than handling one 15-ton shipment. In addition, containerized freight usually pays lower rates than non-containerized freight because the carrier saves many handling costs.

U.S. shippers dealing with conferences either pay the tariff rate or enter into service contracts with the conference. Discussed first will be conference rates; then service contracts.

Carriers publish tariffs and they must charge shippers the rates published in those tariffs. A tariff is a book of rules and rates. The rules section of the tariff constitutes part of the contractual agreement the shipper agrees to when he tenders a shipment. The bill of lading is the other part of the contract. The rules section specifies a variety of conditions of carriage including such items as how long a shipper has to pay the freight bill, how much brokerage fees forwarders will be paid, how long a container may be in the possession of the shipper before demurrage (a per diem rental fee) must be paid, how cargo is to be measured for the purpose of assessing freight, what geographical range is covered by the tariff, what surcharges exist, and so on.

Freight is also classified. From the description of cargo shown by the shipper or his forwarder on the bill of lading, one finds the basis for the rating (pricing) of freight. This is referred is to *freight classification.* Classification has to do with the physical nature of the freight, not its volume nor its origin/destination.

Tariffs list commodities from very general descriptions to very specific. The most specific classification is the legal rate classification. For example:

Classification	Rate in U.S. dollars per short ton
General cargo NOS	250
Foodstuffs NOS	195
Canned vegetables	180
Canned beets	275
(note: NOS means not otherwise specified)	

Only one classification, and corresponding rate, would apply to a shipment described as "canned spinach"; it would be the "canned vegetables" class and rate. This is true because "canned spinach" is more specific than "foodstuffs." A shipment of canned beets would be subject to the "canned beets" rate even though beets are a foodstuff and the foodstuff rate is lower. The law provides that the more or the most specific classification is the correct one.

Dried beets in bags would be subject to the foodstuffs rate even though both a "canned beets" and "canned vegetables" classification exist, because the tariff has been specific as to the packaging.

A shipper may not pick and choose to get the lowest classification and rate. The closest, most specific rate always applies. Consequently, it is important that the correct classification be shown on the bill of lading including the tariff item number if it is known. In obtaining freight quotations the shipper should always ask for both the classification verbiage and item number as well as expiration date of the rate or next scheduled rate increase date. This information should be communicated to the forwarding agent for inclusion on the bill of lading.

A common mistake shippers make is assuming that freight forwarders are experts in classification and that they use tariffs to prepare bills of lading. While it is true that forwarders are better at classification than export generalists, they are not experts on the particular commodity being shipped. Carriers are not experts on the commodity being shipped either. Thus trade names or ambiguous descriptions should never be used, as these will more than likely result in the application of NOS or general cargo rates, which are often higher. (However, shippers sometimes defraud carriers by misdescribing their cargo in order to obtain a lower classification.)

Many tariffs today list commodities by the harmonized number covering the commodity in the Harmonized Tariff Schedule of the United States (or TSUSA). This is the number shown on export declarations and used by shippers and is a number that most shippers know or can get. Typically, the first four to six digits of the nine digit harmonized number are used. Carrier-specific variations beyond the base number can be used to create special subcategories.

Today, all tariffs are computerized. In the U.S. trades, the law requires that they be electronically accessible. That has been accepted as meaning they must be accessible over the Internet. Tariffs can be accessed by going to the FMC website, then clicking on the carrier to be accessed. These links do not always work. This is a problem the FMC polices regularly. Figure 6–2 shows printed rates on Christmas trees in the Transpacific Westbound Rate Agreement. This comes from the tenth revision of page 587 of the tariff.

Shippers frequently apply for specific commodity descriptions. They do so because the more generic existing classifications and rates are considered too high. If sufficient volume exists, the shipper can file an application for the establishment of a new commodity description to cover his product. This can be done by direct application to the conference, if the rate is to be applied across conference carriers, or to the carrier if it is nonconference. A shipper can also have the conference lower his product's classification if he improves its handling characteristics, that is, making it easier for the carrier to haul.

A principle of law in these matters is that the lowest applicable rate applies to a shipment. A shipper cannot be penalized by the application of a higher rate because of his ignorance. What this means is that if a lower applicable rate is discovered, even after the fact, the shipper may claim a refund and the carrier is compelled to refund the excess. Freight auditing companies exist that do exactly this. They research tariffs in search of lower applicable rates, file claims on behalf of their clients, and split the savings.

Consider now rate structures. The ocean liner operator has costs in port and at sea. With the advent of containerships, less time is spent in port, and more productive days each year are spent at sea. "The individual shipping line considers the voyage as its basic production unit."[12] What is a voyage, what is a leg? In

---

[12]Jan Owen Jansson, "Intra-Tariff Cross Subsidization in Liner Shipping, *Journal of Transport Economics and Policy,* September, 1974, p. 296.

```
W TPWBA012,W PAGE=587,LP
Word          =   PAGE=587
****** RATES SEARCH (WITH PRINT) IN PROGRESS ******
****
```

(C) NOT SUBJECT TO SUPPLEMENT NO. 11 JANUARY 1, 1993 GRI INCORPORATED INTO RATES TRANSPACIFIC WESTBOUND RATE AGREEMENT WESTBOUND LOCAL AND INTERMODAL FREIGHT TARIFF FMC NO. 12	Orig./Rev.	Page
	10th Rev.	587.
	Cancels	Page
	9th Rev.	587.

FROM: U. S. Ports and	TO : Northeast Asia Ports	Effective Date
Points (See Rule 1-A)	and Points in Japan, Korea, Taiwan, Hong Kong and P.R.C. (See Rule 1-B)	JANUARY 1, 1993
		Correction No. 94533

Except as provided rates apply per ton of 1,000 kilos (W) or per cubic meter (M) whichever produces the greater revenue.

COMMODITY DESCRIPTION AND ORIGIN	RATE BASE	JBP	KOR	TWN	HKG	PRC	ITEM NO.
TREES AND PLANTS - Refrigerated							
Christmas Greens, including Wreaths, Boughs, Garlands CRF035!							006-5245
WC	W	610 (1) m360					
(1) Includes CY Receiving Charge (m360) Min 6KT/PC20 (m426) Min 11KT/PC40	W	413 (1) m426					
Christmas Trees, in Refrigerated Stowage CRF035!CRL7Bc!							006-5250
WC -From Portland, OR	W	433 (1) m426	423 (1) m426	423 (1) m426	431 (1) m426		
(1) Includes CY Receiving Charge							
-From Seattle, WA	W	412 (1) m426	402 (1) m426	402 (1) m426	411 (1) m426		
(m426) Min 11KT/PC40							
CRF035! CRL7Bc!	Subject to Refrigerated Rule 35. (For AP only) Rates in this item may be prepaid at destination.						

```
For explanation of abbreviations and reference marks, see Page 11 - 13.
****
```

Figure 6–2 Printed rates on Christmas trees in the Transpacific Westbound Rate Agreement. Courtesy OOCL (USA) Inc.

conference shipping, where one thinks of back-and-forth or repetitive movements, the complete movement is probably the relevant measure. The balance of trade in each direction is crucial; usually there is imbalance: a thick (or more lucrative) leg and a thin (less lucrative) leg. One can ponder how in a multi-leg (round-the-world) route does one allocate costs? There is high cross-subsidization in liner rates. In most markets, the flow in terms of tonnage and value of cargoes is not the same in both directions. Traditionally, developing economies traded large volumes of bulk raw materials for smaller volumes of manufactured products. While in this instance the value might be balanced in both directions, the tonnage would not be.

A problem in many container trades is imbalance. This shows up in the rates charged. At the end of 1999, the average rate (expressed in dollars per TEU) for containerized goods moving from Asia to the United States was $2,181, while for goods moving from the United States to Asia the average rate was $736—a disparity of about 3 to 1. The fast description of this commerce has been that the Asians were sending electronic goods to the United States, while the United States was sending scrap paper and cardboard to be made into more packaging to enclose more electronic products bound for the United States. The difference in rates between Europe and Asia is also significant, although not as acute. At the end of 1999, the average rate per TEU moving from Asia to Europe was $1,615, while from Europe to Asia it was $774.[13] Transatlantic trade was closer to being in balance: from the United States to Europe the rate in late 1999 was $1,030, and from Europe to the United States it was $1,127.

While eggs are sold by the dozen, and shoes by the pair, ocean transportation is sold by the ton. Unfortunately, a ton is not one number. It can be any one of several numbers. Before defining these, it is useful to consider that a ship has a finite capacity to carry. One can fill a ship with ping-pong balls or sink it with lead. A shipload of ping-pong balls would not weigh very much. Lower holds solidified with lead would leave a half empty ship.

If carriers only priced by weight, one can see that ping-pong ball shippers would drive them into bankruptcy. Because of this, carriers charge on the basis of weight or cube, whichever generates the higher revenue. Cube is calculated by squaring off freight to the space it occupies. For example, the cube of a drum is calculated as the height times diameter squared. With that in mind, tons are defined as:

Short ton: 2,000 pounds

Short ton, or 40: 2,000 pounds or 40 cubic feet

Long ton: 2,240 pounds

Long ton, or 40: 2,240 pounds or 40 cubic feet

Metric weight ton (kiloton), or tonne: 1,000 kilos (2204.6 pounds)

Metric ton: 1,000 kilos or cubic meter (35.3 cubic feet)

Rates are quoted on one of the foregoing bases (although any single tariff would probably be restricted to one type of ton). A typical quote might be $250 per short ton or 40 cubic feet, subject to a $175 minimum, plus a 15 percent bunker surcharge. To calculate freight on a particular shipment:

---

[13]United Nations Conference on Trade and Development, *Review of Maritime Transport 2000* (Geneva, 2000), p. 54. European trades covered here do not include the Mediterranean. At the end of 1999 we see this annualized flow, expressed in millions of TEUs: Asia to the U.S., 5.9; U.S. to Asia, 3.4; Asia to Europe, 4.1; Europe to Asia, 2.9; U.S. to Europe, 1.4; and Europe to the U.S., 1.8.

1. Determine the correct freight classification
2. Note the applicable rate
3. Divide the total weight by the appropriate weight per above
4. Divide the total cube by the appropriate volume measure given above
5. Multiply the higher of the two (weight ton or measurement ton as quoted) by the rate
6. If this number is lower than the minimum charge, the minimum charge applies
7. Calculate and add any applicable surcharges.

Surcharges are charges aside and apart from the base freight applicable to a commodity classification. Surcharges apply to all cargo, regardless of the classification. A *bunker surcharge* is an additional charge arising from oil price increases, such as happened in late 1990 and early 1991. "The bunker costs became the single largest cost item in the running of ships after the second oil crisis in 1979."[14] A *congestion surcharge* is a charge applied on a port-by-port basis to compensate the carrier for inordinate time the ship must wait to unload due to congestion at a port. A *currency surcharge* is assessed where currency fluctuations result in reduced net revenues. For example, it might take more U.S. dollars to purchase the foreign currency necessary to pay port charges in another country. As an example of surcharges, the Transpacific-Westbound Rate Agreement had a fuel adjustment factor of $160 per 40-foot container, $128 per 20-foot container, $8 per revenue ton (of uncontainerized traffic), and $80 per auto; plus currency surcharges of 8 percent to Singapore and Korea, 10 percent to Taiwan, and 33 percent to Japan.[15] In 1999, some conferences serving Europe imposed a "container-repositioning" surcharge to help defray their expenses in moving empty containers. For example, shippers moving imports from the Mediterranean to Montreal were charged an additional $250 per container.[16] In late 2001, the India-Pakistan-Bangladesh-Ceylon Conference, whose members carry cargo to and from Europe, announced an increase of $300 per TEU for containers moving in and out of Sri Lanka's Port of Colombo, "after international insurance underwriters declared the entire country a war-risk zone."[17]

Figure 6–3 is an ocean carrier's bill of lading. In the lower left see two sur-

---

[14]Niko Wijnolst and Tor Wergeland, *Shipping,* (Delft: Delft Univ. Press, 1997), page 218.

[15]*Daily Commercial News and Shipping Guide,* March 19, 1991, p. 1.

[16]*The Journal of Commerce,* September 3, 1999, p. 6.

[17]*JoC Shipping Digest,* August 27, 2001, p. 6.

OOCL ORIENT OVERSEAS CONTAINER LINE

*** NON-NEGOTIABLE ***
BILL OF LADING
(Not Negotiable Unless Consigned to Order)

SHIPPER / EXPORTER (COMPLETE NAME AND ADDRESS) 00877188	BOOKING NO. 22101660 / BILL OF LADING NO. OOLU22101660
CHEMICAL INT'L INC. HOUSTON TX 77056 USA	EXPORT REFERENCES 414545 / 93-I-007-1 4050-0031 2/11/93 REF 1-3207-93BR
CONSIGNEE (COMPLETE NAME AND ADDRESS) 99999999 TO THE ORDER OF INDUSTRIAL BANK OF KOREA	FMC NO. 1-3207-93BR CO.,INC., 314 P.O.BOX HOUSTON, TX. 77001 FMC.NO. POINT AND COUNTRY OF ORIGIN OF GOODS TX
NOTIFY PARTY (COMPLETE NAME AND ADDRESS) OSHU0002 ABRASIVE MFG CO LTD. C P O BOX SEOUL KOREA	ALSO NOTIFY PARTY-ROUTING & INSTRUCTIONS

PRE-CARRIAGE BY	PLACE OF RECEIPT BY PARTICIPATING CARRIER/CARRIER HOUSTON		ORIGINALS TO BE RELEASED AT HOUSTON
INTENDED VESSEL / VOYAGE / FLAG USA PRESIDENT JEFFERSON 093W	PORT OF LOADING SEATTLE, WA	LOADING PIER / TERMINAL	
PORT OF DISCHARGE BUSAN KOREA	PLACE OF DELIVERY BY PARTICIPATING CARRIER/CARRIER BUSAN KOREA	TYPE OF MOVEMENT (IF MIXED, USE DESCRIPTION OF PACKAGES AND GOODS FIELD)	

(CHECK "HM" COLUMN IF HAZARDOUS MATERIAL) PARTICULARS FURNISHED BY SHIPPER

CNTR. NOS. W/SEAL NOS. MARKS & NUMBERS	QUANTITY PACKAGES	H M	DESCRIPTION OF PACKAGES AND GOODS	GROSS WEIGHT	MEASUREMENT
ABRASIVE MFG. CO. SEOUL, KOREA VIA-BUSAN NO. 1/UP MADE IN U.S.A.	20 DRUM		X 55-GAL.DRUMS X DIETHYLENETRIAMINE, CLASS 8 (CORROSIVE MATERIAL) UN 2079 PG II IMDG 8161 F.P. 210 DEG. F. / DETA DIETHYLENE TRIAMINE 3,900KGS SHIPPED IN PARTIAL ONE X 20-FT. CONTAINER	4101KG 9040LB	6.060M3 214CF
TOTAL : ***20*** PACKAGES				4101KG 9040LB	6.060M3 214CF

SHIPPER'S LOAD AND COUNT; CONTAINERS SEALED BY SHIPPER CY/CY
FREIGHT PREPAID CLEAN ON BOARD 021093 G-DEST
** TO BE CONTINUED ON ATTACHED LIST **

NOTICE: For Carriage to or from the United States of America, Clauses 23 and 24 on the reverse hereof limit the Carrier's liability to a maximum of U.S.$500 per package or customary freight unit by virtue or incorporation of the U.S. Carriage of Goods by Sea Act, 1936, unless the Merchant declares a higher cargo value below and pays the Carrier's ad valorem freight charge.

Declared Cargo Value US$_____ . If Merchant enters a value, Carrier's limitation of liability shall not apply and the ad valorem rate will be charged.

FREIGHT & CHARGES PAYABLE AT / BY: HOUSTON BUSAN	SERVICE CONTRACT NO.	ROUTE CODE	COMMODITY CODE	EXCHANGE RATES:	
CODE	TARIFF ITEM	FREIGHTED AS	RATE	PREPAID	COLLECT
1 099-1822		1.000	484.29	484.29	
BAF BUNKER ADJU		1.000	19.59	19.59	
CAF CURRENCY AD		484.290	4.00	19.37	
DDF CFS DESTINA		6.060	2200.00		73932.00 KRW

DATE CARGO RECEIVED FEB.10,93
DATE LADEN ON BOARD FEB.10,93
DATED FEB.10,93

	USD	523.25	
	KRW		73932.00

SIGNED FOR THE CARRIER(S) OR MASTER(S) SEVERALLY BUT NOT JOINTLY
BY: OOCL (USA) INC. AS AGENT (S)

Figure 6–3 Ocean carrier's bill of lading. Courtesy OOCL (USA) Inc.

charges, one for bunker and one for currency. Note in the center that the cargo weight and cubic dimensions are both stated, and the carrier would choose whichever yield the greater revenue. Shippers tendering cargo routinely give both weight and measurements. Figure 6–4 shows a tank destined for export. On the side are stenciled its weight in pounds and in kilos and its dimensions in both inches and centimeters.

Figure 6–4 Tank destined for export, showing weight in pounds and kilos and dimensions in inches and centimeters. Courtesy of Superior Packing, Inc. HAL, Inc.

Surcharges are also applied to unusual cargoes. Extra length and extra weight surcharges are applied to cargoes with those peculiarities to compensate the carrier for additional handling costs. Some dangerous goods are also subject to surcharges.

Some rates are quoted on a per-ton basis based on the per-ton value of the cargo. Other rates are quoted on an ad valorem basis (on the basis of value). Mixed commodity and *FAK* (freight all kinds) rates are often used by NVOs. The lump-sum charge is divided by the expected average utilization. This results in a "buying rate." To this is added handling and administrative overhead on a per-ton basis, along with a provision for profit. The resulting number is the NVO's selling price (rate) that he charges shippers.

In addition, containerization has introduced bulk-type rates applicable to full containers. *Lump sum* rates apply to full containerload (FCL) shipments. *FAK* rates apply to containerloads regardless of the contents. Mixed commodity rules usually provide lower rates for containers of mixed commodities provided certain proportions are present. The proportions are specified in the tariff. *FCL* are full containerload rates, and *LCL* are less than containerload rates.

Published tariff rates may not be acceptable to the shipper for a number of reasons. From a landed cost[18] basis, the rate may be too high to permit sale of the product. A reduced rate may be needed to make the product competitive. The reduced rate may also be necessary to compete with producers in another country with lower rates into the same destination. In these two examples a rate adjustment would benefit not only the shipper but also the carrier, since it would also enjoy increased business. A true partnership exists. Another case would one where the shipper finds that another very comparable product moves under a specific commodity item description that carries a much lower rate. In short, there are a variety of legitimate business reasons for needing a rate adjustment. To the extent they are legitimate both the carrier and the shipper benefit.

When only a single carrier is involved, application for the adjusted rate, or new tariff item, proceeds normally through direct discussion and negotiation with the carrier. The shipper should present the facts as they are as well as the rationale for the rate sought.

If the shipper would like the rate to apply to the various members of a conference, then application needs to be made through the conference itself. The process need not be very different. The shipper does his research, contacts the carriers involved, explains what he is doing and why, then files the application with the conference rate-making committee. The committee consists of the member lines. The conference staff may ask for additional information and may request that the shipper attend a rate-making meeting to explain the request further.

The application is then voted on by the representatives of the member lines. Most applications are eventually approved. At times the rate is somewhat different than that which was requested, usually higher. What the rate comes in at depends on how well the shipper made his case, what the impact will be on the overall revenue and rate integrity of the conference members, and what the competition will be likely to do.

A conference may elect to reject the application as well. The shipper then has various options. One is to ship through non-conference carriers, if they exist. Another is to ship through other ports using other conferences, if that is feasible. Perhaps the shipper should explore using a non-vessel-operating common carrier. Note that for some products, shipment by air is a viable alternative. The shipper may check to determine whether membership in a shippers association would help obtain the needed rate.

The shipper may also request a member of the conference to establish the rate

---

[18]"Landed cost" is the total cost of item at its intended place of use.

independently of the conference. The right to independent action on rates and service items by conference members is assured under the Shipping Act of 1984. If the carrier decides to do so, the conference is notified by the carrier intending to take the action of the intent, and the conference then has the option of establishing the rate for all its members within ten days of the notification. When many independent filings are made by a conference's members, this is also evidence of the conference's overall weakness in terms of maintaining rate stability.

Service Contracts

Shippers or shippers associations can sign *service contracts* with carriers or conferences. These must be true and bona fide contracts that unambiguously commit the parties for a stated period of time and volume of traffic, and which provide real remedies or penalties for breach by either party. The "essential terms" of service contracts must be published by the conference or carrier and filed with the FMC, although confidential information is not published. Service contracts operate outside the tariff structure. The terms are negotiated between the parties just as in any commercial contract. A vast number of service contracts are signed every year. During OSRA's first year, 46,035 new service contracts and 95,627 amendments were filed with the commission.[19] Most contracts are signed for a period of one year and are renegotiated annually according to prevailing conditions. (Larger shippers are more likely to enter into contracts. As of early 2001, it was estimated that between five and ten percent of the traffic on the North Atlantic still moved under the Trans-Atlantic Conference agreement, rather than under service agreements.[20])

The law does require that the contract be a real contract and not simply a means of circumventing the published tariff. Thus there must be a stated duration, a stated minimum volume, a stated rate, a stated list of covered commodities, a stated origin and destination, a defined service expectation, and remedies for breach of contract. Discounts are given if the carrier can operate from door to door, without specifying the ports through which the cargo must be routed. Discounts are also given for quick release of containers, and for shipping in off-peak seasons.

---

[19] *JoCWeek,* July 3–9, 2000, p. 12.

[20] *JoCWeek,* January 29–February 4, 2001, p. 27. The carriers in this market need to remain in a conference because European Union rules do not allow "discussions" outside of the conference framework.

A service contract consists of: "a commitment by the shipper to the conference or carrier of a minimum volume of cargo, usually expressed in TEU (20-ft container equivalent units) with rate levels indicated as intermodal, point to point, or port to port. The contract is always for a specific period of time. The carrier or conference must guarantee . . . regular service, perhaps a particular port rotation and specialized equipment."[21] There are also clauses for damages, in case the shipper doesn't live up to its commitment—the shipper's problem may be loss of overseas sales (a common problem during times of recession). Most contracts cover containerized cargo, and in the past many had a most-favored shipper clause, meaning that if the conference gives another similarly situated shipper a better rate, then the initial contracting shipper also gets it.

For some year 2001 rates, two agricultural products will be cited. Frozen poultry is high value and requires a container that can maintain freezing temperatures. Rates for 40-foot containers were: Atlantic/Gulf ports to Pusan, $2,774; to Gdynia, Poland, $3,767; to Manila, Philippines, $3,973; to Singapore, $3,484; and to Shanghai, $4,321.[22] Hay is a low-value commodity and used to fill containers bound for Asia that would otherwise be empty. Hay rates reported for 2001 for 40-foot containers from the U.S. West Coast to Japan ranged between $550 and $650; and between $350 to $450 for hay going to Taiwan or Korea.[23]

Summary

The ocean liner industry consists of independent carriers and carriers that have joined together into conferences. Ocean liner conferences consist of liner operators serving in a certain market area who get together and agree to reduce competition among themselves. While this is anti-competitive, the requirement that carriers in conferences have a "right of independent action" assures competition. Today almost all traffic in the United States moves under service contracts. These contracts specify the services expected to be provided and the rates shippers are willing to pay for those services. Shippers have the option of shipping their goods under contract or not under contract through conferences, individual conference members, or nonconference carriers. Shippers can also ship goods through non-asset-based carriers known as non-vessel operating common carriers, or NVOs.

---

[21]"Are Service Accords Destined to Survive?" *Handling and Shipping Management,* February, 1987, p. 27.

[22]USDA ocean rate bulletin website.

[23]*JoCWeek,* May 7–13, 2001, p. 14. Before being loaded into the export containers, the hay is compressed by hydraulic compressors to achieve a density of 25 tons per 40-foot container.

End-of-Chapter Questions

1. What are economic cartels? Give some examples.
2. What were some of the provisions in the first conference contract (involving trade between India and the U.K.)? Why did the vessel operators enter into the contract?
3. What is the difference between an "open" conference and a "closed" conference?
4. Why do conferences need to "police" their various members?
5. What are "pooling" arrangements?
6. What is a carrier's "right of independent action?"
7. What is freight "classification?" What purpose does it serve?
8. What causes traffic imbalances between nations?
9. What are some of the surcharges that are frequently added on to one's freight bill?
10. What is a service contract? When would one be used?

CASE • *Gitomer Container Leasing Company*

Lynn Gitomer was the founder of a small container leasing company that had offices in Los Angeles, Antwerp, and Melbourne and operated through agents elsewhere in the world. The firm's main function was to lease twenty-foot and forty-foot dry containers to steamship lines. Initially, the steamship lines had provided most of their own containers, but soon, leasing companies were providing an increasing share of oceangoing containers throughout the world. This happened because the steamship lines were reluctant to handle containers belonging to other steamship lines, and the industry never worked out the sophisticated equipment-interchange arrangements of, say, the U.S. railroads or the world's airline industry.

Leased containers were neutral and would be handled by any line. Steamship lines liked to use them in unbalanced markets, so that they would not have to reposition their own empty equipment. In the early days of oceangoing containers, the major movements were back and forth between the principal industrialized nations of the world, but now containers were being shipped nearly everywhere, including many areas that had no cargoes to load for an outbound haul. The majority of container traffic moving though U.S. ports was to and from Asia. In that instance the tonnage in each direction was equal, but the value was not. Imports from Asia were high-value electronic goods, while many U.S. exports to

Asia were scrap paper and cardboard that would be converted into packaging material. Looking at major container trade routes worldwide, imbalances were the worst between the Far East and South America, with two to three times as many loaded containers going from the Far East to South America than returning.

Mark Morris, who had recently graduated from Penn State University, was starting the sixth—and final—month of his probationary period with the Gitomer firm. So far, he had spent most of his time learning the business. His biggest problems had been keeping track of containers and finding enough empties to meet the needs of a few good markets. He quickly learned that steamship lines wanted to use leased containers only for one-way shipments into markets where there were few outgoing cargoes. Currency fluctuations were also important; often, nations with strong currencies saw their flow of exports drop to nearly nothing, merely because their usual trading partners could no longer afford to buy from them.

Morris hoped to become a regional manager for the Gitomer firm. The regional manager's main duty was to find and cultivate ship lines that would use Gitomer's containers in a trade pattern that was about the same as Gitomer's desired flow of containers. If Morris passed his probationary period, worked in the home office for about one year dealing mainly with equipment control, and got some experience in both equipment maintenance and sales, he had a good chance of becoming a regional manager in as little as two years.

Gitomer called Morris into her office and said, "Next week, we'll be bringing in two new people, fresh out of college: a fellow from Clemson, and a woman from Syracuse. I'll put them directly into sales, one here and one in the Pacific Northwest. Right now we're developing a one-month orientation program for them. You've been doing a good job so far, and I want you to explain the problems we have in pricing our containers and getting them moved from areas of low or no cargo to areas with more cargo offerings. That's the key to success in the container leasing business. According to an article I read once in *American Shipper,* 21 percent of all container moves by ship are empty, and repositioning costs the industry about 3.5 billion dollars per year."

"What exactly should I cover?" asked Morris.

"Tell them the six ways we use to reposition containers," responded Gitomer as she stood. "Excuse me," she added, "I'm off to the Pacific Union Club to do some networking."

Morris didn't lunch at the Pacific Union Club yet. Instead, he waited for the lunch truck's whistle and walked out of the office complex and bought his usual coffee, ham and cheese sandwich, and a juicy California orange. As he sat on a bench, soaking up the rays, he looked at several copies of *JoCWeek.* An article in the October 30–November 5, 2000 issue said that a container leasing company executive "estimates that 100,000 empty containers owned by leasing companies are in storage yards scattered around the Port of New York and New Jersey, with perhaps another 50,000 owned by shipping companies." The same article quoted the CEO of a San Francisco-based container leasing company who said that "repositioning costs—including movement in and out of container depots, trucking and ocean freight—can exceed $1,000." An article in the February 26–March 4, 2001 issue said: "New dry containers now cost an estimated $1,525 to $1,600 per TEU. ... Nearly all containers are built in China, where labor is cheap and there is a plentiful supply of export cargo to be loaded in a container's first transit."

Morris thought out the six ways to reposition an empty container:

1. Pay a carrier (steamship, rail, or truck line) to move the empty container to a place where it was needed. The Gitomer firm paid for transportation and earned no revenue (although the carrier hauling the container might, on its own, find some "last minute" traffic and use the empty container to carry it).

2. Find a customer in an area with a surplus of empty containers with a shipment of freight going to a spot where there is a shortage of containers. ("A fine theoretical solution," he planned to exclaim to the two new trainees next week, "but not very applicable because—by definition—such shippers would be hard to find.")

3. Give the steamship line some "free" days, not charging them the usual daily fee for the container's use, if they move the container to an area of higher demand. When this happens, the steamship line may find some lower-revenue cargo—such as hay or cotton—that may pay enough for the steamship line to cover the (reduced) charges for the container's use.

4. Lease the container on a round-trip basis only when the initial destination is an area without much return business.

5. Lease on a one-way basis out of low-demand areas, to make certain that the problem is less likely to be repeated.

6. Work out deals with steamship lines, combining in one transaction the leasing of containers moving to good markets with the leasing of containers going to slow markets.

Questions for *Gitomer Container Leasing Company*

1. List and discuss the advantages and disadvantages to the Gitomer firm of the first alternative on Mark's list.

2. List and discuss the advantages and disadvantages to the Gitomer firm of the second alternative.

3. List and discuss the advantages and disadvantages to the Gitomer firm of the third alternative. How many "free" days should be allowed?

4. List and discuss the advantages and disadvantages to the Gitomer firm of the fourth alternative.

5. List and discuss the advantages and disadvantages to the Gitomer firm of the fifth alternative

6. List and discuss the advantages and disadvantages to the Gitomer firm of the sixth alternative.

7. No cost, demand, or revenue data have been present with this case. What kinds of numbers or values would one need to have before deciding answers to the questions posed above?

7

International Air Transportation

Introduction

This chapter deals with air transportation. It emphasizes movements of cargo, rather than passengers. It is difficult to separate the two since considerable freight moves on aircraft that also carry passengers. A very small percentage of the world's commercial airline aircraft carry cargo exclusively. Airlines that carry both passengers and cargo give higher priority to the movement of passengers, and flights are scheduled to capture passenger markets. In terms of value, air cargo is very important. Estimates are that air cargo accounted for over 32 percent of the value of intercontinental trade in 1998.[1]

Some supply chain managers also have responsibilities for moving people throughout the world. In some instances, this merely means providing them with airline tickets; in other instances, contracts may be entered into with airlines for movements of groups of people. Firms with large volumes of travel may have outside travel agencies assign certain personnel to serve their specific needs only, or the firm may have its own travel agency as a subsidiary, earning for itself the commissions on ticket and accommodation sales.

Some airlines specialize in carrying small parcels and documents, and several well-known overnight document/package delivery companies in the United States are expanding their operations overseas. Speedy international delivery of documents is important to many export/import operations, since all documents relevant to a shipment must be present at its point of importation. Air transport is often relied upon to make certain the documents are present when the vessel ar-

---

[1]*American Shipper,* August, 1999, p. 28.

rives in port (although, eventually, many of these documents will be transmitted electronically).

Development of Aviation

Aviation development has taken place completely within the 20th century. The first use of aircraft for moving materials occurred in India, in 1911, when 6,500 pieces of mail were carried for a distance of five miles. Two other early mail flights, taking place in the same year, were in Denmark and in England.[2] One associates airline development as starting just after World War I. In the 1920s, most airlines started operations by carrying mail, and air mail subsidies paid by governments were used to stimulate the development of airline companies. Planes of this era were leftovers from World War I, of wood, wire, and fabric construction. Figure 7–1 is a 1919 photo showing an early movement of air cargo. Airline aircraft were twin-engined and similar to World War I bombers.

Figure 7–1   Early movement of air cargo. Courtesy of Lufthansa.

---

[2]*Exxon Air World,* no. 1, 1982, pp. 26–27.

Legal scholars were calling for the concept of "freedom of the air" to follow the idea of "freedom of the sea"; however, World War I had shown the military potential of aircraft and that the risks of free skies were greater than those of free seas.[3]

In 1919 six European airlines formed the International Air Traffic Association (IATA) for the purpose of developing standardized airline tickets and interline reservations. By 1929, 23 airlines had joined. Airlines developed in all major western European countries. In the U.S., airline development was initially slower than in Europe, and in the United States air mail carriage was more important than passenger carriage. Carrying mail did give pilots experience with schedules and night flying. By 1930, distinctive civilian aircraft, such as the Ford Tri-Motor, were developed. Three-engine aircraft became the airline standard for the early 1930s. Radio communication with the ground was used, although airline aircraft flew VFR (visual flight rules, meaning pilot can see ground). By 1930, U.S. airlines carried as many passengers as the rest of the world's airlines combined. This pattern would hold until after World War II.

Little mention is found of air freight in this early period; much of what moved probably went as air mail. There was great interest—and competition between nations—in using air transport to reduce air mail times across the oceans. Some swift ocean liners would carry a small plane loaded with mail and launch the plane, using a catapult, while the ship was still a few hundred miles from its destination. This would cut a day off of the mail's time. Lufthansa used seaplanes, and had permanently placed tender ships stationed across the North Atlantic. Seaplanes would land, take on fuel and fresh crews, and be catapulted into the air in order to continue across the ocean. One could see that air transport was capable of shrinking the globe. Air mail was also important to international airlines, since payments for carrying air mail were the vehicle through which they were subsidized. Inaugural flights of flying boat service across the Pacific were completely loaded with mail with special "first day" cancellations provided by the post office. (This was at a time when stamp collecting was very popular, with two of the world's best-known stamp collectors being President Franklin D. Roosevelt and England's King George VI.)

In the early 1930s, Pan American Airways extended its routes into Latin America. Western European airlines extended into Africa, the Middle East, and Asia. Government-subsidized airlines were formed in Australia. In Canada, bush pilots were important in opening up undeveloped territories. The Japanese started their airline, and KLM reached the Dutch East Indies. Only in China did there

---

[3]Nawal K. Taneja, *U.S. International Aviation Policy,* (Lexington: D.C. Heath, 1980), p. 1.

seem to be no airline development. A major technological advance came in the United States, where both Lockheed and Northrup introduced clean monoplanes with higher wing loadings made possible by more powerful radial engines. These evolved into the Boeing 247 that appeared in 1933, and the Douglas DC-2, appearing in 1934. The DC-2 soon evolved into the DC-3, which became the cornerstone of modern airline and airport development.

During the 1930s in the United States, which was not preparing for war, expenditures went for civil aviation, and this gave the United States a lead that it holds to the present time. Big domestic lines were Eastern, United, TWA, and American. Pan Am was the overseas carrier, the "chosen instrument," which expanded to Latin America, then across the Pacific, and the Atlantic. As the chosen instrument Pan Am received generous air mail subsidies and help from the State Department in dealing with foreign governments. The negotiation of the landing rights was left to the individual carrier and foreign government. Juan Trippe [Pan Am's president] had taken advantage of this situation by negotiating exclusive traffic rights from the foreign nations. The United States did not oppose Pan American's initiatives to negotiate traffic rights on its own, since it relieved the government of an obligation to grant reciprocal rights.[4]

In dealing with foreign nations, Trippe tried to tie up everything in his deal. Sometimes he would buy foreign carriers who had rights to the United States. Very small nations would welcome Pan Am because they lacked resources for a comparable airline of their own. Large nations were more difficult. The United Kingdom wouldn't give up anything without reciprocal rights. Trippe was blocked for two years in being able to cross to Europe because of this. The United Kingdom wouldn't give fueling rights in either Bermuda or Newfoundland unless they received comparable rights that only the U.S. government, and not Trippe, could provide. An agreement was finally reached and Pan Am and a British carrier were to each have two trans-Atlantic flights per week. However, the British lacked suitable equipment and nothing happened. Pan Am began talking about flying to France instead, and the British decided to let Pan Am fly to Great Britain without reciprocal service by a British carrier. World War II then intervened.

While Pan Am no longer exists, one cannot say enough about its significant role in the economics and politics related to the development of international aviation. R.E.G. Davies, the Smithsonian's aviation curator, said that Pan Am's greatest influence may have been in the development of commercial aircraft that it forced U.S. manufacturers to build (ranging from flying boats in the 1930s

---

[4]Taneja, p. 3.

through the 747). By meeting Pan Am's visionary and exacting requirements, U.S. aircraft manufacturers turned out such superior planes that they dominated the world's airline aircraft market.[5]

In Europe, each nation's airline developed at a modest scale, although most interest there was in the development of military aviation. European airlines were owned by their governments. Service to colonies expanded, and subsidies were justified on the basis of European nations' holding together their respective empires. Aeroflot was formed in 1932 and by 1935 had a route that reached the Pacific. By 1939, IATA membership climbed to 33.

During the 1930s, Britain developed flying boats, necessary to serve its empire. Pan Am used several types of U.S.-built flying boats. Flying boats were about 20–25 percent less efficient than land-based aircraft because of weight and the design of the hull, which could float. However, they were needed because of the lack of airports. There were also German dirigibles, with routes from Germany to North and South America. Commercial dirigible service ended with the Hindenburg disaster.

World War II

World War II was very important to the continued development of aviation. Military training resulted in many pilots who had experience with night flying, poor flying conditions, and flying large planes. The United States also developed a worldwide network of meteorological stations. Two technological developments were radar and jet aircraft, the latter introduced by Germans. In the early days of the war, Britain and the United States divided up war production. Britain built small fighter planes; the United States built planes of all sizes, including four-engine bombers and transport aircraft. Two large, four-engine transport aircraft were introduced during this period, the Douglas DC-4 and Lockheed Constellation. They could carry 50–60 passengers at 200–250 mph, and they required 6,000-foot runways. Some had sufficient range to fly over the oceans. At the war's end, land-based aircraft displaced flying boats. This was because the U.S. military had built runway landing strips and airports throughout the world, because they needed to ferry land-based bombers and transports across both the Atlantic and the Pacific oceans. During the war, aviation had proved its value in many logistical operations, of both short and long duration. An example of a short-time assignment was dropping paratroopers and then the immediate re-supply of troops after they landed on the Normandy beaches, before ports in France could

---

[5]R.E.G. Davies, comments made in San Francisco, April 3, 1993.

be reopened. A long-term supply commitment was flying supplies to China "over the hump" in Burma, keeping China alive in its long struggle with the Japanese.

During the war, U.S. airlines kept operating, with load factors (percent of capacity utilized) of 90 percent. Seats were rationed. By the war's end almost no other nation had operating airlines. And, as the war ended, the United States had virtually the only operating airlines, and the only large aircraft production facilities. There were many surplus aircraft—and trained pilots—left at war's end. In the United States, several new categories of airlines came into being, including those that chartered their aircraft only (non-skeds), and all-cargo carriers. The best-known of the latter group was Flying Tigers, which in 1989 was taken over by FedEx.

After the war, virtually every nation developed its state-run airline, and used U.S.-built DC-3s for the job. In 1949 there were 1,600 DC-3s in airline service in the free world. By 1950, U.S.-built four-engine aircraft were used on major international routes. Other nations were unsuccessful in building competing aircraft. By 1950, 43 percent of the world's airline traffic was in the United States, and Pan Am was the world's dominant international carrier.

Commercial Jet Airliners

In 1953, the British introduced the turbo-prop Vickers Viscount, which was moderately successful. At about the same time, they also introduced the De Havilland Comet, a jet, which was commercially unsuccessful, in part because of a spotty safety record. "An interesting feature of European progress, despite the dependence on U.S. equipment of most of the airlines most of the time, has been the lead which the continent has been able to give in the introduction of entirely new types of equipment. Thus, the world's first turbo-prop network was established in Europe (with the Viscount from 1953), the first long-haul jet network (with the Comet from 1952) and the first short-haul jet network (with the Caravelle from 1959). A lead had also been given, particularly by the United Kingdom, in other technical fields such as airworthiness requirements, approach lighting, navigation aids, air traffic control techniques and automatic landing."[6] While Europe led in commercial aviation development, manufacturers in the U.S. benefited from the Europeans' mistakes, and were able to introduce equipment that was much more successful commercially.

Lufthansa reappeared in 1954; prior to WWII it had been a prominent

---

[6]Peter W. Brooks, "The Development of Air Transport," *Journal of Transport Economics and History* (1967), p. 177.

European carrier. JAL also appeared during the 1950s. The major international carriers we know today all used this decade to spread their routes throughout the world. In 1957, for the first time, more passengers crossed the Atlantic by air than by sea. In 1950, 60 percent of air passengers across the Atlantic flew on U.S. airlines; by 1960, this would drop to 40 percent.[7] The Boeing 707 jet went into service in 1958, followed by the Douglas DC-8, and the smaller Boeing 720s, and some lesser-known jets. The U.S.S.R. also introduced their own jets at about this time, although they were never used widely outside of China and Eastern Europe.

Air freight became significant for both domestic and international airlines. Larger aircraft had more space than was needed to carry passengers' baggage and mail. One reason was that aircraft fuselages are circular, and as they increase in size, there is correspondingly more space below the passenger deck. Jet aircraft had more lifting capability than propeller-driven aircraft, meaning that they could carry a denser mix of cargo. Air freight rates were relatively low, usually covering only out-of-pocket costs.

The Emery-SRI Report

In the early 1960s, Emery Air Freight commissioned the Stanford Research Institute to study how a carrier might identify potential users of air freight. A summary of the report said:

> Air shipments have virtually eliminated distance as a factor in obtaining many items from suppliers and providing products to customers. This had forced a reassessment of transportation policies. No longer is it enough for the traffic manager to seek out the transportation carrying the lowest rate. No longer is the purchase of low-cost transportation the sole criterion of good performance by the traffic department. So many benefits stem from air freight speed that transportation cost must be appraised in terms not only of the "lowest total cost," but also of the total company benefits.
>
> Among forward-looking concerns, transportation is considered an integral part of a company's operation—an extension, as it were, of both ends of a production line—on the one hand for procurement; on the other for distribution. In these areas, it can be used to promote sales, open new markets, provide better utilization of plant and equipment, cut inventory costs, reduce warehousing requirements, accelerate return of capital investment, and add sales profits.[8]

---

[7]Brooks, pp. 174–175.

[8]*The Role of Air Freight in Determining Company Policy* (Wilton, CT: Emery Air Freight, circa 1963), p. 3.

The report was based on interviews with many users of air freight and then placed them into categories according to the user's rationale for choosing the air cargo mode. Some of the rationales, and examples of international movements were:

To speed delivery on perishable commodities, to lengthen useful market life. Examples were strawberries from California moving to Europe; baby chicks from Florida to Latin America.

To speed delivery on production parts, to prevent down time. "Hosiery-knitting machines were purchased by a German company in Pennsylvania, and 230 were airlifted to Germany at a cost of $224 per unit, as opposed to an ocean freight transportation cost of $37.80 per unit. Delivery time was 10 days shorter by air, and this 10-day saving gave the German manufacturer time to produce 207,000 pairs of hosiery."[9] Another example dealt with handling household goods of employees being transferred between countries. By not having to wait for these to arrive, the newly-transferred individual and his family could become "settled" more quickly.

To speed delivery on products or services seeking wider markets from a fixed facility. A U.S. firm decided to buy European-built equipment after the manufacturer guaranteed that repair and replacement parts would be shipped by air.

To cut inventory and storage costs (while improving service) where the market is untested, and demand undetermined. A new Latin American dealer for a U.S.-built auto was able to avoid having to make an immediate large investment in repair part inventory.

To cut inventory and storage costs (while improving service) where lower levels of inventory reduce servicing requirements. The example dealt with the distribution of vaccines in foreign countries where refrigerated storage was difficult to find and malfunctioned frequently.

To take advantage of superior conditions of carriage where higher insurance cost applies in other transport. A Swiss watch manufacturer found that insurance on a shipment of watches to Singapore by air was less than half the amount by water.

To take advantage of superior conditions of carriage where premium handling, difficult co-ordination or documentation prevails in other transport. During a 12- to 14-day shipment of British-made tractor parts to Switzerland, it was impossible to keep in touch with the goods in transit or control the progress of the shipment. Airlines moved the goods in less than 48 hours, giving control throughout the movement.

To take advantage of superior conditions of carriage where duty at destination is assessed on gross weight. Several examples were given of shipments to Latin America where duties were based on the package's total weight.

---

[9]*The Role of Air Freight . . .*, p. 14.

Air transport was shrinking transit times, and an increasing use of air freight was shipping small, expensive merchandise where the principal advantage was collecting payment faster. Assume a shipment worth $10,000 at a time when interest rates are 12 percent. Interest charges run $3.28 per day. If the buyer paid upon delivery, and transit time could be cut from 20 to two days, the seller would save about $60. That may or may not sound like a big deal, but air freight salespeople handed out blank forms upon which potential users could make their own calculations, using their own values.

Air freight was—and is—more dependable than ocean freight in the sense that there was less variability in days early or late on either end. (Today, in major markets, ocean liners do a better job of adhering to schedules; one reason is competition from air.) Later, some of the concepts of reducing both time in transit and variations in arrivals and departures would be applied more broadly to issues of overall logistics system design. Air freight permits the seller (especially multinationals) to keep fewer inventories in fewer locations by responding relatively quickly to market demands from central repositories of stock or even from the production line itself. Affiliates of multinational companies and customers tend to keep lower safety stocks in the field as well when the supply source consistently, reliably, and quickly resupplies their needs. Field inventories have freight, duties, and markups attached to them, and therefore are more costly. In addition to the economies of reduced overall investment in brick, mortar, receivables and inventory, air cargo transport is less rigorous than sea freight in most instances. The effects of motion and stress are minimized compared to ocean transport. Salt water and condensation damage is less likely. That means less protective packaging is required. Expensive crating and boxing costs can be minimized, although not eliminated. Insurance premiums tend to be lower for air cargo consignments as well.

The Emery-SRI report was an important document. It allowed both the sellers and potential users of air cargo to analyze more carefully the mode's advantages and disadvantages. Secondly, it demonstrated an early "total-cost" approach to logistics problems; and it stands as one of the premier post-World War II documents responsible for forming private-sector logistics thought.

Wide-Bodied Jets

In the late 1960s, jumbo, or wide-bodied jets were introduced: the DC-10, the Lockheed 1011, and the Boeing 747. The 747 was a spin-off from a government contract for a large aircraft that Boeing lost to the C-5A. The L-1011 was also considered to be a fine plane technologically, although it was unsuccessful commercially.[10] Later, a West European consortium, Airbus Industries, began producing jumbo jets also and today is considered to be the equal of Boeing.

The 747 became very important to the air freight industry since it had so much carrying capacity. Even with a load of passengers, it could carry more freight than all-cargo versions of the previous generation of jets. Lufthansa operated the first 747F, designed to carry cargo only, and used it across the North Atlantic. A later version of the 747 was introduced in the mid-1980s. It was the 747-400 that looks the same except for six-foot winglets at the end of each wing. It has a two-man crew, and extra fuel is carried in a tank in the tail. Range is over 7,000 miles, and the first big order (for ten) went to Northwest, for trans-Pacific operations. The 747-400's main use was to be connecting the U.S. and Japan and Japan and Western Europe. "The three target markets that helped define the dash 400s performance . . . were Singapore-London, Los Angeles-Sydney and Chicago/New York-Seoul,"[11] although at these extremes, little cargo could be carried. The plane's weight capacity is 122 tons, 20 tons more than the 747-200. By 1997 there were over 140 747 all-cargo planes in use. Some had been ordered new, others were converted passenger models. In 2000, Boeing delivered 25 new 747-400s, and 15 of these were freighters. In 2001, Boeing announced the freighter version of a longer-range 747-400 passenger plane; the freighter could carry an additional 35,000 pounds of freight or fuel (and that weight of fuel would extend the freighter's range by 600 miles).[12] Airbus was also announcing plans for larger models.

Not all cargo is flown on jets. The Hercules, a Lockheed-built freighter powered by four turboprop engines, is widely used in many charter operations, and some versions are used by the military. The plane can carry about 25 tons and flies at 325 mph. It can operate in and out of rougher airstrips than can most airline-type aircraft. Other propeller-driven freighters can be spotted throughout the world. Most of these planes were converted from passenger configurations. Figure 7–2 shows a twin-engine propeller freighter used by Merlin Express to carry cargo in the U.S., Canada, and Mexico.

Another propeller-powered transport, based on a modified Boeing Stratocruiser (an airliner of the late 1940s) was nicknamed the Super Guppy. The modifications to a handful of Stratocruisers took place in the early 1970s. The craft was given a much larger freight compartment and looked as though the fuselage was

---

[10]John G. Borger, "Transport Aircraft—progress and problems," *Exxon Air World,* 1984, no. 2, p. 22.

[11]*Air Transport World,* Nov. 1986, p. 49.

[12]*Shipping Digest,* May 14, 2001, p. 8.

Figure 7–2 Propeller-driven freighter. (Courtesy of Merlin Express, a Fairchild Aircraft Company.)

bloated compared to the dimensions of the landing gear and wings. The Super Guppies were used in the construction of the European Airbus A300 jumbo-jet airline aircraft. Production of one A300 involved eight Super Guppy flights. The aircraft picked up wing boxes made by British Aerospace and flew them, two at a time, from Manchester to Bremen. There they were fitted with flaps, slats (made in Amsterdam), and internal systems. The Super Guppy then flew the wings, one at a time, to Toulouse. Fuselage sections and tail fins also moved in the Super Guppies.[13] More recently, the Super Guppies were replaced by a fleet of five similarly oddly-shaped jet-powered planes, using modified Airbus airframes. This plane model is called the "Beluga" because of its whale-like shape. The five planes are in almost constant motion between Airbus assembly plants in Spain, Germany, and the United Kingdom. (In the year 2001, as Airbus was planning for a larger aircraft seating over 500, one of their challenges was how to move its components since they are too large for the Beluga. "No one knows yet whether the Cargolifter, a new version of the zeppelin that has yet to prove its worth in practice, will be able to guarantee a just-in-time supply of components. At EADS in Hamburg, therefore, a very traditional method of transport

---

[13]*Exxon Air World,* No. 1 (1982), p. 12.

comes to mind: the Airbus yard is located directly on the river Elbe, which customarily carries oceangoing vessels."[14])

Air Cargo Containers

Today, nearly all air cargo is containerized, since the only way to load or unload a large aircraft is through use of containers. Air cargo containers are known as unit load devices (ULDs), and they have differing shapes, designed to take into account the plane's curved contours. Each airline uses only containers that fit into its own aircraft. Many air cargo containers are interchangeable between different models of aircraft. There are about 20 different sizes of containers and pallets. (Air cargo pallets are flat platforms, on which cartons are placed and held down by netting. There is also an auto-transport pallet that is flat but has tiedowns.) The largest air container is 8 x 8 x 20 feet, and it looks like the rail/truck/water container. However, its tare (empty) weight is much less, and it is engineered to higher standards because it is designed to be an integral part of the loaded aircraft. That container is used on the main deck of wide-bodied aircraft. The next smaller is half that size, 8 x 8 x 10 feet, also designed for the main deck on wide-body planes. There are igloo-shaped containers for main deck placement on smaller all-cargo jets, and lower-deck containers with one of the bottom corners tapered. Container placement on KLM planes is shown in Figure 7–3. Some air containers can be temperature-controlled, and there are containers that can be used for carrying livestock and race horses. Some containers have racks at the top for hanging garments. Northwest Airlines owns 500 garment containers and uses them to carry garments from the Caribbean and from Asia.

Air cargo containers are loaded and unloaded at airports or in container stations located off airport property. Forwarders, for example, load containers with their various clients' shipments and carry the loaded container directly to the side of outgoing aircraft, where it is expected. On the other end, the forwarder accepts the complete, closed container from the airline and takes it through customs and to his place of business, where it is further unpacked and the goods delivered to various consignees.

The Airline Industry

International air cargo, as it has evolved, is not a homogeneous industry. It consists of various segments: forwarders, couriers, integrated express services, and

---

[14]*Lufthansa Cargo's Planet,* 1/2001, p. 24. EADS stands for European Aeronautic Defense and Space Company.

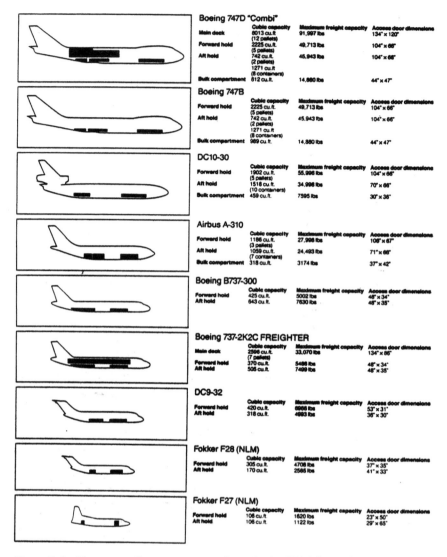

Figure 7–3 Placement of cargo space on planes in the KLM fleet. (Courtesy of KLM Royal Dutch Airlines.)

both scheduled and unscheduled airlines. The distinction between these sometimes clouds. Airlines offer small package services and forwarders own or operate their own aircraft. Scheduled airlines own charter airlines. There are many contracting and subcontracting operations in which a firm in one segment of the industry works closely with a firm in another segment. All sizes of aircraft are used. Carriers offer more than one level of service, meaning that the shipper has some choices as to how quickly the cargo will move and what additional services he is willing to pay for. The order of discussion here will be passenger-cargo airlines, all-cargo airlines, integrated air express services, couriers, air mail, and forwarders.

Passenger-Cargo Carriers

Direct air carriers are the "traditional" airlines, some dating back to 1920. Direct air carriers own or lease the aircraft they fly as well as ground equipment and facilities. Most of the world's airlines today are principally passenger carriers who sell excess belly capacity to cargo shippers and forwarders. The emphasis on the more lucrative passenger traffic has an implication for cargo shippers. During more heavily traveled seasons, holidays and so on, where passenger luggage, mail, and express packages take priority over cargo, it is common for air freight shipments to be "bumped," that is, left behind.

A few of the world's major airlines own all-freight aircraft, usually 747s, and these will be discussed in the next section. However, another form of 747 that is very popular on trans-ocean flights is a "combi" that has a movable bulkhead on the main deck. Passengers sit in front of the bulkhead, and cargo containers are placed aft. This allows the plane to adjust to varying balances of passengers and freight that occur because of seasons, and because of fluctuations in the value of the passengers' home currency that affects the flow of both passengers and freight. There is also an airplane with a cabin configuration that can be changed quickly (within an hour) from all-passenger to all-cargo. The removed seats are stored in a van and placed back into the plane when needed. During the 1970s, several U.S. airlines used these models, carrying passengers by day and cargo at night. In 1993 Lufthansa began using seven "quick-change" Boeing 737s on routes linking Frankfurt with nearby Sweden, Finland, and Denmark. These flights carried mainly forwarder traffic.[15]

In the 1990s alliances were formed between or among some of the world's major airlines. Most of the coordinating efforts have dealt with passenger service, code sharing, and scheduling, and dealing with ground handling and terminal operators. Very few efforts have been made in the air freight sector. However, in 2000, "Air France began selling all of Delta's belly space on its flights from its three French gateways—Paris, Nice and Lyon—to the United States."[16] The two airlines merged most of their cargo sales teams. "Alliances are the

---

[15]*The Journal of Commerce,* April 7, 1993, p. 3B.

[16]*JoCWeek,* October 23–29, 2000, p. 28.

major contributing factor influencing the trend for outsourcing the terminal and ground-handling operations. In the past, airlines had to maintain their own handling services or be forced to use the services offered by the national carrier at the destination they were serving. Nowadays airlines can outsource these activities to an alliance partner that has assumed the investment, on behalf of the alliance at a specific regional hub."[17] In mid-2001, another alliance that appeared to be moving aggressively into the air cargo markets consisted of Lufthansa, SAS, and Singapore Airlines.

All-cargo Carriers/Charter Cargo Flights

At the end of World War II, the U.S. Civil Aeronautics Board, which then regulated commercial aviation, allowed a category of all-freight airlines to be formed. Flying Tigers was the best-known U.S. firm, and there were also three others. They flew both domestically and internationally. For many years, the U.S. Department of Defense was their best customer.

In the 1970s, a number of U.S. passenger airlines operated all-cargo aircraft but—with one exception—they gradually disposed of them. One reason was that the new jumbo jets had so much belly cargo capacity that they could meet the needs of most markets. The problem was that passengers like to fly during the day, while shippers of freight like to have it move by night, so some large U.S. forwarders began operating their own all-freight aircraft. Foreign passenger/cargo airlines still fly all-cargo craft.. One of Lufthansa's all-cargo 747s is shown in Figure 7–4.

Charter flights involve an entire aircraft being leased or chartered, usually with a crew and fuel, for either a specific flight or time period. The Chicago convention in 1944 that established the rules for postwar civil aviation made no mention of charters. By 1956, European nations had met and developed an agreement concerning charters. Today, as nations agree to exchange additional aviation services, one provision might be that nation A will allow a specified number of charter flights between itself and nation B to be performed by a specified nation's charter airline aircraft. Chartering is cheaper than other forms of air cargo because there is less selling cost to airlines and, usually, the plane has a higher load factor when it takes off. Indeed, the user usually does not think of chartering unless her or his load will fill a plane.

Another regular use of all-cargo aircraft is for the movement of livestock.

---

[17]Efstathios Efstatiou and Niclas Anderson, "The Swedish Air Freight Industry," Master's Paper, School of Economics and Commercial Law, Gothenburg Univeristy, 2000, pp. 76–77.

Figure 7–4   Courtesy Lufthansa.

Journeys by sea are very difficult for many animals, and it takes some species months to recover. Moving by air reduces the trauma of travel and the recovery time that is needed. Usually special aircraft are employed. They have stalls to prevent shifting loads, and special protection against animals' hoofs penetrating the fuselage. For several days prior to the flight, the animals are fed a food mixture consisting of shifting amounts of food they have received and food that they will be getting in their new home. Some animals are sedated for their trips, and they are given small, increasing amounts of the sedative for several days before their trip so they do not have a major negative reaction to the sedative on the day of their travel. Most airlines insist that livestock receive a veterinarian's certificate that substantiates the vaccinations status of the animals and the tests required by the receiving country. The livestock are subject to inspection when they arrive at their destination.

Figure 7–5 shows an oversized mobile communications van being loaded aboard an all-cargo plane, the Antonov 124, that had originally been built for military use in the U.S.S.R. The Antonov 124's cargo-carrying dimensions is considerably larger than those of the 747. For example, the height of its open nose door is 4.4 meters, compared to 2.5 meters for the 747. There are about two

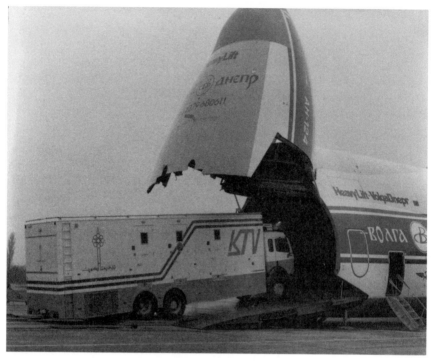

Figure 7–5   Courtesy HeavyLift Cargo Airlines.

dozen commercial Antonov 124s in the world; they are spread among three airlines.

Somewhat similar to the ocean vessel market, there is a surplus of used airline aircraft in storage that could, if the market picks up, be brought back into service. Many of these aircraft are stored in deserts in the southwestern United States. They could be brought back as passenger planes or as cargo carriers. It is more likely that they would be cargo carriers; that is a common second use for one-time passenger airliners. A 747-200 passenger plane can be converted to an all-cargo plane for $20 to $30 million, while a new 747-400F (freighter) costs about $150 million.[18]

Integrators

The fastest growing segment of the international air cargo industry is the integrators, once known as air express services.

---

[18]*JoCWeek* December 11–17, 2000, p. 20. The 747-400F has greater range and carrying capacity, and requires a crew of two, rather than three.

What is it that the integrators do? Why are they called integrators and not forwarders, since they do the same job as them? They are labeled as integrators because they offer other services than just plain consolidated airport-to-airport and some door-to-door transport service like the traditional forwarder does. They mainly operate in business-to-business markets and they specialize in offering door-to-door transport solutions. Value-adding services function as a complement to these door-to-door transport solutions making them more attractive to potential clients. Overall, the integrators are the service providers responsible for connecting all the markets around the globe.[19]

Over the years, the weight limitation, per parcel and consignment, have continued to rise so that to some destinations shipments of several hundred pounds can be moved competitively. Integrator services are fast becoming serious competitors to traditional freight forwarders and should be considered as part of the overall transportation system each exporter or importer designs for her or his company. FedEx, UPS, DHL, Airborne, and TNT (an Australian-based firm) are extending their high quality small package services to major European and Asian markets. All are well-known, and stress door-to-door deliveries. FedEx (then Federal Express) revolutionized the air express business in the U.S. UPS is a major carrier in the U.S. relying on rail, truck, and air to carry its shipments. In 2000 it also entered into an ocean container service that handles packages shipped from China to the U.S.[20] Figure 7–6 shows a UPS street poster displayed in Gothenberg.

The UPS International Air Service Guide is simple, comprehensive, and straightforward, and describes their services from the U.S. to over 175 countries. Early pages cover the services offered such as electronic tracking, collect services, customs clearance; packaging, labeling, documentation (the commercial invoice, the shipper's export declaration, the UPS pickup record, and the UPS waybill); and some notes on consolidations and pricing. Then, about one-half page is devoted to each nation to which a parcel can be shipped. Information for each includes a zone number (used for rates); estimated time in transit; area; service notes—mainly days of weeks when deliveries can or cannot be made; lists of articles commonly considered as documents (and probably exempt from customs); and prohibited materials. UPS also handles inbound shipments from about 100 of these countries and additional information is available concerning that service. This booklet does not contain rates; the user must consult a separate rate card.

---

[19]Efstathios Efstatiou and Niclas Anderson, "The Swedish Air Freight Industry," Master's Paper, School of Economics and Commercial Law, Gothenburg University, 2000, p. 109.

[20]*The Journal of Commerce,* January 18, 2000, p. 1.

Figure 7–6   A UPS sidewalk display photographed in Gothenburg, Sweden.

Currently, the air express companies charter small aircraft from Europe's commuter airlines to fly at night. In addition, they are contracting with European parcel services to provide the truck deliveries and pickups. Between 1989 and 1992, UPS acquired 16 firms in Europe, and has been expanding into the Pacific Rim, Latin American and Mexican markets as well. The firm expected "to lose more than one billion dollars before its international operations become profitable. . . , the company's chief executive said."[21] In 2000, UPS acquired Fritz Cos., a large, well-established international forwarder. In the 1990s, Federal Express, somewhat surprisingly, found itself overextended and had to withdraw from some European markets, contracting with others to continue its surface segment. In the late 1990s both the Dutch Post Office and the German Post Office

---

[21]*American Shipper,* January 1993, p. 26.

acquired some private carriers and expanded into the air express/integrator market. In 2001, UPS obtained rights to fly to China, where it will compete directly with FedEx, which has been in that market since 1995.

The most formidable potential competitor to the air express companies for document delivery are e-mail, FAX machines, or other EDI operations. (However, retail sales conducted electronically often generate business for the integrated carriers since the buyer wants fast delivery.)

These newly developing integrated overseas services deserve considerable credit for creating a more user-friendly environment for the first-time or occasional overseas shipper. They have simplified both the documentation process and coordination of document and shipment flow. They have knocked down some of the psychological barriers to world trade. They should be recognized as logistics partners. The integrators also specialize in offering third-party logistics services. Assistance by specialists for third-party logistics services enables a firm in a given industry to integrate its own distribution and procurement processes and thus realize tremendous savings in doing so. The statement of Brian Clancy, a principal of MergeGlobal Inc. that: "The express companies are highly efficient flying warehouses," best summarizes the role of the integrators.[22]

Couriers

Couriers, once restricted to documents, now carry cargo in limited quantities. Larger courier companies offer worldwide services to most if not all major international destinations. One thinks of couriers as flying on passenger planes, accompanying several bags of documents. As passengers, they and their baggage clear customs more quickly than conventional cargo. An ad for one New York-based courier appearing in a trade journal indicated that the courier provided overnight service to 75 foreign cities, including twice-daily service to Amsterdam, Frankfurt, Paris, and Zurich, and service three times a day to London. The integrated carrier services mentioned above have cut into the courier market.

Air Mail

Air-mail service is offered throughout the world by the postal services of all nations. The postal agencies contract with various international airlines to carry the mail. In nearly all instances the service is dependable and swift, and should be considered by firms shipping small parcels and messages.

---

[22]Efstathios Efstatiou and Niclas Anderson, "The Swedish Air Freight Industry," Master's Paper, School of Economics and Commercial Law, Gothenburg Univeristy, 2000, p. 109.

Forwarders

If direct airlines are the wholesalers of space, air freight forwarders are the retailers. They are indirect air carriers. Forwarders function as consolidators of smaller shipments tendered to the airlines in volume lots under the forwarder's name as shipper. The difference between the volume or contract rate offered by the airline to the forwarder and the forwarder's own tariff rate to the shipper is the forwarder's gross yield on the shipment. From that yield must come all the forwarder's handling, administrative, and sales costs. Forwarders offer specialized services for certain markets. Here is a list of a Philippine forwarder's charges for export shipments, 1996, in U.S. dollars.

Airway bill fees:	$30 per house airway bill
Documentation:	
Garments/handicraft	$25 per house airway bill
Integrated circuit boards	$10 per house airway bill
Live or perishable shipments	$15 per house airway bill
Handling:	
Flat packs (minimum)	$10 per house airway bill
100k & above	$20 per house airway bill
Garments on hangers per airline container	
LD3	$30 per house airway bill
LD7	$50 per house airway bill
Cartage	
Within Metro Manila:	$20 per house airway bill
Flat pack	0.04 per kilo
Garments on hanger per airline container	
LD3	$75
LD7	$100

Higher cartage rates were cited for areas beyond metropolitan Manila.[23]

Currently, forwarders feel threatened by the expansion of the integrated services. The integrated service firms offer a high quality of service and are relatively easy to use from the standpoint of the shipper. Forwarders can, however, handle larger size shipments than most integrators.

Rate Making and Rates

The air freight industry equivalent to ocean liner conferences is IATA, which is controlled by the scheduled airlines. At one time, IATA set rates, and U.S. car-

---

[23]*American Shipper,* February, 1997, p. 70.

riers, which were very efficient, had considerable influence. IATA had an enforcement branch, but cheating (discounting) was a problem that could not be controlled. For example, Arab air carriers complained of problems "caused by operators which land at Gulf airports en route between Europe and the Far East. For them any revenue they can collect from fill-up traffic is a welcome addition with the result that many are not too fussy about charging the official passenger fare or cargo rate."[24] As a rate-making and policing body today, IATA has ceased to function effectively. In recent years, one sees no references to IATA's role in setting air freight rates. Currently, there are limited on-line auctions of unused air cargo capacity being conducted on websites.

IATA convenes meetings of participating airlines periodically to discuss rates and attempt to agree on practices, such as air waybill formats. IATA continues to serve as a airline trade association promulgating industry rules and coordinating policy on, for example, forwarder commissions, development of computer/EDI links with customs, and regulations on the transport of live animals. IATA also functions as a clearinghouse through which airlines reimburse each other for interline tickets and cargo charges. The clearinghouse has been self-supporting because of interest on float of funds.

Airline rates can be grouped in several categories. The first are the traditional tariff rates that one finds in printed booklets. The cargo is classified by general description, and then the rates are given between two specific points. Rates are expressed in cents per pound (or in some other currency per kilo) and are less per pound for larger shipments. Here are some rates charged by Air Jamaica for movements from Toronto to Kingston, expressed in Canadian cents.

Minimum Weight

Commodity described	Minimum charge	1	100	220	440	880	1100	2200	4400
		rate in cents per lb.							
Foodstuffs, spices, & beverages	40.60	156	119	119	119	119	104	104	104
Textiles	—					54	49	49	
Shoes	—					47	47	47[25]	

Note that for shoes and textiles, one would need to be shipping 1,100 pounds or over to use these rates. The vast majority of rates in the tariff booklet applied to

---

[24]*Air Transport World*, March, 1985, p. 65.

[25]*Shipper's Air Tariff, January 1988* (Miami: CRS Publishing, 1988), p. 54.

"general commodities" only, meaning that it made no difference what commodity was shipped. Tariff rates are not restricted to specific shippers.

A second form of air cargo rate, not shipper-specific, is for shipments in containers or unit load devices (ULDs). The same tariff document gave these rates for general commodities in a certain style of container moving from New York City to Buenos Aires on Lan-Chile Airlines: $6,000 with a pivotal weight of 4,409 lbs, with additional weight being charged at the rate of 60 cents per pound.[26]

The third category of rates are contract rates negotiated between airlines and forwarders or shippers or between forwarders and shippers. Often, they are expressed as a price per kilo or per kilo depending on volume:

Weight in kilos	Rate per kilo
1–49	$6.00 (Minimum Charge=$50)
50–99	4.00
100–499	3.60
500–999	3.00
1,000–4,999	2.45
5,000–9,999	1.90

In the foregoing example the airline offers a rate of $2.45 per kilo for shipments of 1,000 kilos. If the forwarder can consolidate 10 shipments averaging 100 kilos each, he qualifies for the 1,000 kilo rate (10 x 100). At 1,000 kilos the forwarder buys space at $2.45. The original shipper would pay the 100 kilo rate ($3.60) if he went directly to the airline. The forwarder therefore has a $1.15 per kilo spread to play with. Since he has to be more competitive than the airline he may offer a rate of $2.90 to the shipper. At $2.90 the shipper saves $.70 per kilo ($3.60 − $2.90) and the forwarder earns $.45 per kilo ($2.90 − $2.45). The forwarder may also offer some additional services, such as cargo pick-up. In the late 1980s, Air France and Lufthansa began to insist that the cargo waybill show "the cargo rate actually paid and the commission (normally 5 percent) charged by the forwarder. In this way, the forwarder could not exact a large middleman's profit . . . without the shipper becoming aware of it."[27]

To some destinations the forwarder may have insufficient volume to amass larger shipments. The forwarder will then team up with another forwarder and co-load to the destination. One of the two becomes the shipper, or *master co-*

---

[26]*Shipper's Air Tariff, January 1988* (Miami: CRS Publishing, 1988), p. 112.

[27]Rigas Doganis, *Flying Off Course: The Economics of International Airlines,* 2d. ed., (London: Harper Collins, 1991), p. 330.

loader. National forwarders with many offices and terminals around the country face a classic linear programming problem every day. Should consolidated shipments be sent directly from the origin terminal to the destination airport, or should they be sent to a central (gateway) terminal for consolidation with other freight destined to the same airport? National forwarding companies and airlines typically use "hubs," like the hub and spokes of a wheel, to gather freight for on-forwarding to destination airports.

Contract rates, and flat rates for a minimum commitment of volume, are not available to all destinations, particularly more remote destinations. Volume discounts for unitized cargo moving on airline pallets are not available to all areas either. Indeed, to some markets there is insufficient traffic to even enable a spread in rates, as in the example above. In these cases consolidation operations simply do not pay.

Forwarders, who are IATA agents, still handle shipments to these places as commission agents of the airlines, not as indirect air carriers. They function in the same way as travel agents and are paid commissions by the airlines to attract traffic and to reimburse the forwarder for her or his work in connection with the shipment. When a forwarder acts as consolidator of shipments, as an indirect air carrier, he issues his own air waybill and assumes the risks of loss and damage. When he acts as an IATA agent the air waybill is issued on behalf of the airline on the airline's form. The airline assumes all the risk of transportation liability. As a forwarder the company charges what it wants. As an agent it charges the airline price for transportation.

In some markets air cargo rates charged by air carriers are controlled by the host government. The Japanese Civil Aeronautics Board, for example, regulates airline rates. They do not regulate forwarder rates. Thus, generally speaking, the air freight forwarding industry is economically deregulated. The shipper and forwarder can negotiate whatever rates are mutually beneficial.

Rates are not the only consideration, of course, when selecting an air cargo carrier. Service is more important. One must also take into account: frequency of consolidation to the places one ships; arrangements at destination (does the forwarder own or control the deconsolidator, and is it a good one?); customer service in answering questions and providing information; tracing; and expertise and consistent quality in the preparation of documentation. The exporter/importer needs to take care to assure himself that the forwarder he selects is capable of providing these services in addition to providing competitive pricing. Specifically, the exporter/importer should satisfy himself that the forwarder is an international specialist and not moving international freight as a sideline.

The chargeable weight of air cargo transportation is based on the weight of the cargo, except that bulky cargo is assessed on a cubic basis. To determine chargeable weight, one multiplies the dimensions of the cargo (in inches) and then divides by 166 to get a number that is a weight equivalent for assessing carrier charges. Hence, if one had a package that was 24" x 36" x 48", multiplying the three yields 41,472; dividing by 166 (41472/166) gives an answer of 250. The airline would then charge for the actual weight of the shipment, or for 250 pounds, whichever yielded the higher charge. This is called *DIM* or *dimensional* weight. Some airlines use 194 rather than 166 as the value.

This is important to keep in mind. One of this book's authors was once asked to see whether freight expense could be reduced. On visiting, he found that one size box was being used regardless of how much was being shipped in the box. Most of the time boxes were half empty, stuffed with cushioning peanuts. He commented that this practice may have simplified the empty box inventory control process, but it cost a great deal in freight. Another way of looking at the 166 value is that airlines want cargo to be packed to a density of at least 10.4 pounds per cubic foot. Hence product and package designers should take this into account. (To give some ideas of densities, here are a few in pounds per cubic foot: cigarettes, 19; cotton gloves, 16; gasoline engines and parts, 28; handbags, 9; magazines, 37; spark plugs, 56; tires, 10; and toothbrushes, 14.)

The reason that airlines desire this density is because carriers can earn the highest revenues if they operate at both their maximum weight and cubic capacity. Most all-cargo planes have about the same ratios between weight and cubic capacity. A Super Hercules can carry 50,000 pounds and has a capacity of 4,500 cubic feet (with palletized cargo); a DC-8-73F can carry about 95,000 pounds and has a capacity of 9,500 cubic feet; and a 747-200C can carry about 220,000 pounds in 25,500 cubic feet. Using the numbers just given, the pounds-per-cubic-foot ratios for the three planes are 11.1, 10, and 8.6, respectively. Airlines also want the proper density, that is, one that fully utilizes the aircraft's cubic capacity and lifting ability. Obtaining the proper density of cargo is important, but difficult for the airline to achieve for each flight, as one can not stockpile freight in order to get the best density. "By the selection of loads and by the creation of stockpiles whereby an easing of the variation in load density can be achieved, it may be possible to approach close to average cargo density. Clearly, however, there are strict limits to the possibility of achieving this on civil or on military aircraft, bearing in mind the significance of high-speed delivery in the promotion of air service."[28]

For air cargo shipments in containers, or on pallets, only the net weight of the

---

[28]Alan H. Stratford, *Air Transport Economics in the Supersonic Era*, (New York: St. Martin's, 1967), p. 182.

shipment is subject to freight charges. This is an inducement to shippers to use airline containers.

Air Cargo Documentation and Insurance

Because air traffic moves so much quicker than sea shipments, documents (invoices, packing lists, and so on), are typically attached to the consignee's copy of the air waybill set. The documents travel with the cargo unless banking is involved. Thus documents arrive at the same time as the freight. To further expedite the clearance process, goods are often consigned directly to the customer's customs house broker. The plane arrives, the broker is contacted, he picks up the documents and arranges clearance. Within the industry, there is a major move toward "going paperless." This would include dealings with customs, with customers, and with connecting airlines. IATA has a goal of eliminating paper air waybills by June 30, 2002.[29]

There are no negotiable air waybills. All air waybills are straight consignments. Someone must be shown as consignee. Airports simply do not have the physical room to accommodate traffic waiting for bank releases. If terms are documents against payment, the shipper should consign goods directly to a bank.

When cargo travels in consolidation, tracing is facilitated by having not only the master air waybill number but also the house air waybill. The *master air waybill* is that issued to the forwarder as the shipper. It is the only number the airline has knowledge of. The forwarder issues individual house bills to cover each individual consignment within the consolidation covered by the master air waybill.

Not all air traffic moves on a direct basis. Earlier mention was made of hubs. Hubs are not just at origin. They are used at destination as well. Moreover, the transport onward from the destination hub may not be by air cargo. A shipment to Paris may actually land at Amsterdam and be trucked by the airline, at its expense and in its own or contracted equipment, to Paris for clearance. A shipment to Hong Kong may be sent to Tokyo for transshipment, by air, to Hong Kong. Transshipments are necessary and common to maximize equipment utilization on the longest leg of the journey (line haul). While this may appear to delay shipments or extend transit time, as it may, waiting for a direct flight may take longer or cost more. This is true of traffic in consolidation as well. A large forwarder may have five or six reserved pallet positions on every flight to a particular destination. If all available space is pre-assigned to forwarders, direct IATA shipments may have to wait for space before they can move.

---

[29] *JoCWeek,* February 26–March 4, 2001, p. 28.

Beginning in 1994, the Federal Aviation Administration required air freight forwarders to certify that all their shipper customers have in place security programs that meet FAA standards. "Forwarders also will be required to sign security certification documents for all shipments. In the case of customers who ship regularly, a single document may be filed once a year."[30] The intent of the regulations, in part, is to shift some of the responsibility for security back closer to the sources of the cargo.

Nearly all shipments moving internationally must be insured, and air cargo is no exception. Terms of sale determine at which point the responsibility for insurance coverage passes from the seller to the buyer. Sometimes the seller's firm or the buyer's firm has a blanket policy that covers owned goods at any site or while in transit. If not, one must determine that the shipment is adequately covered. Airlines provide protection against losses that are their own fault but only up to a certain amount of coverage, usually $9.07 per pound. If shipments are worth more than that, then an additional fee is charged, usually ranging between ten cents to a dollar for each additional $100 in value. Note that this is not considered complete coverage. One usually purchases insurance to protect against theft, loss, breakage, and so on. One may also desire additional coverage against acts of governments, war, and of terrorism and hijacking. Rates for this coverage depends upon areas of the world involved. Sometimes these rates change hourly.

Lufthansa offers cargo insurance for its customers and divides the world into insurance zones. Zone 1 is Europe; Zone 2 is Canada and the United States; Zone 3 is all other America; Zone 4 is Asia, Russia, and Oceania; Zone 5 is Africa and the Near East; and Zone 6 is Australia/New Zealand. A table of six rows and six columns is then used to display relative rates. Shipments with Zone 1 cost the least to insure; shipments between Zones 4 and 5 cost three times as much.

Air Cargo Growth

Air cargo has shown phenomenal growth. One issue is what the source of future traffic will be. Air cargo transport has proven to be a realistic option, especially for higher-valued commodities and those particularly subject to damage. Of course, some cargoes only move by air cargo, such as jewels, artwork, currency, perishable foods, and short-lived commodities such as radioactive isotopes and biological materials. Hence, part of the air cargo marketing strategy will be to increase the percentage carried in those higher-value weight categories. Note that

---

[30]*American Shipper,* January, 1994, p. 48.

as an exporter, the United States is moving toward being a service supplier, rather than a product supplier; hence many of its future exports will be in the form of documents, many of which will be transmitted electronically.

Most of this traffic is not created; much is taken from vessel lines. In about 1990, at the Port of New York, the value of exports and imports moving by air became greater than the value of exports and imports moving by water. Airports handled over half the value but less than two percent of the tonnage. Large aircraft are very productive; a 747 carrying 100 tons at 515 miles per hour produces 51,500 ton-miles per hour; an ocean vessel carrying 15,000 tons moving at 18 miles per hour produces 270,000 ton-miles per hour. The gap between the two is closing. Not shown in ton-mile figures is the fact that the air cargo pays a much higher rate than ocean cargo, so while the tonnage losses of the air carriers may be negligible, the revenue losses are not. A matter of further concern to ocean vessel operators is that the new integrator air express services, which are going to great efforts to make export/import efforts easy for first-time shippers, are creating a new generation of shippers who probably think that the only way for freight to cross an ocean is by airplane.

Chapter 2 mentioned international restrictions placed on aviation in terms of nations having to agree on exchanges of airline routes and services. These practices have restricted the growth of air cargo in some markets, especially the movements of all-cargo craft. Each nation has its own priority when it comes to assessing the relative values of moving persons and moving cargo. Each nation's airline industry is also split on this issue, with all-cargo carriers viewing matters differently from those carriers who handle both passengers and freight. Patterns of use differ; about 90 percent of passenger movements are back-and-forth, while many cargo moves are in one direction only.

Air cargo is expected to continue to grow. Boeing projects air cargo growth in the period 1999–2019 to be at the rate of 6.4 percent per year. Growth in the intra-Asia market is expected to be the highest, followed by these markets: North America-Asia, Europe-Asia, North America-Europe, and North America-Latin America. Growth in these markets is expected to be above the 6.4 percent average. Below average growth is expected in these markets (in descending order): intra-Europe, Europe-Middle East, Europe-Africa, Europe-Latin America, and North America.[31] Boeing also predicts that the worldwide fleet of air cargo aircraft will increase from 1,742 in 2000 to 3,523 by 2020. Most of the additions to the fleet will be wide-body aircraft.[32] In a separate, and slightly lower

---

[31]International Air Cargo Association website, July 9, 2001.

[32]*JoCShipping Digest,* August 20, 2001, p. 13.

forecast, Airbus Industrie also divided the growth into belly cargo and cargo carried on all-cargo planes. They projected belly freight to grow at the approximate rate of 5.7 percent and cargo on all-cargo planes to grow at about 6.1 percent per year.[33]

Summary

On smaller shipments it is important for the shipper to consider the total cost of transportation before making a routing decisions. Trucking from an interior point to an airport, pier charges, forwarding, freight, insurance, customs clearance, and delivery all need to be compared to the costs associated with direct air freight from the nearest airport. International air cargo is much faster than shipments by ocean carrier. This speed results in fewer carrying costs for the owner of the goods. Also, the journey by air usually requires less packaging, resulting in additional savings. Even if if the cost is not lower, the movement by air is often considered to be more hassle free.

Aviation has developed during this century, with air freight achieving importance after World War II. Service is provided by a variety of carriers, who often contract and subcontract amongst themselves. The majority of freight is carried aboard passenger airlines on passenger flights. There are also all-cargo aircraft flown by passenger airlines; all-cargo airlines; charter airlines; and air express services. Air freight forwarders play an important role in moving air freight. Most air cargo moves in containers that are shaped to fit inside aircrafts' curved fuselages.

The International Air Transport Association (IATA) is a cartel made up of all international airlines. At times, it established both passenger fares and cargo rates. At present, its rate-setting ability is not very strong, and most rates are negotiated between shippers and carriers.

In the past decade, several well-known U.S. air express services, also known as integrators, have expanded their markets overseas. This has been perceived as a threat by the traditional partnership of established airlines and air freight forwarders.

End-of-Chapter Questions

1. What is the relationship between airlines' carriage of passengers and carriage of freight?

2. What were some of the influences of World War II on the development of the international airline industry?

---

[33]*American Shipper,* October, 2000, p. 13. By the year 2017, the amounts carried as belly freight and on dedicated all cargo planes were expected to be equal.

3. With regard to the Emery-SRI report, list three different situations where air freight was likely to be used.

4. Discuss the importance of the Boeing 747 to the international air cargo industry.

5. What are some other large air freighters (besides the 747)?

6. Why are air cargo containers used?

7. What are international airline "alliances?"

8. When are "charter" cargo flights used?

9. What are air express "integrators?"

10. What are air freight forwarders? What functions to they perform?

CASE • *Burt & Gert's Forwarding Co.*

Gert and Burt own and operate a small international air freight forwarding company. They have been married five years, and Gert wishes to cut down on her work hours so they can start raising a family. Both Gert and Burt can perform just about any operation in the forwarding firm, so the time saving for either one can become more time for Gert to spend at home. (Burt and Gert can also share the tasks of child care, a point they are negotiating as this case is being written.)

Their biggest problem at the terminal is loading outbound containers in the evenings. There are delays in either the paperwork or the freight, and outbound trucks carrying the loaded containers cannot leave without both. Drivers and terminal workers often stand around while Gert or Burt supervises the paperwork.

While attending George Mason University, both Burt and Gert had studied (or at least heard of) PERT. *PERT* (Project Evaluation and Review Technique) involves looking at related tasks and taking into account which ones have to be completed before others can start and which can be completed with little or no dependence on the completion of others. At any point, work can be done on one or more, but usually not on all, of the tasks. The tasks are diagrammed in sequential order; those that must be completed first are on the left. The time necessary for completing each is indicated. The various paths leading from tasks that must be completed to tasks that can then be started are drawn, from the start of the first task to the completion of the last task. Several paths are drawn, one through each sequential linking of tasks, with time values calculated for each path. The path that takes the longest is called the critical path, because it is this path that controls the total time necessary for project completion. If one wishes to speed up a project, improvements must be made along this path.

Here's an example of PERT. Assume that Gert or Burt wants to bake an apple pie. Six tasks are listed here, along with the time it takes to accomplish them in minutes (in parentheses):

A. Buy ingredients. (15)

B. Drive home. (12)

C. Prepare crust and place in pie tin. (10)

D. Peel and slice apples. (20)

E. Place apples in pan. (3)

F. Bake in oven. (60)

The six tasks must be done in sequence, with one exception: Tasks C and D can be done at the same time if, say, Burt helps Gert (or Gert helps Burt) with one or the other. Here's how a PERT chart would look:

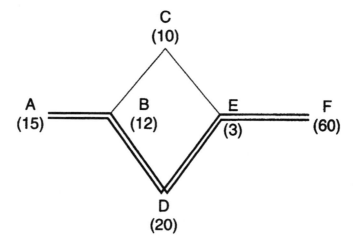

The critical path (A-B-D-E-F) is indicated with a double line; its value is 110 minutes. If Burt and Gert want to speed up their pie-making process, improvements must be made along this line. Speeding up Task C is of no help. Note that if one helps the other, he or she can make the crust (C) and then help with the apples (D). If he or she spends five minutes helping with the apples, the total time for D would be cut to 15 minutes, and this would shave 5 minutes off the critical path and the overall time necessary to complete the pie.

If one refused to help and Tasks C and D both required the other's entire efforts, then they might have a sequential relationship or might be grouped into a single Task C, involving the preparation of both pie filling and crust, lasting 30 minutes. It would then take 120 minutes to make the pie.

Now, looking at the situation in their terminal, Burt and Gert have constructed Case Table 1. On the left are listed the tasks. In the center is the time necessary to complete each task. On the right is the indication of which tasks must be completed before others are begun.

Case Table 1

Task	Time to completion (in minutes)	Precedence relationship: task on right of < can't start until task on left of < is completed
A. Receive incoming freight accompanied by some documents	30	A < B, C
B. Match paperwork with documentation that has already been prepared	20	B < D, E
C. Match freight to outgoing containers	10	C < F
D. Assign workers to loading containers	10	D < E
E. Load containers	40	E < F
F. Prepare and verify manifests listing cargo in each container	20	F < G
G. Seal containers	10	G < H
H. Give documents to truck drivers	10	H < I
I. Trucks depart	10	

Questions for *Burt & Gert's Forwarding Co.*

1. Arrange these tasks into a PERT chart. What is the shortest amount of time it will take to accomplish the evening's work in the terminal?

2. How necessary is computer software, which would reduce the time it takes to perform Task C from ten to five minutes? Why?

3. How necessary is a cargo conveyor system, which would reduce the time it takes to perform Task E from 40 to 20 minutes? Why?

4. Assume that labor can be reassigned within the terminal. From which tasks would you take workers and to which new tasks would you assign them? Why?

5. Additional forklift trucks will speed up Tasks A and E. To which should they be purchased and assigned? Why?

6. Unfortunately for Burt and Gert, their operation is a target of union organization. The union wants two job classifications within the terminal: clerks for handling paperwork only (tasks B, C, & F) and freight handlers for moving cargo only (tasks E & G). Should Burt and Gert resist this move? Why?

8

Surface Transport to and from Ports, and to and from Canada and Mexico

Introduction

The first and last stages of import and export movements involve the transportation of the goods between inland points and ports of import or export. For bulk products, the loading/unloading facility may be located at water's edge in a port. However, for most shipments, arrangements must be made to haul the goods to or from port, usually by truck or by rail. Intermodal transportation has become more important for international movements. There are myriad definitions of intermodal. For purposes of this book, *intermodal transportation* will refer to a shipment within "a container or other device which can be transferred from one vehicle or mode to another without the contents of said device being reloaded or disturbed."[1] Also, the shipment usually travels on a single, door-to-door bill-of-lading. While intermodal can mean any two modes, for international movements one tends to think of containers transferred between ship and rail, and moved by truck between the railroad's intermodal ramp and the shipper or consignee. Nearly all air cargo movements are intermodal, in the sense that truck and air are the two modes involved.

This chapter will cover movement by land between inland points and ports, intermodal movements, and movements by land to and from Canada and Mexico. Some of the intermodal discussion will include domestic movements; however, the technology is the same for either domestic or international moves, and railroad container trains carry both domestic and international shipments.

---

[1] Barton Jennings and Mary Collins Holcomb, "Beyond Containerization: The Broader Concept of Intermodalism," *Transportation Journal*, Spring 1996, pp. 5–13.

Intermodal land–sea operations developed initially on domestic shipping routes of U.S. ocean carriers, that is, trade between the U.S. mainland and Hawaii or Puerto Rico. Ocean liner conferences, which controlled international traffic, were less receptive to the container innovation.

Movements to and from Ports

Choice of port is discussed a number of times in this book. Usually the choice depends upon a combination of port facilities and services offered by railroads and vessel operators. At a time when there was more structure in railroad rates, rails offered export and import rates that were lower than rates for comparable domestic movements. The rationale for these lower rates was either that of marginal cost pricing or an understanding that export/import traffic was more sensitive to transportation costs. In order to qualify for the lower export/import rate, the shipper needed to attach a copy of the shipment's ocean bill of lading.

Today, in the United States, railroads have great influence on the choice of port used. Indeed, the shipper may not make the choice at all; the loaded containers are tendered to the railroad and the railroad sends them to a port where it makes connections with an ocean carrier. (At one time the shipper had several railroads to choose from; because of rail mergers, that no longer holds.) Sometimes, rather than going directly to a seaport, the railroad will deliver the containers to an inland consolidation point where they wait until it is time for them to be taken to the seaport for immediate loading. Inland consolidation points are needed because sufficient land needed for a container facility cannot be found in the seaport.

Traditionally, most inland movements to and from port were by rail, with trucks used for only short distances—say, under one or two hundred miles. An exception was export shipments out of California, which might be carried by truck for distances over 1,000 miles. The reason was that the truckers wanted to come to California so they could pick up desirable hauls of agricultural produce moving from California into the Midwest. That pattern holds today. However, nationwide, it is believed that railroads' share of container traffic connecting with ocean vessels is increasing. One reason is that many heavily loaded containers weigh too much to be hauled legally on public highways.

When a shipper or forwarder books cargo on a vessel he is informed when and where to tender the cargo or loaded container to the vessel operator. If the shipper is relatively close to the port facility, the load is drayed (a term for local trucking) or moved by rail. Hazardous cargoes must sometimes be delivered to the vessel operator earlier since their processing involves additional paperwork and load planning.

In almost all instances cargo does not move directly from the rail or truck aboard ship. Instead, it arrives early and waits. If it is loose, break-bulk cargo, it is stored in a transit shed (a warehouse next to the dock). If it is in containers, the containers are stacked in a yard near to where the vessel will moor. Many general cargo docks still have conventional rail tracks along their edges. Sometimes rail flatcars are spotted (placed) there and oversized or very heavy cargo moved directly between the vessel and the rail car. In port areas, barges are sometimes used to carry the cargo between the shipper/consignee and the ocean vessel. The barge ties up next to the ocean vessel on the side away from land and either the ship's tackle or a floating crane is used to transfer the cargo. This process, known as lightering, is often used for oversized cargo. Figure 8–1 shows a pleasure craft being lightered from a barge to an oceangoing ship.

For imports, the movements described in the past two paragraphs are reversed with one important distinction: the goods must move through customs and sometimes other forms of inspection. Once cleared, they may be sent by truck or rail to the consignee. (To avoid these delays, one large West Coast auto assembly plant has established a foreign trade zone adjacent to its plant, about 30 miles from port, which it pays to staff with customs inspectors. Containers move di-

Figure 8–1 A pleasure craft being lightered from a barge to an oceangoing ship. Courtesy Nordana Line.

rectly from the ship to truck/trailer chassis and move "in bond" to the plant's for-eign trade zone, where they are presented to customs for clearance. The order in which they are presented to customs is determined by how quickly each con-tainer's contents are needed on the assembly line.)

The discussion to this point has emphasized movements of intermodal con-tainerized traffic, which shall be discussed in more detail shortly. Rail is often used and one picks the port where the combined rail and vessel charter charges, and port-handling costs are minimized. Sometimes ports will be avoided because of labor problems.

Intermodalism

The term *intermodalism* is nearly synonymous with *containerization,* with the container holding the cargo that is exchanged between modes. For international movements, we consider intermodal transportation to be the carriage of goods by more than one mode of transportation under a "through" bill-of-lading.

From the shipper's standpoint, an additional advantage of containerization, made possible by the fact that cargo is loaded in boxes, is that containers need not be loaded within the port area. Indeed, they can be loaded anywhere reach-able by truck or rail. This proved to be even more momentous to shippers than the efficiencies containerization enabled in terms of working the vessel. Cargo can be loaded in Cleveland in a 40-foot container, trucked to a railroad ramp, piggybacked on a flatcar to Baltimore, drayed to an awaiting container ship in the port of Baltimore, carried by vessel to Rotterdam, moved by truck to a ferry, carried across the English Channel up to Dublin, then finally drayed to a con-signee's door in Ireland. All this is done without the cargo within the container being unloaded or rehandled. As can be seen from this example, a number of dif-ferent carriers are involved in a single intermodal move. Through transportation arrangements involve a single intermodal bill-of-lading and both the shipper and consignee are relieved of the burden of making the various interconnecting arrangements that would otherwise be necessary. The advantages to this kind of transportation to the user are obvious: simplicity, less paperwork, reduced dam-age because of fewer handlings, and greatly reduced pilferage owing to reduced exposure of merchandise.

Intermodal Equipment

We can look at intermodal transportation in a number of ways. One is by type of equipment, containers, vehicles of different modes for carrying them, and equipment used to transfer them between modes.

The vast majority of containers are 20 feet long, eight feet high, and eight feet wide, and the term "TEU" (20-foot equivalent) is a measure of cargo that would fill such a container. Surface containers that can move by sea, rail, or truck are 10, 20, 28, 35, 40, 48, or 53 feet long. For a time, it appeared that containers would become higher (9.5 feet), which vessel operators would prefer, because a container ship could be loaded or unloaded in fewer moves. However, with the advent of double-stack container trains in the mid-1980s, the 8.5 feet height limit became more necessary because railroad tunnels in the United States could not accommodate double-stacked trains carrying higher containers. The truck trailer on permanent wheels can also be considered a form of container. (Within domestic U.S. markets, a wider container is used to take advantage of an increase in allowable widths for highway vehicles. In Western Europe a "swap body" is used; it is transferable between truck and rail but cannot be stacked.)

Air cargo containers have differing shapes, and they are designed after taking into account the plane's curved interior contours. Most air cargo containers are interchangeable among several types of aircraft. There are about 20 different sizes of air cargo containers and pallets. Some are loaded and unloaded away from the airport property at a forwarder's place of business. The forwarder gives loaded containers to the airline. For unloading imports, the containers are usually unloaded at the airport, where they are subjected to customs inspection. The goods are then picked up by the customshouse broker and delivered to the consignee.

There are floating containers, LASH, and Seabee barges that are guided by tugboats between shoreside facilities and the "mother" ship that is moored off shore. Conventional surface containers also move by barge on inland river systems.

Figure 8–2 shows a worker building up a load inside a container. In terms of sizes of containers, 20-foot containers represent the largest number. Most are constructed of steel or aluminum and are general purpose in that they can carry almost any type of packaged freight. Figure 8–3 shows the closed doors at the end of a container. Many of the world's containers have been built (and repaired) in Korea and Taiwan. More recently, the majority of new container construction has been occurring in China. There are also many specialized intermodal surface containers that carry tanks for holding liquids, gases, new automobiles, or insulated or refrigerated cargo.

As for vehicles, there are the truck tractor and the trailer chassis. Railroads have flatcars and double-stack cars for containers and flatcar and skeleton-frame cars ("spine cars") for piggyback. Aircraft have both belly and main decks for cargo. There are LASH, container, and Ro/Ro vessels. In Western Europe, there are many barges operating on inland waterways for carrying containers. Brus-

Figure 8–2 A worker building up a load inside a container. Courtesy Superior Packing Inc./HAL, Inc.

sels, for example, has barge service for container movements to and from northeast France, Netherlands, and Germany. In nations such as the Philippines, containers are ferried to and from outlying islands by barge or other small vessels.

There are interchange agreements covering the exchange of containers and chassis between connecting carriers. They deal with maintaining the equipment's quality, handling damages, determining charges for equipment use, amounts of "free time" before charges become applicable, and so on. It is very important to have interchange agreements in effect in order to ensure the continuous functioning of a massive interchange system at a near error-free level.

In container yards, containers were originally handled by port heavy-lift equipment, though now special cranes are used. They are also moved by straddle cranes and side-lift loaders, especially off and on to railcars. Truck tractors are used to carry containers on semi-trailer chassis, both on highways and around container yards near ports. Some third-generation container yards have conveyor systems for handling blocks of containers. There is sophisticated equipment for carrying and loading/unloading aircraft containers on to and off planes. All-cargo aircraft also have devices for moving the containers and pallets inside the aircraft.

Containerships were mentioned in an earlier chapter. Demand for new

Figure 8–3   Closed doors at the end of a container. Courtesy of Superior Packing Inc./HAL Inc.

containerships of all sizes continues to be high. By way of example, in January 2001, there were 27 new containerships delivered worldwide. Half of them, in terms of capacity, were intended for use in the Europe-Asia market. Here is a listing of the TEU capacity of the 27 new ships, in descending order: 6,788, 6,600, 5,551, 4,038 (3 ships); 2,476, 2,078, 1,875, 1,740, 1,728, 1,644, 1,618, 1,432, 1,078, 901, 706, 640, 590, 519, 509, 426, 401, 330, 264, and 213.[2]

---

[2]*Containerization International,* March 2001, p. 27.

Development of Intermodal Traffic

Between World Wars I and II there was experimentation with land containers that could be transferred between flatbed trucks and rail flatcars. A few U.S. railroads also carried truck trailers on flatcars. In the 1950s, the U.S. military used 8 x 8 x 10 foot containers for household goods of military personnel. In the late 1950s, containers were introduced to some U.S. domestic movements. The first recorded movement was on April 27, 1956, when Malcolm McLean's ship the *Ideal X* loaded 58 truck trailers lashed to the deck on a New York-to-Houston voyage. In 1958, Matson Navigation Company commenced its containership operations on the West Coast–Hawaii trade. On January 7, 1959, the world's first container crane was put into service at the Encinal Terminals in Alameda, California.[3] Containerships required far fewer stevedores to load or unload. Indeed, one longshore worker, "upon noting the shape of the container, referred to it as 'the ILA's coffin.' "[4]

Intermodal transportation has greatly simplified the movement of large volumes of cargo. Coupled with other technological advances, such as computerized navigational systems and the construction of giant containerships, this has greatly reduced the per-ton cost of shipping internationally by water. To give an idea of the growth of intermodal traffic worldwide, consider these statistics from the Port of Antwerp for containers handled during the 25-year period, 1975–2000:

Port of Antwerp Container Traffic Loaded and Unloaded (in TEUs)

Year	TEUs (in 1,000s)
1975	356
1980	724
1985	1,243
1990	1,549
1995	2,329
2000	4,082[5]

[3]From commemorative program, sponsored by the American Society of Mechanical Engineers, celebrating the crane's 25th anniversary.

[4]Thomas W. Gleason, "Containerization and the Labor Equation," VIA Port of NY-NJ, April, 1986, p. 27. The late Mr. Gleason was president of the International Longshoremen's Association (ILA).

[5]*www.portofantwerp.be* website, July 11, 2001.

Intermodal Carriers

It is usually the intermodal carrier who looks at the total picture, determining whether one mode, or two, or three will deliver the cargo in a dependable manner at the lowest cost within the allowable span of time. This is the nature of intermodal transportation: a marriage of modes, combining the best aspects of each, acting in concert to carry freight and documents.

New and far-reaching advances in transport technology, along with changes in shippers' expectations, have accelerated developments in intermodal transportation. Entire ocean ships are built to hold nothing but containers. In the rail industry, there are new, low, articulated cars (joined together, but able to bend), five car-lengths long, carrying ten double-stacked containers. Much of the spectacular growth in both domestic and international air freight has been in the overnight parcel services, which combine large fleets of planes and trucks offering overnight services between many of the world's major cities.

In ports, new high-capacity equipment handles containers efficiently and quickly. Vessel turnaround time in port, once measured in days, is now measured in hours. Cargo loading and unloading rates per man-hour of stevedore labor have improved tremendously.

Another important factor assisting in the development of intermodal traffic has been computers and electronic tracking and message systems. They allow intermodal systems to keep track of paperwork, vehicles, containers, and shipments. Computer programs also help determine routes, loading patterns, and scheduling. Customers have access to the carriers' systems so that they may make specific inquiries involving service or tracing.

Intermodal Movement by Rail

For the railroads, intermodal transportation once was synonymous with *piggyback,* which meant a truck trailer on a railroad flatcar. One thinks of railroad piggybacking as developing over the past four decades. Animosity between U.S. railroads and truckers kept them from implementing many coordinating, or sharing, arrangements. Railroads also found that they had to give their highest priority to trains loaded with piggyback cars if they were to compete successfully with over-the-road motor carriers. Trailer-on-flatcar (TOFC) is still used exclusively in rail-truck combinations, while container-on-flatcar (COFC) is more likely to be generated by vessel/rail combinations. By 1993, U.S. railroads were loading more containers than trailers.[6]

---

[6]*Railway Age,* March 1993, p. 8.

Railroads and ocean carriers, working together, also developed what became known as *land-bridge* traffic moving East–West across the United States. The container was off-loaded at a U.S. port, shipped cross-country on a flatcar, and loaded on a vessel for continuation of the movement to another continent. The type of haul just described is now called a *maxi-bridge*. A *mini-bridge* is a container on flatcar (COFC) shipment that originates or terminates in a U.S. port other than the one where it enters or leaves the country. An example would be a container of traffic bound for Europe that originates in Seattle and is tendered to an ocean carrier there; the ocean carrier ships the container by rail across the United States to New Jersey, where it is loaded aboard a vessel and sent to Europe. A *micro-bridge* is the routing by rail of a container between a port and an inland point.

Weight of both trailers and flatcars and aerodynamics become important whenever fuel prices escalate. Truck trailer lengths vary from about 28 to 53 feet and widths are either 96 or (more recently) 102 inches. The operating challenge often is to combine similar-sized equipment at one time. This results in a higher degree of utilization and fuel efficiency (a train of identical containers or trailers is less resistant to the wind than a train loaded with a collection of trailers and containers of assorted sizes).

Most TOFC railcars in the United States are either 85 or 89 feet long, and they can accommodate both trailers and single-stack containers. By repositioning the hitches on an 89-foot railcar, it is possible for the car to carry two 45-foot trailers. Similarly, the same railcar can haul three 28-foot trailers through insertion of a single knock-down hitch in the middle of the railcar. Thus, critical to the design of any rail flatcar for carrying trailers is its ability to carry trailers of varying lengths. Of course, railcar dimensions and allowable highway dimensions and weight limits differ in other parts of the world.

Containers originally moved on rail flatcars. Use of double-stack trains has grown in the past two decades. Stack trains now use special long drop-centered cars with five segments joined together permanently, capable of carrying five 40-foot containers on the drop-centered bottom plus five containers 40-feet or longer on top. Figure 8–4 shows a portion of a long double-stack railcar.

Ports and railroads are working together to expand intermodal container-handling facilities. Most of these double-stacked trains are operated by or for steamship lines. They control such large blocks of traffic that they can make the idea work. Some railroads deal only with specific vessel operators, while others run generic container trains that any shipper (usually an ocean carrier) can use. Some railroads also offer the truck service that moves containers between the railroad and the shippers and consignees. Sometimes railroads rely on consolidators to perform this function. Some steamship lines also offer truck service; American President Trucking performs the service for APL customers.

Figure 8–4   Two segments of a five-segment double-stack container rail car. Courtesy American President Lines, Ltd.

Congestion problems occur at intermodal hubs, especially as they become busier. These include backed-up trucks with trailers, inadequate transfer equipment, documentation delays, and misplaced and damaged containers. Larger operations rely on computers, and some containers are equipped with transponders (radio devices that will answer the query signal of another). Time is also consumed in inspecting the container as it moves from the responsibility of one carrier to another. The delays are sometimes called "dwell time," for at least those durations of time when the loaded containers are sitting in one place.

> Part of the problem ... is that many receivers ... harbor negative perceptions of intermodal service and do not feel that they can count on having shipments arrive on time. As a result, many will build delay time into their production planning and therefore are less inclined to schedule delivery appointments the same day that shipments actually arrive at destination hubs. ...
>
> Receivers ... don't think the shipment is going to arrive on time so they say, "We don't need it now, just deliver it tomorrow." That tends to perpetuate the perception problem because when carriers then analyze their performance ratings for door-to-door service, the ratings usually reflect significant amounts of dwell time, which pushes up the total "turn time" of each average load.[7]

A survey of industrial transportation managers conducted in 1996 reaffirmed the managers' lower opinion of intermodal service, compared to that by motor

---

[7]*American Shipper,* September 1989, p. 70.

carrier. One respondent said: "When the merchandise is not hot, we generally route shipments intermodal."[8]

Container trains also operate elsewhere in the world. In 1997, container trains operated between the Port of Rotterdam and 22 other cities with a frequency ranging between two to 12 trains per week. The cities served were principally in Austria, Belgium, France, Germany, Hungary, Italy, Poland, and Switzerland.[9] In the United States there are major container routes leading to and from most coastal ports, and some have all-container trains operating every day.

One other U.S. railroad intermodal equipment innovation should be mentioned. It is the Santa Fe Railway's "10-Pack fuel foiler," initially designed to carry truck trailers but being reengineered to handle containers as well. It is a series of long, articulated, skeleton-like flatcars that have only a beam down the center; are small platforms for the trailer wheels and a hitch for the fifth wheel. Gone is the large deck one associates with flatcars, which allows the new railcars to weigh 35 percent less.

In the United States, several different methods or plans are used to determine the railroad charges for the service. First of all, the majority of piggyback and container-on-flatcar traffic moves under contract rates, agreed on between the railroad and a major shipper. In addition, there are piggyback plans that are applicable to container on flatcar traffic as well and cover nearly all variations of who does what and who owns what equipment. Major plans are:

PLAN I Motor carrier provides trailer and assumes responsibility for door-to-door haul. Railroad carries trailer on the long haul.

PLAN II Railroad provides trailer, rail, door-to-door service, and uses a single bill-of-lading.

PLAN II 1/4 Same as PLAN II, except railroad provides either door-to-ramp or ramp-to-door service, but not both.

PLAN II 1/2 Railroad provides everything, but shipper delivers to and consignee picks up at ramp.

PLAN III Railroad provides flat car and carries trailer from ramp-to-ramp. Shipper provides trailer and bill-of-lading.

In late 1992, the American National Standards Institute adopted new

---

[8]Donald F. Wood and Richard S. Nelson, "Industrial Traffic Management: What's New?" *Transportation Journal* vol. 39, no. 2, Winter 1999, p. 29.

[9]H. Arjen van Klink and Geerke C. van den Berg, "Gateways and Intermodalism," *Journal of Transport Geography,* vol. 6, no. 1 March, 1998, pp. 4–8.

intermodal service codes as a part of EDI (electronic data interchange) standards. Seventeen different two-digit codes are used, and they are categorized by ownership of the unit, service provided by carrier, and determination of carrier.

Intermodal Movement by Over-the-Road Trucks

The trucker's role is very important at either end of most intermodal hauls. In the United States, long-haul truckers cannot compete with double-stacked container trains in terms of cost and have difficulty in competing with them in terms of service in markets where railroads choose to run trains on a regular basis. The hub-and-spoke concept was mentioned earlier; one expects to see more trucking resources serving as "spokes," mainly because they cannot compete on the long haul. Figures from a few years ago showed typical over-the-road operating costs for a Teamster-driven motor carrier were between $1.25 and $1.30 per mile, and for a non-Teamster truck, between 90 cents and $1.25; railroads could carry the same haul for between 60 cents and $1.10 per mile.[10] Note the overlaps. Several partnerships between major railroads and major motor carriers for handling intermodal containers were announced in the 1990s.

The rear view of a truck trailer chassis is shown on Figure 8–5. Note the pins at each side that fit into the container's frame. On the highway, the rig looks like a conventional truck tractor/semi-trailer (Figure 8–6). It is obvious that a chassis must be placed under the container for the container to move. In recent years shortages of chassis have occurred in various ports or in major transport hubs, such as Chicago. At other times, these areas suffer from a surplus of chassis, which are difficult to store. Shortages and surpluses of containers also occur. While chassis (and containers) are often mechanically interchangeable, they are owned by different parties who may resist allowing their equipment to be used. Owners of the land where containers and chassis are stored are adopting pricing policies that encourage equipment owners to move their containers and chassis out promptly. In early 2001, some vessel conferences began adding a $40 to $60 chassis fee to shipping charges, to help recover some of their costs in owning and operating chassis.[11]

A current problem associated with moving containers on U.S. highways is that the combined weight of the container and truck-trailer is sometimes greater than allowed by highway weight restrictions. Each state sets its own weight restric-

---

[10]Donald F. Wood and James C. Johnson, *Contemporary Transportation,* 4th ed (New York: Macmillan, 1993), p. 244.

[11]*WERCsheet,* January 2001, p. 4.

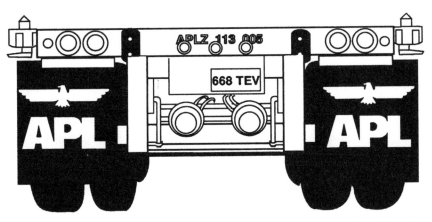

Figure 8–5   Rear view of a truck trailer chassis. Courtesy American President Lines Ltd.

tions (except on interstate highways), so there is no uniform minimum. In some states, it is possible to meet the law by adding a third axle to the trailer chassis in the rear or adding an extra dolly with axle at the front. In California, one port bought the nearby local roads from the state, so that state weight limits won't be enforced on them.

Yellow Freight, one of the best-known LTL (less-than-truckload) motor carriers in the United States, entered into agreements with a European motor carrier that served 16 nations in the European Community. Yellow offered a one-invoice

Figure 8–6   Front/side view of a truck and trailer chassis. Courtesy American President Lines Ltd.

system for European shipments, with container stuffing through the Port of New York and New Jersey for shipping on one of two steamship lines, the Taiwan-based Evergreen Line or the Germany-based Hapag-Lloyd. The company offered comprehensive cargo tracing and expert advice in customs clearance and freight forwarding.

In the 1990s, five well-known U.S. LTL motor carriers developed connections with motor carriers on other continents. In addition to Yellow, the carriers were: ABF Freight System, Con-Way Intermodal, Roadway Express, and A-P-A Transport. They all had connections in Europe, and one or more had also developed connections in Asia, Australia, South America, South Africa, Chile, or the Middle East. The trucking companies also had to develop partnerships with ocean carriers and port terminal operators who handled the consolidation. Some of the U.S. motor carriers were geared to handle exports from the U.S. only; the others handled both exports and imports.

Intermodal Movement by Air

Air freight is intermodal because pickup and delivery service is provided by truck. The U.S. airline industry has had an affiliation, through Air Cargo, Inc. (ACI), with local truckers at airports to perform pickup and delivery service for all air carriers using that airport. They pick up and deliver both domestic and international shipments.

The development and growth of parcel and express carriers such as UPS and FedEx continues to spread overseas. These carriers' fleets of trucks and planes are being augmented by contracts with parcel and express carriers in foreign countries to perform the pickup and delivery services necessary to complete an international movement. For the most part, these carriers use their own equipment, but they will contract space with other carriers if that proves to be advantageous.

Surface Intermodal Facilities

Western Europe and the industrialized nations of Asia have container ports that are as sophisticated as those found in the United States. Each year, an increasing share of the world's general cargo moves via container. Some shippers are forced to use containers because container ships are the only ones readily available. Often, the only way to load cargo aboard a container ship is to load it into a container.

An issue in developing countries is the ability of ports and inland transport to handle and benefit from the use of containers. Developing nations complain of being forced into containerization. The experience was described this way: "Just imagine how uncomfortable you will be when you are asked to buy a pair of very expensive shoes which do not fit, and then you will have to shape your feet to wear them."[12] While a port has to invest in expensive container-handling cranes, this is offset by not having to construct buildings to store the cargo while waiting in port, since the container provides protection. It is also believed that in many developing countries the containers are loaded/unloaded at port, and other means of transportation haul small quantities to and from port. Note that in many trades, a container load of any good represents an investment that would be excessive for many firms, either buying or selling.

Another impact that increased intermodalism has had in many nations is the increase in door-to-door international movements. This means less activity at ports. One somewhat dated study of the decrease in transloading (unloading containers and reloading their contents into trailers and railcars) at West Coast ports found that retailers were having containers loaded with imports move through the port to some inland point. This was for three reasons:

1. The development of cost efficient double-stack rail service and its promotion by ocean carrier has made it more attractive to ship containers intact to inland destinations under mini- or micro-bridge rates, using a single bill of lading. . . .

2. The growth in both double-stack rail systems and U.S. exports has encouraged ocean carriers to allow more containers to move inland rather than offering allowances to transload the containers on the West Coast. A few years ago, transloading was used by ocean carriers to avoid the expense and delays associated with allowing the containers to move inland. . . .

3. The growing shift in manufacturing from the Far East to Southeast Asia has also contributed to the shift to offshore consolidation. Because many manufacturers in Southeast Asia are small and cannot manufacture enough product to fill a 40-foot container for a particular importer, the importer must buy from a number of manufacturers in various countries and will ship partially loaded containers from these sources to places such as Taiwan or Hong Kong for . . . consolidation. This practice is often referred to as "multi-country consolidation."[13]

---

[12]Cited by H. C. Brookfield, "Boxes, Ports, and Places Without Ports," *Seaport Systems and Spatial Change* (New York: Wiley, 1984), p. 72.

[13]*Intermodal Market Survey,* (Chicago: Trailer Train Co., 1989), p. 19.

Air–Ocean Movements

One last type of intermodal movement to be mentioned is when an item moves part of the way by ocean and part of the way by air. A common ocean–air movement for the West Coast of the United States is fresh pineapples that arrive by sea and then are distributed to inland points by air. Ordinarily air rates have to be unusually low for such a move to take place. Another move is from Japan to Latin America. Goods move from Japan by water to southern California, and then by air to Latin America. In this case, the reason is that ocean service between Japan and Latin America is inadequate and air service between Japan and Latin America is too expensive.

Land Transportation to and from Canada and Mexico

First of all—and this applies to international borders almost everywhere in the world—there is a brisk trade carried on by pedestrians who cross borders daily and return with shopping bags filled with goods that are cheaper or only available "on the other side." One can observe this at any of the border towns along the U.S.–Mexican border. Just south of the U.S.–Canadian border, grocery stores distribute lists of products that Canadians can carry home duty-free. Somewhat related to cross-border shopping are the duty-free shops one sees in port and airport areas. While technically all of what has been described are considered as domestic sales, the markets consist of foreign people.[14]

This remaining part of the chapter deals with situations in shipping to and from adjacent countries where all-rail and all-truck options become viable. Actually, the situation is quite common since many nations' best trading partners are their immediate neighbors. That is true for the United States, whose best trading partners are Canada and Mexico, respectively. Air and ocean shipping could be used, but this discussion will ignore them. Some Canadian/U.S. trade moves by water on the Great Lakes/St. Lawrence Seaway system (technically not the ocean). Iron ore is loaded in Seven Islands, Quebec and delivered to U.S. steel mills on Lake Erie.

Goods might also be routed through Mexico or Canada on their way to still another destination. Transportation managers of large U.S. firms often feed a small, continuous flow of traffic through one or more Canadian ports as insur-

---

[14]Susanne Bygvra, "The road to the Single European Market as seen through the Danish retail trade: Cross-border shopping between Denmark and Germany," *The International Review of Retail Distribution and Consumer Research,* vol. 8, no. 2, April 1998, pp. 147–164.

ance against a strike closing down U.S. ports. As regular shippers through Canadian ports, their additional traffic will receive priority over that of first-time users who are obviously diverting their cargo because of the U.S. dock strike.

The North American Free Trade Agreement (NAFTA) has increased trade among the United States, Mexico, and Canada. The United States can expect more even trade with its two neighbors. There have been two additional changes. First, some supply chain systems have been designed that employ facilities and labor in all three nations. Second, there have been increases and improvements in North/South operations of many U.S. carriers. In the United States, the major trade routes historically have been East/West. That is changing.

Shipments to and from Canada are handled by the same equipment used in the United States, and the equipment is interchangeable. Canadian railroads own some trackage in the United States. Rail cars from Canada can run in the United States and vice versa, and so can trucks and truck trailers, assuming that they are adequately licensed. When moving goods between Canada and the United States, there are delays for documentation checks and problems with tariffs, quotas, and so on. At present, some truck shipments are pre-cleared electronically, meaning the truck driver merely has to pause briefly while crossing the border. Logistics systems work about the same, although there are differences in packaging and labeling.

Since U.S. motor carrier deregulation, Canadian firms have set up U.S. trucking subsidiaries to handle the U.S. leg of haul; initially, U.S. truckers could not do the same in Canada. The U.S. Motor Carrier Act of 1982 required Canada to lift their restrictions on U.S. motor carriers to reflect U.S. trucking deregulation. Canada generally accepted this.[15]

In general terms, there are very few differences in logistical practices or equipment or language when shipping to or from Canada. Prior to Europe 1992, the Canadian/U.S. border was probably the easiest border in the world to cross or to conduct trade across. Those trucks that are not pre-cleared for customs are probably delayed about an hour, depending mainly on the time of day and queue of trucks. Most delays are caused by the trucker's documentation not being in order. In 1990, when a Canadian government workers' slowdown closed border crossings for about a day, a number of automakers had to close down their assembly plants because of lack of parts.

Shipping goods to and from Mexico is not considered to be as easy. The U.S. Motor Carrier Act of 1982 also required Mexico to lift their restrictions on U.S.

---

[15]See Clarence Woudsma, "NAFTA and Canada-U.S. cross-border freight transportation," *Journal of Transport Geography,* June 1999, pp. 105–119.

truckers, but Mexico did not. At present, prohibitions against U.S. trucks in Mexico are strictly enforced. Within the United States, however, foreign trucks are allowed to operate in special commercial zones within selected metropolitan areas. (Commercial zones were established by the former Interstate Commerce Commission in most urban areas; they are considered as one origin or one destination for rate making purposes.) The sizes of these zones are determined by the population of the U.S. border community. The commercial zone for Mexican carriers in the San Diego area includes the city and 15 miles outside of the city. For the border towns of Tecate, Calexico, and Andrade, the commercial zone extends only three miles past city limits. U.S. trucking interests complain that U.S. restrictions are not being enforced and that the Mexicans operate outside the zones, have unsafe equipment, and pay lower wage rates than U.S. firms. During the first half of 2001, a NAFTA tribunal ruled that the United States should allow Mexican truckers further entry into the United States; however, that was not happening. Mexico replied with a threat to ban U.S. trucks from Mexico.

Cargo is often transferred between U.S. and Mexican equipment because better U.S. equipment will be stripped once it is south of the border. After the Mexico City earthquake in the 1980s, U.S. trucking firms that carried relief supplies insisted on transferring the relief cargo to Mexican equipment at the border; if not, they would have made an additional (and involuntary) contribution. In the past few years, northbound traffic crosses the border very slowly because of detailed, time-consuming inspections for drugs and aliens.

There is a huge volume of trade between the United States and Mexico, with the main reason being that the low Mexican wage rate has made the area just south of the border the site for many manufacturing and assembling operations, known as *maquiladoras*. The early entrants to the border areas were mainly electronics and clothing manufacturers and some wood-products companies. Initially, most of the jobs that these firms brought to Mexican laborers were simple and labor intensive. During the late 1960s and early 1970s, however, an increasing number of jobs requiring more skill were brought to the border areas. Also, in the mid-1970s, U.S. automobile manufacturers—most notably, Ford—began building state-of-the-art plants in Mexico. Some firms located in Mexico in order to avoid the increasingly stringent worker safety and environmental protection regulations in the United States. By 1999 there were over 3,000 maquiladora plants in Mexico, employing over one million workers.[16]

Going south, virtually all freight going to the maquila plants along the California border travels by truck. Many high-tech electronic components are made

---

[16]*World Trade,* July, 1999, p. 36.

in California and are then sent to the maquilas for final assembly. Some materials come in through the ports of Los Angeles/Long Beach and travel in-bond to the maquilas.

One practice that inhibits international trade between the United States and Mexico requires that a trailer bound for the maquilas must be picked up at a U.S. point by a Mexican union driver in a Mexican tractor. However, Mexican drivers are limited to driving only in the international border areas, which means that the pick-up site must be close to the border. From this point the Mexican driver can take the load to the border to be cleared by Mexican customs and then deliver it to the maquila plant. Although it is assumed that only Mexican truck drivers can transport freight on the southern side of the border, in fact, U.S. drivers are allowed to move trailers in Mexico. The Mexican Ruiz Cortines Presidential Decree of 1955 states that U.S. equipment can be operated in Mexico, with these two stipulations: 1) the U.S. carrier must have legal title to the goods being transported, and 2) the carrier can only operate in border communities.

All for-hire Mexican trucking companies must have a certificate of registration to be allowed to enter U.S. border communities' commercial zones. To receive a certificate, a carrier must pay a one-time $200 fee. The motor carrier must declare that it is in compliance with existing requirements for minimum insurance and vehicle safety and that it is current on its payment of U.S. road taxes.

A minimum of day-trip insurance is required for all Mexican haulers who use U.S. roads and highways. Proof of insurance and documentation showing the date of expiration must be kept on board the truck. U.S. state and federal laws require Mexican truck drivers to purchase insurance policies from companies that are licensed to sell insurance in that particular state. The difficulty lies in finding an insurance company that is willing to write insurance for Mexican national truck drivers. The main problem associated with insuring Mexican drivers is that Mexico does not have a centralized system for tracking a driver's history. Some Mexican nationals are able to obtain a California drivers license and therefore can be insured. Their driving record in Mexico is unknown; they can only be insured at the expensive rate of assigned risk. Insurance companies also want to be compensated for their increased risk exposure associated with Mexican truckers' equipment. Tractors and trailers that originate in Mexico are believed to be less well-maintained than their U.S. counterparts. The result is a situation where Mexican drivers are required to have insurance that very few companies are willing to offer.[17]

---

[17]Telephone interview with Jorge Cacho-Sousa, MexiPass International Services, Inc., South Pasadena, California, November 12, 1991.

Highway transportation equipment is still another issue. To operate in California (along with Arizona and Texas), all Mexican motor carriers must meet the federal safety standards that were set in the Federal Motor Carrier Safety Assistance Program.[18] This set of standards states that Mexican equipment must comply with the same federal regulations as U.S. equipment in their entirety except for one: Mexican vehicles are not required to have front-wheel brakes.

The U.S. parent corporations of the maquilas do not make the same complaints as the trucking companies. The reasoning seems to be that if the maquilas are not permitted to use their own trucks and drivers, then they are willing to use the comparatively low-cost Mexican drivers instead of the U.S. drivers. Besides, the Mexican drivers offer the added advantage of being able to haul goods to the interior of Mexico when needed. In an effort to overcome some of the cross-border trucking problems, some U.S. motor carriers have affiliated with Mexican firms to form subsidiaries to handle trailers south of the border.

Through the mid-1990s, Mexican railroads were government owned and their operations were chaotic. U.S. railroads would sometimes embargo rail shipments to Mexico until the Mexican railways would release certain numbers of U.S. railcars that U.S. railroads felt were being held hostage. In 1997, the Mexican government decided to privatize their railroads. They divided their rail system into four parts, and most of the bids to purchase came from U.S. railroads that wished to connect with them. Kansas City Southern Industries purchased TFM (Transportacion Ferroviaria Mexicana), which gave KCS (Kansas City Southern) a direct route between Kansas City and Mexico City. KCS purchased 150 new diesel engines for use south of the border and upgraded the track and signaling systems. Transit time between Mexico City and Nuevo Laredo (across the border from Laredo, Texas) was cut from four to two days.[19] TFM established a large customs inspection area south of the border where U.S. Customs agents could inspect northbound trains without having the stopped train blocking the main line. In 2001, BNSF (Burlington Northern/Santa Fe) entered into a cross-border intermodal partnership with TFM and named the service "Mexi-modal." The UP (Union Pacific) Railroad also acquired a Mexican line and that new railroad is called "Ferromex."

Shipment documentation for goods crossing any border is always a problem that adds to costs and to delays. The Mexican Maquila Decree of 1989 refined some of the bureaucratic process of setting up a maquila operation in Mexico.

---

[18]Glick, Leslie Alan, "U.S. Laws Affecting Mexican Carriers," *Twin Plant News,* March 1990, p. 45.

[19]Nathan Muhlethaler, term paper, San Francisco State University, December 9, 1999.

However, it is still necessary for a company to get permission to establish a maquila facility and begin temporary imports. Once all of the permits are granted the firm must carefully account for all incoming materials and outgoing products during operation.

First, a company wishing to start a maquila operation must get permission from the Mexican government. This is accomplished by filing an application with the Secretaria de Comercio y Formento Industrial (Department of Commerce and Industrial Development, or SECOFI). The information supplied must include the corporate structure of the maquillage and the products it plans to make in Mexico. The maquillage operation must also indicate the quantity and value of the equipment that will be used in the assembly plant and the exact amount of raw materials that will be temporarily imported into Mexico. In addition, an accurate account of all finished goods that will be exported to the U.S. must be stated in advance.[20] The quantity of temporarily imported raw materials and equipment listed on the maquila license application will establish the import quota placed on the maquillage for these articles. These quotas will be monitored by SECOFI during the operation of the maquiladora plant.[21] Maquilas that are registered under the Mexican National Registry of Importers and Exporters have the option to clear customs at their own domiciles (plants or factories).

The U.S. government requires that U.S. companies acquire the appropriate export licenses from the Commerce Department or the State Department. More than one export license may be required, which can be confusing and time-consuming. A shipper may be required to obtain a Special Export License, a Certificate of Registration, an Export Declaration for Drawback, or a Shippers Export Declaration (SED). There are licenses that are valid only for a specific quantity of materials (some of which may have to be returned to the United States), and some licenses may be valid for only a certain period.

During the production phase, each shipment of goods to or from the manufacturing plant must have the appropriate accompanying paperwork for the shipment in order to cross the border. Mexican and U.S. customs agencies use the Harmonized Tariff System (HTS) to classify goods that are being imported into their respective countries. However, matters become complicated because the two agencies use different customs accounting methods. Only a Mexican customs broker can clear goods through Mexican customs. A U.S. broker has no authority to clear goods out of Mexican customs. Likewise, only a U.S. broker has

---

[20]Cacheaux, Rene and D'Ambrosio, Nicholas, "The New Maquila Decree," *Twin Plant News,* February 1990, p. 20.

[21]Wright, Jeff, "Maquila Software," *Twin Plant News,* July 1989, p. 40.

the authority to clear a shipment out of U.S. customs. Usually the operation on the Mexican side of the border selects which Mexican broker is to be used. Customarily, U.S. brokers at the border have a working or financial relationship with Mexican customs brokers.

In addition to border crossing documentation, both U.S. and Mexican governments demand maquilas to regularly track and report various operations information. The Mexican government requires maquilas to prove what happens to all of the imported raw materials within a maquila cycle (usually six months). This is known as the *pedimento*. The total imports to the maquillage plant must equal exports plus waste. The accounting method used during the maquila cycle must list the materials by SECOFI permit classification instead of a specific part number. An experienced Mexican broker can be hired to monitor the pedimento to avoid possible delays at the border. Implementation of NAFTA should also remove some of the documentation requirements.

Another cost of crossing the border was known as a *mordida* (or bribe). In the past, delays at the border were avoided by paying a mordida to Mexican customs officials. Interviews indicated that this practice is decreasing along the California border with Mexico. A customshouse broker said that it had been six months since he was last approached by a Mexican official seeking a mordida. The broker made the decision not to pay $200 but had to wait five weeks for the goods to be cleared from Mexican customs. The broker said that formerly, it had been the practice for Mexican customs brokers to be expected to handle the mordidas as well as the documentation requirements for importing into Mexico. An interview with a manager of a large consumer electronics firm also indicated that the mordida is on the decline. The reason given was that his company, and others like it, never paid a single mordida because it would be too expensive in the long run.

Summary

This chapter has covered the land movements to and from ports, and the land aspects of intermodal traffic. Several types of equipment were discussed including both vehicles and their accompanying containers.

Land movements to and from Canada and Mexico were also covered. More attention was paid to movements to and from Mexico. Transport to and from there is not seamless, and other practices also inhibit the movement of products.

End-of-Chapter Questions

1. Define intermodal transportation.
2. Give some examples of intermodal transportation.

3. What was port equalization as it might have been viewed by a shipper in mid-America?

4. What is a TEU?

5. Do you think that intermodal surface containers are standardized or not? Discuss.

6. What is land-bridge traffic?

7. Why might developing nations be less enthusiastic about intermodal traffic than developed nations?

8. To which country is it easier to ship goods: Canada or Mexico? Why?

9. What is a maquiladora? Why are they used?

10. What are some of the problems on either side of the Mexican/U.S. border regarding the use of trucks? Why?

CASE • *Kokomo Diesels*

Founded in 1939 as an Indiana corporation, Kokomo Diesels built a high-quality stationary diesel engine that was widely used for powering electric generators and pumps. Units ranged from 10 to 100 horsepower. In addition to its home factory, the firm had smaller factories in Brussels, Belgium and Pusan, Korea. In recent years, most production was shifted away from the Belgian factory because of the high labor costs; however, it still served as an important warehouse and distribution point for diesel repair parts. Kokomo diesels were sold in North and South America, Europe, Asia, and a few nations in Africa. Sales in the Americas were handled out of Kokomo; those in Europe and Africa, out of Brussels; and those in Asia, out of Pusan. Each of the three major offices had its own customer service standards. Inconsistencies became apparent as some global customers complained that customer service elements that were free in some areas were charged for in others.

Diesel engines in general, and Kokomo Diesels in particular, were very durable, and easy to maintain and repair. Some had been in daily operation for decades. Repair parts now accounted for over 15 percent of Kokomo Diesel's annual sales, although very little of this contributed to profit, as the parts operation was supposed to only break even. This was because it was felt that the product's long life and ease and low cost of repair were an important selling point for new equipment. However, each year, repair part sales were increasing faster than the company's overall sales, and one result of this was that the company's overall profit on sales was declining.

Questions for *Kokomo Diesels*

1. Toward the end of the first paragraph it says: "Each of the three major offices had its own customer service standards. Inconsistencies became apparent as some global customers complained that customer service elements that were free in some areas were charged for in others." What different types of customer services do you think a diesel engine manufacturer should offer? List them.

2. Should Kokomo Diesels offer the same level of customer service everywhere in the world? Why or why not?

3. How might Kokomo Diesels measure the levels of customer service offered by competitors?

4. Should Kokomo Diesels require some or all of their dealers to stock certain repair parts? If yes, how would you determine which parts?

5. Should Kokomo Diesels place some repair parts in dealers on consignment, meaning that the dealer will pay for the part only after he has sold it? If yes, how would you determine which parts?

6. Kokomo Diesels owns repair parts inventories in Kokomo, Pusan, Brussels (and in some dealerships—depending upon how you answered question 5). Each nation has its own currency, and each currency fluctuates daily. For accounting purposes, how should Kokomo Diesels evaluate their repair parts inventory?

7. Should Kokomo Diesels change its pricing policies for repair parts? Why or why not?

8. In the year 2001, North Korea appeared to be thinking about opening its window to the world. They represent a potential market for stationary diesel engines. How might Kokomo Diesels prepare to enter this market? How might they create a distribution system to function within North Korea? What types of customer support and service should they be prepared to offer there?

9

Seaports, Airports, Canals, and Tunnels

Introduction

The transportation mode choice for many international shipments comes down to a decision between air and water transportation. This chapter will discuss some of the major man-made nodes and links that facilitate international water and air transportation. Specifically, this chapter discusses seaports and airports (nodes), as well as canals and tunnels (links). Seaports and airports act as transfer points for cargo and passengers from ocean vessels or airplanes. Canals serve to connect bodies of water separated by land, whereas tunnels and bridges link land bodies divided by mountains or water.

Seaports

Although the term *port* is often used generically, ports can be classified as 1) sea, 2) lake, 3) river, or 4) canal, depending on the type of business that is transacted there.[1] Since this book deals with international logistics, our focus will be on seaports. As a result, most references to ports will mean seaports. Figure 9–1 shows the Port of Longview, Washington, a small port in the Pacific Northwest.

Ports are important economic catalysts for the regions that they serve, in that they provide employment in and of themselves (for dockworkers and administrative officials) as well as by generating jobs in the surrounding region. It is estimated, for example, that the Port of Singapore is responsible for approximately

---

[1]M. L. Fair, *Port Administration in the United States.* Centreville, MD: Cornell Maritime Press, 1954, Chapter 1.

Figure 9–1 Longview, Washington, located on the Columbia River. In the foreground is a transit shed (a warehouse for handling inbound and outbound breakbulk cargo); toward the rear, some grain elevators. (Photo courtesy of Pat Burt).

5 percent of Singapore's entire Gross Domestic Product (GDP).[2] And, according to the Port of Baltimore's website, "The Port of Baltimore is a significant economic engine for the entire region, generating $1.4 billion in revenue annually and employing nearly 126,700 Marylanders in maritime-related jobs."[3]

Ports may also play important roles in the national defense of individual countries by allowing for efficient transportation to support overseas military operations. Indeed, commercial ports in the United States and allied nations were instrumental in the successful outcome of the Persian Gulf conflict of 1990–1991. These ports handled all of the petroleum shipments and approximately 95 percent of all cargo shipments in support of military operations for Desert Shield/Desert Storm.[4]

Responsibilities for the ownership, operation, and other aspects of port management fall to port authorities. This responsibility can involve either public (that is, government) or private interests. With respect to public entities, port control and management by the federal government has historically been more prevalent in non-U.S. countries such as Egypt, Malaysia, and Indonesia. Non-federal control and management of ports tends to be most prevalent in the United States, and includes operation by city (Port of Milwaukee), county (Port of Seattle), and state (Virginia Port Authority). With respect to management and control by private interests, Hutchison Port Holdings (HPH) has responsibilities at over 25 ports in countries such as China, Panama, and the United Kingdom.[5]

The tremendous growth of companies such as Hutchison Port Holdings highlights one of the key issues in contemporary port management, namely, the degree to which port operations should be privatized. In its purest form, privatization involves the ownership and operation of an enterprise by private concerns. With respect to ports, however, privatization refers to a reduction (or elimination) of government control over port operations. During 2000, for example, the Egyptian government implemented partial privatization by allowing individual port authorities total control of revenue streams as well as control of the various government agencies (for example, customs and cargo inspection, among others) that may operate at them.[6]

---

[2] *www.mpa.gov*

[3] *www.mpa.state.md.us/info/history*

[4] E. Thomchick, The 1991 Persian Gulf War: Short-term Impacts on Ocean and Air Transportation. *Transportation Journal,* Winter 1993, pp. 40–53.

[5] *www.hph.org*

[6] J. Prescott, Egypt: Government Sets Port Privatization in Motion. *Lloyd's List,* March 14, 2000, p. 8.

Proponents have argued that privatization can make ports more competitive as well as providing better access to funding. With respect to competitiveness, privatization is argued to improve port efficiency, in the sense that port assets can reduce relevant costs and/or increase port revenues. As an example, Saudi Arabia's first year of port privatization witnessed traffic growth of over 10 percent, largely attributable to improved cargo handling efficiency.[7] Likewise, India's Kakinada Port, in the state of Andhra Pradesh, expected a tonnage increase of approximately 50 percent during its first year of privatization.[8]

Alternatively, opposition to port privatization has focused on several issues. One is that privatization may result in ports selling their most valuable assets—the real estate of the port location. Other opponents argue that rather than increasing efficiency, private operators will actually decrease port efficiency. This decreased efficiency has resulted from labor resistance to privatization efforts. As an example, the Port of Santos in Brazil has experienced many worker strikes since being privatized in the 1990s; these strikes have led to cargo being moved through other Brazilian ports.[9]

Since 1990, port privatization efforts have occurred in many regions of the world, including Africa (Kenya and South Africa, among others); Asia (Bangladesh, India, among others); Europe (England, France, and Portugal, among others); and South America (Argentina, Brazil, and Chile, among others).

Unlike other countries, port privatization is not likely to be widely implemented in the United States because of capital constraints to purchasing and maintaining port facilities. In addition, because port facilities are public entities, interest payments on their debt is exempt from federal income taxes, which means they can borrow money at a lower rate than could a comparable private sector undertaking. Labor opposition, in the form of unionized stevedores, has also been a barrier to U.S. port privatization. This topic will be more fully discussed later in this chapter.

Determination of the world's major cargo seaports can be problematic, in the sense that there are a number of different ways to measure port output, such as the total number of vessel calls, the dollar value of cargoes, the tonnage of cargo throughput, and the number of containers. Because containerization appears to be the most common measure of port output, it will be used here as well.

Table 9–1 provides a listing of the world's ten top container ports, in terms of

---

[7]M.G. Ali Khan, Ports Witness 12 Percent Growth. *Arab News,* March 2, 1998, retrieved from Lexis-Nexis Academic Universe.

[8]A. Mitra, India: Kakinada Port—Privatization = Prosperity. *Financial Times Information,* August 30, 1999, retrieved from Lexis-Nexis Academic Universe.

[9]*Lloyd's List,* Showdown Time in Santos as Stevedores Make Final Stand. April 3, 2001, p. 18.

Table 9–1   Top Container Ports (In Millions of TEUs), Calendar Year 2000

Port (country)	Volume
Hong Kong (China)	18.10
Singapore (Singapore)	17.09
Pusan (South Korea)	7.54
Kaohsiung (Taiwan)	7.43
Rotterdam (Netherlands)	6.28
Shanghai (China)	5.61
Los Angeles (U.S.)	4.88
Long Beach (U.S.)	4.60
Hamburg (Germany)	4.25
Antwerp (Belgium)	4.08

Source: *JoCWeek*, July 9–15, 2001; pp. 20+

TEUs (20-foot equivalent units). Note that the top two ports, Hong Kong and Singapore, handle over twice as many containers as the third ranked port, Pusan. Moreover, the top four ports and five of the top six ports are located in Asia. Three of the top ten ports are found in Western Europe, with the remaining two in the United States. Figure 9–2 shows the port of Singapore.

Port Competition

Given that approximately 60 percent of cross-border trade moves via water transportation, seaports are key participants in international logistics systems. A confluence of factors over the past twenty years—containerization, explosive growth in cross-border trade, emphasis on cycle time reduction, acceptance of the integrated logistics concept as well as the emergence of the supply chain concept—have had a profound impact on port competition. Several important aspects of this competition will be discussed below.

Load centers, or "a major port where thousands of containers arrive and depart per week,"[10] are one of the most important topics in port management. Conceptually, load centers work much the same way as hub airports, that is, large amounts of traffic moving through limited facilities. There are definite efficiencies and economies to handling a larger number of containers at one time. Container handling equipment requires a large fixed investment, and, as with any

---

[10]J.C. Johnson, D.F. Wood, D.L. Wardlow, and P.R. Murphy, Jr., *Contemporary Logistics,* 7th edition, New Jersey: Prentice Hall, 1999, Glossary.

Figure 9–2 Singapore, one of the world's busiest container ports. (Photo courtesy of the Port of Singapore Authority).

high fixed-cost option, larger output (in this case, the number of containers handled) leads to lower unit costs.

Moreover, the development of larger-capacity ocean vessels provides the opportunity to carry more containers. As a result, ship operators have found that it can be uneconomical to stop at a number of ports in a particular region to pick up/deliver limited amounts of freight; rather, operators of large ocean vessels prefer to stop at only one port in a particular area.

And, as vessel sizes increase, the number of ports of call may decrease even further. Indeed, when the first edition of this book was produced in the mid-1990s, a 6,000 TEU containership might have been considered large. As this edition is being written, there is talk of ships capable of carrying 10,000 or more TEUs. According to some experts, if these large ships come to pass, then the relevant economics could dictate no more than five or six load centers, spread throughout the world, with many other ports providing feeder traffic to the "mega" ports.[11]

One example of the mega-port concept involves Maersk and Sea-Land, who in 1998 indicated that they would prefer to consolidate the majority of inbound and outbound container traffic to and from the U.S. Midwest and Northeast through one U.S. East Coast port. Maersk/Sea-Land solicited bids from interested ports, and in 1999 named the Port of New York/New Jersey to be the chosen mega-port. As part of the 30-year contract, the Port agreed to deepen its channel to 50 feet in order to accommodate larger containerships.

Load centering has several key implications for port operational characteristics, such as container handling equipment, storage space for containers, and rail accessorial service. As an example, requirements for Maersk's U.S. East Coast mega-port included the capability for 750,000 annual container lifts; 16 post-Panamax container cranes; storage space for 12,000 40-foot containers; and on-dock nearby rail facilities for two railroads.

The development of load centers may also require port expansion (to store containers) and the dredging of existing harbors (to accommodate larger vessels). Unfortunately, both port expansion and dredging present various environmental problems. Port expansion may mean the reduction of wetland areas and the consequent disruption of the surrounding ecosystem. In addition, port expansion may lead to vehicle congestion and subsequently higher levels of air pollution. Environmental considerations with port dredging tend to focus on disposal of the channel sediment because of the possible presence of toxins, heavy metals, and cancer-causing chemicals. While environmental considerations of port dredging

---

[11]J. Parker, Big Ship Economics. *Traffic World,* July 2, 2001, pp. 39–40.

have long been associated with western, industrial countries, these considerations have become more prominent in recent years in less-developed countries such as China, Ecuador, India, and Malaysia.

There have been several types of strategic responses by ports with respect to load centering. As pointed out earlier, some ports will end up providing feeder traffic to the mega-ports. Others are choosing to focus on a particular cargo niche(s), as illustrated by the Port of Baltimore. Baltimore, which was one of the three finalists for the Maersk/Sea-Land East Coast mega-port, has decided to deemphasize container cargo in order to focus on automobiles, heavy equipment and paper products.[12] A surprising number of ports—many of whom are seemingly undaunted by projections of five to six mega-ports worldwide—are pursuing ambitious expansion projects in the hopes of being one of the surviving mega-ports. Examples of the latter include Freeport, Dubai, and Port Klang (Malaysia).

Port labor continues to be one of the major impediments to efficient port operations. This focus on port labor has been intensified in recent years by the various competitive forces mentioned earlier, such as privatization, multi-country trade alliances, and containerization. Because many ports can no longer count on formerly captive hinterlands, inefficient labor practices, which may have been tolerated because customers had limited service options, have become major targets for reform.

Inefficient labor practices can have an important influence on port costs and operations. With respect to costs, for example, a typical Singaporean container crane operator makes about $20,000 per year, while his or her counterpart at the U.S. Port of Los Angeles can make over $100,000 per year—more than five times as much.[13] As for labor's influence on port operations, some Asian container ports like Hong Kong can handle over 15,000 TEUs per acre per year, compared to less than 2,500 TEUs per acre per year at the Port of New York/New Jersey. One reason for such productivity per acre involves container-stacking practices at the various ports. Asian ports often stack containers seven or eight high, whereas U.S. ports are hesitant to stack more than three or four high because of safety concerns.

A discussion of port labor would be incomplete without a look at strikes, which have long been used by port labor to achieve particular goals such as higher pay and more favorable working conditions. From labor's view, these

---

[12]P. Adams, New Deals Point Way for a Changing Port. *Baltimore Sun,* January 21, 2001, p. 16P.

[13]D. Machalaba, US Ports Are Losing the Battle to Keep Up with Overseas Trade. *The Wall Street Journal,* July 9, 2001, pp. A1, A13.

strikes have often been an effective tactic because they adversely impact port operations while costing large sums of money. For example, a 17-day strike at India's Port of Chennai was estimated to cost the Port approximately $1.5 million in lost revenue, along with two to three weeks to catch up on backlogged imports and exports.[14]

While these strikes may benefit dockworkers, their impact on ports are more problematic. Because shippers, carriers, and forwarders now have a multitude of cross-border logistics options, port strikes may do little more than cause these parties to take their business elsewhere, as illustrated in the comments of one US port administrator: "I can't move my wharf. But ships can go anywhere."[15] Moreover, in recent years, even the threat of a labor strike has caused freight to be diverted from one port to another.

Port management throughout the world is recognizing that labor effectiveness and efficiency is critical to maintaining, and increasing, port traffic in today's global economy. This has led many ports to attempt to institute labor reform, such as Great Britain's abolishment of the National Dock Labour Scheme that promised guaranteed employment to port laborers. Such labor reforms have generally led to a reduction in dockworkers along with higher productivity expectations. Not surprisingly, port labor reforms have met with strong resistance from the dockworkers. This resistance can consist of riots, strikes, cargo theft or destruction, damage to port equipment and property, assaults, and even killings.

Choosing the Port

Port selection choices made by various logistical constituencies can play an integral role in the efficiency of cross-border trade. A poor choice of ports can cause higher shipment costs, delays in either pickup or delivery of cargo, lost or damaged freight, among other inefficiencies. A basic consideration in port selection involves cargo compatibility, that is, the port's capability of handling particular types of freight. The Port of Houston (Texas), for example, specializes in petroleum and petroleum products as well as organic and inorganic chemicals.

The emergence of mega-ports for containerized shipments suggests that the relative power in port selection may be shifting to the ocean carriers. This, in turn, has important ramifications for the relative importance of various factors in the port selection process. For example, location is no longer the overriding factor that it once was in port selection. Rather, today's large container lines are

---

[14]N.V. Rao, Indian Port Clearance Could Take Three Weeks. *JoC Online,* May 25, 2001, p. WP.

[15]Machalaba, *The Wall Street Journal,* July 9, 2001.

concerned with harbor depths, rail connections, simplified transfers between modes, and port productivity issues.[16]

Free Trade Zones

Another important issue associated with today's ports involves *free-trade zones*, which can be defined as "part of an economy, geographical or functional, in which the rules and other institutions for the production and distribution of goods and services differ from those in the rest of the economy."[17] Free-trade zones offer the potential for attracting nondomestic investment to generate jobs and spur economic development. The most prominent types of free-trade zones are foreign trade zones, special economic zones, and export processing zones. Free-trade zones typically are located adjacent to, or in close proximity to, water ports, but these trade zones can also be located at airports.

Although free-trade zones have been in existence for hundreds of years, their worldwide popularity has increased dramatically over the past 25 years, from approximately 80 free-trade zones at the beginning of the 1980s to over 600, and counting, at the present time. Reasons for the increased number of trade zones include globalization and its emphasis on cost competitive goods and services as well as the adoption, to varying extents, of economic reforms in Asian, European, and Latin American nations.[18]

Free-trade zones offer a variety of incentives to parties engaged in global commerce. Due to the diversity in the types of free-trade zones (foreign trade zones versus export processing zones) as well as diversity in their rules and regulations (one trade zone might permit manufacturing activities while another trade zone doesn't), the benefits to free-trade zones vary from country to country (and may vary from free-trade zone to free-trade zone within a country). As a result, a definitive listing of free-trade zone benefits is not possible. What all free-trade zones share in common, however, is that "goods can enter duty-free and remain duty-free unless, and until, they enter the customs territory of their country."[19]

---

[16]B. Mongelluzzo, A Warning to Ports. *JoC Week,* January 29, 2001, p. 33.

[17]*Business Wire,* India: Alchemy of Special Economic Zones. June 17, 2000.

[18]R. Barovick, Zones' Adaptability Held Key to Success. *Journal of Commerce,* October 20, 1997, p. 6A.

[19]Barovick, *Journal of Commerce,* October 20, 1997.

Airports

Airports have been characterized as ". . .harbors on the ocean of air."[20] This description, taken from the early days of commercial air travel in the United States, was meant to demonstrate that airports serve a purpose quite similar to that of water ports—that is, transfer points for freight and passengers. Although there are several types of airports, such as general aviation, military, and commercial, our focus in this chapter will be commercial airports. Figure 9–3 shows how aircraft developed during the 20th century.

Table 9–2 provides a listing of the world's ten busiest airports in terms of passenger throughput. This is of importance to shippers of freight because a great deal of air cargo moves in the belly of passenger flights. The world's busiest passenger airport is Atlanta Hartsfield, followed by Chicago O'Hare and Los

Figure 9–3 Evolution of aircraft used by KLM. Courtesy KLM, The Royal Dutch Airline, Cargo Division.

---

[20]J. A. Wenneman, Municipal Airports. Cleveland: The Flying Review Publishing Company, 1931.

Table 9–2   World's Busiest Passenger Airports (Year 2000)

Airport (country)	Passengers
Atlanta Hartsfield (US)	80,171,036
Chicago O'Hare (US)	72,135,887
Los Angeles International (US)	68,477,689
London Heathrow (UK)	64,607,185
Dallas/Ft. Worth (US)	60,687,122
Tokyo Haneda (Japan)	56,402,206
Frankfurt Main (Germany)	49,360,620
Paris Charles DeGaulle (France)	48,240,137
San Francisco International (US)	41,173,983
Amsterdam Schiopol (Netherlands)	39,604,589

Source: *www.airports.org/traffic/passengers*

Angeles International. A listing of the world's ten busiest cargo airports, in terms of metric tons, is presented in Table 9–3. Memphis International, the main hub for FedEx, is the leading cargo airport. Hong Kong Chep Lap Kok and Los Angeles International follow Memphis.

Comparison of the data in Tables 9–2 and 9–3 provides evidence of the globalization of the world's economy. Five of the top passenger airports are located in the United States, four in Western Europe, and one in Asia. Five of the top cargo airports are located in the United States, four in Asia, and one in Western Europe. Note that only two airports, Los Angeles International and Frankfurt Main, appear on both the passenger and cargo lists.

Table 9–3   World's Busiest Cargo Airports (Year 2000)

Airport (country)	Volume (metric tons)
Memphis International (US)	2,489,070
Chep Lap Kok (Hong Kong)	2,267,175
Los Angeles International (US)	2,054,212
Tokyo Narita (Japan)	1,932,694
Anchorage International (US)	1,883,825
Inchon International (South Korea)	1,874,228
New York Kennedy (US)	1,825,906
Frankfurt Main (Germany)	1,710,144
Changi Airport (Singapore)	1,705,410
Miami International (US)	1,642,484

Source: *www.airports.org/traffic/cargo*

Because many commercial airports are designed to serve passengers first and cargo second, passenger considerations generally take priority in airport decision-making. However, the fact is that airport services and layouts designed to facilitate efficient passenger travel may contribute to inefficient cargo movements. As a result, many countries throughout the world are considering (India), are in the process of implementing (Cambodia), or have implemented (Brazil, Panama, and the United States) commercial air facilities solely devoted to cargo movements.[21] Advantages to such facilities include reduced congestion from fewer flights as well as facility designs that emphasize freight loading docks and the protection of freight from loss and damage.

Issues in Commercial Airport Management

There are a number of issues concerning commercial airport management, including their ownership and operation; airport congestion; airport safety and security; and environmental concerns. Each has important ramifications for the efficiency of cross-border movement of freight and passengers.

Ownership and Operation

In the United States, the ownership and operation of most commercial airports is carried out by some type of public authority, including city (Phoenix Sky Harbor International Airport, under the jurisdiction of the city of Phoenix), regional (Pittsburgh International Airport, under the jurisdiction of the Allegheny County Airport Authority) or state governments (Baltimore-Washington International Airport, under the jurisdiction of the state of Maryland). Historically, public ownership and operation of U.S. commercial airports has been preferred because these public authorities have the ability to issue municipal bonds to raise funds for airport capital needs.

Airport privatization refers to placing the ownership and/or operation of commercial airports with private (nonpublic) entities. During the latter part of the 1990s and into the early 2000s, airport privatization has become an increasingly popular option throughout the world. Ironically, a primary reason for this popularity is that in non-U.S. countries, privatization often provides airports with a better opportunity to raise funds for their capital needs. Although federal legislation in 1996 made privatization of U.S. commercial airports easier, few airports to date have opted for this alternative.

---

[21]*Financial Times Information,* India: Cargo Airports: The Efficient Alternative. October 12, 2000.

As with water port privatization, airport privatization has resulted in companies that specialize in the management and control of airports. Perhaps one of the best known of these companies is the British Airports Authority (BAA), which was formed to manage and control major British airports such as London Gatwick and London Heathrow. BAA also operates one U.S. airport (Indianapolis International Airport) as part of a contractual agreement with the Indianapolis Airport Authority.

Airport Congestion

It will come as no surprise to anyone who has flown through a busy airport that airport congestion is an acute problem at many of these facilities. During the first part of 2001, for example, a study of the U.S.'s busiest airports discovered that over 25 percent of the flights were at least 15 minutes late; similar results were reported during this time period at Western Europe's busiest airports. This congestion is caused by a variety of factors, including inadequate physical facilities, inadequate air traffic control systems, increased passenger and cargo traffic, and an increased number of takeoffs and landings during particular time periods.

One response to airport congestion is to construct new airports or to expand existing ones. This is often easier said than done, however, particularly in industrialized nations. For example, the costs of constructing new commercial airports or expanding existing ones can be quite prohibitive. South Korea's new Inchon International Airport, for example, cost approximately $6 billion to construct when all was said and done.[22]

Moreover, modern airports capable of handling the aircraft needed for international air transportation require large amounts of land in order to have sufficient runway space for approaches, takeoffs, and landings. Because large parcels of land are often difficult to find near major cities in industrialized countries, a new airport must be located well away from the central business district. As an example, Milan's Malpensa International Airport is located over 30 miles from downtown. Expansion is often not a viable option at many existing commercial airports because of land constraints around individual facilities.

A look at new airport construction in different countries reveals an uneven pattern. For example, the last major new airport constructed in the United States, Denver International Airport, opened in 1995, and no major airports are scheduled to be constructed through 2005. By contrast, the construction of new com-

---

[22]*Bangkok Post*, Aviation Fingers Crossed as Inchon Airport Prepares for Debut. March 28, 2001, p. 1.

mercial airports is quite prevalent in many of the world's developing nations. As an example, new airports are planned for, or are currently under construction in, Punta Areans (Chile), Dakar (Senegal), Guangzhou (China), and Mexico City (Mexico), among others.

Airport Safety and Security

Airport safety and security are matters of continuing concern. Worldwide acts of terrorism involving both airports and aircraft first became commonplace in the 1970s, and continued through the 1980s, 1990s, and into the early years of the 21st century. A turning point for terrorism directed at airports and airlines appears to have occurred in 1985.[23] During 1985, there were several high-profile airplane hijackings, along with bombings at airports in Frankfurt, Rome, and Vienna. The mid-1980s rash of terrorist acts led many airports to begin checking up on passengers before flights as well as tightening control over airport personnel with access to aircraft or airport security points.

The bombing of Pan Am Flight 103 in the late 1980s showed that the tighter security measures were still not sufficient to combat certain kinds of terrorism. Although airports and airlines throughout the world have worked tirelessly to come up with more sophisticated security devices to improve the safety of air travel (and continue to do so), the safety and security of the world's airports are far from uniform. Airport security measures in developing nations are often limited by resource constraints, so that in some cases major airports do not have even basic security equipment, such as metal detectors. Contrast this situation to the United States, where the Airport Security Improvement Act of 2000 mandated fingerprint checks for all airport and airline employees.[24] Despite these heightened airport security measures, the terrorist activities of September 11, 2001—airplanes used as bombs—demonstrated the need for even more stringent security precautions at U.S. airports.

Environmental Concerns

Environmental concerns that are important to airport management include air, water, and noise pollution, along with the potential disruption to natural ecosystems that can be caused by airport constructions projects. Environmental

---

[23]L.J. D'Amore and T.E. Anusa, International Terrorism: Implications and Challenge for Global Tourism. *Business Quarterly,* November 1986, pp. 20–29.

[24]*PR Newswire,* Digital Biometrics Ships Live-Scan Systems to Seven Major U.S. Airports. January 24, 2001.

considerations tend to be more difficult to address at existing facilities than at newer airports, in part because the newer facilities have been, or are being, explicitly designed to deal with environmental issues.

Noise pollution, in the form of aircraft noise levels, continues to be perhaps the most prominent environmental concern facing airport management. In reality, the only way to eliminate aircraft noise levels would be to ban all aircraft flights—clearly an unrealistic option. And, while a number of different approaches are available to reduce the inconvenience caused by aircraft noise, these approaches have important implications for airport and airline operations. As an example, approximately 40 nations currently are involved in the Coalition for a Global Standard on Aviation Noise, a group that seeks a global standard for aircraft noise reduction. While certainly a laudable objective, such a standard would likely entail significant costs for many airlines, either to retrofit existing aircraft or to purchase new aircraft.

Dealing with environmental concerns often requires a delicate balancing act for airport officials, because actions taken to deal with one environmental problem can impact another environmental issue. For example, airport expansion in the form of new and/or lengthened runways is often championed as having the capability for reducing runway delays—hence less congestion, less fuel consumption, and less air pollution. However, construction of new and/or expanded runways can potentially disrupt the natural ecosystem, meaning that airport authorities will have to take corrective measures (for example, wetland relocation) before receiving construction approval.

Canals, Tunnels, and Bridges

Canals, tunnels, and bridges are of great significance to international logistics because they lessen barriers to travel and trade. As a point of reference, *canals* are man-made waterways that can be used for either transportation or irrigation (our focus will be transportation). Whereas canals provide water linkages between bodies of water separated by land, *tunnels* and *bridges* generally provide methods of connecting land masses separated by bodies of water. The primary difference between tunnels and bridges is that tunnels are constructed under waterways or mountains, while bridges are built across waterways.

Most modern canals, tunnels, and bridges have been constructed for economic purposes, such as to speed the movement of freight and passenger traffic. However, they can also have important political and/or military importance. While canals, tunnels, and bridges may be located within a particular country (for example, San Francisco's Golden Gate Bridge), our discussion will be on those that link two or more countries.

Canals

The world's two largest canals (in terms of tonnage), the Suez Canal and the Panama Canal, have long and colorful histories and both have played important economic and political roles in the regions they serve. The Suez Canal, which connects the Mediterranean Sea and the Red Sea, is a 90-mile waterway that was opened to traffic in 1869. From an economic perspective, the canal cut off half the distance by water between Europe and Asia, and, as a result, transit times between Europe and Asia declined dramatically.

The Suez Canal has been much more than just a conduit of goods between the Mediterranean and Red Seas. For example, the canal allowed Moslems living in Asian nations to make pilgrimages more easily to the holy city of Mecca. In addition, the canal has served as a focal point in the politically volatile Middle East; political tensions have periodically caused the canal to be closed to commercial traffic.

The Panama Canal, a 50-mile facility designed to link the Atlantic and Pacific Oceans and avoid long ocean trips around Cape Horn in South America, was opened to traffic in 1914. Once completed, the canal cut nearly 8,000 miles, and many days of transit time, off the existing water route from New York to San Francisco.

Politically, the Panama Canal represented an example of the global reach of the United States, in the sense that the United States was largely responsible for its construction and funding. Moreover, the United States controlled operations of the Panama Canal from 1914 until late 1999, at which time Panama took control of the Canal. Despite some apprehension about this transfer of power, the transition on December 31, 1999, appears to have gone smoothly: ". . . a week later, the sky hadn't fallen, the canal hadn't caved in, and no foreign troops had seized it. It was business as usual . . ."[25]

The changing nature of international supply chains, particularly in terms of increased north–south trade and the emergence of larger container ships, has important implications for the Suez and Panama Canals. While the Suez Canal currently can handle the world's largest ships—albeit not fully loaded—it is only operating at about 50 percent of its potential capacity. One reason for this underutilization is not physical constraints, but rather, that the Suez ". . . Suez is a victim of world trade patterns."[26] For example, the so-called North–South

---

[25] *Journal of Commerce,* Business as Usual. January 10, 2000.

[26] J. Drummond and H. Saleh, Too Big for World Trade Demands. *Financial Times,* May 9, 2001, p. 11.

Corridor between Central Asia and Russia would bypass the Suez Canal and link India, Iran, and Russia by rail, highway, and water. When fully operational, this corridor is expected to result in at least a 10 percent drop in Suez traffic.[27]

The Panama Canal, by contrast, continues to be challenged by physical constraints. Currently, the largest vessels that can traverse the canal are so-called Panamax ships, with a width of approximately 106 feet, a length approaching 900 feet, and carrying capacities of about 65,000 tons. As this edition is being prepared, there is talk of building a bypass that could accommodate container ships capable of carrying up to 10,000 TEUs.

Bridges and Tunnels

Some of the world's most prominent international bridges are those involved in facilitating movements between the North American Free Trade Agreement (NAFTA) countries of Canada, Mexico, and the United States. Since implementation of NAFTA, cross-border trade volumes have skyrocketed; this increased volume has put tremendous pressure on the existing infrastructure. In 2000, for example, a fourth bridge linking Laredo, Texas and Nuevo Laredo, Mexico was opened—and this new bridge is a cargo-only facility. Likewise, in 2000, a bridge was completed between Sweden and Denmark that connects the northern Scandinavian countries with mainland Europe.

Tunnels can specialize in either road traffic (the Detroit-Windsor Tunnel) or rail traffic (Channel Tunnel). One of the world's most famous cross-border tunnels is the Channel Tunnel (Chunnel), which runs under the English Channel and provides rail linkage between Britain and France. Moreover, the Channel Tunnel allows for high-speed rail service between the key European economic centers of London, Paris, and Brussels. In recent years, the Channel Tunnel, which was plagued by construction and financial difficulties prior to its opening in 1994, has suffered from various operational problems, including periodic worker strikes and a fire in 1996.

Although there have been important advances in engineering and construction for both bridges and tunnels, accidents and failures still occur. These accidents and failures are important because of their potential human and business consequences. Bridge collapses and tunnel fires, for example, often result in the loss of multiple lives and economic disruption to the surrounding communities. This is well illustrated by the March 1999 fire in the Mont Blanc Tunnel, in which approximately 40 people were killed. This seven-mile tunnel, which connects

---

[27]E. Watkins, North-South Corridor Puts Suez on Notice. *Lloyd's List,* November 16, 2000, p. 7.

France and Italy, carried nearly 50 percent of the truck traffic between the two countries. During the tunnel reconstruction, this traffic was diverted to the Frejus tunnel, adding both time—at least three hours—and monetary costs.[28] The Mont Blanc tunnel was expected to reopen in late 2001—two and one-half years after the tragic fire.

Summary

The chapter looked at some of the man-made links and nodes that help to facilitate international trade. Seaports and airports were the two nodes that were discussed, while the links discussion focused on canals, tunnels, and bridges.

A general discussion of port operations was followed by analysis of various aspects of port competition, including load centers, port labor, and free trade zones. Selected issues in airport management included airport ownership and operation, airport congestion, as well as airport safety and security.

The chapter concluded with a look at canals, tunnels, and bridges. Two of the world's most prominent canals, the Suez and Panama, were highlighted. The discussion of bridges focused on their importance in facilitating trade between NAFTA countries, while the tunnel discussion highlighted the Channel Tunnel that links Great Britain and France.

End-of-Chapter Questions

1. Do you believe that water ports (airports) should be operated by public or private authorities? Why?

2. How do load centers influence the dynamics of international logistics?

3. How does port labor contribute to the efficiency/inefficiency of port operations?

4. Discuss the importance of free trade zones.

5. What are the major causes of airport congestion?

6. Do you believe that the policies and procedures for airport safety and security should be standard throughout the world? Why or why not?

7. Discuss the various environmental concerns associated with airport operations.

8. Distinguish among canals, tunnels, and bridges.

---

[28]R. Graham, Painful Consequences of Severed Artery. *Financial Times*, June 28, 1999, p. 1.

9. Discuss how the changing nature of international trade has impacted the Suez and Panama Canals.

10. Do you believe that the construction of the Channel Tunnel was a good idea or a bad idea? Why or why not?

CASE • *Paula's Food Products*

Paula's Food Products (PFP), located in Cleveland, Ohio, specializes in packaged snack foods such as potato chips, corn chips, and pretzels. PFP uses one manufacturing plant, located on Cleveland's southeast side, to supply its U.S. customer base. The Cleveland manufacturing plant is also the source for products that are exported to Canada and the United Kingdom, PFP's two current non-domestic markets. PFP's board of directors has recently approved expansion into two additional European markets, France and Germany. Initially, at least, PFP will export its snack products to these two countries.

Questions for *Paula's Food Products*

1. Do you agree with the choice of France and Germany as the next two European markets? Why or why not? If not, what other European country (ies) would you prefer that PFP serve?

2. PFP currently uses the Port of Hampton Roads (Norfolk, VA) as the exit port for shipments moving to the United Kingdom. Should Norfolk also be used as the U.S. exit port for the shipments to France and Germany? Why or why not?

3. PFP's U.K. shipments enter through the Port of Felixstowe (England). With the addition of France and Germany as new European markets, would you send all the European shipments through Felixstowe, or would you opt for shipping through ports in each of the three countries? Support your answer.

4. What are the most important factors that PFP should consider when selecting its U.S. port of exit? What are the most important factors that PFP should consider when selecting its European port(s) of entry? Are your answers the same? Why or why not?

5. Transit times by container ship from Norfolk to England, France, and Germany range from 11 to 13 days. Although snack foods are a relatively low-value product, can you think of any instances in which air transportation would be used to move shipments to the United King-

dom, France, and/or Germany? If yes, how would your answers to Questions 2, 3, and 4 be similar? How would they be different?

6. Several members of PFP's board of directors are urging that the next non-domestic market to be entered after France and Germany be either China or India. What kinds of information about China and India's water ports should be relevant to this decision?

10

International Logistics Functions
and Intermediaries

Introduction

There are no airtight definitions of logistics or logistics systems. Experts increasingly see logistics and logistics systems as activities facilitating four different cycles in the supply chain: the customer order cycle, the replenishment cycle, the manufacturing cycle, and the procurement cycle.[1] As used in this book, *logistics* is the organized movement of materials, information, and sometimes, people. Logistics implies that many separate, related activities are undertaken and are coordinated.

International logistics involves movements that cross borders, and these movements are considerably more complex than domestic ones. Many international movements go aboard ship, and the entire process of moving through ports and being at sea is time consuming. Complicating matters, differences between time zones can limit the hours when verbal communications can take place. Also, the documentation required for international shipping is varied and complicated, often requiring the services of experts. And today, inventory-in-transit is managed as if it were inventory-in-place, increasing the information management complexity and demands of international logistics.

The firm's international logistics department is responsible for the management, communications, control, and planning of the logistics activities. Specific activities or functions, all of which fall under the business firm's international logistics umbrella, include the following, which may be categorized in terms of

---

[1]Gupta, Sunil and Peter Meindl (2001), *Supply Chain Management: Strategy, Planning, and Operation*, Upper Saddle River, NJ: Prentice-Hall, p. 8.

usually being associated with outbound movements, inbound movements, or overall logistics management:

Demand forecasting, order management, packaging, labeling, documentation flow, customer service and parts and service support are typically associated with outbound flows. They will be discussed in both this chapter and Chapter 14, although the treatment in Chapter 14 will be from the exporter's viewpoint. Production scheduling, procurement, and the handling of returned products associated with inbound movements will be mentioned here and are covered also in Chapter 15.

Logistics activities that are related to both sales and procurement include: inventory management, materials handling, transportation management, warehouse and distribution center management, returned products, salvage scrap disposal, inter-plant movements, plant and warehouse site selection, and movement of people. All logistics functions today are assisted by information systems as well, and many firms consider information systems related to logistics functions as themselves a part of logistics management.

The various separate logistics activities listed will be discussed, but one should realize that they must be planned and executed in coordination with each other and with other functions in the firm's supply chain. Forever present is the idea of cost trade-offs: the logistics manager may pay more for one element of service in order to save an even larger amount on a different element. For example, if one uses air freight, an expensive form of transportation, one saves money on packaging because airlines are more careful with cargo than are many ocean carriers. In addition, one will receive quicker payment since the goods will be delivered more quickly. Also, current logistics thought holds that improving the level of customer service has its own reward in the form of increased sales.

The second topic to be covered in this chapter is related to the first, and it deals with firms that specialize in performing the various logistics functions. These firms are referred to as *facilitators* or *intermediaries*. Intermediaries exist because they improve the efficiency of marketing channels. In addition to covering routine logistics functions, they perform literally hundreds of specialized tasks associated with import/export movements. Take translators, for example. They may be needed for verbal translations, say, in trade negotiations and in promotional videotapes, and for written translation of trade documents or users' manuals. A translator must be able to work with at least two different languages; consider the number of different language pairs for which translations might be needed!

The best-known intermediaries in international trade are the freight forwarders.

Conventional wisdom continues to hold that they should be used by all first-time exporters. And many firms with long experience in exporting and importing continue to use forwarders for all but the most routine and repetitive of activities. Some companies use firms known as third-party logistics service providers, or "3PLs". These 3PL firms are capable of handling all or part of a firm's logistics service needs and are thus comprehensive in scope.

Outbound Logistics Functions

Outbound logistics for the exporting firm are covered both here and in Chapter 14. In this chapter, the goal is to list and define the activities. Those mostly associated with marketing include demand forecasting, order management, packaging and labeling, and documentation. Note that every firm has its own methods of selling overseas, and often uses different arrangements in different markets.

Demand Forecasting

Demand forecasting is carried on in conjunction with the firm's marketing staff and its principal overseas distributors and is used by the firm to project sales. This translates to production and procurement needs for the next planning period. These in turn translate into direct logistical requirements that include both delivery to customers and receipt of raw materials or components for assembly. Since the logistics staff is also involved with order management, it also has very early information about what customers are actually ordering. This is important intelligence for others in the firm who are planning and scheduling production and may wish to make alterations because of changes in demand. Note that the free flow of accurate demand forecasts is essential among the members of a supply chain to ensure a smooth flow of goods from origin to final consumer. Thus demand forecasting is equally important to managers of inbound movements.

Order Management

Order management starts with the receipt of an order from an overseas customer. It may be obtained by the firm's salesperson, be telephoned or faxed in, come by mail, or arrive electronically through EDI, email, or the World Wide Web. The first step in most international order management systems is to verify the accuracy of the order; that is, make certain that the various documents accompanying the order contain no internal errors that might mean the customer was uncertain about what he or she was ordering. The next step is to verify the customer's credit, or ability to pay. At this point, terms of sale become important, and they are covered in the next chapter. One would be concerned, for example, about insurance coverage for the shipment. A decision is made from which inventory point to ship the goods, and instructions are sent to that warehouse to fill the order. At the warehouse an order picking list is given to a warehouse worker who assembles the specific order. In the packing area, it is checked and packed for shipment, and the package is labeled. While this has been going on, the export traffic manager has been preparing the transportation documents and making arrangements for the forwarder or carrier to pick up the shipment. Various inventory and financial records are updated.

Packaging

Three purposes are served by packaging: identifying the product, protecting it, and aiding in handling. Identification serves a variety of purposes, from automated recognition of the product through bar coding to promotional purposes: packages make the product stand out on a store shelf and say "take me home" to the customer. The protective function is to protect the product and, in some instances, to keep the product from damaging surrounding items. Packaging also makes handling the product in distribution a much simpler task. The choice of packaging materials is influenced by concerns for environmental protection. Containers that can be recycled, or are made of recycled materials, are enjoying increased demand. Some nations are mandating their use.

Most retail products are packed in a hierarchy of packaging. The concept is of building blocks with the smallest size being the container placed on the shelf that the customer buys and takes home. These containers fit into a master carton that is typically one to two cubic feet in dimension; master cartons are unloaded, item by item, by the person stocking the shelves. Master cartons are stacked on pallets, usually wooden (though increasingly today recycled molded plastic) platforms six inches high and 40 inches by 48 inches along the top. Sometimes slip-sheets are used instead of pallets. Loaded pallets are moved by fork-lift trucks into and out of warehouses, intermodal containers, railcars, and trucks. Pallet loads are also called "unit-loads," and are the most common way of handling packaged freight.

Labeling

Labeling has several functions, the principal of which is to describe the contents of a package. Labeling is usually in the language of the exporting nation, although it is often advisable to have it in the importing nation's language as well. The buyer may intend to have the same shipping carton used for the international move serve for the domestic move as well, in which case additional labeling may be applied. Today, a common request would be to have bar code labels applied. (Providing them would be an example of value-added service.)

Documentation

Documentation is the preparation and handling of all the documents accompanying a shipment. In international movements, all documents must be present at the point where the goods are passing through the importing nation's customs and inspection posts. In recent years, computers and the electronic preparation and presentation of documents through EDI and the World Wide Web have made documentation less of a burden.

International shipments require many more documents than domestic shipments. The typical number ranges from six to ten, but the number can climb far above that. An example would be that livestock must be accompanied by a veterinarian's inspection certificate. Documentation also links the shipment to payment for the product, a form of control necessary to insure that goods are not shipped without regard to their payment status.

Customer Service

Customer service involves an array of activities to keep existing customers happy. "It makes sense to focus on customers you already have, encouraging repeat business. Barring that, you'll spend a lot of time and effort refilling a leaky bucket as you chase an ever-replenishing supply of new customers."[2] Servicing equipment in the field and training new users are other examples of customer service. As another example of customer service, FedEx pioneered the use of Web-based tracking of customer-shipped packages in 1994, empowering the customer with real-time information on the shipping status of packages.[3]

Customer service functions are important to a firm's success. In a survey of logistics practice worldwide, firms listed customer service performance ahead of six other performance variables in terms of importance to the success of logistics within their firm. Customer service ranked ahead of such concerns as lowered logistics costs and delivery speed and dependability.[4] In comparing firms

---

[2]Timm, Paul R. (1998), *Customer Service,* Upper Saddle River, NJ: Prentice-Hall, p. 6.

[3]*Wall Street Journal* (1999), "FedEx CEO Smith Bets His Deal Will Recast the Future of Shipping," p. 3.

[4]Global Logistics Research Team at Michigan State University (1995), *World Class Logistics: The Challenge of Managing Continuous Change,* Oak Brook, IL: Council of Logistics Management, p. 273.

globally on customer service performance, the same study found that the most successful firms differed significantly in their performance on six key customer service measures as compared to the poorest performing firms. Those performance measures were fill rate, stockouts, shipping errors, cycle time, complete orders, and overall reliability. Clearly, the customer service functions are strategically important.

Customer service levels are more challenging to maintain in international distribution systems. Repair parts, supplies, catalogs, warranties, and return policies must take into account the hurdles of crossing borders.

Parts and Service Support

Parts and service support are another element of customer service. Equipment that has been sold must be maintained. Buyers of capital equipment insist on knowing that their purchase will be kept in running order for many years, and thus prompt delivery of repair parts is necessary. Air freight is often used for that purpose. One large U.S. tractor manufacturer retains an outside firm to request, at random, specific repair parts from its own dealers and competitors' dealers throughout the world to measure how long it takes to fill the part orders.

Repair parts inventories are expensive to maintain and often must be justified on different criteria than are used for the main product lines. Parts and service support is an element of customer service although, in fact, buyers of a product may shift to another firm for long-term service support. In many trades special parts lists exist showing the interchangeability of various competitors' parts.

In an era when long-term partnerships are increasingly common, manufacturers of capital goods are recognizing that post-sales activities are important. Mercedes Benz trucks, for example, leans heavily on this approach: Before expounding on the trucks' features, the West German company uses advertisements to ask the enigmatic question: "Are you buying a vehicle or an iceberg?" In studying documents, one soon learns that the company in fact is referring to the total-cost concept to buy, operate, and replace the equipment. Mercedes Benz is happy to remind buyers that the price to buy a truck now only constitutes about fifteen percent of the total cost estimated for the average life of this kind of equipment. The company's sales directors thus advise clients to calculate the provisional costs—taking into account Mercedes Benz fuel-saving systems, rental or finance terms, and especially the large number of vehicles in stock, thanks to high quality production and efficient after-sales service—before choosing a supplier. Beyond maintenance services, which are complemented by an accelerated spare parts distribution system, the company also develops software packages for fleet management or delivery planning, as well as numerous training programs in economical driving or upkeep.[5]

Inbound Logistics Functions

Three functions associated with inbound logistics are production scheduling, procurement, and handling returned products. Either a manufacturing firm or a wholesale/retail firm must first forecast demand, and then determine what must be purchased for use in the production process or to stock inventories. Handling returned products is more of an issue for domestic transactions than for foreign ones because the difficulties in returning a product across borders may erase any advantages of doing so.

Production Scheduling

Scheduling of production is done with the assistance of the logistics staff. Production is scheduled in an attempt to balance demand for products with plant capacity and availability of inputs. In the international arena, one must take into account anticipated changes in relative values of currencies, longer distances and times for materials to travel, quotas on imports, etc. Some firms are truly international in stature and try to develop products that can be manufactured and sold in many parts of the world. One example is the Ford Focus, which is a "world designed" vehicle that one can spot variants of in many countries.

Inbound materials and components must be scheduled to fit into the production process. The production process itself is scheduled to fulfill existing and planned orders, and is thus dependent on accurate sales forecasting. Manufactured products must be scheduled for shipment to wholesalers, retailers, and customers. The logistics staff advises as to costs of moving materials. They hope to develop back-and-forth hauls of materials in order to better utilize transportation equipment. Just-in-time manufacturing philosophies call for disciplined, on-time deliveries. When just-in-time systems are used in supply chains, forecasts must be shared with suppliers so that they can better make their own plans. NUMMI (a GM-Toyota joint venture) in Fremont, California sends a seven-week forecast to its North American suppliers each week. The forecasts show potential ship quantities for the week by individual part numbers. Parts from Japan are handled in two ways: for optional parts, a three-day stock is maintained at the plant store-

---

[5]Mathe, Herve (1990), Service-Mix Strategies, Cedex: France: European Center for Research in Operations and Service Management, p. 51.

room and fed to the assembly line on a JIT basis. The other parts, such as engines that are used on all autos, move in response to seven-week plans. No safety stock of them is kept; they move in containers directly from the port to the assembly line.

Procurement

Closely related to production scheduling is procurement (or purchasing), since many of the inputs needed for production must be procured from outside sources, known as vendors. Boeing, for example, relies on about 10,000 vendors worldwide. The logistics staff advises as to the transportation services that must be used to insure that the purchased materials arrive in good condition and on schedule. If the vendor assumes responsibility for delivery of the inputs, the buyer's logistics staff monitors the delivery performance. The logistics staff will also attempt to consolidate the shipments of various inputs, to reduce their overall transportation costs. U. S. retail chains, buying in Asia, have consolidation points at major Asian ports, and have vendors ship goods to the consolidation points where the buyer's agent takes possession, places them into containers, and ships the full containers to the United States.

The procurement cycle has been visualized as having four major components in a process that is an input to manufacturing. First, an order is received based on a manufacturer's production schedule or on a supplier's stocking needs. Second, the supplier schedules the necessary production. Third, components are manufactured and shipped. And fourth, the components are received at the manufacturer's location.[6] The cycle is then repeated for a given manufacturer-vendor pair, and is similarly repeated for manufacturer-wholesaler and wholesaler-retailer pairs.

One issue in international sourcing is to learn about and rate the political stability in the nation from which one is buying. The risks are greater than for exporting to that nation since depending upon a single nation as a source may place at risk one's total production. Currency exchange rates are always an issue: in what currency does the supplier want to be paid? One must also evaluate the vendor firm and determine the quality of its product and its ability to maintain a given quality. Systems of testing and assuring quality of product should be agreed on. Often this involves use of a mutually agreed-on third party to perform such testing and assurance.

---

[6]Gupta, Sunil and Peter Meindl (2001), *Supply Chain Management: Strategy, Planning, and Operation,* Upper Saddle River, NJ: Prentice-Hall, pp. 12–13.

Sourcing decisions are made after determining total acquisition costs, which include the price of the product, transportation, inventory investment, packaging, and so on. From what source will the "landed" (or delivered) price be the lowest? On-time deliveries are also important. For example, U.S. catalog merchants are required by law to ship products to their customers within 30 days or refund their money within 90 days after the order is placed. The merchants incur extra costs as shipments to their customers are delayed beyond 30 days.

Returned Products

In domestic markets, there are many categories of returned products. A few are subjects of product recalls, meaning that a safety defect or hazard has been discovered and the products are removed from the shelves and both retailers and consumers attempt to return them to the manufacturer or to some intermediary. Some returned goods are those that have been on the shelves too long, and are no longer fresh. In the United States many food products have a "pull date" code on the package, indicating that the product should not be sold after that date. Then there are products that the customer is returning to be repaired or replaced. Some products are returned to be recycled in some way or another. Finally, there are products that may have been placed on consignment, never sold, and are being returned.

The firm doing business internationally will have to realize that in many national markets where the product is being sold, some returns can be expected for reasons given in the previous paragraph. Reverse flow channels must be established within those nations. Strict accounting controls are necessary to protect all parties in these sorts of transactions. Some care is also needed to insure that the returned product, thought to be scrapped, does not "reappear" to compete with one's other products in the same or perhaps in a different market.

Increasingly firms are using information technology to facilitate reverse logistics flows. One important function that requires specialized information systems is gatekeeping. Firms accepting returns must categorize, approve, and specify procedures as far forward in the distribution channel as possible. Such gatekeeping functions can now be pushed down to the point of end-customer return, typically a retail store. Returned products may be examined for completeness and condition, scanned into the reverse logistics information system, and appropriate final disposition determined before the good leaves the retail location. Firms typically outsource the design and operation of such sophisticated reverse logistics systems.[7]

---

[7]Naber, Mark A. (2001), *Reverse Logistics and Internet Technologies,* unpublished master's thesis, San Francisco State University, pp. 55–57.

It is possible, although unlikely, to have products returned to the nation where they were manufactured. This does not happen frequently because of logistics costs and uncertainties regarding the items' value at its final destination point. Quite often returned products are disposed of inside of the nation in which they were sold to the end customer. This may involve repackaging and sale, salvage sale, or disposal (usually requiring some level of destruction to prevent the resale of defective goods).

Overall Logistics Activities

Some logistics functions are not specific to import or export operations. Terms of sale may assign responsibility for them to either the buyer or the seller. Most common of all logistics activities are inventory management and transportation management. Also covered here are materials handling, warehouse and distribution center management, salvage and scrap disposal, interplant movements, plant and warehouse site selection, and moving people.

Inventory Management

Stocks of goods or materials are inventories. They often are located at points where there is a change in the rate and unit of movement. A grain elevator might receive grain from local farmers at the rate of six or seven truckloads a day during the harvest season, and hold the grain until it is shipped out at the rate of several railcars a week over a 12-month period.

Since inventories are used as buffers between differing rates of inflow and outflow, in the design of systems they are also placed as buffers to protect against unforeseen demands, lags in resupply, or managerial error. Inventory protects a firm's customers from these three sources of error. Modern logistics thinking is critical of inventories; all other things being equal, a system with fewer or smaller inventories is judged to be superior. An important logistics management function deals with management of inventories. In some firms, it is the single most important decision, since decisions concerning the locations of inventories and their directions and patterns of flow do, in fact, reflect the design efficiency of the total system.

Inventories also represent an investment that the owner hopes to sell. (Sometimes they represent an "involuntary" investment that occurs when goods are produced faster than they are sold. If a demand forecast is too high, surplus inventory can begin quite early in the supply chain.) There are costs associated with holding inventories, including interest on the money invested in the inventory, storage costs, and risks of deterioration, obsolescence, and shrinkage. *Inventory shrinkage* is the term that acknowledges and measures the fact that most inventory records show more goods have entered an inventory than can be found. In some trades shrinkage is so pronounced that it is designed into the system, with a common example being the shipment of tropical fish.

Carrying costs are significant. Inventory carrying costs in the U.S. declined from 5 percent to 4 percent of Gross Domestic Product during the ten year period ending in 2000.[8] This was due largely to improved inventory management. While a 1 percent decline may seem small, that represents some $99.6 billion dollars saved in 2000 through logistics efficiencies.

Many different classes of products are kept in a firm's inventory. They may include company supplies, work-in-process goods, finished goods (made by the firm), packaging materials, labels, promotional materials (catalogs and samples), raw materials and components, resale goods (purchased from other firms for resale—a firm that manufactures air cleaners may buy filters from an outside source), returned goods made by others, returned products made by the firm, scrap and waste to be disposed of or recycled, spare parts, and traded-in goods of a competitor's or one's own brand.

For products that are traded internationally, there are additional inventory classifications: the country of origin, since import duties or charges sometimes vary by country of origin; countries where goods can or cannot be sold, an example being that some foreign autos cannot be sold in the United States because of emission control and crash safety requirements; and the specific languages used on the product or package or in catalogs. For these categories, the phrase *committed* might be applicable. Committed inventory is pledged for a certain market, use, or customer, and cannot be freely drawn upon for other purposes.

Maintaining accurate records of international inventories is more difficult because of the length of the pipeline through which the products travel and the fact that there many more places where the inventory can hide. It is vital to understand that inventory ages at each of these hiding places. Guidelines should be established for maximum holding periods at each location, as well as when to ship such inventories back to the factory or to an alternative customer. Inventory valuation is also difficult because if goods are valued in the currency of where they are produced, that value will usually fluctuate vis-a-vis the currency value in the nation where they are stored. Import quotas also affect the value, since goods that have been admitted under the quota may be sold, while those outside the quota must wait. Some international companies use an internal "company" currency for consistency.

---

[8]Delaney, Robert V. and Rosalyn Wilson (2001), "Managing Logistics in the Perfect Storm?" *Twelfth Annual State of Logistics Report*, St. Louis, MO: Cass Information Systems.

There are different standards for maintaining inventories throughout the world. Factors given for international variations in manufacturing stock levels include: industrial structure, length and reliability of lead times, proximity to international markets and material sources, cost of storage space, standards of inventory management, nature of quality control systems, diversification of product ranges, cyclical activity in the national economy, government economic policy, structure of the distribution system, and speed and reliability of transport.[9] The rule of thumb here is: The less well developed the logistics infrastructure and the less sophisticated the logistics processes, the more inventory will be required to support a given level of customer service.

Transportation Management

Planning, arranging, and buying the international transportation services needed to move a firm's freight is known as *transportation management.* It is probably the single most costly element of international logistics. The transportation manager is concerned with freight consolidation, carrier rates and charges, carrier selection, certain documentation, tracing and expediting, loss and damage claims, demurrage and detention, movements of hazardous materials, employee moving services, and use of private carriage. Transportation management for export shipments is discussed in more detail in Chapter 14.

Freight consolidation means the assembling of many smaller shipments into a smaller number of large shipments. The reason for this is that the carriers charge less per pound for handling larger shipments since less paperwork and individual handling are involved. Hence, a transportation manager would like to see a customer's daily orders consolidated into a single weekly order, or have orders for seven customers in a foreign country handled as a single shipment to that country, and then broken down inside that country for delivery to each of the seven. Carriers establish their rates in several ways, as discussed in chapters dealing with transportation. Transportation managers must know how to determine rates and, in some markets, be able to negotiate for even lower rates.

Carrier selection is a two-step phase. First the company must decide which mode—water, rail, pipeline, truck, or air—to use for each segment of traffic it handles. Air is the fastest way to carry international shipments, but it is also the most expensive. Once the modal choice decision is made, the transportation manager must choose which carrier firm or firms should get the company's

---

[9]Dimitrov, P. and S. Wandel, cited in Alan C. McKinnon (1991), "Regional Variations in Manufacturing Inventory Levels," *International Journal of Physical Distribution and Logistics Management,* 21 (6), 4 (1991).

business. After the selection is made, the carriers' performance is monitored to make certain that its quality does not deteriorate. Increasingly, transportation managers are purchasing transportation services from intermodal carriers who creatively combine modes under single ownership for point-to-point transportation solutions. Several of these intermodal carriers offer Web-based real-time access to global shipment information by their customers. APL has its HomePort website *(http://www.apl.com)*, and Orient Overseas Container Line has its CargoSmart website *(http://www.oocl.com)*.

MSAS Global Logistics is a British global logistics services provider that manages the selection of both air and ocean freight carriers. Each carrier is evaluated in five performance areas: general operation efficiency; administrative performance; people relationships/communications; route profiles; and rates. What emerges from the evaluation is a set of preferred carriers who currently handle over 70 percent of the firm's shipments. Carriers who don't make the preferred list are given feedback and asked to improve their operations to be considered for preferred status in the future.[10]

Transportation managers must also know how and where to combine modes. One example of this can be found in Japanese manufacturers who located assembly plants in Brazil. The sea service was slow and undependable, so a route was developed consisting of an ocean carrier from Japan to Los Angeles, and then an air carrier from Los Angeles to Sao Paulo, Rio de Janeiro, and Manaus. If the goods went solely by sea, the cost was 60 to 75 cents per kilo, while all air costs were about ten times as high. The sea/air link cost about $2.75 per kilo and transit time averaged 16 days, compared with 45 to 60 days by sea. The variability in time via sea made just-in-time type of discipline difficult. An added disadvantage of long transit times was that Brazil's inflation changed the results of financial calculations very quickly.[11]

Tracing and expediting are related; both involve paying attention to a shipment that is in the carrier's hands, somewhere. *Tracing* is the effort to find a delayed or misplaced shipment. *Expediting* is the attempt to have a specific shipment move faster through the carrier's system because it is needed immediately by the consignee. An example would be components needed for an assembly line. Tracing and expediting are today facilitated by real-time shipper access to carrier and customs databases through the Internet.

Loss and damage claims require the transportation manager to attempt to col-

---

[10]Beddow, Matthew (1999), "Carrier Selection," *Containerisation International,* October 1999, pp. 45–47.

[11]*American Shipper* (1990), January 1990, pp. 69–70.

lect the amount of the damages from the insurance company and from the carrier. Demurrage and detention reflect the traffic manager's responsibility to load and unload carrier equipment promptly. If he does not, then the carrier assesses daily detention or demurrage charges until the transportation manager's firm frees the carrier's equipment. This is to prevent the shippers and consignees from using the carriers' equipment as warehouses.

Hazardous materials movements require special attention. Sometimes only certain routes, ports, warehouses, and vehicular equipment can be used. For example, there are a number of hazardous materials that may be moved by land or truck but which are prohibited in air transport. For some hazardous material movements specialized carriers must be used. Containers and vehicles have special markings and additional documentation is needed to accompany the shipment.

The transportation manager is also responsible for dealing with the household goods carriers that move the families of employees being transferred from country to country. Private fleet management involve control of railcars, trucks, vessels, or airplanes that the company owns for carrying its own products.

Mention should be made of "turnkey" projects. They involve the building, finishing, and turning over to new owners a complete, operating project, such as a power dam. Logistics in these situations would involve assembling all the materials, as needed. Projects are often in remote areas, and transportation and housing facilities must also be provided. Some projects built by Bechtel Engineering, a large San Francisco-based contractor, generate a million tons of cargo over a four-year period.

Materials Handling

This term is used in several different ways. *Materials handling* often covers movements of goods that are under the firm's immediate control, such as within a plant or warehouse complex or between plants. The term is also associated with procurement, that is, what to do with materials after acquiring ownership. Lastly, the term sometimes refers to the handling of bulk products. Examples are iron ore, coal, and grain that move in trainload, truckload, and shipload lots. The materials are loaded, unloaded, and transferred by large mechanical devices. Liquids such as petroleum are pumped through pipelines. Flour and cement are moved between dry tanks pneumatically, that is, by large vacuum-cleaner-like devices.

Materials flow is another term that is used. Dell Computer uses a sophisticated set of software tools through its extranet with component suppliers, logistics and transportation companies, and value-added resellers all over the world.

Time-sensitive information regarding materials flow, including orders, inventory levels, manufacturing inputs, and shipping order status are shared with all of the firms participating in Dell's supply chain.[12]

Usually one does not think in terms of an entire international move fitting under the materials management spectrum. However, that is not impossible. As firms exercise increasingly rigorous and tight control over their international logistics system, they may consider it to be part of their materials management system. To repeat, the distinction is relative; the term usually applies to those segments of the move where the company's control is complete.

Warehouse and Distribution Center Management

This logistics activity involves the management of the locations where the firm's inventories are stored. Warehouses and distribution centers are similar but the latter places more emphasis on moving the goods through promptly. In international logistics, one usually thinks of having overseas warehouses managed by third parties who are providing a bundle of services for an exporter/importer, of which inventory maintenance and warehousing is but one part. Consider this: "In most Hispanic countries, the warehousing business . . . is a tight club. Third-party warehousing has been largely organized under banking laws, with providers operating as branches of the bank." And, ". . . most Mexican warehouses operate on a system of 'ad valorem pricing' in which customer charges are based on the value of the cargo. . . . That system is popular among warehouse operators . . . because it shields them from inflation or currency devaluations."[13]

Salvage and Scrap Disposal

A firm's waste materials must be managed. Ordinarily, one associates scrap disposal as a domestic activity. Many firms sell their scrap to other firms which specialize in disposal and recycling. However, there are a few international aspects of scrap disposal. Old ships are sailed or towed to nations in the world where labor is very cheap. India is one country with an active ship dismantling and recycling industry, for example. Auto batteries are shipped for recycling to nations with weak worker safety and environmental protection controls. These practices can raise ethical questions. Firms must also be wary of companies offering dis-

---

[12]Reeve, John (1999), "E-commerce: What Role for Intermediaries?" *Containerisation International,* November 1999, pp. 51–55.

[13]*American Shipper* (1992), December 1992, p. 38.

posal services to make certain that they dispose of the materials in legal and environmentally sound ways. The public is becoming increasingly concerned about each firm's environmental scoreboard, and more and more care is needed to make certain that environmental concerns are addressed in the firm's scrap disposal methods.

Markets for many used products are worldwide, although the demand elsewhere must be sufficient to cover all the added costs of international movements. Usually firms other than the original manufacturer handle these transactions. Some production equipment is sold overseas, where it continues to produce styles that may no longer be fashionable in U.S., Japanese, or European markets.

Interplant Movements

During the production process a firm moves products among its various plants. A large manufacturer might have several thousand suppliers feeding parts into dozens of factories that assemble components that will be used by a few assembly lines. Flows must be controlled and altered to meet changing demands. A continual challenge is reducing the size of work-in-process inventories.

At this point one should discuss the importance of *bartering* (a form of countertrade) to international transactions, because it may have an additional impact upon the seller and the seller's interplant logistics operations. Barter is often used by buyers in nations with scarce supplies of hard currency. Sometimes even a three-way trade will be insisted upon. The buyer will insist that the seller also ship or accept goods from a third party with whom the buyer is also attempting to settle accounts. Responsibility for carrying out the logistics arrangements can fall on any of the parties. Bartering can have several effects upon a firm's logistics. If the firm can use the product, then they must enter it into their internal goods flow and control system as they would any other input. If the firm is not going to use the product, they must determine a way to dispose of it profitably.

Sometimes a specific product will not be bartered, but the buyer will agree to make a certain volume of purchases from a firm or from a nation. A common example is in the export sale of new airline aircraft to airlines owned by governments of foreign nations. The aircraft manufacturer will agree to spend a certain amount of money in the nation buying the planes. This is called an *offset transaction*. Boeing encourages the offset process by sending material in kit form to be assembled in a particular country and then returned to the United States as a complete unit. Boeing also ships near-complete aircraft kits to China for final assembly for use in the Chinese domestic market.

International interplant movements are subject to customs scrutiny because they are related party transactions. Duties are taxes levied on imports, and ad valorem duties are duties based on the value of goods. If one were a customs inspector reviewing an import invoice from a related party, might one not wonder whether the value shown represents the true or fair market value of the goods covered by the invoice? *Fair market value,* or FMV, roughly means the price at which a willing seller will sell to a willing buyer under similar conditions. Since willing infers that neither party is under any compulsion, an important aspect of fair market value is missing in related party, or intercompany, transactions. The possibility is that the product is intentionally underpriced in order to avoid paying the full amount of duty due. Hence, when making plans for intercompany transactions, one of the cost items to be controlled is customs payments as the materials cross borders. Consider this:

> A recent trend among U.S. firms has been to set up final-assembly plants in Europe for goods partially assembled elsewhere. The goal: these plants in low-tax countries—Ireland and the Netherlands are the two favorites—sell the half-finished products to the final assembly plants at ridiculously low prices, and concentrate profits there as a means of reducing a firm's overall tax bill. But Uncle Sam has been cracking down on this, and the sneak who thought he could dodge the IRS through final-assembly sleight of hand is now finding that the transfer of profits back to the U.S. is often accompanied by a hefty tax bill.[14]

Plant and Warehouse Site Selection

Firms often must find the location for a new facility. Usually this decision follows a process of system analysis and design wherein a determination is made of how many facilities the firm should be operating. As an example, a firm needing to distribute repair parts overnight within fifty industrialized nations could probably reach nearly all markets by air from five or six warehouse locations, if the firm were willing to use air express services. Or a growing firm may decide that it needs a new warehouse to serve a certain region. Several layers of analyses would be performed, each with a finer focus.

After a world region is selected, then a country within the region is chosen. Criteria to this point include markets, membership in a trade bloc, availability and wage rates of labor, tax rates, political stability, energy costs, proximity to suppliers and to markets, customs charges, import quotas, climate, and transportation. Trade agreements between that nation and nations with which the facility would be doing business are relevant; many Asian manufacturers have located plants in Mexico to take advantage of NAFTA, for example. Finally, a city

---

[14]*World Trade* (1992), June 1992, p. 97.

is chosen and, within that chosen city, various sites are examined, with one taking into account land-use controls, street traffic capability, room for expansion, soil stability, environmental protection requirements, water and sewer line capacity, police and fire protection, presence of unions, proximity to rail tracks, freeways, ports and airports, free trade zones, and so on.

Some firms serve contracting, or shrinking, markets. They must decide which production or distribution facilities to close, and the closure and withdrawal must be scheduled in a way that reduces adverse impact on the firm's overall operations.

We defined bartering as trading goods for goods. Another form of bartering occurs when a seller will agree to locate a plant, assembly operation, or distribution center in a specific nation and will employ a specified number of local citizens.

Most levels of government provide subsidies to encourage the location of production facilities. They do this to increase job opportunities for their citizens. Subsidies can and do take many forms. The direct payment of money to a producer is a simple example. A government may make such direct subsidy payments in order to keep workers employed. There are subtler subsidies as well. Paying a part of employee compensation, training, or benefits, or underwriting the cost of factory construction or energy expense, are all subsidies that reduce the producer's costs artificially and thus the price at which the firm may sell. Another form of subsidy is the granting of special tax relief to a particular beneficiary industry or even company. Tax concessions are extremely important as they often determine the profitability of a given business. Nations subsidize exports in order to increase the level of economic activity and to earn foreign exchange. However, other nations, importing these goods, require that these subsidies be taken into account when determining the cost of an imported good. The practice is known as imposing countervailing duties. A *countervailing duty* is one that is imposed on the invoice value of a transaction (the "transaction value") in order to compensate for subsidies granted to the exporter/producer by the exporting country. Again, this must be taken into account when determining where in the world one wishes to locate economic activity.

Moving People

Little has been said about the logistics of moving people. This can be handled in two ways. Individuals can be given instructions to meet at a certain point, either nearby or far away. They then assume responsibility for making their own travel arrangements and showing up as directed. If larger groups of people are to be moved, a firm may assume responsibility for a group move and charter an

airplane and arrange for a block of hotel rooms. When large projects are constructed in remote areas, it is necessary to build housing for the construction
workers and to continually supply them with food and other goods.

A firm that transfers employees around the world also must relocate their families and household possessions. There are third-party firms that provide this
service.

Some nations often supply the workforce used in other nations. The workers
are recruited in their home nation and moved to where they are needed. Recall
that during the war in Kuwait, many of the persons living in Kuwait were common laborers from other nations.

Coordinating and Managing Logistics

This concludes the discussion of the individual elements of a firm's logistics system. How are they tied together? The first way is by the firm's management
structure. It may have a separate logistics department that is equal in status with
other major departments such as finance, production, marketing, and so on. Today, some firms rely on third-party logistics, whereby they contract with an outside firm to coordinate, manage, and sometimes perform the various functions.

Communications links are important and are also obviously complex, although
EDI and the Internet are being used for buyer-seller, shipper-forwarder-carrier,
and importer-exporter-customs linkages. Many ocean carriers allow cargo to
be booked by computer. Maersk Sea-land allows shippers direct access to its
computer network. The customer can bypass a Maersk Sea-land customer service representative and, using a connection to Maersk Sea-land's website
(http://www.maersksealand.com), can:

Perform cargo tracking, learn shipment status

Request vessel schedules

Book space (via the website)

Make direct queries about information on specific bills of lading, that is,
charges, piece counts

Email queries to other Maersk Sea-land offices anywhere in the world

Learn cargo availability (imports)

Book facilitating services from Maersk Sea-land or cooperating intermediaries

Obviously, the task of managing an international logistics system is challenging and calls for one to be able to understand, control, and lead all the elements
covered in this book.

Logistics Intermediaries

The first part of this chapter covered a wide range of activities that fit under the logistics umbrella. On occasion, mention was made of the fact that third parties, meaning outside firms, were often retained to perform these specific services. In this chapter these firms will be referred to as intermediaries or facilitators. The term *third-party logistics,* or 3PL, is widely used in logistics circles these days, and it has a somewhat broader meaning—namely the outsourcing of all a firm's logistics activities to another firm that then manages them, without taking an ownership position in the inventories.

One intermediary with whom readers may have dealt is the travel agent. The travel agent represents a client's desire to travel and finds the transportation and lodging accommodations best suited to his or her needs and pocketbook. Airlines and hotels pay the travel agent a commission for their selling efforts.

Intermediaries abound in foreign trade, and they cement relationships between parties in the supply chain. Whole armies of specialists and generalists exist to help the firm with its export or import shipments. One listing of economic activities associated with ports handling international cargoes shows nearly 100 different types of ancillary services.[15] One can find very specialized activities from groups that collect used books to be placed on ships where they might be read by merchant seamen, to an agency that monitors workmen's compensation claims by seamen to insure that the claim for the same disablement is not filed against two different vessel operators.

At times the carriers have attempted to eliminate these intermediaries, feeling they could perform all these functions themselves. For the most part, the intermediaries have survived. Writing of marketing channels, Bowersox and Cooper say: "The demand for functional performance coupled with complexity leads to a high degree of specialization in . . . channel arrangements. Specialization and its related benefits represent . . . [a] motivation for the formation of channel arrangements. Specialization is fundamental in advanced industrial societies."[16]

For the authors, it is a challenge to decide which intermediaries to discuss and which to ignore. Some exist in certain geographic locations; some are associated with certain types of cargo, such as livestock or zoo animals. ("With a Dutch expert [the intermediary] KLM has shifted its method of dolphin transport from wet slings . . . to Styrofoam-lined chests, shaped to hold fins and tail safely, with

---

[15]Wood, Donald F. and James C. Johnson (1996), *Contemporary Transportation,* 5th edition, Englewood Cliffs, NJ: Prentice-Hall, p. 422.

[16]Bowersox, Donald J. and M. Bixby Cooper (1992), *Strategic Management of Marketing Channels,* New York: McGraw-Hill, p. 20.

battery-operated pumps that keep the dolphin doused in water."[17] Some are generalists, many are specialists. Complicating the matter is that many firms are "shells" set up to minimize liabilities or taxes or to establish residency in other nations. Some of the intermediaries that are discussed are well known; others are more specialized.

Freight Forwarders

The most common intermediary in international logistics is the *freight forwarder*. After the sale is completed, a freight forwarder can handle nearly of all the logistical aspects of the transaction. Indeed, large forwarders may assume responsibility for managing the firm's international distribution and supply channels. Smaller forwarders often specialize in air or ocean movements. Forwarders have a number of advantages, including daily pickup and distribution; global shipping capacity with choices from multiple carriers; local staff who are familiar with the shipper's needs; advice and preparation of documents; consolidation of freight from multiple shippers to a single destination, thus saving freight costs; and because of bulk booking of freight space, they will often have capacity available when the carrier reports "sold out."

In early 2001, United Parcel Service (UPS) bought the Fritz Companies, leaders in freight forwarding and customs brokerage. UPS is combining freight forwarding and customs brokerage services into its other services in transportation and logistics, thus providing one-stop shopping for small shippers (*http://www.ups.com*).

NVOCCs

A second form of intermediary, somewhat similar to the forwarder, is the non-vessel operating common carrier (NVOCC). They are also called consolidators or NVOs. NVOCCs provide scheduled ocean shipping services without operating ships, sometimes by leasing containers, paying flat rates (or FAK—freight all kinds) rates for the containers, and then selling space in the containers to less-than-container load (LCL) shippers. NVOCCs also provide a variety of services required for point-to-point movement of goods, many of which overlap forwarder functions. The relationship of forwarders to NVOCCs is that a foreign freight forwarder may select an NVOCC instead of an ocean liner for the ocean segment of the cargo movement for LCL shipments.

---

[17]*KLM Cargo Directory of Services*, 1990, p. 19.

NVOCCs can be independent companies or be owned by freight forwarders, subsidiaries of large U.S. transportation companies, or large overseas transportation companies. Many NVOCCs are small entrepreneurial firms. The total shipping handled by NVOCCs in the United States has amounted to about 10 percent of annual volume.

NVOs are thought of as "shippers with respect to carriers and carriers with respect to shippers." They came into being as shipping conferences offered discounts for heavier shipments, or full container loads. Today, the future of NVOCCs is somewhat clouded by the rapid consolidation in the shipping industry that took place at the turn of the 21st century. A number of small parcel express shippers have purchased major freight forwarding firms, allowing the new combined organization a number of advantages over NVOCCs.[18]

One of these advantages is in information management. Many small shippers wish to have comprehensive information on the movement of their goods. Combined industry behemoths like UPS/Fritz (a global delivery firm and a freight forwarder) provide an attractive array of Internet-based tools allowing the small shipper to manage freight in transit. NVOCCs have been slow to adopt similar technologies. According to Paul E. Victory, president of the NVOCC Dieterle and Victory International Transport Company:

> Outside of rates, most of our shippers just want to know where their freight is . . . We're not talking rocket science here . . . [With regard to the internet as a sales tool], it's something you do because you have to. I don't believe that it helps you move freight any faster. A box is a box: you still have to load it correctly and get it to where it's supposed to go.[19]

With continued consolidation likely in the global freight transportation industry, the competitive climate for NVOCCs is uncertain at best. As Alan E. Baer of NVO Ocean World Lines says regarding the large parcel carriers, "We know they're out there. They're large, money-backed organizations that will attack the business."[20]

Export Management Companies

Export management companies (EMCs) are intermediaries that market another firm's products overseas. They have three to five-year exclusive representation

---

[18]*American Shipper* (2001), "UPS Acquires Fritz Cos.", February 2001, p. 8.

[19]*American Shipper* (2001), "UPS Acquires Fritz Cos.", February 2001, p. 8.

[20]Gillis, Chris, op. cit.

contracts, investigate potential customers' credit standing, and can handle complementary, non-competitive products. EMCs are professional exporters. An EMC does not manufacture. The business of the EMC is finding and servicing markets overseas on behalf of domestic manufacturers. Servicing the market includes many of the functional areas covered in this chapter. Preparing documentation; appointing forwarders; arranging for special packing; procuring insurance; providing special documents, such as consular documents; and negotiating rates are all functions provided by the EMC. In addition, and more important for many firms, the EMC provides a marketing and sales capability the manufacturer lacks. The EMC will conduct market research on behalf of the product and develop promotional materials designed specifically for the target market. The EMC will also advise the manufacturer on modifications needed in order to promote the success of the product.

Fitting the product to the market is an essential part of international business. Product presentation and promotional methods are not always directly transferable to foreign markets. With respect to promotion, colors, words, phrases, and graphics (such as cartoons and photographs) can connote different things in different countries—sometimes with disastrous results. A scantily clad woman on a billboard in California may sell sun-screen lotion, but the same ad would be unthinkable in Arab countries. For these and similar reasons, manufacturers find a need to utilize specialists familiar with the intricacies and the norms of particular markets. What will work and how it should be structured is the business of the EMC. When the EMC designs promotional literature, represents the manufacturer at a trade show, responds to an importer's inquiry, appoints a local distributor, or goes on a sales trip, she or he is doing so with expert knowledge of the market area and its distribution channels. In addition to marketing and forwarding expertise, the EMC brings export finance and credit capability to the manufacturer.

Commission arrangements with EMCs are an alternative to buy-sell contracts with export trading companies. As indicated above, the EMC simply represents the manufacturer in its marketing effort. The exporter sells and ships directly to the foreign buyer, assumes all of the credit risk and usually makes all of its own arrangements. There are over 1,100 EMCs in the United States.

Export Packers

Export packers will be discussed in chapter 13. They are examples of a specialized intermediary. They assist the exporter with special packaging requirements needed to reach some export markets.

Customshouse Brokers

Often tied to freight forwarders in exporting nations, the *customshouse broker* meets the importer's shipment, and guides it through customs seeking to use tariff classifications that involve the smallest charges. Then he or she delivers the goods to the importer's place of business.

Publication Distributors

Another example of specialized intermediaries are *publication distribution firms.* KLM, the Dutch airline, has a publications distribution service that includes wrapping, destination sorting, addressing, database management, and so on, for magazines. Also handled are business reply mail and collections of subscription payments in local currency. Magazines move overseas by air and then are turned over to post offices for delivery, saving on international postage costs. Sometimes, the wrapping and labeling is done in the country of destination to save the weight of wrapping materials going by air.

Goods Surveyors

Goods surveyors are frequently referred to in international trade. They are retained by the buyer, the seller, or both to inspect the quality of goods, measure the weight, or determine the extent of damage that may have occurred while the goods were in transit. This is necessary to consummate some sales agreements where there is an apparent discrepancy. This is an extensive activity; in the Port of Antwerp, for example, are 15 surveying companies, employing a total of 2,500 workers. "Most companies have their own specialty. Some only survey grains, or oil or petrochemical products. There is even a company which only does sugar. Similarly, they might just inspect the quantity, or quality."[21]

Parts Banks

Several firms, often airlines, offer a parts bank service. This permits manufacturers to store important repair parts throughout the world, where they can be quickly flown to customers with equipment "down."

---

[21]*Hinterland* (1992), March 1992, p. 12.

Container Leasing Companies

Container leasing companies also facilitate intermodal movements because they can relieve individual carriers of the financial burdens and control responsibilities they would have if they had to own all of their equipment. The largest container leasing company in the world is GE Seaco, with over 1.1 million TEUs available for lease. GE Seaco's website *(http://www.geseaco.com)* provides a wealth of information regarding container leasing and industry trends, including an interactive map showing container availability in ports worldwide. These companies lease containers on both a short- and long-term basis. Each retires between five and ten percent of its containers each year because of wear.[22] Within the industry are niches filled by container leasing firms that specialize in different types of containers, such as reefers or tanks. Some firms also own fleets of container chassis that they lease out.

Export Trading Companies

Finally, one distinctly different intermediary is the *export trading company* (ETC). ETCs go one step further. They actually buy the manufacturer's goods, take title, and then sell these goods in the export market. ETCs are not merely representatives. They are customers of manufacturers in selected markets. Some of Japan's largest firms are ETCs. ETCs were allowed in the United States by 1982 legislation that lessened antitrust restrictions that would hamper cooperation needed for overseas selling.

Financial risk is an issue. By selling to an ETC instead of the importer, the manufacturer removes himself from some of the financial risks associated with exporting, such as those associated with political instability, the importer's creditworthiness, the country's creditworthiness, and the risk of unavailability of foreign exchange. Instead, the creditworthiness of the ETC becomes the only issue.

Summary

Two separate but related topics have been covered in this chapter. One dealt with the numerous functions or activities that fall under the logistics umbrella. They included demand forecasting, order management, packaging, labeling, documentation flow, customer service, and parts and service, all of which are usually

---

[22]*Port of New Orleans Record* (1990), May 1990, pp. 9–10.

associated with exporting. Then discussed were production scheduling, procurement, and the handling of returned products, all associated with inbound movements. Also discussed were logistics activities that are related to both sales and sourcing, including inventory management, materials handling, transportation management, warehouse and distribution center management, salvage and scrap disposal, interplant movements, plant and warehouse site selection, and movement of people.

The second part of the chapter dealt with logistics intermediaries. These are firms, often small, that specialize in performing one or more of the logistics tasks. They include freight forwarders, NVOCCs, export trading companies, and customshouse brokers, along with others. Often, they are the glue that holds the supply chain together.

End-of-Chapter Questions

1. Make a list of common international logistics channel intermediaries and their functions.

2. Explain the concept of a cost trade-off, and give an example from international logistics business practice.

3. Make lists of the common inbound and outbound international logistics functions. Which functions are common to both outbound and inbound movements?

4. Explain the relationship among demand forecasting, production scheduling, procurement, and inventory management. Give examples of cost trade-offs and information management issues that may affect the relationship among the four functions.

5. How are transportation management, warehouse location and management, and materials handling concepts related to each other? Give examples to illustrate your discussion.

6. What are the functions of a freight forwarder?

7. What are the functions of an NVOCC?

8. What are the functions of an export management company?

9. Describe three different logistics situations in which it would make good sense to choose (a) a freight forwarder; (b) an NVOCC; and (c) an export management company.

10. What is the main difference between an export management company and an export trading company?

CASE • *Betty's Brownies*

Growing up in Chicago, Betty Budris always enjoyed baking: cookies, cakes, sweets of all kinds. As Betty's children grew up, all their friends knew that Betty was the neighborhood source for homemade treats. But once Betty's children had gone off to college, she was left with lots of time-tested recipes but few "consumers." Her son Kenny was working on his MBA in marketing at Northwestern University when he suggested to his mom that they go into business together and bring Betty's treats to the sweet tooths of the world.

They started small, with a walk-in bakery shop in Evanston, Illinois, not far from the Northwestern campus. Wildly successful with the college crowd, they expanded by building a baking plant in Gurnee, Illinois, where they could concentrate on making packaged cookies and brownies with modifications to Betty's old recipes.

One of Betty's first corporate customers was ABC Sky Kitchen, an airport-based caterer who specialized in assembling meals for in-flight food service. One of their customers was Japan Airlines, and soon Betty's Double Fudge Brownies were being served warm to business- and first-class passengers on JAL. It wasn't long after ABC Sky Kitchen began to serve the tasty brownies that Kenny received an email message from Ryuji Fujikami in Tokyo. Mr. Fujikami had enjoyed a Betty's Brownie on his return flight to Tokyo, and was interested in the possibility that Betty's might want to export their brownies to Japan. Mr. Fujikami was a food buyer for a major Japanese department store chain, and thus presented an immediate overseas expansion opportunity to Betty's Brownies.

Kenny was excited at the prospects for the company's first step into a distant market. He called Mr. Fujikami to discuss developing a business relationship, and Fujikami responded with an offer to purchase an initial order of 40,000 individually wrapped Double Fudge Brownies. Each packaged brownie would weigh 100 grams (about 3.5 ounces). He asked that the products be labelled in both English and Japanese (for the promotional appeal of the American product), but that Japanese manufacturing standards for food would have to be used to insure that the brownies would pass customs and agricultural inspection.

The initial order of 40,000 brownies would be shipped to the department store chain's distribution center near Osaka, Japan. But Fujikami asked that future shipments be presorted and packaged for direct delivery to the individual retail store locations throughout Japan. Kenny immediately grasped the complexity of this new customer's requirements, and sat down with Betty to consider what kinds of assistance they would need to expand their business into the Japanese market.

Questions for *Betty's Brownies*

1. With just one customer in Japan, should Kenny and Betty be handling all aspects of this relationship? What logistics functions might make sense to outsource? Which should they consider keeping in house?

2. If they decided to outsource the entire relationship, would an export management company or an export trading company make more sense? Why?

3. What transportation modes should be considered for this product? What kinds of transportation intermediaries might be useful?

4. Are there roles for specialized logistics intermediaries? List some functions that might be handled by specialists.

5. Assume that Betty's Brownies are a smash success in the Japanese market, and the Gurnee plant begins to receive inquiries from Japanese food retailers and manufacturers. Given the possibility of expansion, revisit your decision on hiring an export management company or an export trading company.

6. Assume the business in Japan grows to a point where it makes good sense to prepare the raw brownie dough in the Gurnee, Illinois plant, but to then cold-transport it to Osaka for baking and packaging. Revisit your decision regarding specialized logistics intermediaries. List some functions that might be handled by specialists.

11

Terms of Sale and of Payment

Introduction

The logistics manager should be concerned with the terms of sale involved in both selling and buying materials. In international transactions, the terms of sale govern the movement of the product, and if the logistics manager plays a passive role, he or she will have to accept logistics decisions made by others along the supply chain. Many of these decisions have an impact on costs and service quality. Also, in every international transaction, there is a point in both time and geography when and where: title to the goods changes; responsibility for insurance and caring for the shipment (say, of livestock) changes; responsibility for paying and arranging for transportation changes; and payment for the goods takes place.

The logistics manager should be involved in establishing policies regarding terms of sale for nondomestic sales and purchases. In addition, the logistics manager will have some responsibility for completing portions of each international sales and purchase transaction. This chapter discusses many small, discrete steps that the buyer and seller negotiate. The logistics manager interested in forming a seamless partnership arrangement must study all these individual elements and their interrelationships to determine how to simplify future negotiations with potential customers and suppliers and others within the supply chain.

Terms of Sale

Terms of sale deal with the cost of the product, the risk of physical loss, and with the costs of moving the product from one place to another. They address the responsibilities of all parties to the transaction. Terms of sale are a subject on which everyone and no one is really expert. A good reason for this is that terms of sale are often manipulated or tailored to meet the specific objectives of the traders. Another is that identification of the point of title transfer, with all that implies, has been the subject of many court cases and interpretations not only in the United States but around the world.

It is important to recognize that U.S. law, precedent, and the Uniform Commercial Code are hardly enforceable in international trade. While that may be debated, the practical fact is that it is highly unlikely a U.S. exporter is going to sue a buyer in the Peoples Republic of China or Costa Rica unless the amount is very significant. Even then the trader will do so under the customs, practices, and laws of the foreign judiciary. The object of this section is not to deal with legal issues but to generally describe accepted trade terms in order to avoid disputes. Individuals in need of more definitive information on terms of sale should seek the advice of lawyers who specialize in international commercial and trade law.

In international transactions there are more risks involved than for comparable domestic transactions. Some of these risks are covered by insurance; others may be factored into the costs. Both buyers and sellers face additional risks. In negotiations, it is conceivable that the risks can be identified and shared to the extent both sides are not adding a cost item that, at worst, only one would have to pay. There is a credit risk to the seller associated with export sales. There are other kinds of risk as well, such as risk of loss during transport from the seller's warehouse to the buyer's warehouse. Who is responsible for what risk and who will the bear the cost of protecting against those risks? A decade ago, when the Asian economy faltered, there were reports that Chinese entrepreneurs "who stand to lose money from falling commodity prices are refusing to claim ordered cargoes when ships arrive, leaving the vessels stranded at Chinese ports waiting to discharge cargo that nobody wants."[1]

There is also the issue of known costs. These include costs of the product, transportation, forwarding, consular fees, duties and taxes. Who will bear what cost? These are the domain of terms of sale. So the terms of sale must take into account risks that must be evaluated and assigned to either party and known costs that are assigned to either party. The topic of risks will be covered first.

Risk of Physical Loss

Every commodity is sensitive to some particular type of loss and all commodities are in peril. High value, easily resold products, such as cameras, cosmetics,

---

[1]*The Journal of Commerce,* October 6, 1993, p. 7B.

liquor, and VCRs, are particularly susceptible to loss through theft and pilferage. Fragile commodities, such as optical equipment and electronic assemblies, are highly susceptible to loss through breakage. Grain can be infested with vermin. Metal objects are susceptible to loss through rust and oxidation. Other products, such as automobiles, are subject to dent and scratch damage. Frozen commodities, such as meat products, and temperature-controlled products, such as fish and produce, are sensitive to heat and humidity, resulting in thawing and spoilage. Seasonal items risk becoming worthless if delayed in transit. Even products of almost no value have been lost in incidents when dishonest vessel captains deliberately scuttled a loaded ship in order to collect hull insurance. The list is as long as there are commodities and perils.

The perils just mentioned include theft, denting, scratching, thawing, breakage, freezing, massing, caking, oxidation, infestation, contamination, and water damage. While these may be music to the ears of insurance agents, they are an ever-present concern and cost factor to traders. And if the foregoing list were not long enough, there are man-made hazards as well, such as war, civil commotion, strikes, negligence, piracy, collision, sinking, fire and other human and natural perils to merchandise in transit.

Well-written contracts can, do, and indeed must cover all these contingencies. They cover them through a thorough and knowledgeable use of internationally accepted sales terms. In brief, most risks are covered by insurance. However, most insurance coverage is often not 100 percent complete in terms of totally covering all contingencies. Costs of insurance and risks for insufficient coverage must still be factored into the sales agreement. (Note that even with good insurance coverage, there are some inconveniences; most individuals who have had an automobile accident lose time filing claims, dropping off and picking up the car that is repaired, waiting to see doctors, and so on.)

Terms of sale have a usefulness, or *utility*. Using this approach, one could say that the first utility is in handling the concepts and the real elements of risk inherent in an international transaction.

Product Cost

Obviously, the cost of the product being traded must be covered. There are some legal ramifications to be considered. If the price for an export product is too low, the seller may be accused of "dumping." If sale is to a country that uses pre-shipment inspections, a price that is too high may be attacked as a method to facilitate hard currency flight from the importing nation.

A global firm might have inventories warehoused in a number of different nations; in addition, the products in these warehouses may have been produced in still another set of nations. The seller may assign stock-keeping units (SKUs) the same value wherever they are; or the value may differ by site of manufacture and site of storage. It is also conceivable that the buyer can take delivery in one of several nations. Both the buyer and seller would have explored which origin-destination set results in the lowest import duties and minimizes other charges.

The second utility of the terms of sale is to handle the price of the product, however defined, that is most advantageous to both parties.

Transport Cost

For a sales transaction being negotiated, cost of transportation is addressed by sales terms as well. Products are worthless, or in economic terms "without utility," until they reach the point of consumption, the customer. But who will pay for that transportation? And where is the customer? The Kansas businessperson exporting to Paris may know where Paris is, but he knows nothing about the French freight transportation system, or French freight rates, or even how to go about finding out. Consider how difficult international trade would be if exporters were required to have that kind of in-depth, detailed knowledge of transportation and distribution systems around the world. The converse is also true. The Saudi buyer may wish to purchase from a manufacturer in East Lansing, Michigan or Columbus, Ohio. But he knows nothing about North American transportation either. Domestically, sellers deliver their products to their customer's door. Internationally, that is still not generally the case, although in some markets, the practice is getting closer to that norm. This is being facilitated by the wide acceptance of intermodalism. Today, it is possible to outsource transport arrangements to a single carrier that will make door-to-door arrangements over multiple modes all under a single bill of lading. Still, there are costs involved that need to be accounted for and paid by either the buyer or the seller.

As with physical risk, sales terms provide a convenient internationally recognized shorthand manner for describing up to where transportation will be provided by the exporter and who will be responsible for what expense and risk. This is the third utility of international terms of sale.

Movement Facilitation

The fourth utility of trade terms is their utility in specifying, again in a shorthand manner, who will be responsible for making the various arrangements necessary to move product from one place to another. A good way to describe that process might be *movement facilitation*. Export/import movements usually involve more than just transportation. They involve clearing the customs of the exporting country and entering the customs territory of another, and that activity, in turn, involves the production and presentation at the proper time and place of various import-export documents of entry, licenses, permits, and various declarations incidental to international trade for that type of merchandise. For example, a buyer in the Peoples Republic of China wishes to purchase a machine containing sophisticated electronic process controls from an exporter in Detroit. The PRC requires all import purchases to be covered by import licenses in order to obtain foreign exchange. The United States government requires that this type of computer control device be licensed for exportation with a validated export license. Who is responsible for what documents?

Selling Terms

Within the United States, domestic sales terms are contained in the Uniform Commercial Code. These terms do not apply in international trade.

International terms of sale are contained in the Incoterms. The *Incoterms* are a set of terms that define respective responsibilities and are published by the International Chamber of Commerce. They are periodically reviewed and updated by delegates selected from many countries in order to reflect current practice and changing technologies. The last revision was in the year 2000, and the publication is referred to as *Incoterms 2000*. Although the International Chamber of Commerce is not a governmental body, the terms are recognized worldwide as legally binding upon the parties to an international transaction.

Before taking a closer look at these definitions it may be useful to consider that what is being discussed are essential elements of a contract. In fact, what is being reviewed are those aspects of the purchase contract that have internationally recognized aspects. Incoterms are commonly and widely accepted practices and definitions employed by the principals to suit and facilitate their needs and in order to protect their interests. That sounds one-sided, but since both sides feel that use of the selected terms works to their own advantage, the net result is both sides are more willing to enter into contracts to sell and move products.

On December 11, 1986, the United States ratified the "1980 United Nations Convention on Contracts for the Sale of Goods." The convention became effective on January 1, 1988, although not all countries ratified it. In its federal register notice the U.S. State Department said of the convention:

> The Convention sets out substantive provisions of law to govern the formation
> of international sales contracts and the rights and obligations of buyer and seller.
> It will apply to sales contracts between parties in different countries bound by
> Convention, provided the parties have left their contracts silent as to applicable

law. Parties are free to specify applicable law and to derogate from or vary the effect of provisions of the Convention.[2]

Thus even where a jurisdiction has not been named by the parties, a "law" governing the nature of international sales contracts exists. (Note that while this chapter makes the agreements seem unwieldy and complex, they can be very simple—and even verbal. Often the contract is simply a purchase order followed by an acceptance of some form, such as an order confirmation or shipment against the purchase order. Other times, the purchase order is pursuant to a more formal contract.)

Aside from the other terms of the articles of the sales contract specifying quantity, quality, delivery, price, service and so on, a crucial element of the contract should be a statement to the effect that the Incoterms apply to the transaction. This is accomplished by stating the Incoterm and the revision that applies. An example would be "DDP Liverpool Incoterms 2000," meaning delivered at Liverpool with the duty paid. Another element that should be included in the contract is a clause regarding *force majeure* conditions. *Force majeure* conditions are those conditions, over which the seller has no control, which may arise and which will prevent the seller from performing under the contract. They are a way out with prejudice. For example, a seller may stipulate that crop failure due to insufficient rainfall will render the contract unenforceable. Such conditional statements are what make each relationship unique. Similarly, Incoterms of sale can and should be modified, with additional language, to cover the particular requirements of both parties.

Definitions

For many years a variety of selling terms evolved that were translated as terms of a seller's cost quotation. Each started with the product and added some additional service. The product and added services are listed below.

EX-Works (EXW)

In this most basic transaction, the seller transfers all risk of loss and all responsibility for expenses to the buyer at his loading dock. In an EX-Works transaction, goods are made available for pickup at the seller's factory or warehouse. Example: EXW Cleveland Incoterms 2000.

---

[2]Department of State, Public Notice 1004, FR 6262, March 2, 1988.

FCA (Free Carrier)

In this type of transaction, the seller is responsible for arranging transportation to a specific carrier at a named place. For example, a shipper (seller) located in Milwaukee may sell FCA Chicago. In this transaction the seller arranges to deliver goods to an agreed-upon carrier in Chicago. The goods are delivered when they are receipted by the buyer's carrier and all risk of loss transfers to seller at that point. Example: FCA Chicago Incoterms 2000.

FAS (Free Alongside Ship)

In this transaction, the seller must arrange for delivery and assume all risks up to the ocean carrier at a port. Ancient, albeit unofficial, usage understands delivery to be "within reach of the ship's tackle." Freight costs up to the ship, risk of loss, and costs of clearance are borne by the seller. Example: FAS Baltimore Incoterms 2000.

FOB (Free On Board)

FOB is a very common term that is used domestically but with a different meaning. It is also used extensively in international settings, often incorrectly. Officially, the Incoterms limit the use of FOB to carriage by water and define the point of title transfer as occurring when the goods have passed over the ship's rail. *In other words, freight to a vessel, loading aboard, and export clearance are the seller's responsibility.* Once the goods are loaded, the risk of loss and costs of transport revert to the buyer.

CFR (Cost and Freight)

CFR is a new term replacing "CNF," which itself replaced "C&F." The "Cost" portion of CFR refers to the merchandise. The "Freight" refers to all the freight, including export clearance, up to the foreign port of unloading. What is not included is cargo insurance from the port of loading. Indeed, risks are shared in a CFR transaction. The seller must deliver over the ship's rail, so any loss up to that point is the seller's responsibility. Once loaded, the risk transfers to the buyer. This term is only used on waterborne shipments. An example would be: CFR Hong Kong Incoterms 2000.

CPT (Carriage Paid To)

This term is similar to CFR, but it can be used for any mode of transport including air cargo. CPT means that the seller will pay all freight costs all the way up to the foreign port and that the buyer assumes all risk of loss beyond the loading port. Example: CPT Paris Incoterms 2000.

CIF (Cost, Insurance and Freight)

A CIF transaction includes the costs of freight and the costs of insurance. The seller retains the risk of loss up to the foreign port of unloading. This term is used on waterborne shipments. Example: CIF New York Incoterms 2000.

CIP (Carriage and Insurance Paid To)

This term is similar to CIF except that it is primarily used in multimodal transactions where the place of receipt and place of delivery may be different from the port of loading or place of unloading. Example: CIP Zurich Incoterms 2000.

DES (Delivered Ex Ship)

In this type of transaction, the seller must pay all the costs and bear all the risk of transport up to the foreign port of unloading, but not including the cost or risk of unloading the cargo from the ship. In the case of large pieces of equipment or bulk cargoes, the costs of unloading can exceed the cost of the main freight. Example: DES New York Incoterms 2000.

DEQ (Delivered Ex Quay)

This is the same as DES except that the term provides for the seller to pay the costs of unloading the cargo from the vessel and the cost of import clearance. Example: DEQ New York Incoterms 2000.

DAF (Delivered At Frontier)

Here the seller's responsibility is to deliver goods to a named frontier, which usually means a border crossing point, and to clear the transaction for export. The buyer's responsibility is to arrange for the pickup of the goods after they are cleared for export, carry them across the border, clear them for importation and, effect delivery. Example: DAF Laredo Incoterms 2000.

DDP (Delivered Duty Paid)

This is a new term mainly used in intermodal transactions whereby the seller undertakes all the risks and costs from origin to the buyer's warehouse door, including export and import clearance and import customs duties. Essentially, the seller pays everything in a DDP transaction and passes all related costs in the merchandise price.

DDU (Delivered Duty Unpaid)

This is the same as DDP except that duty is not paid. Since the importer is generally better informed on local customs, a DDU transaction makes a great deal of sense even when the buyer does not want to deal with transportation and insurance issues. Example: DDU Milan Incoterms 2000.

Just which Incoterm to use depends on the bargaining position of both parties and their willingness to assume, relinquish, or assign responsibilities. Figures 11–1 and 11–2 are simplified decision charts for buyers and sellers to give preliminary guidance as to which terms to choose. (They were actually drawn when

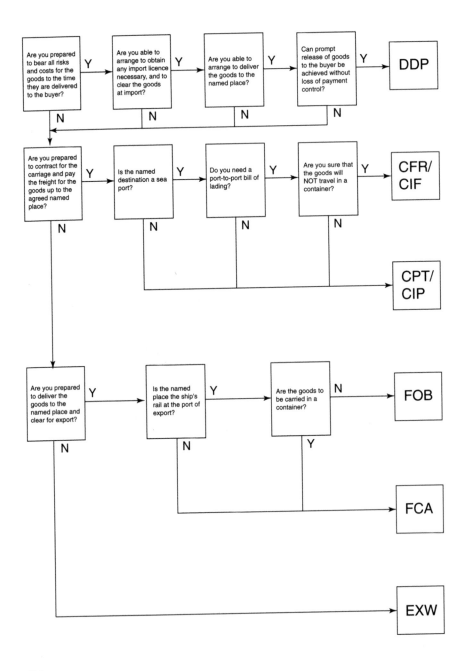

Note:

This chart is for broad guidance only. Once it has been used to select an Incoterm, the rules of the chosen Incoterm should be consulted to ensure that you are prepared to undertake all the detailed responsibilities of the Seller set out therein.

Figure 11–1 Simplified decision chart for seller's choice of Incoterms, 1990. Courtesy: P & O Containers, "The Merchants Guide, North American Edition," August 1992, J. W. Richardson, editor.

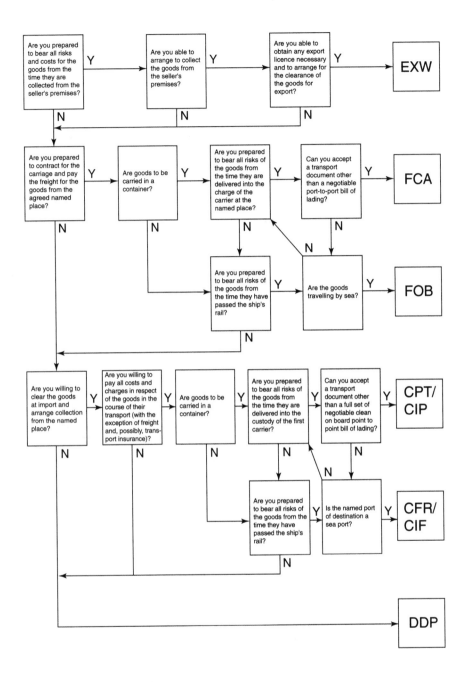

This chart is for broad guidance only. Once it has been used to select an Incoterm, the rules of the chosen Incoterm should be consulted to ensure that you are prepared to undertake all the detailed responsibilities of the Buyer set out therein.

Figure 11–2   Another simplified decision chart for seller's choice of Incoterms, 1990. Courtesy: P & O Containers, "The Merchants Guide, North American Edition," August 1992, J. W. Richardson, editor.

a slightly different set of Incoterms was in use.) Both buyers and sellers must be willing to take some risks in terms of making arrangements. There would be no trade if all sellers insisted upon selling ex factory and all buyers insisted on some other terms. Part of the process of growing into being a global firm is the willingness to use terms of sale that carry the firm's and the logistics manager's scope of responsibilities outside of the firm and outside the nation. Indeed, one should not leave it to one's customers or suppliers to determine the terms of sale. There are additional profits to be earned or lost in the process of negotiating and fulfilling an international sales or purchase agreement.

In this book the current Incoterms are briefly summarized. They are widely used, and even if a buyer and seller preferred some other arrangement, the easiest way to describe that arrangement would be to take the closest Incoterm and then list and describe the exceptions agreed to. For example, if the buyer requires special packing and the cost of export packing is substantial, and not usually included in the merchandise quote, there is nothing to prevent the parties from agreeing to "CIF [named point] plus export packing." This term makes it clear that while freight and insurance will be procured and billed and part of the price, export packing will be extra. "In some commodity trades, there are standard international contracts of sale which relate to specific Incoterms. In these circumstances, neither the buyer nor the seller has any choice to make."[3]

The International Chamber of Commerce has a number of publications that describe and explain the Incoterms 2000 in more detail. These publications may be obtained from their various offices.

Sometimes the government of the country where the buyer or seller is located will also have some influence. Nations with weak currencies may insist on terms that allow carriage and insurance to be provided by firms of that nation, thus minimizing the need to import those services (in a national accounting sense).

Choice of Incoterm is also a matter of bargaining. Figure 11–3 shows the allocation of responsibility and risk that fall on each party. From the standpoint of the logistics manager, once her or his firm is committed to the responsibility, the manager becomes responsible for carrying out all those tasks within time deadlines specified in the sales agreement. As the sales agreement was being negotiated, the logistics manager should have provided advice and cost estimates to her or his firm's negotiators so that whatever allowances were made for the firm's logistics operations related to the transaction were more than covered by the price agreed to. This is important, because negotiators on the other side also want to profit from handling the logistical aspects of the entire transaction.

---

[3]P & O Containers, "The Merchants Guide, North American Edition," (East Rutherford, NJ, 1992), p. 6.

INCOTERMS RESPONSIBILITIES & RISKS (S = Seller, B = Buyer)													
Responsibility	**EXW**	**FCA**	**FAS**	**FOB**	**DES**	**DEQ**	**CFR**	**CIF**	**DAF**	**DDU**	**DDP**	**CPT**	**CIP**
Commercial Invoice	S	S	S	S	S	S	S	S	S	S	S	S	S
Export License	B	S	S	S	S	S	S	S	S	S	S	S	S
Import License	B	B	B	B	B	B	B	B	B	B	S	B	B
Supply Product	S	S	S	S	S	S	S	S	S	S	S	S	S
Inspect Shipment	B	B	B	B	B	B	B	B	B	B	B	B	B
Cert. of Origin	S	S	S	S	S	S	S	S	S	S	S	3	3
Export Packing	S	S	S	S	S	S	S	S	S	S	S	S	S
Vehicle Loading	B	S	S	S	S	S	S	S	S	S	S	S	S
Move to Port	B	S	S	S	S	S	S	S	S	S	S	S	S
Ocean Documents	B	B	B	B	S	S	2	2	S	S	S	3	3
Select Carrier	B	B	B	B	S	S	S	S	S	S	S	S	S
Load Ship	B	B	B	S	S	S	S	S	S	S	S	S	S
U.S. Pier Costs	B	B	B	S	S	S	S	S	S	S	S	S	S
Ocean Transport	B	B	B	B	S	S	S	S	S	S	S	S	S
Ship to Quay	B	B	B	B	B	S	S	S	S	S	S	S	S
Foreign Customs	B	B	B	B	B	S	B	B	B	B	S	S	B
Foreign Inland Trans.	B	B	B	B	B	B	B	B	4	4	4	S	S
Marine Insurance	B	B	B	B	6	S	B	S	S	5	5	B	S
War Risk Insurance	B	B	B	B	6	S	B	1	S	5	5	B	B
Unload Foreign Vehicle	B	B	B	B	B	B	B	B	B	B	B	B	B
Risk													
On U.S. Vehicle	B	S	S	S	S	S	S	S	S	S	S	7	7
To U.S. Pier	B	S	S	S	S	S	S	S	S	S	S	7	7
On Board Vessel	B	B	B	S	S	S	S	S	S	S	S	7	7
Ocean Transport	B	B	B	B	B	S	B	B	S	S	S	B	B
Ship to Foreign Quay	B	B	B	B	B	S	B	B	S	S	S	B	B
On Foreign Vehicle	B	B	B	B	B	B	B	B	4	4	4	B	B
Foreign Transport	B	B	B	B	B	B	B	B	4	4	4	B	B
Foreign Veh. to Buyer	B	B	B	B	B	B	B	B	B	4	4	B	B

1. Buyer must pay cost for B/L.
2. Seller must furnish buyer with clean B/L at his expense.
3. Seller obtains, but buyer must pay all costs for documents including certificate of origin.
4. Seller to frontier, buyer from frontier to destination.
5. No obligation for either seller or buyer, but seller bears risk of loss during ocean shipment.
6. No obligation for either seller or buyer, but buyer bears risk of loss after tender to ocean carrier.
7. Buyer bears risk after tender to first carrier regardless of mode.

Figure 11–3 Incoterms 1990 viewed in terms of assigning responsibilities and risk. This chart originally appeared in "The Language of Foreign Trade," by Thomas A. Foster, *Distribution Magazine,* October, 1990, pp. 86–90, published by the Chilton Co., Radnor, PA.

There are two other matters of logistics concern. Today, there is great emphasis placed on a value-added approach to marketing logistics services. In negotiations, the party attempting to provide the service should stress that if they do it, there will be some value added to the product in the eyes of the buyer. For example, if the seller assumes responsibility for the first part of the haul, the seller might label the parcels in shipment using bar codes that can be utilized by the carriers and warehouses used by the buyer and others along the supply chain. The more value an exporter can deliver in terms of service, the better off he is from a sales and service perspective. Secondly, logistics partnerships are stressed today, which means that the negotiators might consider terms of sale that are advantageous to a longer-term commercial relationship rather than to a single transaction.

However, many non-domestic markets and potential sources of supply are considered volatile, and the prospects for stable, long-term relationships appear remote. Or, one may question the integrity of a prospective customer or source, or doubt the political and economic stability of the nation with whom the trade will be conducted. Or the uncertainty might be with something in between, such as ocean freight rates that are fluctuating wildly. One trade journal said:

> The Transpacific-Westbound Rate Agreement [a liner conference] . . . , keeps a variety of charges and surcharges on tap covering documentation, equipment, value-added tax, fluctuating fuel prices and currency rates, terminal handling at both ends, and container freight-station deliveries. In addition, shippers in just about any trade can expect to pay stiff congestion charges to locations suffering from dock strikes or lacking state-of-the-art cargo facilities. Or they might be slapped with a $500 charge [per container] to regions—like Scandinavia— that lie off the main trade routes.
>
> Not all charges are applicable in every trade; they come and go with regularity, depending on the situation in a particular country. To add to the confusion, carriers might announce a surcharge weeks in advance, only to implement a much lower rate at the time of implementation. . . . Customers might not know what they're paying until virtually the last moment.
>
> That's a big problem for exporters who sign contracts with buyers up to a year in advance of delivery. Often they have to eat the increase. . . .[4]

If one party is uncertain and unwilling to take risks, then he or she might choose a selling or buying term that puts the majority of responsibility on the other party. This cautious strategy is often employed by first-time exporters and importers. They should realize that if they allow other parties to assume all the risks, these other parties will collect more than enough to compensate themselves for this risk-taking.

One of the signs of growth or maturity in a firm engaged in international trade is whether it controls its inbound and outbound moves. This depends in part on the company's size. That's no secret. High volume can command a high level of service at a relatively low price, as this quotation from the early 1990s shows:

---

[4]Robert J. Bowman, "Sea Saw," *World Trade* (October, 1992), p. 84.

"With regard to shipments from Korea to the U.S., up until about five years ago, between 60 percent and 70 percent of the cargo that came . . . from Korea moved free-alongside-ship or free-on-board—that is, the cargo came under consignee's control at [Korean] dockside or upon loading. . . . Now [1992] the ratio is reversed, between 60 and 70 percent moves cost-insurance-freight, meaning under control of Korean exporters. . . ."[5]

Another factor that influences who will procure transport and thus which term will be used is the respective buying leverage of the parties in the particular trade and globally. Since today global service contracts can be negotiated, a shipper with a large volume in one trade lane may be able to negotiate a lower rate in a second lane even if the volume is relatively small. It might also be the case the importer has volumes of traffic from multiple origins or even multiple vendors in the same origin. Those volumes can be leveraged in negotiating the lowest inbound rates. So it is important to determine who is in the best position to negotiate freight when sales terms are being determined.

Terms of Payment

Terms of payment refers to the manner by which the seller will be paid for his goods. Terms of payment can range from insisting on cash in advance to conventional billing of regular customers on, say, a monthly basis. Payment can also be in the form of another good, which is known as bartering or countertrade.

The Importance of Credit

Credit is more than a convenience. In today's world it is an economic necessity. At times, the federal government itself relies heavily on credit to finance government operations. But to most consumers credit means installment buying. At a given point in time one may not have the cash to purchase an item, even though that item may be essential to one's well being. It may be a raincoat, a washer, or even a badly needed vacation.

It is not that one cannot afford the item. If that were the case then credit would not be extended, no matter how badly one needed the item. On the contrary, credit is extended only to people or companies who can afford the expense over time. How much time is allowed is a function of the amount of credit extended and the ability to repay the obligation at each installment, including interest. The ability to repay is a function of income. Thus, one might buy a camera on credit

---

[5]*American Shipper* (June, 1992), p. 14.

today in anticipation of being paid next week. Moreover, one might be willing to pay more for the item just to get the current utility. The exact same model camera may be worth more to a buyer because it can be purchased on time.

Business entities work in much the same way. Indeed, the discussion of credit serves to introduce one of the most important topics in international trade in merchandise: trade terms. Essentially, trade terms define the amount of credit the seller is willing to extend to the buyer. The similarities to consumer credit should be kept in mind. Businesses sell products or services. In order to sell those things they must first make, buy, or position themselves to do so. That costs money. It costs money to be in business, even before the first product is sold or before the cash register rings for the first time. And it costs money to continue making or delivering those products or services between rings of the cash register.

Where does the money come from? It comes from one of three sources: 1) investment by owners (capital); 2) sales; or 3) creditors. Most companies could not survive very long without a continuing source of both profits from sales and credit resources. Credit is essential to stay alive between rings of the cash register in order to keep making the things or providing the services that produce profit.

U.S. exporters are often thought of as being too conservative in the extension of credit to foreign buyers. This conservatism is said to be detrimental to U.S. exporters in exploiting the markets of the world. In the same way that consumers generally prefer to buy from stores that extend credit, so do foreign companies prefer, for good business reasons, to buy from exporters willing to help finance their businesses through the extension of favorable terms of sale. In some countries, extended terms are mandated by the central governments as a condition to exporting to their manufacturers.

Risk of Loss

While it may be good business to extend credit, it is even better business to assure or insure being paid. The seller is also concerned about the amount of time it takes to get paid. Time is money. If it takes the seller six months to get paid for a sale, he has lost six months' use of his funds. If he had to borrow himself to finance his business, then the sale would have netted him several percent less than the face amount of the invoice.

Thus both the borrower (buyer) and the seller must put a great deal of emphasis on payment terms. The seller is concerned that he will be paid for his goods. The buyer is concerned he will receive the goods he pays for. Both parties have an interest in the way the transaction will be financed, that is, the length of time before payment is to be made. The international banking system addresses these issues. Before talking about the banking system, we will discuss some common payment alternatives.

A buyer can pay for the goods before they are shipped. In some risky situations, the seller might insist on payment in advance. In such cases, a *sight draft* is sometimes employed. A draft is a demand for payment. A draft at sight is payable on presentation "at sight." Typically, the demand matures at the time of arrival of goods at the destination port. Under these terms, the buyer must pay for the goods before he can obtain possession of them but after they have been shipped to him. Remember that export trade requires that goods travel long distances. A sea freight shipment can routinely take 25 to 40 days between dispatch and arrival. Thus the difference between paying for the item before it is shipped versus later can be significant. Sight draft terms can be compared to a domestic cash on delivery (COD) sale.

The terms *date draft* or *time draft* require that the buyer pay for the goods at some specified time after shipment. Typically, but not necessarily, the draft matures, or becomes due, sometime after delivery of the goods at the buyer's warehouse, after the buyer has taken possession. This would be similar to use of a credit card where indebtedness occurs which is due sometime after the buyer has taken possession of the merchandise.

Both sight and time drafts employ the banking system as collecting agents of the seller. The seller entrusts a bank to demand payment according to a specified set of instructions. There is yet another way to employ the banking system for collection purposes: the letter of credit, to be discussed below. However, it is possible, indeed increasingly common and in many cases preferable, to deal directly with the buyer.

Domestically, one often sells to a valued customer on net-30-day terms, the invoice being due in thirty days. There is no reason why that cannot be done internationally and it is commonly the case in trade among developed countries between firms that have an ongoing relationship. Such terms are referred to as an *open account.* In an open account transaction the seller trusts the buyer will pay the invoice on the specified date. The credit extended is unsecured, which is to say the seller holds no collateral, even though the buyer can and does take possession of the goods.

Progress Payments and Options

Progress payments, also known as percent of completion terms, are involved when the item involves a major capital investment to be spread over a period of many months, or even years. An example might be building a new ship, which takes 12 months. In that situation the agreement might be that the buyer pay 30 percent down before construction starts, 20 percent at the end of four months, 20 percent at the end of eight months, and the balance on delivery of the ship. The payments at the end of four and eight months would also be subject to certain amounts of work being completed and tested, and this would usually be certified by a third party.

Options are used for multi-unit sales. The agreement is firm for a certain number of units and includes the option of allowing the buyer to purchase additional units at the same (or some other stated) price within the period of the option. New airline aircraft are sold in this manner: an airline may place a firm order for six, and have an option to buy three more at the same price, provided that they exercise the option within two years of the initial order date.

Both types of orders are of some concern because they usually have some provisions for speeding up or slowing down the order's completion date. In the ship example given above, there might be a different payment schedule that takes effect in case the buyer decides that either an earlier or a later delivery date is desirable. The logistics manager would have some input in calculating costs of speeding up or slowing down the entire production process. Some contracts also have bonuses for early completion and penalties for late completion.

Documents Related to Terms of Sale

Documents are of significance to the logistics manager for three reasons. First, documents such as the letter of credit specify how the shipment must be handled. Second, part of the challenge of international logistics is handling all the documents themselves. The logistics manager must know how they relate to each other in a processing sense. Last, the logistics manager is responsible for inputting much of the data contained in some of the documents.

Foreign trade documentation is complex and will be covered in Chapter 12. However, documents directly relevant to the terms of sale will be covered here. In the discussion of basic payment terms above we referred to the use of drafts. A *draft* is a demand for payment, the opposite of a check, which is a demand to pay. Drafts, like checks, are processed through banks. As bills of exchange, drafts can be used to exchange goods for money. Obviously, physically exchanging goods themselves for money (payment) would be somewhat awkward. Drafts substitute for the goods in the exchange process. This is facilitated, in marine cargo shipments, by the bill of lading.

Title to goods in international trade is evidenced by the ocean bill of lading. (Strictly speaking, terms of sale denote where title transfers. However, the bill of lading serves as documentary evidence of title and a basis of claim for the goods.) Bills of lading also will be discussed in greater detail later. Suffice here to say that a bill of lading is legal evidence of title, hence ownership.

Goods covered by a bill of lading are owned by whomever is named as consignee in the document. The bill of lading is issued by the ocean carrier to the shipper. The carrier's contractual obligation is to release the goods only to the consignee, (that is, the party to whom the goods are to be delivered). If no consignee is mentioned by name on the bill of lading then the document becomes negotiable upon endorsement by the shipper. That is to say, the goods belong to whomever possesses the bill of lading. The form of consignee is, "To Order Of Shipper." When the shipper, or his agent, endorses the bill of lading (signs the back), the document is referred to as a "blank endorsed bill of lading."

The blank endorsed, or negotiable bill of lading, is very useful to accomplish exchanges. Since it represents title to the goods it covers, it can be traded for cash, or an obligation to pay. This is what the bank does when it handles documents for collection purposes. It offers the bill of lading to the buyer in return for the amount of money demanded on the draft, or alternatively, in return for the buyer's promise to pay the draft on its date of maturity.

Payment required on presentation of the draft is referred to as a *sight draft/documents against payment* transaction, or SD/DP. Exchange of title in return for an obligation is referred to as a *date draft/documents against acceptance.* When the buyer pays, or accepts, the draft (according to the terms of payment), he is given the bill of lading and with that document he can demand the goods from the ocean carrier.

It may be appropriate at this point to consider how much protection is afforded through use of these two payment modes. In an acceptance situation the buyer gains control of the goods simply against his signature. There is the obvious risk that he will not pay when the draft matures. The maturity date is the date on which the payment is due. The *tenor* is the length of time to maturity (for example, 60 days). In considering this risk, weight is given to the importance all businesses put on their credit rating. Thus, a buyer who accepts a draft and then fails to make payment to a bank risks jeopardizing his all-important credit standing and may be liable for damages. Nevertheless, the chance of default remains a risk.

In sight draft/documents against payment transactions, the buyer cannot gain possession of the goods without paying the bank first, the bank serving as the seller's collecting agent. This is relatively risk-free but still not without risk. Should the buyer decide not to pay the draft, the seller has no recourse but to arrange to return the merchandise and absorb the expense—or to abandon the cargo.

There is also the possibility that foreign exchange may not be available for remittance, or even that the collecting bank itself may become insolvent. In the case of foreign exchange shortages, the buyer must either wait for exchange to become available or elect to discount the draft.

Documentary Letters of Credit

A letter of credit is a guarantee issued by a bank that it will pay the beneficiary upon presentation of certain documents evidencing the conditions of the credit have been satisfied. The letter of credit substitutes the credit and creditworthiness of the issuing bank for that of the buyer on whose behalf it is issued. The bank comes between the two parties.

Indeed, where letters of credit are employed, two new contracts come into existence. First is a contract between the buyer and the opening bank (also known as the issuing bank). Second is a contract between the bank and the beneficiary (the seller). This second contract obligates the bank to pay the beneficiary upon satisfaction of the terms.

It is important to recognize the nature of this second contract. The buyer is out of the picture as far as the beneficiary is concerned. A credit may, for example, stipulate that shipment is to be made by air cargo. In direct communication the buyer, learning of the cost, changes his mind and directs the seller to ship by sea freight instead. The seller does so and presents an ocean bill of lading to the bank. The bank refuses to pay, properly so, because the beneficiary has failed to comply with a specific provision of the documentary credit contract.

The buyer is out of the picture as far as the negotiating bank is concerned. Direct agreements between the buyer and seller have no relevance to the bank and carry no weight whatsoever. Any change to the contract must come through the bank in the form of an amendment to the original credit. Until the seller has received and accepted the amendment, it must not act differently than stated in the original document.

Documentary letters of credit are called *documentary* because they deal strictly and exclusively in documents; specifically, the documents stated in the credit. This proper narrow-mindedness causes exporters unnecessary problems and expense. These problems can be avoided by complying exactly, without deviation of any kind, with the stated provisions of the credit.

Depending on its form, letters of credit can eliminate many of the risks described under drafts and with regard to open-account transactions. No two letters of credit are exactly the same. For practical purposes all letters of credit are different and must be treated as unique.

The principal forms of letters of credit are *confirmed* and *advised* and *irrevocable* and *revocable*. An *irrevocable credit* cannot be canceled prior to expiration without the consent of the parties. The expiration date of the credit "for negotiation" is the last date (excluding weekends and certain holidays) that the contract remains an enforceable contract. For practical purposes, it is the last date presentation of documents can be made under the credit. Some credits also specify last shipment dates. This is always on or before the expiration date. It is the last day shipment, as evidenced by the appropriate transport document, may be made.

Confirmed credits are letters of credit that have been guaranteed by a second bank, usually in the beneficiary's country. The confirming bank adds its guarantee of payment and substitutes its own credit for that of the opening banks.

There are various reasons why confirmation may be required. Assume a credit is opened in Iran through an Iranian bank. The exporter may have no more faith in the Iranian bank than in the buyer itself. In requesting confirmation by a prime New York bank, the beneficiary assures himself payment will be made.

Also, aside from the question of faith, there is the issue of protracted payment delay attributable to lack of foreign exchange. The confirming bank assumes that risk when it adds its confirmation. The beneficiary no longer need concern itself with the risk of exchange shortages. Confirmation is therefore more common in cases where political or economic risks are associated with the opener's country, and less common in stable environments. U.S. import letters of credit, as an example, are infrequently confirmed.

An *advised letter of credit* carriers no such third-party guarantee or protection. The advising bank is simply notifying the beneficiary that a credit in its favor has been opened and what the requirements under it are. The advising bank may also be the recipient of documents under the credit, and check them for compliance. But until it is authorized to pay by the opener, the notifying bank will not remit funds and is under no obligation to the beneficiary. If the instruction to pay is delayed, for any reason, the notifying bank simply will not remit to the seller.

An example of a requirement which might seem superfluous in sales between related parties is the use of letters of credit. Letters of credit serve to guarantee payment to the seller. They are issued by banks and are payable to the seller upon presentation of certain documents, provided the seller has complied with terms and conditions.

Does IBM U.S.A. need that kind of assurance when selling to its own affiliate in Manila? Perhaps not, from a credit point of view. But letters of credit might be required anyway for a variety of possible reasons, including a government edict imposed in order to control the outflow of foreign exchange.

The rules underlying letter of credit and draft collections are found in another periodically updated International Chamber of Commerce publication, *Uniform Customs & Practices For Documentary Letters of Credit, Publication 500.* UCP 500 defines bank responsibilities and obligations. Buyers and sellers agree to the terms of UCP 500 whenever they accept letters of credit and process drafts through an international bank for collection. The ICC also provides a dispute settlement mechanism for those instances where disagreements on the meaning of UCP 500 arise.

Obtaining Foreign Exchange

In very simplified terms, when a seller must be paid, the buyer goes to his local bank and, using local currency, must buy the foreign currency of the seller's nation, and use that currency to settle his account.

For most firms, receiving payment in their home nation's currency is the norm. It is not, however, without its own complexities. For example, Widget Co. finds a customer in Mexico willing to pay the right price to buy widgets. The Mexican firm is financially sound and an excellent potential distributor for the product. The only problem is it cannot obtain U.S. dollars. It has plenty of pesos but no dollars. Widget, on the other hand, has no need for pesos. It cannot pay its employees or suppliers in pesos. Thus, even though the potential for business exists, the unavailability of foreign exchange prevents consummation of the deal.

Foreign exchange is the currency of another nation. In the United States pesos would be foreign exchange. In Mexico, U.S. dollars are foreign exchange. The dollar is the most important denomination of foreign exchange because it is widely used internationally for foreign settlements (payments).

An obvious question becomes, "How does a country get foreign exchange?" The answer is that countries earn foreign exchange as a result of export sales. For example, when American companies buy shirts made in Hong Kong, they pay for the shirts in U.S. dollars. Hong Kong's reserves of foreign exchange are thus increased. A Hong Kong firm can use these dollars to buy Japanese-made sewing machines, thereby decreasing its own dollar reserves and increasing Japan's. Japan can in turn buy Kuwaiti oil, and so on. Exports increase foreign exchange reserves. Imports decrease foreign exchange reserves.

Barter

The form of payment may be in other goods, or even services. Non-currency transactions are referred to as *barter transactions*. Barter is not only an ancient way of conducting business, it is also very modern and can range from a simple two-way deal to a complicated set of transactions.

For example, Cuba bought oil from the Soviet Union and paid in sugar. How much sugar would buy a barrel of oil was dependent on a variety of factors, not the least of which were world availability of both sugar and oil. If oil were in surplus it would obviously have bought less sugar than if it were in short supply.

Barter arrangements are of great interest to the logistics manager, since he or she must evaluate the goods being offered by the other parties in terms of costs needed to make them useful or marketable. Of no small concern is the geographic site at which the goods will be made available. Barter and cross-trading arrangements are complicated, risky, and best performed by expert brokers in the field who specialize in this increasingly important means of conducting international trade.

Banking and Bank Documents

As discussed in the previous section, one of the most important factors in the negotiation of a sales agreement is the negotiation of mutually acceptable payment terms. Payment terms are the means by which the transaction will be financed. Two prime considerations for both parties are the protection of assets and the cost of trade financing.

In discussing the various payment modes, five were identified as commonly used: 1) cash in advance, 2) open account, 3) date drafts/documents against acceptance, 4) sight drafts/documents against payment, and 5) letters of credit. The risks associated with each of these payment modes were also discussed. This section will amplify what has been said thus far and examine the way banking documents are prepared and used.

First, reconsider the five basic payment modes in terms of relative risk, from most safe to least safe. Clearly, the most safe option for the exporter is cash in advance. It is not only risk free, but it also carries the least financial burden. Next safest is letter of credit. With a letter of credit as the operative financial instrument, a bank has guaranteed payment to the seller. This third-party guarantee makes letter of credit financing a safe option. Figure 11–4 is a bank's simplified chart showing the two-step nature of the letter of credit process.

Next in order of safeness would be the sight draft (s/d d/p) option. The buyer cannot get his hands on the goods without paying for them. This is relatively risk free, but it is neither without risk nor is it without cost. One risk is that the buyer simply will not take the goods, and the other is that exchange may not be available for remittance.

Next, there are date drafts and acceptance drafts. Acceptance drafts have all the same risks of sight drafts. There is additional financing cost (time is money) and there is the possibility the buyer will not honor the draft at maturity even after having accepted the obligation. There are risks involved, but the buyer's concern with respect to his creditworthiness makes capricious default unlikely.

Finally, there is the open-account transaction. All the risks associated with acceptance drafts are present. Concern over default probably was not much of an issue if these were the terms selected.

From the buyer's point of view, all the opposite considerations are true. Cash in advance is both expensive and risky. The order may be delayed in shipping,

First Phase: Application, Issuance, and Advice of a Letter of Credit

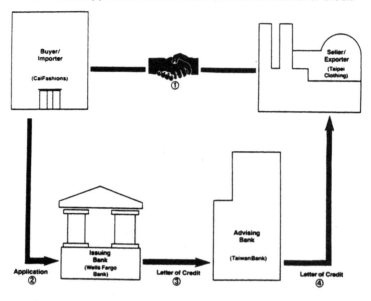

Second Phase: Presentation of Documents and Payment

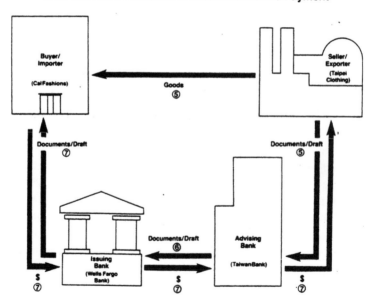

Figure 11–4   Bank chart (simplified) showing two-step nature of letter-of-credit process.

the wrong product may be supplied and, indeed, there is the possibility the or-der may not be shipped at all. At the other extreme, depending on the terms, open-account terms involve practically no risk at all to the buyer.

Letter-of-credit financing, where it is used strictly for commercial purposes, may serve the needs of both parties. The buyer is required to tie up his credit line. He may need access to this credit but if it is tied up in an open letter of credit he cannot use it. Depending on the financial condition of the buyer and lo-cal requirements, some, or as much as all, of the credit amount may be required by the bank on deposit as collateral against the credit.

On the other hand, the buyer can stipulate exactly how the order should be handled, what documents are to be supplied, when the goods are to be shipped, by what mode, and so on, in the letter of credit. This helps assure the order will be handled exactly as required.

In some cases, the decision to use the letter of credit is not left to the buyer or seller. The central bank of the importing country may require letters of credit as a means of controlling exchange transactions and imports. In these cases, stipula-tions may be required to be contained in the letter of credit that would not other-wise be necessary; for example, a requirement that the invoice list customs clas-sification numbers and nomenclature. Whatever the reason that letters of credit are used, they cost money. Who pays the bank charges is a matter for negotiation be-tween buyer and seller. Bank commissions can be anywhere from one half of one percent to two percent or more, with minimum fees. Confirming banks also charge for their services, as do advising banks. Charges can amount to several hundreds of dollars and should be considered, particularly in the case of small transactions.

It is not uncommon for letters of credit to be written in such a way that bank charges outside the importer's country are borne by the seller and bank charges within the importer's country are borne by the buyer. In this case, the buyer pays the opening bank and the seller the confirming bank in the form of a deduction from total proceeds against the credit.

Sometimes, the buyer unwittingly agrees, by shipping under the letter of credit, to pay all bank charges. The deduction from the proceeds can be quite large, to the seller's surprise. Often, buyers, in order to discourage deviations from the original sales agreement, stipulate that all amendment charges are to be borne by the beneficiary. These can amount from $50 to $100 per amendment. Profits can easily disappear.

Working with Letters of Credit

After a letter of credit is accepted by both parties, one or the other may want to change its terms. An example of actual requests was:

> Please extend shipment date until 1/31/01
> Please extend expiration date until 2/15/01.[6]

An amendment requested in another situation read:

> Please amend as follows:
> 1. Original documents must be sent together with shipment. Copies can be presented to negotiating bank.
> 2. Letter of credit terms changed to read C and I. The freight charges will be paid in Honduras.
> 3. Letter of credit amount increased by USDLRS 690.50 and now must read USDLRS 7,902.25.
> All other conditions unchanged. Please advise beneficiaries urgently and acknowledge receipt by mail.

This request was to cover both an increase in product price, and the buyer's assumption of transport costs.

Letters of credit and amendments to them need not be accepted by the other party. An unacceptable condition in a letter of credit or in an amendment should not be accepted. The credit or the amendment should simply be returned to the bank with a letter stating the reason that it is not being accepted. Good sense dictates the customer should be informed as to what one is doing and why.

Identification of unacceptable conditions is a critical part of working with letters of credit. Typically, the buyer applies for the import letter of credit based on data provided by the exporter in a pro forma invoice. (This is also true of import licenses where the pro forma invoice itself is presented.) A *pro forma invoice* is a form of commercial invoice. It is an advance invoice and provides all the particulars of the seller's regular commercial invoice. Indeed, the final invoice should be a virtual duplicate of the pro forma invoice.

The buyer uses the pro forma invoice to complete the letter of credit application. Details such as the exporter's name and address, description of the goods purchased, price, quality, and quantity are included. Often, incidental expenses are listed as well, such as freight, insurance, packing and consular fees. Other details, such as "ship by date," are included in the application as well. The banks add their own boilerplate language and eventually the document arrives in the buyer's office.

Today, major banks facilitate and expedite the process by electronic means that permit the buyer to apply for the credit through a personal computer and

---

[6]This, and other quotes, are taken from real letters of credit.

print letters of credit in the beneficiary's office through a personal computer and modem.

However, when the credit arrives, it is vital, from both a financial and customer service sense, that the letter of credit be reviewed in minute detail immediately upon receipt. The review process will include various individuals within the company. The treasurer or credit manager may wish to review financial aspects. The logistics manager must contact the materials or manufacturing managers to confirm availability of product; and the export transportation manager will be asked to review the document to assure transportation and documentation specifications can be complied with. Some exporters send copies of the letter of credit to their freight forwarders for review as well. Every aspect of the contract must be reviewed carefully and early on in order to assure problems will not surface on the day of shipment.

Few things are more annoying to a buyer that to receive piecemeal requests of amendments. As indicated earlier, amendments are costly and time consuming. The piecemeal approach demonstrates lack of professionalism and suggests a lack of caring as well.

The letter of credit review process is conducted in some firms with use of a letter of credit checklist and routing form. What kinds of questions will the review address? Certainly, can shipment and presentation of documents be made within the validity period? Where will the shipment originate? Is a particular port named? Is it the most advantageous port? Is the mode of shipment as per the pro forma invoice or quotation? Are special documents required? How many? What will it cost to produce them, and will this result in logistical hurdles?

Another line of questioning should include the dollar amount involved. What price was quoted? How much is being ordered? Does one multiplied by the other exceed the credit amount? How much was quoted for freight? Is the right amount provided in the credit? How old is the quote? Was the price based on a minimum quantity? Are partial shipments allowed? How have transportation rates gone up? Are there new surcharges? (Some forwarders issue daily sheets showing changes in bunker surcharges and currency adjustment surcharges to different areas of the world. In one such sheet, for shipments from the U.S. West Coast to the Far East, the bunker adjustment factor (BAF) was $96 for a 20-foot container and $120 for a 40-foot container. The currency adjustment factor (CAF) was 33 percent for Japan, 5 percent for Korea, 12 percent for Taiwan, and 10 percent to Singapore.[7])

Transportation restrictions should be carefully considered as well. Does the

---

[7]Sheet issued by J. E. Lowden & Co., of San Francisco.

credit restrict choice of carrier? Does it require under-deck stowage when cargo must move on deck? Does it prohibit transshipment of cargo or use of a consolidator? Does it require the exporter to use a freight forwarder he does not know, or knows and prefers not to deal with?

All of the problems and potential problems with the transactions should be methodically identified upon receipt of the letter of credit. Those problems should be communicated at once to the buyer and, if necessary, there should be a single request that the credit be modified through amendment. Thereafter, it becomes a matter of policy based on one's relationship to the buyer to make a decision to ship or wait until the amendment is accepted before going ahead with either production or shipment. But one thing is matter of policy, and that is that until one physically receives the amendment, he does not have one and is bound by the stated original terms of the credit.

Uniform Practices

Commercial letters of credit and documentary sight drafts are usually subject to the provisions of *Uniform Customs And Practices For Documentary Letters Of Credit,* ICC Publication 500 or *UCC For Documentary Sight Drafts.* These publications are rules promulgated by the Banking Committee of the International Chamber of Commerce.

When traders use letters of credit or drafts subject to these rules, they are agreeing to the provisions. Neither publication is very long and it would helpful to read and understand them. Doing this will avoid disagreement and confusion. For example, Article 3 says: "Credits, by their nature, are separate transactions from the sales or other contract(s) on which they are based and banks are in no way concerned or bound by such contracts even if any reference whatsoever to such contract(s) is included in the credit."

In another article, ICC Publication 500 clarifies when a credit is and when it is not revocable. It reads: "All credits . . . [are either revocable or irrevocable and] . . . should clearly indicate whether they are revocable or irrevocable. In the absence of such indication the credit shall be deemed to be revocable."[8]

From time to time the Banking Committee updates these rules in order to keep up with changing technologies and practices in the underlying businesses. These determinations can be very specific. Following is an edited example of an interpretation distributed to members and posted on the ICC's website. It treats the matter of what an original document is as defined in Article 20(b) of UCP500.

---

[8]Article 7 (b) (c).

Correct interpretation of sub-article 20(b)

General approach

Banks examine documents presented under a letter of credit to determine . . . whether on their face they appear to be original. Banks treat as original any document bearing an apparently original signature, mark, stamp, or label of the issuer of the document, unless the document itself indicates that it is not original. Accordingly, unless a document indicates otherwise, it is treated as original if it:

1. appears to be written, typed, perforated, or stamped by the document issuer's hand; or
2. appears to be on the document issuer's original stationery; or
3. states that it is original, unless the statement appears not to apply to the document presented (e.g., because it appears to be a photocopy of another document and the statement of originality appears to apply to that other document).

Hand signed documents

Consistent with. . .above, banks treat as original any document that appears to be hand signed by the issuer of the document. For example, a hand signed draft or commercial invoice is treated as an original document, whether or not some or all other constituents of the document are preprinted, carbon copied, or produced by reprographic, automated, or computerized systems.

Facsimile signed documents

Banks treat a facsimile signature as the equivalent of a hand signature. Accordingly, a document that appears to bear the document issuer's facsimile signature is also treated as an original document.

Photocopies

Banks treat as non-original any document that appears to be a photocopy of another document. If, however, a photocopy appears to have been completed by the document issuer's hand marking the photocopy, then, consistent with . . . , the resulting document is treated as an original document unless it indicates otherwise. . . .

Telefaxed presentation of documents

Banks treat as non-original any document that is produced at the bank's telefax machine. A letter of credit that permits presentation by telefax waives any requirement for presentation of an original of any document presented by telefax.

Statements indicating originality

Consistent with . . . above, a document on which the word "original" has been stamped is treated as an original document. A statement in a document that it is a "duplicate original" or the "third of three" also indicates that it is original. Originality is also indicated by a statement in a document that it is void if another document of the same tenor and date is used.

Statements indicating non-originality

A statement in a document that it is a true copy of another document or that another document is the sole original indicates that it is not original. A statement in a document that it is the "customer's copy" or "shipper's copy" neither disclaims nor affirms its originality.

What is not an "Original"?

A document indicates that it is not an original if it

1. appears to be produced on a telefax machine;
2. appears to be a photocopy of another document which has not otherwise been completed by hand marking the photocopy or by photocopying it on what appears to be original stationery; or
3. states in the document that it is a true copy of another document or that another document is the sole original.

Note that while this language seems excessive it really is not, when one considers that banks never actually see merchandise. A $50 million draft presented under a documentary letter of credit will be paid simply on the basis of documents presented. Fraudulent documents, such as reproduced bills of lading, are a reason that banks are particularly cautious about the way words like "original" will be interpreted.

Banks subscribing to UCP500 are legally liable for performance as stipulated in the document. If a bank fails to comply with the terms of UCP it is "on the hook" for any money involved. Not all international banks subscribe to UCP500. Indeed, if a letter of credit does not indicate it is subject to Uniform Customs & Practices Publication 500, it is not! An exporter accepting an LC that is not covered by UCP500 is at serious risk. The exporter must make determination of this point a part of the letter of credit review process upon receipt.

Discrepancies in Letters of Credit

Discrepancies are deviations from the terms and conditions of the credit. Failure to present a required certificate of origin is a discrepancy. Discrepancies void the letter of credit as far as the beneficiary is concerned. Unless the discrepancy can be corrected, one no longer has the protection of a letter of credit. Letters of credit must be perfect; if not, the bank will refuse to pay. In 1980 there was story about a sunspot (a dark spot on the sun linked to disturbances in the earth's magnetic field) which caused an extra "L" to creep into a telexed message involving the letter of credit associated with a shipment of watches. The buyer's bank refused, then, to honor the letter of credit.

> Ordinarily, bankers say, the buyer authorizes payment despite such insignificant mistakes. [A spokesman for the importer said] the watches arrived too late [i.e., after the Christmas sales period] and were useless.[9]

---

[9]"How a Glitch Can Ensnarl Foreign Trade," *The Wall Street Journal,* November 4, 1980, p. 1.

When the negotiating bank receives documents presented under the credit it checks for discrepancies. Checkers compare documents line by line against the letter of credit. If discrepancies are found the bank will communicate with the beneficiary or his agent requesting correction. If the discrepancy can be corrected, it must be done so before expiration. The bank will then be obliged to pay.

If the discrepancy cannot be corrected, the credit is null. The only options left to the beneficiary are to (1) request the bank to "cable for approval to pay" with the discrepant condition; (2) request an amendment (which is usually not feasible); or (3) request that the documents be forwarded to the opening bank on an approval basis. This type of problem is compounded when the market price of the product sold has changed dramatically since the original sales terms were agreed upon.

To forward on *approval* (also known as a collection basis) is fundamentally the same as sight draft/documents against payment transaction. Documents are forwarded to the openers, where they are examined by the bank and the customer. Only after that review has taken place and the documents have been accepted can the credit be paid. Neither the confirming nor the issuing bank is under any obligation to pay. In short, one has gone from a letter of credit to an ordinary sight draft.

Documentary Credits and Drafts

In this and the previous section the discussion has been about documentary letters of credit and drafts. That means they are negotiated against underlying shipping documents. This is important to keep in mind. When a checker in a bank checks documents, he or she is checking documents and not merchandise. Banks deal in paper, not merchandise. It is the paperwork that must be correct in order get paid on time and without difficulty. Article 4 (ICC Pub 400) says: "In credit operations all parties concerned deal in documents, and not in goods, services and/or other performances to which the documents may relate."

The bank knows nothing and cares even less about the business of the traders. This sometimes leads to oddities in the negotiation of credits. For example, an invoice generated by the exporter's domestic order billing system describes a product as "sodium chloride." The credit reads "salt." Even though sodium chloride may be the same as salt, the bank will balk at paying the credit. A credit requiring shipment from "Cleveland" would be rejected if the port of loading is shown as "Baltimore," even though Baltimore may be the natural port of exit for Cleveland.

The concept to keep in mind is that banks deal in paper, not in merchandise. The less imaginative the exporter the easier it will be to comply exactly with the terms of the credit.

Documentary Sight and Date Drafts

Documentary drafts are called "documentary" because they are literally attached to documents. When documents are not attached the draft is referred to as a "clean" draft. The draft itself resembles a check. It should read and be prepared like a letter from the top down.

> Exchange for US $12,000, New York, September 29, 2002; At sight of this first of exchange (second unpaid), Pay to the Order of [the seller]; twelve thousand U.S. dollars. To: [The buyer] Signed [Joe Smith] [Company].

As in the case of bills of lading, the draft can be endorsed in blank or to the order of another party. The endorsement makes the draft a negotiable instrument that can be sold by the drawer of the draft, the collecting bank, or anyone else.

An exporter who has extended 120 days credit to the buyer (a 120-day time draft) may not wish to wait 120 days for his money. He can sell the draft for an amount less than the face value in the same manner as a bond, which is also an indebtedness, can be sold before maturity for less than the face amount. Selling drafts for less than their worth at maturity is referred to as *discounting* or *discounted drafts*. The amount of the discount is a function of prevailing interest rates and the risk associated with the country on which the draft is drawn.

(The notation *first* and *second* of exchange refers to presentation. The first draft is presented first to the drawee. If he fails to acknowledge, the second is sent with the preprinted notation that the first is still unpaid. This anachronism is also found in bills of lading).

Bank Letters

The letter of instructions to the bank, or *bank letter,* provides the bank with the drawer's specific handling instructions. All major international banks have their own prenumbered forms. Major exporters can also print their own forms. Forwarders often use their own. The form used is not important. The content is.

The bank letter states the draft number (usually the same as the exporter's invoice number), the tenor and amount of the draft, and currency denomination. It also states what documents are attached. If the transaction is a SD/DP, the original endorsed ocean bill of lading would be attached along with original commercial invoices and miscellaneous other original documents.

The bank letter also shows the name of the carrying vessel or airline and contains a general description of the merchandise being traded. These data elements tie the invoice, bill of lading, and bank letter together.

Next the bank letter provides very specific instructions to the bank as to how the collection is to be handled. For example, "deliver these documents against payment or acceptance. Forward my money by cable, or by mail. Charge the drawee (the customer) for the cable but me for all other expenses. If the buyer accepts the draft but fails to pay on time notify me by telex. Also file an official notice of action against him ('protest'). Or do not file a notice of action."

An important instruction in all bank letters is what to do in the event of problems. "If you need help, contact Harry Hornblower [in the country itself] who is/is not authorized to do whatever he feels necessary; or, who is only authorized to assist in the collection."

Thus the bank letter is one of the essential documents for international traders. It should be prepared under the direction of the treasurer or controller of the exporter, who should set policies to be followed for different kinds of transactions. For example, a policy may provide that if the amount is over $2,000 the funds should be cabled. For less than that, they should be mailed.

The bank letter provides the banking institution with all the information it needs to collect the item, take corrective action if needed, and credit the drawer's account. The specific details should be agreed in advance by the seller and buyer. The buyer should advise what bank in his country he would like the collection to come through. If no bank is indicated in the bank letter, the documents will be sent through the originating bank's correspondent (a bank with which it has a banking relationship) in the importing country.

Presenting documents to a bank in the exporter's country for forwarding overseas to a local collecting bank takes time. With today's fast ships the possibility the cargo may arrive before the documents is a potential problem. Also, given management's desire to minimize accounts receivables, this entire process becomes an issue.

To help minimize the amount of time it takes to get documents to the importer's bank, *direct collection letters* are used. These instruments are exactly like regular bank letters except that they are sent directly by the exporter or his forwarder to the collecting bank overseas. The forms are usually prenumbered on the originating bank's letterhead. Blanks are supplied to the exporter. When shipment is made the first one or two copies go directly overseas along with the controlling /underlying documents. Copies of just the bank letter go to the exporter's bank for follow up and proper crediting. When the collecting bank overseas receives the document package, it proceeds exactly as if it had received the documents directly from the exporter's bank.

Summary

Terms of sale for an international transaction are complicated. The buyer and seller must agree as to where to exchange the goods and the payment and assign responsibility for freight charges and insurance. In international trade matters, it is difficult to fall back into law courts in case of a commercial dispute; therefore international transactions must be carefully documented. International shipments (and payments for them) are also subject to risks that must be assumed.

Incoterms 2000 were adopted by the International Chamber of Commerce, and these terms recognized changes in logistics technology, especially the increased use of containers for door-to-door service. There are 13 different terms ranging from ex-dock to delivered, and they cover most trade situations. Exactly which term is chosen is a matter of bargaining between the buyer and seller. It is important to know that the party who assumes risks also expects to be compensated for that exposure.

Terms of payment were also discussed, and they ranged from payment in advance to adding to an existing open account. Often letters of credit are used to settle transactions. These banking instruments offer protection to both the buyer and the seller. Several other documents related to payment were also mentioned.

End-of-Chapter Questions

1. In a global setting, what are terms of sale?
2. What are some of the risks to buyers in an international transaction?
3. What are some of the risks to sellers in an international transaction?
4. What are Incoterms? When should they be used?
5. Which Incoterms place the heaviest burden on the seller's logistics staff? Why?
6. Which Incoterms place the heaviest burden on the buyer's logistics staff? Why?
7. Why do business firms use credit, rather than cash, for many global trade transactions?
8. What is a bill of lading? What functions does it perform?
9. When is barter used in international transactions?
10. What is a letter of credit, as used in international transactions? Why would one be used?

CASE • *Van Bemmel Steamship Company*

Van Bemmel Steamship Company was a small U.S.-flag carrier operating only one vessel on a regular route between the East Coast and Japan via the Panama Canal, with intermediate stops, in both directions, at San Juan, Long Beach, and

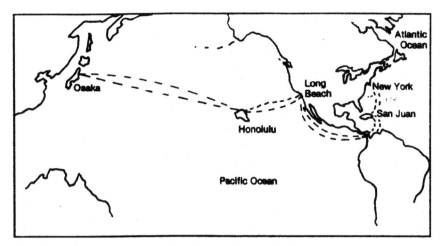

Case Figure 11–1 Route of the Van Bemmel Steamship Company.

Honolulu. Its approximate route is shown on the map in Case Figure 11–1. A round trip would be New York, San Juan, Long Beach, Honolulu, Osaka, Honolulu, Long Beach, San Juan, and back to New York. At each port of call, the vessel spent an entire day discharging and taking on containers. The vessel's time at sea between ports (in either direction) was New York–San Juan, two days; San Juan–Long Beach, five days; Long Beach–Honolulu, four days; and Honolulu–Osaka, six days. (These days are in addition to the single day spent in each port whenever the vessel stopped.) The vessel made about nine round trips per year, and it could carry 1,200 containers, either full or empty. Loaded containers that it picks up at a port were left off at the previous call.

Case Table 11–1 shows the number of full containers that the Van Bemmel vessel carried between the ports on its route. At present the firm is attempting to determine its costs of carrying containers between the different ports it serves.

Case Table 11–1 Number of Full Containers Carried on the Van Bemmel Company's Route

Source	Destination				
	New York	San Juan	Long Beach	Honolulu	Osaka
New York		100	100	200	100
San Juan	100				100
Long Beach	100	200		300	200
Honolulu	100	100	100		
Osaka	200		100	100	

Questions for *Van Bemmel Steamship Company*

1. Assume that the Van Bemmel Company wants to use its own containers exclusively. Any containers it picks up at a port (either full or empty) will have to have been left at the port on a previous voyage. Using Case Table 11–1, calculate the minimum number of containers the company must own. Show your work.

2. How much ship space could be saved if, instead of owning its own containers, Van Bemmel Company leased them for one-way hauls only and therefore carried only containers loaded with freight?

3. Can the Van Bemmel Company switch to using a "flag-of-convenience" vessel registered in another nation that has lower labor costs? Why or why not?

4. Given the facts in the case, if the company wants to fill up the containers it is currently carrying empty, what markets (from point to point) should it emphasize?

5. Assuming that business is increasing uniformly, between which ports will the vessel's capacity first be reached? Once this happens, what should the firm do?

6. A major U. S. railroad approaches Van Bemmel with a proposal for land-bridge service, using rail, rather than water, to carry containers between Long Beach and New York. The cross-country rail trip would take four days, plus one day each in terminals in Long Beach and New York. Outline how you would determine the value to Van Bemmel of this proposal.

12

Documentation and Insurance

Introduction

For the logistics manager whose experience is limited to domestic commerce, both the documentation and the insurance requirements of international movements will be an additional challenge. Indeed, Gray and Davies even used the definition of international logistics to mean "a system in which documentation flows are as much a part of the main logistical flow as flows of product."[1]

Usually about ten documents are required for an export shipment; the number can run to over 100. Assembling all the documents is a major logistical exercise in itself. Nearly all of the documents must be ready at the port of export; all are required at the point of importation. In U.S. foreign trade, "the average cost of processing a single set of documents for a shipment of goods in 1982 was $395. In general, the process involved six different handlers and 16 different types of documentation. . . . The British calculations were similar [with estimates] that between 3 percent and 4 percent of small and medium-sized British import and export company overall expenses are spent on trade facilitation."[2]

Here's another quote from Britain: "The direct cost per consignment due to documentation for an exporter not employing one or more of the various systems

---

[1]Cited in G. J. Davies, "The International Logistics Concept," *International Journal of Physical Distribution & Materials Management,* vol. 17, no. 2, 1987, p. 20.

[2]*American Shipper,* August, 1984, p. 16.

available to aid the management of export administration, can be estimated by using the formula

$$\text{Current retail price index} \times 0.23\text{''}[3]$$

From these quotations, one can see that documentation is a major cost item. In the late 1990s, one airline official complained that, ". . . it still takes as long to process an air cargo shipment [now] as it did 26 years ago in a process which involves up to 36 separate handling functions, generating up to 16 individual documents."[4] Assembling all these documents is a time-consuming task, which must be coordinated with the flow of the product through the distribution channel. Documents have their own logistical requirements. Often a logistics manager's first understanding of the importance of documentation will be when he or she learns that an important shipment is being delayed because of a single missing document.

Today, computers are helping to reduce facilitation costs. In 1999, for the international airline industry, it was estimated that using paperless (electronic) documentation had the potential to save $5 to $6 per shipment,[5] although the industry has not yet converted. Software is developed that can perform most of the documentation functions. Each logistics manager must decide in which instances to have documents prepared by computer; when they should be produced manually in house; and when to rely on an outside freight forwarder to complete the function. For many firms, as a segment of the order processing system, a checklist of documents is generated as an order is logged. A list of all the bits of information that will be needed to complete all the documents is also generated. Several parties at different locations input information; the packer may give the final shipment weight, the vessel operator will supply the container number, and so on. Time requirements for information bits as well as for completed documents are programmed in, and one can tell—in advance—when and what missing data will be causing a problem.

As for insurance, which will be covered later in the chapter, we will say here that all foreign movements should be covered by insurance, and it is the logistics manager's responsibility to make certain that the goods are properly insured whenever they are owned by or the responsibility of his or her company.

---

[3]Gary Davies and Charles Freebury, "The Management of Documentation by British Exporters," *International Journal of Physical Distribution and Materials Management,* vol. 17, no. 6, 1987, p. 15.

[4]*KLM Cargovision,* (January 1997), p. 3A.

[5]*www.cargolaw.com,* August 12, 2001.

Documentation

Recognizing that such impediments to free trade are not in the best interests of prosperity and economic growth, a number of organizations exist to facilitate trade. The most important of these is the GATT, which stands for General Agreement on Trade and Tariffs. GATT itself is an international treaty, with well over eighty national signatories, that has been entered into for the express purpose of removing barriers to trade, including high duty rates, quotas, documentary red tape, and artificially imposed barriers, such as unnecessary health and safety requirements.

GATT was formed at the end of World War II as a consequence of the generally accepted conviction that the Depression of the 1930s had been aggravated and prolonged by the trade barriers nations set up in the rush to protect their home economies from the spreading economic blight. It is now part of the World Trade Organization (WTO).

Why, then, do such strange and seemingly senseless documentary requirements, such as the need to legalize documents, still exist? Sometimes they are a form of nontariff trade barrier. The requirement that an importer obtain an import license before he can purchase goods overseas is such an example. An *import license* is a government-issued permit to import that specifies the commodity to be imported, the quantity, the value, and other particulars. Importers must adhere strictly to the terms of these licenses or face denial of exchange, fines, and even confiscation of the imported goods. Where import licenses are required, the exporter is given very specific instructions by the buyer on how documents must be prepared and on how the shipment is to be made.

Specific instructions exist for completing each document; some must be in a foreign language and some must be processed by the importing nation's consular offices located in the exporter's country. This requirement for consular legalization approaches being a nontariff barrier. Mideast countries and some Latin American countries are the most likely to insist on consular legalization of U.S. exporters' documents. One U.S. exporter said, "all the embassies really want to do is collect money."[6] Most consular services charge $20 to $40 per transaction. Embassies have their own documentary requirements. Jordan requires legalization of certificates of origins and commercial invoices, in addition to certifying the documents through the National U.S.-Arab Chamber of Commerce. The Dominican Republic requires that the documents be in Spanish.

Usually the instructions for completing each document are about as long as the document itself, although one could devote a chapter in a book to the finer

---

[6]*The American Shipper,* June, 2000, p. 74.

points associated with some of the documents. For example, the Certificate of Origin becomes very difficult to complete when the product consists of components that have differing origins. It is overused to the extent that the exporter is trying to say where the product is not coming from in order to get past an illegal boycott.

Many firms sell preprinted documents, and one such firm, Unz & Co., allowed us to reproduce their brief description of about 40 documents. See Figure 12–1. This is a partial list, although in most instances a shipment would require only five to ten documents. Perusing Figure 12–1 should give the reader an idea of the wide array of documents that might be a requirement at one time or another. The most commonly used documents are the certificate of origin; commercial invoice; consular invoice; dock receipt; insurance certificate; letter of credit; ocean bill-of-lading (or airwaybill); shipper's export declaration; and shipper's letter of instructions.

It is wise to obtain outside advice for first time shipments. Some of the documents deserve additional discussion here, especially those with logistical ramifications. When the time does come to ship, it is necessary that the shipper prepare the basic documents of international trade. The most important of these is the commercial invoice.

Commercial Invoice

The commercial invoice is a summation of the entire transaction. Terms of sale and payment, quantities, prices, additional charges, shipping marks, dates, remittance instructions, and references are all contained. A properly prepared commercial invoice should provide all the information relevant to the transaction. It is very different from and much more comprehensive than a domestic invoice. The international commercial invoice is important not only because it is a collection document, but because it is used by governmental authorities. Duty and even admission under quota are assessed on the basis of the information provided in the commercial invoice.

The preparation of the invoice is a critical step in assuring the smooth flow of goods and payment. Information to prepare it must come from many sources, including the buyer's purchase order; licenses (if any apply); the letter of credit, if there is one; internal departments, such as credit; and reference to publications such as the *Exporter's Encyclopedia* published by Dun & Bradstreet and the *Shipping Digest's* summary of export documentary requirements.

The National Committee on International Trade Documentation (NCITD) has identified, and for its Cargo Data Interchange System (CARDIS)—a data telecommunications format—has specified, what data elements should appear on international commercial invoices.

AIR WAYBILL — The Air Waybill is a non-negotiable Bill of Lading, and is used as a receipt for cargo and a contract for transportation between shipper and air carrier. Unlike an ocean carrier with a "to order" ocean bill of lading, the air carrier must deliver the shipment to the consignee named on the non-negotiable air waybill. International Air Waybills, or "airline air waybills," are used by the air carriers: "House Air Waybills," or "neutral air waybills," are used as receipts by Freight Forwarders who then consolidate them with the air carriers International Air Waybills.

CERTIFICATES OF ORIGIN — This document certifies that goods were manufactured in the United States. It is signed by the shipper, and may also be certified by a local chamber of commerce, notarized, and even visaed by a resident foreign consul. A Certificate of Origin may be required by a foreign government for control purposes, or by the foreign importer to ensure that he receives U.S. goods. Specific C/Os are required for duty reductions with Canada (U.S./Canada Free Trade Agreement) and Israel (U.S./Israel Free Trade Area).

CHARTERPARTY — A Charterparty is a contract signed between a ship owner and a charterer who hires the vessel for a period of time (Time Charter) or for a particular voyage (Voyage Charter). There are many types of Charterparties, most codified by various shipping associations.

COLLECTION LETTER — A collection is the procedure whereby the exporter entrusts the movement of his commercial documents to a remitting bank for further processing through a collection bank for settlement from the buyer. A Collection Letter is the document used by the remitting bank to relay complete and precise instructions to the collecting bank.

COMMERCIAL INVOICE — A Commercial Invoice is the basic statement of the seller to the buyer for payment of the goods shipped. It must conform to any Letter of Credit requirements, foreign government requirements, and U.S. export control requirements regarding destination statements. It is used as one of the primary documents in the collection process, and is the main document used by foreign Customs for control, valuation, and duty determination. The C/I should contain a full description of the goods, pricing, terms of sale, payment and delivery, bills of lading numbers, method of shipment, and ship date. Letter of Credit numbers, import license numbers, shipper and consignee names, and shipping marks and numbers. Commercial invoices are usually signed by the exporter.

CONSULAR INVOICE — Prepared from the information on the Commercial Invoice by the buyer's consulate or embassy in the shipper's country, these documents are usually stamped with an official seal. They may be specific forms required by the destination country's government or simply copies of the Commercial Invoice. Consular Invoices are required for control of certain commodities and to ensure valuation control.

CUSTOMS INVOICE — Certain countries require special invoices containing specific information for the Customs clearance and valuation of imported shipments. These documents contain most of the elements of the Commercial Invoice, and are usually in the language of the importing country. The Canadian Customs Invoice is the most popular of this type.

DELIVERY INSTRUCTIONS — Also called Delivery Orders, these documents provide specific information to a carrier regarding delivery to a specific port, pier, terminal, airport, or steamship line. They show the shipping carrier, delivery deadlines, name and address of consignee, and the contact name and telephone number of the shipper in case of delivery problems.

DOCK RECEIPT — The Dock Receipt provides the exporter with a receipt indicating that the ocean terminal operator has taken custody of the shipment on behalf of the ocean carrier. It is basically a proof of delivery of the goods from the exporter to the pier.

DRAFT — Sometimes called a bank draft or bill of exchange, the draft is a negotiable instrument which contains an order to pay. It must be signed by the drawer (seller) and be payable at sight or by a certain time. The draft must contain an unconditional order to pay a certain sum of money to the drawee (buyer). Drafts are used in both collection and Letter of Credit methods of payment.

ENTRY/IMMEDIATE DELIVERY — Customs Form CF3461 allows the Importer or Customs Broker to take immediate delivery of imported goods prior to payment of duties and processing of an Entry Summary for most types of merchandise. The importer has ten days to file the Entry Summary and pay the appropriate duties.

ENTRY SUMMARY — Customs Form CF 7501 is filed by importers and Customs Brokers for merchandise entered into the U.S. for consumption, warehousing, or temporarily in bond. It is used for computing duties and fees owed upon importation, for control purposes, and for the compilation of import statistics. Its use is governed by the U.S. Customs Regulations.

EXPORT LICENSE — Under the Export Administration Act, the U.S. Bureau of Export Administration (BXA) is charged with controlling and licensing most items exported from the U.S. for reasons of national security, short supply, and foreign policy. There are two basic types of export licenses: Individual Validated Licenses which must be applied for and received from the BXA; and General Licenses, which are not documents but rather published authorizations covering commodities not subject to validated licensing.

Figure 12–1   Glossary describing international shipping documents (part 1). Reprinted with permission of Unz & Co., 190 Baldwin Avenue, Jersey City, NJ 07306.

FORM A — "Form A" refers to an origin declaration document, required by importers from their foreign suppliers, to enable the importer to receive favorable Customs duty considerations for goods imported under the Generalized System of Preference (GSP). These documents may be supplied only by the foreign shipper, and are not available in the U.S.

FORM B — "Form B" would refer to the U.S. exporter's version of an origin declaration, and is represented by the U.S./Israel Free Trade Area Certificate of Origin used by U.S. exporters for shipments to Israel.

HARBOR MAINTENANCE FEE — Customs form CF349 is used by both exporters and importers to report, on a quarterly basis, all shipments which used a U.S. water port. A fee of .125% of the value of the shipments is collected and used to maintain U.S. harbors.

HAZMAT BILL OF LADING — The Research and Special Programs Administration (RSPA) of the Department of Transportation provides specific regulations for shipping papers documenting hazardous material shipments in the U.S. The Hazmat Bill of Lading, usually based on a straight, non-negotiable Short Form Bill of Lading, includes areas to report the additional requirements of the RSPA.

IMPORT LICENSE — Many countries have currency exchange controls which serve to limit the amount of currency available for the purchase of foreign merchandise. The import license is used to control orders sent to foreign exporters. It is important for exporters to understand their foreign buyer's licensing requirements as payment negotiations are made prior to any exportation.

INLAND BILL OF LADING — The Inland Bill of Lading, usually a non-negotiable document, evidences the receipt of goods by an inland carrier for transport from the point of origin to the point of export. These bills of lading include the following export information: "for export," marks and numbers, "freight prepaid," and special delivery/notification instructions.

INSPECTION CERTIFICATE — To protect themselves, many foreign firms request a Certificate of Inspection. This may be an affidavit by the shipper, or by an independent inspection firm hired by the buyer, certifying the quality, quantity, and conformity of the goods to the Purchase Order.

INSURANCE CERTIFICATE — An insurance certificate gives evidence of risk coverage for merchandise shipped. It is sent to the bank with other collection documents, and normally is used only when required by Letter of Credit or Documentary Collection procedures. There are many types of insurance policies available. Coverage requested is usually 110% of the value of the cargo shipped.

INTERNATIONAL IMPORT CERTIFICATE — This document is the Bureau of Export Administration (BXA) form number BXA-645P. It is required for the import of selected commodities from COCOM nations. The U.S. importer would supply this form, after authorization by the BXA, to the foreign exporter so that he could apply for an export license.

IN-TRANSIT DECLARATION — The In-Transit Declaration, Department of Commerce form 7513, is prepared for shipments in transit from one foreign country to another which pass through the continental U.S., the U.S. Virgin Islands, or Puerto Rico. Also used for merchandise exported from General Order warehouses and for imports rejected by the U.S. government and re-exported.

LETTER OF CREDIT — The Letter of Credit is a financial instrument issued by an importer's bank (opening bank, on behalf of the importer. The opening bank substitutes its own credit for that of the importer, and undertakes a committmer to a designated beneficiary (the exporter) to pay a stated amount within a stated time frame, provided that the exporter complies with all the terms and conditions of the Letter of Credit.

LOSS AND DAMAGE CLAIM — This document is used to claim insurance compensation for goods lost or damaged during exportation. The items lost or damaged must be fully described. Supporting documentation would include copies of the Commercial Invoice, Bill of Lading, and Insurance Certificate.

MANUFACTURER'S CERTIFICATE — A Certificate of Manufacture is used when a buyer intends to pay for goods prior to shipment, but the lead time for the manufacturing process is lengthy and the buyer does not wish to tie up funds too far in advance. Usually, the goods are manufactured after a small down payment. When the goods have been manufactured, the seller prepares a Manufacturer's Certificate stating that the goods ordered have been produced in accordance with the contract with the buyer. Upon receiving the certificate, the buyer forwards both payment and shipping instructions, and the shipment is made by the seller.

OCEAN BILL OF LADING — The Ocean Bill of Lading serves three main purposes: it is a contract to deliver the goods; it serves as a receipt from the ocean carrier for the goods shipped; and it becomes a certificate of ownership, which covers the goods noted thereon. If it is made out "To Order" and endorsed and delivered to another party, the title of the goods passes on to the other party. The "order" party can demand delivery of the goods at the port of destination.

Figure 12–1   Continued

PACKING LIST — This important document describes all items in the box, crate, pallet, or container, plus the type, dimensions, and weight of the container. It is used to determine total shipping weight and volume (cubes) by Customs officials to check cargo, and by the buyer to inventory merchandise received. Prices and item values are usually omitted from the packing list. Shipping marks, reference numbers, and carton numbers are also important additions to the packing list.

PHYTOSANITARY INSPECTION CERTIFICATES — Also referred to as "plant health" certificates, these are required by many foreign countries for shipments of plants and plant products. They serve to certify conformity to local plant quarantine import regulations with respect to pest and disease infestations.

PRO FORMA INVOICE — The Pro Forma is used primarily to document to the buyer, in advance, the cost and terms of sale of a proposed export. It is used by the foreign buyer as a quotation from the exporter, and also to assist in applying for a Letter of Credit from his bank. The Pro Forma Invoice serves as the basis for the subsequent Commercial Invoice.

POWER OF ATTORNEY — Exporters and importers authorize Freight Forwarders and Customs Brokers to act as their agents, for export control and Customs purposes, with this document. Completed Power of Attorney documents, however, do not relieve importers or exporters from liability to the U.S. Government in the event of export control or entry errors.

SHIPPER'S DECLARATION FOR DANGEROUS GOODS — Under the regulations of the Department of Transportation, the International Air Transport Association (IATA), and the International Maritime Organization (IMO), snippers and exporters are required to declare dangerous cargos to the air and ocean carriers they use for shipment. Both the IMO and IATA require specific documents to report hazardous goods, and these requirements are published in their respective Codes. IATA also provides a document specifically for non-restricted articles.

SHIPPER'S EXPORT DECLARATION — The Department of Commerce (Census Bureau) form 7525-V serves the dual purpose of providing export statistics and export control. This document reports all the pertinent export data of a transaction such as parties to the transaction, transportation details, description. Schedule B classification, and value of the goods, as well as necessary licensing information and certification signatures. Completion and requirements of the SED are governed by the Export Administration Regulations.

SHIPPER'S LETTER OF INSTRUCTION — These instructions, often prepared along with a Shipper's Export Declaration, are the exporter's directions to the freight forwarder on how to handle the exporter's shipment. The information prepared on an SLI includes a description of the goods and containers, the ultimate consignee, shipping method desired, insurance requirements, and special instructions pertaining to the shipment.

SINGLE ACCESS DOCUMENT — Also referred to as "SAD," the Single Access Document is required for movement of goods through the countries of the European Economic Community. It is generally prepared by Customs Brokers in Europe for imports entering the EC.

TRANSMITTAL LETTER — The Transmittal Letter, commonly prepared with a bank draft, is the document used to send shipping documents to a remitting bank for processing either a collection or payment/negotiation under a Letter of Credit. It contains the shipper's precise and complete instructions on how the documents are to be handled and the payments remitted.

USAID LABEL — These labels and aluminum placards bear the new (1991) logo of the Agency for International Development. All merchandise exported under an A.I.D. program or contract must be labeled with the USAID emblem.

WEIGHT CERTIFICATE — The Weight Certificate, usually a certified copy of the Packing List is occasionally required by the foreign buyer for control purposes. This type of certification may be made with an export inspection company.

Figure 12–1   Continued

Consular Invoice

Regarding the consular invoice, "Required by some countries, this document is used to control and identify goods shipped to them. It usually must be prepared on special forms and may require legalization by their consul."[7]

---

[7]"Common Export Documents," prepared by the Port Authority of New York and New Jersey, circa 1980.

Dock Receipt

The *dock receipt* is used to transfer responsibility and accountability between a land carrier and the ocean vessel line. The forwarder or shipper prepares the document and it is signed by the ocean carrier or the carrier's agent, such as a stevedoring firm. The dock receipt need not be as comprehensive as the bill of lading itself. It is not necessary to show the consignee or even the tariff classification on the dock receipt. It must, however, be complete enough to permit the bill of lading department to match the dock receipt to the corresponding bill of lading.

Insurance Certificate

An *insurance certificate* is issued by an insurance company or agent and is proof that the shipment is insured to the extent stated (and no more).

Letter of Credit

Letters of credit were covered in Chapter 11. It is suffice to say that they tie together payment for and movement of the goods. Their list of conditions specifies which documents must be presented, and where. Also, they often spell out many of the specifications of the shipment's journey.

Ocean Bill of Lading

The rules section, together with the published rate and bill of lading, constitute the entire agreement between shipper and carrier. The bill of lading itself can be legally defined as 1) a contract of carriage; 2) documentary evidence of title; and 3) a receipt for goods. The title aspect of the bill of lading was briefly discussed in the section on banking and controlling documents. The front of one bill of lading is shown in Figure 12–2.

When cargo arrives at the carrier's terminal, notification is sent to the carrier's bill of lading department that the cargo has been received. In ports using dock receipts, the notification is a copy of the dock receipt. The bill of lading department then matches the dock receipt to the non-executed bills of lading. The form is prepared by the forwarder and sent to the carrier along with the shippers' export declaration. The carrier then rates (computes the freight charges), numbers, and signs the bill of lading. Original bills of lading (usually three are signed) are returned to the forwarder.

The same process is followed by non vessel operators (NVOCCs). The shipper/forwarder receives the NVO's bill of lading. The NVO issues a bill of lad-

COMPANHIA MARITIMA NACIONAL

Rio de Janeiro - Brasil

SHIPPER/EXPORTER	BOOKING NO.	BILL OF LADING NO.
COMPANHIA MARITIMA NACIONAL 120 WALL ST SUITE 2501 NEW YORK, NY 10005	NYC 105	NCNUJXRJTB 0001

EXPORT REFERENCES

INV NU 800012

CONSIGNEE	FORWARDING AGENT REFERENCES
COMPANHIA MARITIMA NACIONAL RUA SAO BENTO 8, 8° ANDAR RIODE JANEIRO , RJ 20090-010 BRAZIL	CMN INTL P.O.BOX 123 NY NY 10005

POINT AND COUNTRY OF ORIGIN

JACKSONVILLE

NOTIFY PARTY (CARRIER UNDER NO OBLIGATION TO NOTIFY)

DOMESTIC ROUTING/EXPORT INSTRUCTIONS

IMPORT LINCENCE NO
12-93/12345-6

PLACE OF INITIAL RECEIPT.	PRE CARRIAGE BY.
NYC	
VESSEL & VOYAGE (OCEAN)	PORT OF LOADING
MERIDA 001	JACKSONVILLE
PORT OF DISCHARGE	PLACE OF DELIVERY.
RIO DE JANEIRO	JACKSONVILLE

PARTICULARS FURNISHED BY SHIPPER

MARKS & NOS./CONTAINER NOS.	NO. OF PKGS.	HM**DESCRIPTION OF PACKAGES AND GOODS	GROSS WEIGHT	MEASUREMENT
ITLU 1234567	01	1 X 40' HOUSEHOULD GOODS & PERSONAL EFECTS FREIGHT COLLECT DATE 01/01/93 "THESE COMMODITES LICENSED BY U.S. FOR ULTIMATE DESTINATION BRAZIL, DIVERSION CONTRARY TO U.S. LAW PROHIBITED."	18.5 K	

FREIGHT AND CHARGES

OCEAN FREIGHT	5.175.00
BUNKER SURCHARGE @ 14%	724.50
CONTAINER RENTAL	270.00

SIX THOUSAND ONE HUNDRED
SIXTYNINE AND FIFTY CENTS

PAGE 230 FMC 27 **TOTAL**   6.169.50

*APPLICABLE ONLY WHEN DOCUMENT IS USED AS THROUGH B/L.
**INDICATE WHETHER ANY OF THE CARGO IS HAZARDOUS MATERIAL UNDER DOT, IMO OR OTHER REGULATIONS AND INDICATE CORRECT COMMODITY NUMBER.

DECLARED VALUE $ _____ [CLAUSE 5. (C) (4)]

Received for shipment the above described merchandise, in apparent good order and condition unless otherwise state, to be transported to the above mentioned port of discharge or so near thereto as the vessel may safely get and be always afloat; and for arrangement or procurement of precarriage from the place of receipt and on carriage to the place of delivery hereon, if applicable. Weight, measure, marks, numbers, quality, contents and value if mentioned in the Bill of Lading were declared by the Merchant and accepted by the Carrier in good faith. The signing of this Bill of Lading does not signify confirmation by the Carrier of such particulars unless the contrary has been expressly acknowledged and agreed to. In accepting this Bill of Lading the Merchant expressly accepts and agrees to all its stipulations, exceptions and conditions, on both pages, whether written, printed, stamped or otherwise incorporated as fully as if they were all signed by the Merchant. In WITNESS whereof the Master of the said vessel has signed 3 (three) original Bills of Lading all of this tenor and date, one of which being accomplished the others to be void.

FOR THE CARRIER:
GULF & EASTERN
STEAMSHIP & CHARTERING CORP, AS AGENTS

PLACE & DATE OF ISSUE:	MO	DAY	YEAR
JACKSONVILLE	01	01	93

Figure 12–2 Front of a bill of lading. Courtesy of Companhia Maritima Nacional/Nacional Line.

ing to the vessel operating carrier showing himself (the NVO) as shipper. This master bill of lading carries the cargo.

The terms of the bill of lading contract are found on the front of the long form bill of lading. Though shippers rarely read either the bill of lading or tariff rules section, the agreement, enforceable in court, is found in these documents. The bill of lading contract specifies the legal liabilities of the carrier.

For example, one carrier's bill of lading states that, "The carrier shall have a lien on the goods which shall survive delivery, for all freight, charges and sums referred to herein and may enforce this lien by public or private sale without notice." In tendering a shipment to this carrier, the shipper agrees that even if freight is collect (to be paid by the buyer), the carrier may sell the goods without notice to recover unpaid charges.

Bills of lading are not uniform except as to general format. Terms and conditions vary from carrier to carrier and from liner conference to liner conference. As a practical matter, although most business people would not enter into contracts without understanding them, shippers, including their general counsel, generally are not sufficiently expert in admiralty law to interpret bills of lading and their consequences. The burden often falls on the insurers of cargo to remedy losses arising while cargo is in the carrier's custody. Brief mention should also be made about bill of lading fraud, wherein a falsified bill of lading is presented as evidence that goods have been shipped, and payment is demanded of the buyer, under a previously arranged credit agreement.[8]

Shipper's Export Declaration

Federal law requires that a *shipper's export declaration* be filed on every export valued over $2,500 and on every export requiring any form of validated license. The declaration is used for export control purposes and for compilation of U.S. trade statistics. Forwarders often prepare SEDs on behalf of their exporter clients. The forwarders accumulate the entries of their clients on computer and forward the computer files to the government. However, responsibility for accuracy and completeness remains the exporter's.

Shipper's Letter of Instruction

Shippers not making their own arrangements need to prepare detailed instructions for their shipping agents to follow as to just exactly how shipments are to

---

[8]*Hinterland,* (4/88) p. 25.

be handled. For example, who should receive what copies of which documents, what and whose insurance should be used, how it should be declared, what special documents if any the buyer has requested, what U.S. documents are required to be filed (such as export license notifications), and how much should be added for trucking. All these items and more, depending on the shipper's and buyer's requirements, and the relationship the forwarder has with the shipper, need to be in writing.

The importance of accurate written instructions cannot be overestimated. Avoiding disputes is good reason to use written instructions. A better reason is to assure that the customer is properly serviced.

"Clean" Documents

One will often hear reference to a dock receipt or bill of lading or some other document as being *clean*. That means that the document has been processed and nobody receiving or checking the cargo has noticed any flaw such as breakage, leaking, or shortage. In the entire chain of product movement, each party who receives the shipment may or may not check it before signing a receipt. If they do check the cargo and notice that something is wrong, they make the notation at the time they sign the receipt. In a shipment of 28 cartons, they might note: "short two cartons." Later, whenever the shipper or insurer attempts to settle the issue, the party who took exception has, in essence, placed the responsibility on some earlier party who handled the goods. Notations like this also delay financial settlement for the entire transaction.

Carnets

An international trading document that is used for accompanying sample goods is known as a *carnet*. It functions like a passport/visa and allows a person to carry a sample into a nation duty free, provided that it is carried out again, without alteration, usually within 12 months. These goods are carried by salespeople or are intended for display in trade fairs. Frequently goods accompanied by carnets are pre-cleared, although some have been subjected to inspection in areas where terrorist activities are a threat.

Hazardous Materials

Movement of hazardous materials internationally requires special labeling, package marking, and special documentation. New United Nations regulations went into effect in early 1991. Special documents include an IATA Dangerous Goods

Declaration and an International Maritime Organization (IMO) Dangerous Goods Declaration. There is also a "Shipper's Certificate of Articles Not Restricted" to be used if material being shipped by air appears to be hazardous but, in fact, is not.

Logistics of Documentation

Each shipment has its own documentation requirements, and each document has its own information requirements. There is a sequential relationship among many documents and it is possible to apply PERT charting to determine critical paths of documentation tasks.[9] Few shipments require the same documents. One can generalize that there are two points in the process when all documents must be ready and in good order. The first point is when the goods are presented to the international carrier. The second point is when the goods arrive in the importing country and must be presented to customs and subjected to other inspections. There are penalties for not having the documents in order, ranging from fines, higher import duties, missing quota windows, or being refused entry into the importing nation. One would have to factor the penalties and probabilities of their happening into any strategy. Lead times are important; some sources for documents charge more for rush service.

In international trade and distribution, computerization is slowly but surely taking hold in every aspect of the business. From computerized trade leads available through the Department of Commerce, to electronic letters of credit, to telecommunicated documents, to computerized freight booking, tracing, and documentation systems, to electronic freight tariffs, to automated freight payment systems, to computerized loss and damage reporting, to automated export license application systems, to computerized duty drawback and customshouse clearance systems, almost everything is being computerized to some extent. Most major nations are also working to develop a harmonized commodity description so that traders everywhere describe the same goods in an identical manner, facilitating the use of computers. Customs and trade statistics will also be reported using harmonized descriptions.

In an export documentation system, the computer should minimally produce an invoice. The invoice will contain information that is fixed and information which is variable. Fixed information is information that does not change. The customer name is information that does not change and the product name is in-

---

[9]Paul Murphy, Daniel Wardlow, and Donald Wood, "Charting International Logistics Channels," *Western Marketing Educator's Association 1996 Conference Proceedings*, 1996. pp. 45–49.

formation that does not change. Fixed data are stored in the computer's database. Thus in producing an invoice the program has to be told which customer record is being used, which product record is being used, and where to print the information on a piece of paper.

What does change from order to order is how much the customer is ordering. That information is variable and has to be put in (input) to the computer with each transaction. Price may change with each order also, so it may be variable. If it is variable, and not fixed, one will have to input price as well. The key to automation is therefore the ability to store repetitive information. The more repetitive, the more the database can be used, and the better the system will function.

Export systems are exceptionally difficult to program. An export commercial invoice contains a great many data elements not found in domestic invoices. A fully exploded export system, capable of producing bills of lading, dock receipts, bank letters, certificates of origin and the other documents involved in export, is very complex and difficult to program without both a strong knowledge of systems programming and a very strong knowledge of export documentation and traffic.

Exporters approach automating their operations in a variety of ways. But before automation can be successfully implemented the exporter needs to have its own house in order. Computers, in a certain sense, mimic what people do. If an analyst were asked to program a manual system that did not work well, then the final product would not work well either.

Thus companies considering automation have a number of up-front determinations to make: 1) They can go outside to buy a canned package; 2) they can buy a canned package and have it modified; 3) they can buy a package to do some things and not others; 4) they can write the entire system in house; 5) they can hire professionals to design and write a system.

Cost is associated with each option. Flexibility is also associated with each option. Canned packages are not flexible. The system does its work its own way. Existing operating procedures must be modified to fit the system. Modifying a canned package may be a good or bad idea, depending on how much modification is necessary. If extreme modification is needed, given the complexity of export systems, the option may be more costly and more troublesome than having the entire system written. Writing a completely new system requires careful consideration of expertise. Does it exist in house? Are knowledgeable persons in export/import documentation and transport available? Are expert programmers available? Are these people familiar with advances in technology outside the company? How much time does one have? How much money?

Whichever route is taken, modification of existing operating procedures and retraining of existing personnel will be required. Implementation will take longer than expected, cost more, and be less than what was finally wanted. Analysis of ongoing advances in the industry should be a fundamental part of the planning process for currently automated exporters and companies considering automation.

The great leap forward has been the ability to telecommunicate data and function interactively with remote computers. This is a relatively recent occurrence. Under the broad heading of electronic data interchange (EDI)—ANSI .X12 domestically and EDIFACT internationally—telecommunication permits the transfer of data, such as documents, and transactional data, such as freight booking data, to carriers, to banks, to customs and even to and from customers.

EDI operates on the simple premise that information can be electronically transmitted and that the various parties along the line use the same pieces of data in addition to others. For example, port of discharge (POD). POD is used by the exporter, the port terminal operator (to know where to load the freight on the ship or airplane), the carrier, the insurance company, the bank (particularly in letters of credit), the customer's customs broker, customs, and of course the customer.

Transmitting data records that can be read by computers belonging to each of these partners or parties assures the correct information without the need to rekey. Transactions are thereby electronically processed much more efficiently than having to produce, send, read and key manual documents. The data originator need not know anything about the next user's computer or even use the same kind of computer. The Internet and EDI are the future of international trade documentation. Some companies and industries have developed proprietary protocols that are not EDI compatible. At an industry level these are fading as customers switch to EDI standards. International data communication problems of both a political and technological nature have impeded progress. But they will be resolved. It is therefore important to program for tomorrow and not just today's needs.

The power of these products has been long recognized by financial and other professionals. They are also of immense use to transportation and distribution personnel. However, the real value of the products, in particular database products, is not realized until data can be downloaded.

Emulation software and other products are available on the market to permit data to be taken off the order billing system, for example, for analysis using one of these commercial products. Freight payment systems, whether in house or contracted, contain invaluable information that can be quickly and easily analyzed.

Thus automation means more than producing invoices. It means creating a system capable of producing and receiving international documents and data streams containing standardized information, in addition to proprietary information, which can be electronically networked to others. It must be capable of generating data that can be used by the average manager in commercially popular spreadsheet and database software products on an ad hoc basis.

There are many software programs on the market. One freight forwarding package includes these features:

Port planning for multiple shipments going to the same port, with automatic creation of a consolidation manifest.

Direct date transmission (via modem or diskette) of shipping data to the U.S. Census Bureau.

IATA Agent/Airline reports for airlines and agents, enabling forwarders to keep track of commissions due.

Printing of shipping labels, shipper's export declarations, intermodal masters, dock receipts, air master and house bills of lading, plus all other necessary documents on both continuous and single forms.

Maintains complete export history on each shipment with tracking by customer, date, house bill of lading and client's reference or purchase order number.[10]

Figure 12–3 shows a diagram that fits some of that software supplier's packages with physical product flow and documentation flow.

Figure 12–4 shows a network prepared by a software developer that specializes in software for large volume exporters who are heavily regulated. ELS stands for *Export Logistics Systems*. The network shows the electronic connections between individual PCs, workstations, and mainframe computers. The system links customers, vendors, warehouses, forwarders, and carriers. It also reports export transactions to the Census Bureau. Figure 12–5 shows data flows through the exporting company and the other parties with which it is linked by EDI. The transactions are monitored by the system to assure compliance with corporate policies, government controls, and hazardous materials regulations. For example, the system checks to make certain that incompatible hazardous materials are not accidentally stowed in the same container. It also checks to make certain that the foreign customer is not listed in the federal Table of Denial Orders (a list of firms to whom exports may not be sent). Modern computing technology enables vast databases to be linked and accessed, and to perform specific, complex functions in the logistics process.

---

[10]Brochure issued by GMS International, Inc., Old Tappan, NJ, ca. 1992.

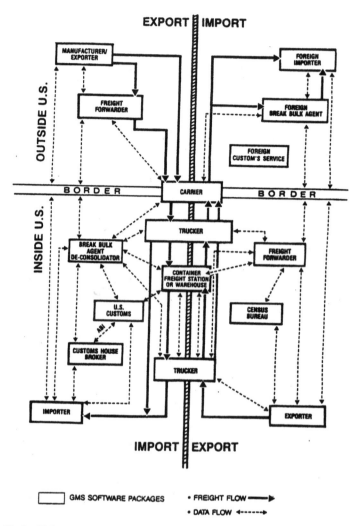

Figure 12–3 Using computer software to integrate documentation and freight flow. Courtesy GMS International Inc. Old Tappan, New Jersey.

ELS
Export Logistics
System

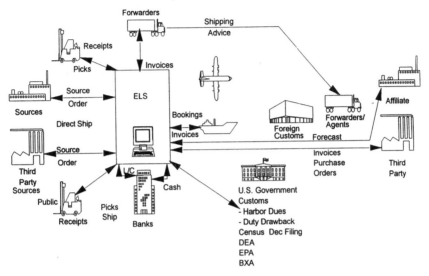

Figure 12–4 Network for heavily regulated, large-volume exporters. Courtesy Syntra, Ltd.

Cargo Insurance

For international shipments, one needs insurance. There are few exceptions to this rule. Under a codification of the Hague rules of 1924, an ocean carrier has an upward limit of $500 per package. "In some jurisdictions, courts have held that a 40-foot container is the package."[11]

The primary purpose of insurance is to redistribute loss and so to eliminate risk. An equally important function of insurance, and one which is more economically creative, is the actual prevention of loss. One is interested in the elimination of risk and the prevention of loss. The cost of risk elimination is the insurance premium. The reason one is interested in preventing loss is that the cost of risk elimination is directly related to loss experience.

Frequency has interesting implications with respect to any discussion of insurance. How often does a particular loss occur? What are the chances it will occur? Consider icebergs as an example. It is certainly true that the chances are

---

[11] *Handling and Shipping Management,* February, 1987, p. 37.

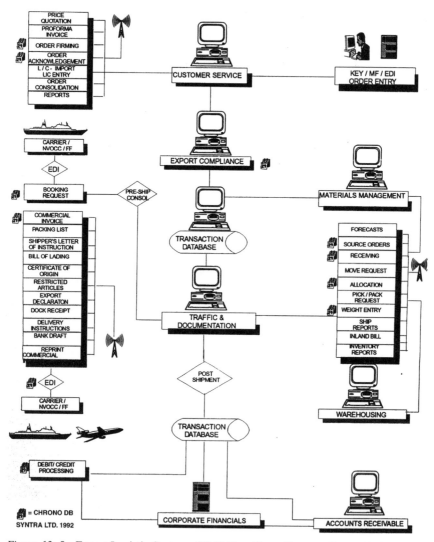

Figure 12–5 Export Logistic Systems (ELS) Data Flow. Courtesy Syntra, Ltd.

slim one's cargo will be lost as a result of an iceberg collision. And yet, it happens. In fact, one can confidently say that losses attributable to iceberg collisions will definitely occur. The question is, how likely is it any particular shipment will be lost?

With hundreds of thousands of shipments made every year and tens of thousands of claims serving as a statistical base, it is possible to answer such questions in terms of odds (probability). For example, assume that the odds are 100 to 1 that any one shipment will be damaged by motion. If one makes only one shipment per year it is unlikely that a loss will occur. On the other hand, if one makes 100 shipments a year the chances are very good that there will be a loss. In fact, *risk* is uncertainty concerning loss. When one insures he does nothing more than reduce the uncertainty regarding the financial impact of that loss.

Again, the purpose of insurance is to redistribute the loss and thereby eliminate risk. How does insurance redistribute loss? It does so by increasing the number of exposures so that loss is certain and by spreading the cost of that loss among all those exposures. Each time one pays an insurance premium he is absorbing a very small loss. One eliminates uncertainty by suffering a loss on each shipment.

People or firms who *self insure,* or buy no insurance from an outside party, apply a portion of each sale to a kitty awaiting the occurrence of a loss, which is sure to come. In this way they are spreading the cost of the loss that does occur over time and over the shipments on which a loss did not occur. All companies do this to some extent. Minor claims are not usually sent to underwriters because the administrative cost of doing so is prohibitive.

The amount of self insurance, per loss transaction, may also be referred to as the *deductible.* Deductibles are a part of the cost of doing business. Over and above deductibles, most companies purchase marine insurance from specialized insurance carriers.

Policies

The most common form of insurance policy for ordinary importers and exporters is the so-called *open marine policy,* or simply *open policy.* An open policy is an insurance contract that remains in force until it is canceled and that automatically covers shipments made and reported under it. The benefits of automatic protection and the convenience of such an arrangement are obvious. But beyond convenience, open marine policies are desirable because they are tailored to the needs of the purchaser.

Customized protection is particularly useful to shippers of unusual commodities or traders to particular remote areas of the world, where unique perils are the issue. The other benefit is that the physical damage or loss premium rate is fixed and known in advance. Finally, there is the administrative efficiency of periodic reporting as opposed to making arrangements on each shipment individually. Periodic monthly or even quarterly reporting results in cost savings to the exporter as well as the insurance company, savings passed on in the form of lower premiums.

Efficiency, unfortunately, is not endemic to international trade. Exporters are often requested, and in letters of credit sometimes required, to provide negotiable insurance certificates, or proof of extant insurance. An insurance certificate is simply an affirmation, usually on insurance company letterhead, that insurance has been provided. The certificate is commonly prepared by the exporter or his forwarder. Many forwarders have open policies (referred to as house policies) that they can use to offer insurance coverage to their clients.

Larger exporters should consider the fact that since forwarder policies cannot be customized, the premium rate is going to be based on the loss experience of all sorts of different commodities. Moreover, shippers unable to purchase economical insurance directly because of high loss ratios do purchase insurance through forwarders. These two facts tend to make forwarder insurance more expensive than individually negotiated premiums. In addition, some forwarders charge extra for arranging insurance. An informed discussion with one's insurance agent or broker may reveal substantial savings opportunities if insurance is being purchased through a foreign freight forwarder.

A special marine policy is more than a certification. When properly endorsed the document becomes a fully negotiable instrument. If a loss occurs, the settlement is payable to the bearer of the negotiable policy. Thus, in a letter of credit situation the bank wants assurance that if a loss occurs after the exporter has been paid, any loss arising under the transaction will be restored not to the exporter but to the bank or its client. This is easily accomplished with a special marine policy.

A point of clarification may be in order. Special marine policies are not separate policies. The document is prepared in multiple parts. The copies sent to the insurance company are used as declarations under the master policy. However, as far as the banks are concerned, special marine policies stand alone as insurance protection.

Insurable Interest

Who insures? Who insures is determined by the sales term negotiated by the parties. The sales term specifies where the risk of loss will pass from seller to buyer. In an ex-works transaction the buyer assumes the financial risk of loss right from the seller's dock and therefore has an insurable interest in the goods.

At the other extreme, using DDP (delivered duty paid) the risk passes from seller to buyer at the buyer's warehouse. Thus all the risks of transport are borne by the seller.

Now assume for that moment that one makes a sale of computers valued at $1,500,000 cif to a Brazilian firm. Payment terms are s/d d/p, and because Brazilian regulations require local purchase of insurance, the buyer is arranging for marine coverage. The sales terms are F.A.S. (delivered to ship) New York.

Forty hours out the carrying vessel breaks up in a heavy sea and sinks. The buyer declines payment of the invoice. The seller telexes the buyer that insurance was under his care according the sales contract. He telexes back that his insurer has informed him that the carrying vessel was over twenty years old, but that the policy will cover the loss. The buyer advises he will make whatever restitution he can depending on how a number of lawsuits are decided, but that may take several years. What does the seller tell his boss?

A good trader would have protected his firm through the purchase of contingency insurance. The contingency was that the buyer's insurance would fail to adequately cover the loss. It should be noted that ownership is not a criterion in the usual sense of insurable interest. Contingency insurance covers in the interests of persons who may be financially damaged by a loss.

Perils

The insurance industry, and in particular the marine insurance industry, speaks an obscure language. Nevertheless, it may be useful to discuss perils in the vernacular.

First, what is a peril? A peril is the nature or kind of loss. It is that which causes a loss, that is, fire, collision, pirate attacks, war, or the like. Firms insure against perils. The word "average," in insurance terms, refers to the extent of coverage. A "particular average" loss is one that affects specific interests only. A "general average" is one that affects all interests in a voyage including that of the vessel itself. Ancient convention has established that all parties to a voyage, shippers and owners alike, share in the benefits of the voyage and should therefore also share in the perils thereto. Thus, should a vessel sink, all interests (that is, persons having an interest) share in that loss.

Both "general" and "particular" average insurance cover against total loss resulting from perils of the sea (that is, the action of the wind and sea). "FPA" coverage (that is, free of particular average) covers only for total (general) loss or partial losses resulting from certain named perils (for example, stranding or fire). That is to say, in the event of a partial loss due to these perils, only a partial amount is recoverable. "With average" or "WA" insurance covers the full amount of the loss. FPA is a more restrictive and narrower insurance than WA coverage. Basically, FPA will cover only in the event of a total loss while WA will allow for recoveries on partial losses.

The so-called "all risk" coverage is most commonly used by traders of general commodities. All risk insurance does not, as the name implies, cover against all risks. Certain risks are specifically excluded, such as those arising from war and losses attributable to delays in transit.

In fact, all risk insurance is an extension of WA insurance in that perils in addition to those of the sea are incrementally covered (for example, all risk insurance protects against theft, pilferage, and non-delivery). Typically, endorsements are amended to the all risk policy to add protection against still other perils. The "S. R. & C. C." endorsement (that is., strikes, riots and civil commotion endorsement) covers against those named perils. In October 1993, when there was obvious unrest in Haiti, "a committee of London underwriters that offer cargo insurance to protect against strikes, riots, and civil disturbances recommended raising tenfold the minimum rate charged for such coverage on transporting goods to and from Haiti."[12]

War and the acts and consequences of war are all excluded from marine policies. In the United States "war risk" insurance is almost always purchased separately and covered by a separate policy. A separate premium is also paid for war risk. The reason is that war risk premiums fluctuate and are frequently updated by underwriters. To certain places in the world, that is, those involved in open hostilities, rates are not prepublished and must be obtained on an individual, shipment-by-shipment, basis—"on application."

Inherent Vice

No insurance will cover against that which is bound to happen. An exporter who ships light bulbs in bulk, thrown loosely into a wooden crate, cannot expect to collect on a breakage claim. Insurance covers against "external risks" of physical loss normally consequent to transport and due solely to external factors. Losses arising from the negligence of the shipper cannot be recovered. Spoilage of fresh produce is often considered as an inherent vice. Also included here may be government confiscation, a problem with high-tech goods.[13]

It is important to keep in mind that the courts have sustained the premise that the shipper covenants to act in good faith to afford reasonable protection to the insured goods. The shipper is bound to act as if there were no insurance operative. Claims rejected on the basis of inherent vice are rejected because the loss was attributable to an internal and not external factor.

Term

Generally, the "term" or "currency" of an all risk policy is from the moment a shipment leaves the exporter's warehouse (or plant) until the time it arrives at the

---

[12]*The Journal of Commerce*, October 25, 1993, p. 14A.

[13]Edgar Rachelson, "How to Reduce the Risks of International Air Carriage," *Inbound Logistics*, January, 1987, pp. 35–36.

buyer's warehouse, including stops in between, provided that the shipment is in "continuous" and "ordinary" transportation. This includes up to 30 days' stay in customs. Beyond 30 days the assured (the party covered by insurance) must contact its insurance carrier for a time extension (and additional premium). The so-called "South American Clause" adds an additional 30 days to the normal Customs custody period.

The concept of *continuous ordinary transportation* should be well understood. For example, if customs were to seize a shipment, it would no longer be in continuous ordinary transportation and insurance would lapse within 10–15 days of the seizure. What that means is that the customer must inform the seller of unusual delays in customs in order to assure rights under the policy are not prejudiced.

Another example of noncontinuous transportation would be a shipment made from Chicago to a Baltimore warehouse, where the shipment is held for an import license or receipt of a letter of credit. Pilferage occurs while the cargo is in the warehouse. The marine policy will not cover this loss because the shipment was not continuous transportation. If, on the other hand, a trucking company moving the cargo from Chicago to a pier for export loses the cargo at the same warehouse, the marine policy will apply.

Prevention

The purpose of insurance is to eliminate risk. That can be done by assuring that one will be made "financially whole" by recovering the loss resulting from the perils of transportation through insurance, or by attempting to prevent the loss from occurring in the first place.

Of course the only way to completely eliminate risk is not to act. Even then risk is not totally eliminated. Nevertheless, risk can be reduced by taking prudent protective measures. Indeed, in order not to prejudice rights under the policy one must take prudent measures to avoid loss as if no insurance were in effect.

In the case of cargo transportation there are various ways of doing this. They all begin with proper and adequate packaging able to withstand the rigors of the most arduous portion of the journey. Adequate may vary from from shipment to shipment and market to market. Adequate will vary from commodity to commodity as well. Figure 12–6 gives an indication of some the forces to which a ship at sea (and its cargo) are subjected.

In the case of consumer products manufactured and packaged in corrugated cartons for domestic sale, additional packing of some sort, or containerization, is absolutely necessary for export. Domestic corrugated cartons cannot withstand the rigors and hazards of sea transportation.

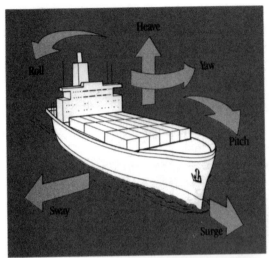

A ship at sea may move in six different directions.

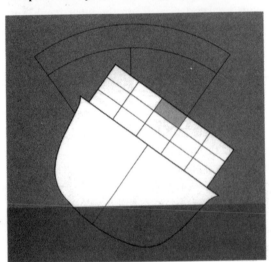

This container may travel 70 feet with each complete roll; as often as 7 to 10 times per minute.

Figure 12–6 Forces encountered by ships at sea and their cargo. Courtesy CIGNA Corporation, *Ports of the World*, 15th edition.

A ship at sea will heave, roll, and yaw. Condensation will collect on the bulkheads and overheads of steel ships moving from one climate to another. Condensation falls like rain onto cargo in the holds of the ship. Heat and humidity surge in confined spaces, including containers loaded on deck. Walls of waves pound ships at sea in storms, drenching the entire vessel with thousands of tons of corrosive salt water.

Cargo shipped in less than containerload quantities may find itself on the floor of containers or holds with tons of other cargo loaded on top. As the ship moves violently, vertically and horizontally, tremendous pressure is exerted on the cargo.

In some ports of the world there are no covered dock facilities. Cargo sits on the open wharf, drenched in the rain and baked in blazing sun or frozen solid in sub-zero temperatures. It is picked and nibbled at by rats, roaches, vermin of all sorts. Pilferers and thieves methodically take cargo for their own consumption or for sale on the black market.

Knowing what conditions one's cargo will be exposed to is the first step in deciding what protective steps must be taken to prevent or reduce loss. Protective greases should be applied to exposed metal surfaces to prevent rust. Fibreboard cartons should be shrouded or shrink wrapped then tightly and securely bound with steel-band strapping. Machinery should be carefully crated or entirely boxed. Green wood, with high moisture content, should never be used. Sensitive electronic equipment should be cushioned from shock and protected with over-wrapping.

"Blind marks" should be used on cartons, crates and boxes. Blind marks do not reveal the contents of the package, an easy tip off to thieves.

These are all examples of steps a prudent person would take to minimize the risk of loss in transit. They are steps one would take were the property his own and without insurance coverage.

Hull Insurance

In addition to insuring a vessel's cargo, the vessel itself is also insured. The term used is hull insurance, and the costs are usually paid directly by the vessel's owners but indirectly by the vessel's users. Insurers look at the vessel's flag, fleet, owner, and management, as well as the political situation. In the 1980s, merchant vessels were operating in some areas where shooting wars were taking place, and our examples given here are from that tumultuous era. A vessel flying a Cypriot flag, for example, in the 1980s was about four times as risky as a U.S. flag and 13 more times than a Japanese. "As a rule of thumb, underwriters in the marine business say that for every dollar Japan pays to insure a fleet of, say, five ships, the Norwegians pay $1.10, the Americans $1.25, and the Greeks, $1.50. U.S. flag hulls are about three times as risky as Japan's, many times more so than Norway's and the high cost of U.S. repairs and crews adds even more to the cost of coverage."[14] This was during the time of military unrest in the Middle East. In 1986 alone, 105 vessels were attacked in the Persian Gulf, 79 of which were tankers. The August 22, 1986 "Iraqi raid of Sirri Island which hit three vessels and killed 19 men, doubled insurance rates for tankers serving the island."[15]

Here is a 1984 article regarding vessel insurance rates for tanker shipments in the Persian Gulf. For ships stopping at Kharg Island (Iran's main oil terminal),

"the rates agreed upon by most Lloyd's underwriters start at 7.5 percent of the vessel's value for a seven day voyage, plus 3 percent of the cargo's value. . . . By comparison, the standard war-risk policy in most other parts of the world costs only 0.1 percent of the hull's value, and 0.0275 percent of the cargo. Tanker owners also buy additional insurance policies, costing about 2.5 percent of the vessel's value to cover other hazards such as storms."[16]

At that time most tankers were valued at $20 million and their cargoes at $40 million. "In August of 1984, underwater mines allegedly planted by Libya damaged 19 commercial vessels as they prepared to transit the Suez. Although damage was minimal, the Canal was effectively closed as minesweeping units from five navies swept the approaches at a cost in excess of $100 million. There is speculation that the ore carrier Mariner II was sunk by one of these mines as late as April, 1985."[17]

Rustbucket fraud occurs when one charters an aged ship that is loaded with goods worth more than the ship. After setting sail, it makes an unscheduled stop, sells off the cargo to the highest bidder and exchanges its regular crew for a "scuttling crew" that takes it out to sea, where it runs into bad weather and sinks in very deep water. The crew manages to escape.

Most of these quotation are over a decade old and they come from a time when maritime shipping was more perilous because of wars in the Iran-Iraq region. A key danger today is piracy, especially on Asian seas. During calendar year 2000, for example, the International Maritime Bureau recorded over 450 pirate attacks on ships, up from 100 attacks in 1990.[18]

---

[14]*American Shipper,* March, 1987, p. 60.

[15]*American Shipper,* March, 1987, p. 60.

[16]*The Wall Street Journal,* May 31, 1984.

[17]*VIA Port of NY-NJ,* December, 1986, p. 11.

[18]*The Washington Post,* June 18, 2001, p. A01.

Protection and Indemnity (P & I) clubs insure vessels. The club in the United Kingdom is the world's largest, insuring about 25 percent of the world's fleet. Typical vessel owner risks covered include injury, illness, and death of crew, passengers, and stevedores; crew repatriation and costs of substitutes; costs incurred when handling refugees, stowaways, and sick people; collision liability; property damage; pollution by oil; cargo loss; shortage and damage; unrecoverable general average contributions; fines; and legal costs. Major types of P & I claims are: cargo, 39 percent; crew injury, 23 percent; property damage, 10 percent; collision, 8 percent; pollution, 5 percent; fines, 2 percent; unrecoverable general average, 2 percent; wreck removal, 1 percent; and other, 10 percent. Major causes of P & I claims are deck officer error, 25 percent; crew error, 17 percent; shore error, 14 percent; structural failure of vessel, 10 percent; equipment failure, 8 percent; pilot error, 5 percent; mechanical failure, 5 percent; engineering officer error, 2 percent; and other causes, 13 percent.[19]

Air Cargo Insurance

The international airline industry is more closely regulated than are ocean carriers. The Warsaw Convention of the late 1920s, as updated by the Montreal Protocol of 1999, set uniform rules for the international air carriers. Airlines are liable for about $23 per kilo of the entire shipment (and the liability is tied to changing values of currency rather than a stated amount, which is reduced by inflation).

Most goods moving internationally by air are worth more than this so they require separate insurance coverage. Airlines sell some coverage themselves, although many traders use a modified form of marine insurance coverage. When moving museum-quality artwork, insurance companies may insist that air freight be used because time that cargo is in an unfamiliar climate or atmosphere is reduced. Also, "for more important works of art, usually there is only one object per flight, thus guaranteeing against the loss of an entire collection in the event of an accident."[20]

FedEx, UPS, Airborne and DHL are called integrated carriers because they own all their planes, vehicles and the facilities that fall in between. They now each serve at least 200 countries. Their air operations are governed by international airline regulations and have their internal systems for processing loss and damage claims promptly.

---

[19]*The Journal of Commerce* January 7, 1997, p. 1A.

[20]"Packing Up the Pieces," *KLM CARGOVISION,* January–February, 1990, p. 14.

Land Transport

Movements over land must also be insured. This could be a truck or rail movement that crosses borders or the move connecting an inland point to a seaport or airport. One must make certain that coverage of this shipment is complete and that there are no gaps. Consider this: "Assault on transport operations now accounts for more than 60 percent of total losses due to theft in Mexico, according to the Mexican Association of Insurance Agencies." To combat these thefts, trucking companies operating in Mexico are advised to remove logos from their vehicles, rotate drivers, change schedules, use exclusively toll highways, and travel in convoys. The thieves, many of whom are ex-policemen, are so well organized they even have their own insurance guaranteeing safe passage to shippers, for a price.[21]

Settlement of Insurance Claims

When a loss does occur certain steps must be taken promptly. The carrier must be notified immediately of a potential claim. A formal claim may follow, but the immediate notification is essential. The notification may be verbal but must be confirmed in writing and receipts obtained.

The insurance company must also be promptly notified of the loss. The local agent of the insurance company must be given the opportunity to physically examine the loss and determine the cause. This is done through employment of independent surveyors of the insurance company who are dispatched to the site of the goods when a loss is reported if the amount is significant.

Immediate steps must be taken to prevent further loss, if that is possible. Photographs or video tapes of the cargo should be taken on arrival. Documents in support of the claim must then be gathered. These would include signed delivery receipts, bills of lading, packing lists,[22] commercial invoices, insurance certificates, photographs, and surveyor reports. The carrier must be given the option of examining the goods as well with its own surveyors.

While piece-count shortages and some damages are clearly visible on arrival, others are not. Losses on cargo shipped in freight containers or otherwise unitized or contained in sealed boxes may not be apparent at the time of delivery.

---

[21]*Business Mexico* (August, 1996), p. 27.

[22]A packing list is placed in each carton of assorted merchandise by the person packing it; and upon receipt the consignee (the receiver of freight) verifies both the count of freight on the carrier's waybill and the packing list's entries for each carton.

These are concealed losses and are more difficult to prove, as having resulted from a covered peril. The consignee should be instructed to inspect goods as soon after receipt as practical in order to determine whether concealed losses have occurred. The longer the period between receipt and discovery of loss, the less the chance the claims will be satisfactorily settled. Having discovered a loss, the customer should take the same steps indicated above.

To assure proper steps are taken and that the customer knows whom to contact and what to do when a loss is discovered, some exporters send along with original documents covering the shipment a written instruction to consignees. The document includes the names and addresses of local settling agents and provides detailed instructions on what steps should be followed in the event of loss.

Typically, the carrier will reject the claim when received from the assured. The assured must make a good faith effort to obtain full or satisfactory settlement from the carrier and evidence of this should be available. The carrier may offer a partial settlement. The assured may decide to accept the partial amount, in order to maintain a healthy loss-to-premium ratio and keep his premiums low. However, having accepted any amount the assured gives up the right to further settlement either from the carrier or the insurance company.

If the offered settlement is not adequate the assured subrogates his rights to recovery to the insurer. *Subrogation* means to transfer all rights against the carrier to the insurance company. The insurance company will pay the claim, if it is properly documented and the loss is covered, then it will file claim against the carrier itself. The insurer may even elect to file a lawsuit against the carrier for full or partial damages. Having transferred rights to it, the insurance company then has the legal right to do so. If, however, the assured has prejudiced its rights, the insurer can no longer obtain satisfaction from the carrier.

Minimizing losses through protective packaging, safe routings, blind marks, and other means are the best way to avoid high premiums and maintain good customer relations. The effort and management creativeness always should be focused on the minimization of loss. Here's an example of a settlement facilitated by a marine cargo surveyor sent to survey a damaged cargo. These are excerpts from a surveyor's report to a vessel operator:

> On . . . we proceeded at the request of . . . to examine the shipment to determine whether it was contaminated by acid. . . .
>
> At the arrival at the above premises, we contacted the Importer [who had set aside] the drums in question. . . .
>
> The drums were marked: ". . . ." They were constructed of a plastic material, with a screw type lid and measured approximately 26″ X 18″ in size, with a gross weight of 350 lbs. each. . . .

Upon examination of the drums we sighted 2 drums #12 and #15 to show evidence of a gray powder residue on the side face of the drums, which was identified as acid. . . .

Based on the type of drum lid and inner lid, we were of the opinion that none of the powder had entered the drum or resulted in contamination of the product. . . .

We advised the Importer of our findings . . . , and he responded that this was a food product, used in the production of . . . and that if the product was to be sold, his firm would require the steamship line to guarantee the product and take responsibility for all liability. . . .

After further discussion, the Importer indicated that the product could be removed from the drums, washed, resalted and repacked into new drums, at which time his firm would accept the product. We were advised that the cost of washing and repacking the 15 drums would be $2000.00. . . . It was agreed that the 15 drums upon washing and repacking . . . would be accepted as sound at a cost of $1800.00 which was to be considered as a full and final settlement.

It was our understanding that the 15 drums had an invoice value of $9,600.00. . . . We are of the opinion that any alternative to the above . . . would result in a greater loss.[23]

Summary

One unique aspect of international logistics is the requirement of a vast number of documents. Often about ten are required, with the most common ones being the commercial invoice, certificate of origin, consular invoice, dock receipt, insurance certificate, letter of credit, ocean bill of lading, shipper's export declaration, and the shipper's letter of instructions.

Computers are being used increasingly to assist in completing many of the required forms. Worldwide harmonization of product descriptions is making the task easier.

Insurance is needed for all international shipments. It covers all ordinary risks, and additional coverage is purchased for other risks. Hull insurance is for protecting the vessel; it is paid for by the vessel owner, but indirectly ends up in the cost of moving freight.

End-of-Chapter Questions

1. In international logistics, what is role performed by documents?
2. What is the commercial invoice? What functions does it perform?

---

[23]Form supplied by a West Coast vessel operator.

3. What is the function of the dock receipt?

4. What would be a clean bill of lading?

5. What is a carnet?

6. In what ways are computers being used to alleviate some of complexities in the international trade transactions?

7. Why must international shipments be insured? Who is responsible for buying the insurance?

8. In marine insurance, what is a general average?

9. What is hull insurance? When is it used?

10. What is the relationship between insurance and the international trade transaction?

CASE • *The Great Bite Peach Company*

An item in today's issue of *Maritime Outlook Weekly* says:

"The first quarter is historically slow for shippers of cargo between Asia and the United States, but ocean carriers in trans–Pacific trades are betting that volumes will rise soon enough—and strong enough—to allow for a $300 rate increase per container on eastbound freight and a second increase in west-bound rates for refrigerated products.

"While importers are relying on the reality of several new entrants to keep tonnage at high levels—a fact that usually mitigates against rate increases—exporters are more realistic that the new increases will hold, coming as they do on the heels of the apparent recovery of Asian economies.

"Carriers, meanwhile maintain that U.S. exports of perishable meat and produce shipments to Asia are growing apace with the region's return to normalcy after the late 1990s economic crisis. As they begin to redeploy costly refrigerated containers in the Pacific along with specially trained personnel necessary to operate, maintain, and repair them, carriers are looking to improve freight rates on westbound hauls.

"Container lines say they have seen increases in reefer cargo volumes ranging from 5 to 11 percent, depending on commodity. They expect the trend to continue for the next six to twelve months as Asian economies strengthen and consumer demand for fresh and chilled meat, fruits, and vegetables from the Americas increases.

"The major carriers in the trade have raised rates on frozen beef, pork, and poultry, French fries and potatoes, fruits and vegetables, juice concentrates, and other refrigerated cargoes beginning January 1, then again February 1, and continuing throughout the year. The lines are expected to implement increases across the board or on an individual basis with amounts and effective dates varying according to commodity, origin, or destination, seasonal shipping cycles, service requirements, and other factors.

"Carriers are attempting to recover mounting losses, a large portion of which resulted from the Asian economic crisis several years ago. The ripple effect of such a catastrophe—falling exchange rates, reduced lending, contraction of the consumer markets, stifling of consumer confidence—hit the US export market hard as demand went through the floor.

"Meanwhile, the relatively strong U.S. economy and falling Asian exchange rates has created a 20 percent surge in eastbound traffic with another double-digit surge predicted for the coming six months. This has created a great deal of demand for containers in Asia but much less so in the United States. Carriers have to get containers back to Asia somehow. They are looking to fill back hauls with very little demand.

"Reefer operators are especially vulnerable because there is very little inbound refrigerated traffic. These lines have been forced to offer discounts westbound. Rates are down across the board. They have fallen to as little as $2,000 per box and less. That is half the rate that existed twelve months earlier for some of the most expensive equipment in the industry.

"But lines report that recent demand has exceeded supply in certain areas for reefer equipment. This specialized equipment now ranges in price from $25,000 to $35,000 per forty-foot box, plus an equivalent amount in repair and maintenance costs over the container's useful life. There are also costs of energy to power the equipment and personnel costs monitoring temperature. Pacific carriers incur further round trip costs because they often are forced to fill their expensive, but less space efficient, equipment at lower rates for nonreefer cargo. Shippers say they are expecting some form of westbound rate increase to hold."

You have just been hired as the westbound logistics manager for the Great Bite Peach Company, headquartered in Michigan. The CEO invites to an early Friday afternoon meeting with senior executives of the company including the chief financial officer, the VP of production, and the VP of Sales and Marketing, Ern Hewill, who is excited about the possibility of opening a vast new market in China. One of your current "A" clients, a major American retailer, is opening a chain of super markets across China and will buy all the fresh peaches you can produce. Upon further questioning, Hewill forecasts 5,000 to 6,000 container loads a year. The VP of production advises there will be no problem meeting the demand. "That's fantastic," says the CEO.

Hewill looks across the table at you. "It's all up to you now," he says. "I must provide a landed cost to our customer as soon as possible, no later than next Wednesday, or they go elsewhere. You get back to your office, call in your freight forwarder and find us a rate."

It's later in the afternoon now in an office overlooking the Seattle waterfront. The sales VP of Pacific Dreams Containership Company has just received a call from Great Bite Peach Company, who has been a customer from time to time. They said that they have the opportunity to sell a great deal of fresh peaches to a major retailer opening a chain of supermarkets across China and need to negotiate an agreement immediately in order to submit to a proposal to their customer. The sales VP arranges a quick meeting with the CEO, Bob Hannus, and the owner's representative. The owner's rep is delighted. "We need this business. Friday's ship has been going out light every week. We have only been operating at 60 percent of capacity westbound for months."

Hannus isn't as animated. He says: "This is reefer cargo. For us to carry this I may have to go out and buy or lease refrigerated equipment. Do you know what that costs?"

The owner's rep says: "We can use the containers on the eastbound with department store merchandise. There is plenty of that."

Hannus looks at his sales VP and says: "Make a deal we can both live with, hot shot. Oh, and by the way, don't come back empty handed."

Questions for *The Great Bite Peach Company*

1. You are the westbound logistics manager for the Great Bite Peach Company and are about to attempt negotiating a contract. What are the issues as you see them?

2. (Continuation of question one.) What other information do you need?

3. You are the sales VP of Pacific Dreams Containership Company and are about to attempt negotiating a contract. What are the issues as you see them?

4. (Continuation of question three.) What other information do you need?

5. How should the carrier explain to the shipper of Westbound cargo that the shipper is also expected to pay part of the cost of returning the empty or less lucratively loaded containers eastward to the U.S. West Coast?

6. Shippers choose carriers on the basis of cost and quality of service. What are some of the service and service quality elements that should be considered here?

7. At your instructor's direction, meet with another student, or as teams, to negotiate various service and service quality items to be incorporated into the contract. Write out those portions of the agreement.

13

Logistics of Export Product Movement

Introduction

As international logistics develops as a field of study, the concept of channels becomes helpful for understanding the behavior patterns of business people. *Marketing channels* are defined as sets of interdependent groups involved in the process of making a product or service available for use, and the channel should be seen as a network that creates value through the generation of form, possession, time, and place utilities. Donald Bowersox described the importance of two specific channels in understanding logistics systems: The transaction channel that handles negotiations, contracts, and continually administers trading; and the distribution channel that provides five functions: adjustment (including the concentration, selection, and dispersion of goods); transfer; storage; handling; and communication. In Chapter 12, mention was made of a third channel, one for documentation necessary for international transactions.

The channels are separated from each other, that is, a firm may locate sales offices in a different set of cities from where it locates distribution warehouses, and documentation may follow a different route, that is, the documents may move by air to be available when the ship carrying the goods enters the port where they will be offloaded. However, the three channels are linked to the extent that sales or payments trigger release of goods to the buyer, and that documentation must be complete before goods can move forward.

In somewhat different terms, Roger Kallock said more about these linkages along and between chains:

> . . . logistics is simply linkage—the interdependent making, moving and selling of products. The "making" integrates production scheduling, master sched-

uling, materials management, and manufacturing; "moving" ties in transportation, materials handling, location design, and finished goods deployment; and "selling" factors in forecasting, order service, customer service, and pricing. Thus the linkage activity is the focal point of improvements on any basis—international or domestic. Linkage across the supply chain is also the framework for logistics systems design.[1]

This chapter will deal mainly with the distribution channel, that is, the physical movement of the product. It is written mainly from the view of the exporter shipping goods overseas. It could also be studied from the viewpoint of the individual responsible for successfully making a shipment who would either perform the functions described or farm some or all of them out to third-party service providers.

International Transaction Channel Activities and Their Influence on the Movement of Goods through the Distribution Channel

Marketing abroad is not the same as selling domestically. From a logistics viewpoint, there will be discussion of two unique aspects in the transaction channel: choosing the terms of sale and handling the payment.

Choosing the terms of sale involves looking at the distribution channel and determining when and/or where to transfer between buyer and selling the following:

1. The physical goods
2. Payment for the goods
3. Legal title to the goods
4. Responsibility for:
   a. insuring the goods
   b. paying for transporting the goods
   c. controlling—or caring for—the goods (in the case, say, of livestock)

Transfer of these can be expressed in terms of calendar time, geographic location, or on completion of some action(s). Thus, when developing the agreement to sell, one must think in terms of both time and location. These dates need not be specific. As Hyundai autos cross the ocean from Korea to U.S. ports, they are

---

[1]Roger Kallock, "The Challenge of Managing Logistics in a Global Environment," *CLM Annual Conference Proceedings, 1988,* vol. 1, p. 87.

initially owned by Hyundai Motor America, which has purchased them from Hyundai Motor Co., and, "often two-thirds or more of a car carrier's capacity, are sold electronically from a carrier vessel while it's at sea."[2] Dealers receiving cars by truck pay for them electronically the moment they are delivered to the dealership. For those arriving by train, the dealer pays when the train arrives. In both situations the money is transferred directly to Korea to pay off Hyundai Motor America's debt to Hyundai Motor Co.

Here, from the seller's viewpoint, is a list of the different locations or stages for quoting a price to an overseas buyer:

1. At seller's dock

2. At seller's dock, packaged for export

3. Loaded aboard surface carrier that will take it to port of export

4. Delivered next to the ship, ready for loading

5. Loaded aboard ship

6. Crossed ocean

7. Unloaded at port of import

8. Passed through customs and other inspections

9. Loaded aboard surface carrier that will take it to importer

10. Delivered to importer's receiving dock.

This is a simplified list and was presented in a slightly different form in Chapter 11. The significance here is that it also determines to or from which point each party has responsibility.

Many terms of payment can be used. Since there is no universally accepted international equivalent of the Uniform Commercial Code as used in the United States, the seller must take extra precautions to ensure that the payment is received. The most common financial device used is the irrevocable letter of credit, an escrow-like agreement between the buyer's bank and the seller's bank to guarantee payment provided the seller meets specified terms.

From a logistics standpoint, the letter of credit's wording controls the shipment's movement, specifying ports, sometimes carriers, departure dates, dictating marking and labeling, and so on. If changes are to be made, both the buyer and seller must agree, and the letter of credit must be amended through the two corresponding banks. The risk is that the value of the product may have changed

---

[2]*American Shipper* (September, 1995), p. 62.

since the date of the original agreement, and one party to the agreement may also want to renegotiate the price.

There is one further difference between international and domestic channels, and that deals with relative fluctuations in currencies of both the buyer's and seller's nations. These fluctuations are in the price of the goods and of most of the logistical services. For example, on shipments from the United States to country X there is a currency adjustment surcharge because it requires more U.S. dollars to purchase the local currency in X to pay port charges there. Another complicating factor is that sometimes making payment is beyond the control of the buyer; the buyer's government may ban the flow of currency out of the country.

How complex is the transaction channel? It depends on the specifics of the actual sale. A decade-old study, done for U.S. customs, had a diagram showing about ten different parties (including banks, forwarders, customshouse brokers, etc.) to a typical international transaction and indicated 24 different interfaces between the parties involving transfer of documents, or payments.[3] To these activities and interfaces would be added all or most of the steps discussed in the remainder of this chapter.

The International Distribution Channel

There is no single domestic distribution channel to use as a norm against which to contrast the more complicated international distribution channel. What we will try to do is follow the approximate order of a goods movement towards a foreign buyer and point out instances where the channel becomes more complicated. Notice that many of these steps are complicated, and some are costly.

Order Management

Order management consists of several closely related steps. The order itself may be in hard-copy form or arrive electronically via FAX , an EDI system, or a website. Today, regular buyers and sellers are linked electronically through EDI. As the buyer's inventories become low, an electronic purchase order is generated. It is communicated to the seller, whose computers will determine that the goods are available, and the seller will respond to the buyer, still using EDI, that the order will be filled and shipped by a certain date. When letters of credit are used, all the stated terms must be studied and should be consistent with whatever

---

[3]*American Shipper,* May, 1988, p. 16.

agreement had been reached previously. For some goods, and for some markets, the exporter must determine that the goods can be exported legally. Or, possibly, the order is for a product that may not prove satisfactory, such as an electrical appliance ordered by a buyer in a nation with different voltage strengths. (In this situation, one should at least first verify that the buyer is aware that the appliance uses a different voltage than is used in his home country.)

Any order must be verified for accuracy, correctness, and completeness. If there is an error or omission on the order, it is necessary to contact the buyer before proceeding (sometimes taking into account differences in time zones). For international transactions, errors in documentation may invalidate the entire order and make it impossible to collect payment. One document, the letter of credit, may include specific instructions related to logistics, such as package marking, name of vessel, sailing date, and so on. The seller must make certain that these requirements can be met. If they cannot, the buyer must be notified. After the order is determined to be correct, several related steps take place.

1. A determination is made from which stocks or warehouses the goods should be supplied. If a firm has inventories of goods in several nations, there may be tariff, quota, and duty benefits from using one location of supply rather than another. The order is picked, packed, and labeled. The goods sometimes are accompanied by instruction sheets, warranty cards, and so on, printed in one or more languages.[4]

2. Transportation arrangements are made, at least to the extent of the seller's responsibility. The mode and carrier must be selected since these decisions influence packaging, document requirements, and so on. In addition, the export transportation department or forwarder is given advance information so that they can think in terms of consolidating this shipment with others.

3. Necessary documentation is prepared in house or by forwarders. One must decide in what language(s) it is to be printed. Arrangements are made to coordinate the flow of the goods with the necessary documentation. Identification numbers on documents must be linked with those used by other parties to the transaction, including banks and carriers.

4. Financial records are updated. These may be complicated for international firms since one may want to use the buyer's currency for purposes of determining duties, and the seller's currency for purposes of consis-

---

[4]One of this book's co-authors once purchased a lawn mower that came with assembly instructions printed only in Japanese.

tency in records. The accounting records should also reflect which duties should be paid.

5. A decision is made whether—and how—to replenish the stock that has just been depleted.

The steps just listed are sometimes referred to as the *order cycle*. For the seller, it would often be measured as the time between initial receipt of the order until when the goods left the loading dock (bound for the port or airport of export). The buyer uses a longer timeframe: from the time his or her order leaves the office until when the goods arrive.

Labeling

Goods must be labeled so that they can be handled in the distribution channel and also so that they can be presented for retail sale in the country of import. Usually this involves use of foreign languages and metric measurements. Many shipments are also labeled with their weight and their width, length, and height. This is because both ocean and air rates penalize cargo that is unusually bulky, and if it weighs too little per cubic meter, then a cubic meter will be converted to, say, a ton of weight for rate-making purposes. Also, and similar to domestic shipments, a customer's purchase order number is often stenciled on the package, facilitating processing at the receiving dock. Labeling also includes cautionary pictures to guide those handling and storing the cargo. Bar codes are also used but to be of maximum value, it is necessary that all parties handling the package have bar-code compatible equipment. Two-dimensional codes are being introduced; they can contain much more information in the same space. In early 2001, General Motors required all of its 11,000 suppliers worldwide to use a two-dimensional label. It is expected that other makers will follow and use the same label system. Eventually some systems will include radio frequency identification labels. "With radio frequency identification label technology, silicon chips are embedded in the label and data can be changed at points along the supply chain."[5]

Sometimes labeling requirements are even more stringent than those imposed by the importing nation. For example, goods sold in Quebec must be labeled in French; this is a Provincial requirement and it has nothing to do with having goods imported into Canada. Once goods are labeled, they are less interchangeable in the inventory. In addition, the importing company may have different

---

[5]*JoCWeek,* March 19–25, 2001, p. 28.

informational types of requirements regarding, say, the nutritional value of the package's contents. Some European countries want labels that indicate whether the product comes from plants or animals that have been genetically modified. Most nations insist that a product be labeled with its country of origin.

Labeling also has some marketing aspects. For example, wine labeled in French has a certain snob appeal. Other information, such as specifications, instructions for assembly, or a warranty, must be easily understood by the potential buyer. Choice of which language to use, or how many languages to use, is difficult. Instruction plates, booklets, and accompanying literature must also be in the language of the buyer. Sometimes it is even necessary to give instructions on how to open the package. Pictures can also be used to both show how to assemble and use the product and to discourage certain unsuitable cargo-handling practices. Some are shown in Figure 13–1.

Sometimes an export label is attached to a product to discourage having the product re-enter the exporting nation and compete with the exporter's domestic product lines.

For moving though the distribution system, the packages must be labeled to the extent necessary, and as required by the buyer and by the carrier. (However, valuable products are sometimes labeled in a manner that does not call attention to their value.) Shippers' *blind marks* are symbols stenciled on the exterior of packages and are referred to in the shipping documents. They are symbols or codes that avoid using the name of the firm or product and are used by carriers to keep multiple parcel shipments together. Some look like cattle brands. On various shipping documents is a column for marks and numbers, and one would draw there the blind mark and indicate how the cartons in shipment were numbered, say 1–9 (meaning that there were nine cartons and they would be identically labeled, except for the numbers which would be 1-1, 1-2, 1-3, 1-4, 1-5, 1-6, 1-7, 1-8, and 1-9). The blind marks should be changed on a regular basis.

In the United States and some other parts of the world, bar codes are used for handling the products for all or part of their move, so today many retail and wholesale packages contain bar code labels as well. In the United States, the bar code is called the Universal Product Code (UPC). In Europe, it's called the EAN (European Article Numbering). The UPC and EAN systems are almost completely compatible. (Carriers also add bar code stickers to the parcels as they move through their system, and their shipment control numbers can incorporate the shipper's control numbers.) Also, many labels are now computer generated, so it is easier to generate numerous variations in terms of design and information content.

Figure 13–1 Labels used to inform cargo handlers how to handle goods. Courtesy CIGNA Corporation, *Ports of the World,* 15th edition.

Protective Packing

Goods are packaged so that they will not be damaged during their movement through domestic distribution channels. When goods move internationally, additional problems are caused by: condensation; pilferage and theft; the rigors of an ocean voyage; or having to lie outside, exposed, for a long periods of time while awaiting inspections. Shrink wrap is commonly used both to protect packages from the elements and by its nature, if ripped or punctured, would indicate that the cargo may have been tampered with.

The same retail package used in the United States can sometimes be used overseas, although in some markets a recyclable container is valued more. Recycling is of varying importance throughout the world, and this has an effect on the popularity and price of different packaging materials. In addition to demanding recyclable containers, buyers want product packages with a certain content of recycled materials. The issue is complicated; an alternative to being recyclable may be for the packaging to be biodegradable, meaning that the material will disintegrate in landfills. Choice of dye materials used in printing on the packages is also a matter of environmental concern. While reusing containers is commendable, there are some potential dangers. A common one is that the container may not have been sufficiently cleaned and the previously carried cargo may contain contaminants. Salmonella bacteria, associated with poultry, will contaminate wooden containers.

In 1999, Western European nations, the United States, and China required that imported packing materials consisting of pine wood be heat treated to prevent the spread of several plant infestations.

Desired density for ocean cargo is usually less than 40 cubic feet (or one cubic meter) to a ton. Cargoes less dense than this usually pay a penalty on ocean ships. Denser cargoes travel for fewer cents per pound. This should influence product design, the extent to which a product is shipped disassembled (knocked down), and the choice of packaging material. Package dimensions are also important. Computer software recommends container packing patterns that maximize the utilization of the container's cube and meet other objectives, such as loading in reverse order of unloading, or determining the center of gravity or weight on axles if the container is to be trucked.

Unitization and *palletization* mean about the same thing, namely, using a building block concept to load packages on to pallets so that the pallet load is 40 x 48 inches along the bottom and piled high enough that two pallets will just fit inside the container or truck trailer (taking into account that pallets have varying thicknesses, and containers have varying heights). The pallet load (or unit load) is then secured by steel straps, shrink-wrap, or both. (Pallets used elsewhere in the world have dimensions that differ from those used in the United States. For example, The "European pallet" is 80 cm. × 120 cm.)

If there are certain quantities of packages that are cheaper or easier to handle than others, this should be reflected in the product's price, in order to encourage buyers to order in these same quantities. One could even back up and say that product design is important. In fact, the combination of the product and package must be considered together. A packaged book can stand rougher handling than a packaged light bulb. It is possible to design many products so that they travel with fewer mishaps or at lower costs. In agriculture, for example, broccoli with less stem and more flowers is valued more per pound than broccoli that has heavier stems.

Parcel and overnight express carriers often make available to customers their own specially constructed packages and large envelopes. Since packages must often pass through customs and other inspections, they are often designed with small openings through which inspectors can peer without destroying the integrity of the package. Large envelopes may have a portion of a flap that opens, again allowing an inspector to look—and even probe—inside.

Export packers are employed to pack cargo so that it will survive the journey. Large exporters employ experienced personnel for this purpose. Private packers travel to the exporter's loading dock or to a cargo consolidation point. Or, they may be an additional node or loop in the distribution channel since the cargo may move to their shops for packaging. Some export packers have rail tracks down the center of their building, and the exporter sends the cargo to them using a switch engine; the packer then packs and labels the cargo, and ships it to the port of export. Figures 13–2 and 13–3 show an export packer building protective crating around plastics refinery equipment.

The shipper might also handle the stuffing of intermodal containers, and if so must be concerned with the bracing of the load inside the container. Even before loading, the container must be inspected for possible leaks. One way to inspect a container is to go inside and close the door. If any spots of light can be seen, the container has holes where water and moisture can enter. Sometimes the shipper will take a picture of the loaded container just before the door is closed and sealed, for possible use in case of a freight claim.

One must know the temperature extremes to which the product will be subject while in transit, as well as other climatic conditions. Moisture from condensation is one of the worst enemies of goods in transit. Desiccants that absorb moisture are placed inside packages before they are sealed. Fresh meats and produce also "breathe," and this process must be slowed or stopped to extend the product's life and quality.

Choice of packaging, or material handling, is also influenced by conditions

Figure 13–2   Export packer building protective crating around plastics refinery equipment. Courtesy of Superior Packing Inc./HAL, Inc.

and equipment at the other end of the haul. For example, in a few parts of the world, grain is still loaded by men carrying baskets on their heads. In Ethiopia, relief grains are unloaded from bulk ships into mounds, then shoveled into burlap sacks, and sacks stitched across top. Not all cargo fits into corrugated containers. Burlap bags, bales, barrels, and so on, are all used for specific products. However, the intermodal container is the common carrying unit into which most general cargoes are fit.

Figure 13–3 Export packer's protective crating for plastics refinery equipment. Courtesy of Superior Packing Inc./HAL, Inc.

This discussion has assumed that the product will be packaged at point of manufacture. This is not always the case. One should explore shipping the product overseas in bulk and having in packaged and labeled in the country of importation. Foreign trade zones are frequently used for this purpose.

Pre-shipment Inspections

Pre-shipment inspections were mentioned in Chapter 3. They are imposed by about 40 third-world nations that are short of hard currency and have problems with illegal flights of currency. U.S. exporters complain for two reasons. The process takes more time, and an outsider is commenting upon an agreed-upon price. "U.S. exporters say their [the pre-shipment inspection firms] practices can be highly disruptive. Delayed shipments, distorted prices of exported goods and sensitive product information leaked to potential competitors are the most common complaints."[6]

---

[6]*The Journal of Commerce* (December 31, 1997), p. 1A.

One can see that pre-shipment inspections add to the cost, time, and travel dimensions of goods in the international distribution channel. Also, to the extent that the pre-inspection agent reviews the contract sales price, he is evaluating—even challenging—actions that took place in the transaction channel. In 1998, Douglas Tweddle, of the Brussels-based World Customs Organization, said: "pre-inspection services can be the equivalent of a tax of up to 1.5 percent on the value of the goods."[7]

Commercial Diversion

Since the discussion is dealing with the concept of channels, it is worthwhile to mention the problem of commercial diversion. *Commercial diversion* occurs when the buyer of the goods misleads the seller about their intended market and often places them into existing channels where they compete directly with the sellers' good. This is sometimes referred to as "gray" marketing.

This is of concern because exporters often price their export goods below domestic prices because of the incremental cost nature of business, or because certain expenses such as domestic advertising or research and development are not allocated to the export price. The difference between export and domestic prices always creates the potential for commercial diversion.

Two examples, from actual cases, follow:

> An exporter receives an order from a Middle Eastern country. He's told that to avoid the (anti-Israel) boycott language issue, the payment will be made in advance through a bank transfer of funds. The exporter is suspicious because the product is to be delivered to a port warehouse for "consolidation." The product is later discovered being sold at a low price in a local discount store.
>
> Another exporter, somewhat smarter, insists on making the shipment himself. The container load of a popular consumer appliance is loaded aboard a vessel, by the exporter as shipper, destined for Naples. From Naples, the even smarter diverter ships the container load overland to Rotterdam and back through New York for sale in the exporter's domestic market.

The exporter must be very careful to suspect diversion whenever the deal sounds too good to be true—because it probably is. Similarly, exporters of goods controlled by U.S. export regulations should be wary of offers that do not make sense, offers of cash payment, buyers with no history in the particular line of business, shipping instructions to domestic warehouses, and buyers who do not seem to know much about the product they are buying.

---

[7]*American Shipper* (May 1998), p. 66.

Transportation Management

Many carriers now supply considerable information about their services to actual and potential shippers on the Internet. Intermediaries also use the Internet to create markets and exchanges for transportation and other services. UNCTAD reports refer to them as "infomediaries." The export transportation manager must be able to use these services as he or she selects routes, modes and carriers, and monitors the shipment as it moves. Here are some examples of some of the online capabilities these websites provide:

Shippers posting their requirements for tonnage, rates, delivery times

Carriers posting their available capacity, rates, routing, and delivery times

Shippers viewing rates and capacity information available from carriers

Shippers responding to service offers posted by carriers

Carriers responding to loads offered by shippers at carriers' posted rates

Carriers and shippers making contracts

Printing and receiving bills of lading

Cargo booking and confirmation

Cargo arrival notification

Payment, and

Tracking and tracing support as product moves along the transport chain[8]

The export transportation manager's first decision deals with choice of mode. When shipping to an adjacent country, one usually has as wide a choice of modes as exist for domestic movements. To reach other markets, one may use ocean ships or air. Aside from physical considerations, perishability, small size, and so on, value per ton is the usual determinant for use of air freight. Much of the rationale for this is that air freight reduces the length of time one's money is invested in inventory. There are also quality ranges of ocean shipping, with containerized shipping providing the highest level of service and being used for the most valuable waterborne cargo. Various combinations of modes that provide intermodal service offer a range of delivery times. Similar to domestic channels, the transport mode selected influences the route, the carrier, the type of packaging, and so on.

---

[8]United Nations Conference on Trade and Development, *Review of Maritime Transport 2000* (Geneva, 2000), p. 84.

One thinks of moving cargoes quickly because of investment in inventory, but this holds only for products that are made and sold immediately. For other products, such as canned goods, waste paper, or Christmas tree decorations, there is less need for speed. Indeed, there is a need for warehousing, so shippers may take a deliberately slow routing, just to save on warehousing costs.

On the other hand, there may be great need for speed. In the case of live chicks (breeding stock) transported by air, they're shipped right after birth. They are born with three days' worth of nutrients in their bodies to sustain them. They must, however, be protected from the outside environment. They have special containers and are transferred directly from hatchery truck to plane. The hatchery's "trucks are outfitted with the same lights and safety equipment required of airport vehicles used within the confines of JFK [International Airport at New York]. The drivers undergo special training to ensure that they are completely familiar with airport operations, security procedures and the regulations that Port Authority personnel must fulfill when servicing cargo planes."[9]

Because of the long length of time that some products are moving, it is conceivable that time priorities change while the goods are en route. This can be accommodated. One example was Burroughs, which received materials from the Far East. As containers were loaded in Asia, information was sent electronically to the United States regarding contents of each. Then, comparison was made of upcoming needs, and a priority list was established. Incoming containers were precleared with customs and containers sorted and shipped according to the priority Burroughs had assigned. Four-day truck, two-day air, or overnight air express were assigned to move goods across the United States.

Within the bulk-carrying ocean mode, it is possible to orchestrate the movement's time to an extent not usually practiced with domestic hauls. The charter (lease) agreement specifies the amount of time the vessel will be in port loading and discharging, as well as the time spent at sea. One takes into account port charges, seamen's labor costs, and fuel consumption before deciding how much time to allow for a trip. These preceding paragraphs have described examples of trade-offs between transportation and inventory costs.

The second choice the transportation manager makes is the choice of port or airport for export. Choice here depends on the importance of the shipper and the size of shipment. If one deals in shipload lots and charters a vessel, the ship will come to the port of his choice. Or, one could charter a cargo plane.

---

[9]*Via Port of NY-NJ,* December, 1986, p. 14.

For most transactions, however, one uses the port or airport that the carrier serves.

When looking at distribution channels, however, there is another alternative. Some ocean vessels will call at little-used ports *on inducement,* meaning that they will make a special stop at a (usually) unscheduled port to take on or discharge a large shipment. One factor in the vessel operator's decision is how booked with cargo the ship happens to be.

Professor Gary Dicer pointed out that the marketing environment of U.S. ports has changed. In the 1970s, each port had its own tributary area. Since then, and because of carrier deregulation, the 1984 Shipping Act, and new technology (the stack train), more and more commodities were shifted to containerized movements. The economics of large containership operation have allowed the steamship operator to absorb some of the costs of inland transportation to obtain the scale of operations needed to make these large ships profitable. As a result, port hinterlands (markets) disintegrated in this new type of competitive arrangement.[10] With the increased availability and use of containers, many steamship lines and shippers have found it more economical to off-load all cargo at a single port. Using the intermodal option frees the container ship from calling at numerous ports or traveling thousands of miles at less than full capacity.

The transportation manager is usually responsible for arranging surface transportation to the seaport or airport. In the early 1990s an issue, mainly in the U.S., was overweight containers, and shippers preferred ports where adjoining highway weight limits were not rigorously enforced.

Sometimes the choice of port is influenced by the desire to consolidate cargo from several inland points. Or one may wish to blend products, since blending is sometimes used to work around an importing nation's tariff specifications.

One must also mention choice of port of import. There must be service between the port of export and the port of import. Rates, time in transit, and material handling equipment compatibility are also of concern.

> Up until mid-1995, nearly all the Hyundais moved through Portland, Oregon, which is 19 sailing days from Korea. The importer then switched to receiving Hyundais through Portland, Los Angeles, Brunswick, and Newark. Processing the cars through Portland took 20 days because of congestion, and to this was added four or five days for a transcontinental rail crossings, totaling 43–44 days

---

[10]Gary Dicer, "Marketing: Crucial for Port Survival," *Traffic World,* Sep. 22, 1986, p. 38.

for a car to reach the northeast. With vessels sailing through the Panama Canal, it takes 31 days from Korea to Newark.[11]

Livestock imported into U.S. must arrive at designated ports that have facilities for receiving and holding the livestock until they can be inspected. They also have quarantine areas for livestock that, for various reasons, inspectors decide to deny immediate entry. At the port of import, there must be customs and other inspection services available. Several years ago, during a trade disagreement with Japan, France insisted that all Japanese electronics products be funneled through an obscure French customs post, which delayed the movement until after the Christmas market had passed.

Choice of carrier is the next concern, although it is somewhat related to choice of port, since some carriers serve only certain ports. Recall from Chapter 6 the discussion of the ocean liner conference system. An initial consideration when using ocean lines in some parts of the world is whether the exporter has signed a conference agreement. In market areas where shipping conferences (combination of vessel lines) are active, shippers sign loyalty contracts with the conference, agreeing to give them all of their business and in return receiving a 10–15 percent discount off published rates. Loyalty contracts are not used by conferences serving U.S. ports, however, they are used in certain other shipping markets.

The existence of conference loyalty agreements in some parts of the world has several impacts. In terms of the distribution channel, the cargo would be routed aboard a conference carrier. However, there are options which might make it possible for the shipper to escape from his obligation to use the conference, in situations where non-conference vessel operators were offering much lower rates. Both of these involve the transactions channel. The first would be that if either the exporter or the importer (but not both) had a contract with the conference, an option would be to select terms of sale so that the party responsible for ocean transportation was the one without the contractual obligation to use conference vessels. The second option is to work through a "dummy" buyer or seller, who does not have an obligation to use the conference.

Today, many U.S. shippers enter into contracts with ocean carriers. Contracts often have incentives for larger volumes of business, which causes shippers to route via specific lines.

---

[11]*American Shipper* (September, 1995), p. 122. At the port, "Hyundai's car preparation companies remove a protective coating from each vehicle and then accessorize every auto with 'PIOS,' port-installed options. These include mud guards, arm rests, floor mats, side moldings, sun-roof wind deflectors, as well as air conditioning units slipped into prepared niches."

Sometimes, the decision would be the flag of the carrier. Cargo preference laws were discussed in Chapter 2, and they require that certain cargoes or proportions of cargo go on vessels flying a specific nation's flag. The buyer of the goods also may prefer that they move on his nation's flag lines. Indeed, the letter of credit may specify what is to be done and limit the options available to the export transportation manager.

If a shipper has the choice of several carriers, additional criteria are used. The standards that Ford used in its picking its carriers and judging their performance, [Ford's transportation director Richard] Haupt said, are their safety records, price-competitiveness, financial stability, transit performance, handling of damage claims, equipment availability and suitability, EDI capability, ease of doing business, and innovative initiatives.[12] In a 1999 survey of shippers that asked their most important criterion for selecting an ocean carrier, 31 percent chose pricing and 22 percent chose on-time performance. Document quality and customer service each received 13 percent, and were followed by shipment tracking capability with 11 percent, and global coverage and information management systems with five percent each.[13] A survey conducted in 2000 asked shippers to rank carriers in terms of their e-commerce capabilities using a 1 to 10 score with 10 being the best. FedEx Corp. led with a score of 7.6, followed closely by United Parcel Service, with a score of 7.5. Third was Con-way Transportation Services, with a score of 6.8, followed by Roadway Express, Inc. which scored 6.5. Respondents felt that "real time tracking and tracing" was the most important attribute, followed by "online service performance reports".[14]

Hazardous Materials Transportation

The subject of hazardous materials transportation is complex and of considerable importance. For the shipper of goods that possess hazardous characteristics, the design and functioning of the distribution channels is more complex. Bayer AG, a large German chemical manufacturer and exporter, announced that it was taking a variety of measures to reduce the chances of environmental disasters. "Since transport is, environmentally speaking, the weakest link in the Bayer chain, checking and rechecking and tightening up safety measures during shipment has become daily work. . . . Should something go wrong, trained specialists are on 24-hour standby at strategic points throughout the world."[15]

---

[12]*American Shipper,* March 1990, p. 52.

[13]*The Journal of Commerce,* Oct 8, 1999, p. 1.

[14]*Shipping Digest,* August 21, 2000, pp. 1-3.

[15]Hans Kops, "Learning by the Numbers," *KLM Cargovision* (July/August, 1988) p. 8.

Specialized carriers and warehouses are often used, meaning that different channels may be used than is the case for less or non-hazardous goods. At times, the packaging, not the goods, is hazardous, with the most common example being dry ice that is used for cooling. The exporter who ships hazardous materials is advised to seek specific advice on the commodity he ships.

Safety in the transport of hazardous materials is subject to regulation by various countries and the United Nations has adopted standards for packaging hazardous materials. This resulted in a shift in emphasis from the protection of the transported goods to preventing the substance concerned from escaping during storage, transport and handling.

The purpose of hazardous materials transportation regulation is to prevent loss of life, limb, and property. This is accomplished through identification, communication, and packaging regulations that have been developed over the years. The regulations pertaining to the transport of hazardous materials in the United States are contained in Title 49 of the Code of Federal Regulations (49 CFR). One of the regulations contains a requirement that persons who transport or ship hazardous goods be trained according to the responsibilities assigned them. Traffic clerks who prepare bills of lading must be trained in the preparation of those documents (use of proper shipping name, class, and highlighting). Warehousemen who pack, mark, and label hazardous material must be trained in the proper procedures to do so. Truck drivers who transport hazardous materials must be trained with regard to co-loading of hazardous materials with other types (classes) of hazardous material and non-hazardous materials that they might contaminate.

The U.S. DOT specifies exactly how hazardous materials in transportation are to be marked, labeled, and described in documentation such as bills of lading. Freight containers carrying hazardous materials must be placarded. The penalties for failing to comply with the applicable regulations are severe; both civil and criminal penalties can and are imposed on not only those directly responsible but on corporate officers and companies as well.

When hazardous shipments move for export or import U.S. regulations make exception to permit use of internationally accepted communication (and to some extent classification) standards, as published in the International Maritime Organization (IMO) Code for sea and the International Civil Aviation Organization (ICAO) Code for air. Exception is by no means an exemption. The shipper must still comply with U.S. packaging requirements and other pertinent parts of the regulations.

Internationally the communication of information about hazardous materials is complicated by different languages and kinds of regulation. Fortunately, international agreements have been developed under the auspices of the United Nations to standardize many of the aspects relative to hazardous materials transport.

As indicated, cargoes moving by air freight and sea freight are subject to different codes. International air carriers limit the kinds and the maximum quantity of hazardous material that may be shipped in one package (in order to minimize release, if there is one) and in the aggregate on one aircraft. The pilot has the final word as to whether he or she will carry the hazardous material. The pilot inspects the hazardous cargo documents and may reject any consignment without challenge. Because of the additional work involved in documenting hazardous materials and the problems of stowage, many airlines add a surcharge to the ordinary freight bill. The regulations applicable to the international carriage of dangerous goods by air are promulgated by the International Civil Aeronautics Association (ICAO).

Regulations applicable to the transport of goods by sea are promulgated by the International Maritime Organization (IMO). Shippers who load their own containers at their facilities must be especially cautious with regard to adequate blocking and bracing within the container to prevent movement. Ships at sea roll, heave, and yaw violently. Trucks on the road brake suddenly, while freight trains are humped in coupling and uncoupling operations. The shipper, not the carrier, is responsible for proper and secure internal blocking and bracing. Although inspection companies are employed by the carriers and federal highway, railroad, and Coast Guard inspectors do open and inspect freight containers for safety compliance, the responsibility is squarely on the shipper.

Companies handling oil must, as part of their response plan, make extensive commitments to have available equipment and trained personnel to deal with spills. Many belong to cooperatives, meaning that they expect to help, and be helped, by each other. There are also large cleanup contractors who can be relied upon. The U. S. Oil Pollution Act of 1990 (OPA) requires owners of tank vessels and facilities to prepare a plan for responding to a worst case discharge of oil or a hazardous substance. For onshore facilities the requirements apply to those that, because of their location, could be expected to harm the environment by discharge in navigable waters or to shorelines. Nearly all modes of transport were involved, as were several government agencies. The most stringent regulations deal with tank vessels, of any size, operating within 200 miles of the U.S. "Approximately 1,500 oil response plans covering more than 6,000 vessels have been submitted to the U. S. Coast Guard."[16]

---

[16]Pamela Garvie and Susan B. Geiger, "Spill Response Planning—All Modes of Transportation Feel the Impact of the Oil Pollution Act of 1990," *Transportation Practitioners Journal*, Vol. 61, No. 3 (Spring 1994), pp. 294–299.

Friction or Fraud in the Distribution Channel?

To this point, the discussion has dealt with the positive forces and activities that coordinate the movement of products forward to the buyers. However, some outside parties continually examine the long links of the overseas distribution channel, searching for vulnerable spots where it might be attacked or robbed. One designing an international channel must be aware of these problems and make certain that the channel is sufficiently strong to withstand these types of attacks.

Tequila Cuervo, the Mexican drink, manufactured in Guadalajara, "has little theft problem in exports out of Mexico or in distribution throughout the country. Not so, however, in Mexico City, where theft is so pronounced it affects the bottom line. Under mandates from insurers, the company now pays for chaperones who accompany the load. It also requires its truckers under contract to use only toll highways, which are extraordinarily costly in Mexico."[17]

Pilferage, which is informal theft of small amounts by one's own employees, is quite common. Figure 13–5 shows wooden crating placed around a utility

Figure 13–5 Wooden crating placed to protect truck contents from pilferage. Courtesy Superior Packing Inc./HAL, Inc.

---

[17]*The Journal of Commerce* (March 4, 1997), p. 5A.

truck body to protect its contents from pilferage. Beers, wines, and fancy food-stuffs are common targets. It may be necessary to pay bribes at borders, or to get workers—or others—to perform their tasks. "Although Southeast Asia has the highest incidence of piracy in the world, it has fewer cases of assaults in port areas and more attacks on the high seas. . . . Many robberies, whether in Brazil or elsewhere, are not reported because keeping a ship docked long enough for an investigation costs a fortune in harbor fees."[18] These are costs of doing business that are, frankly, added to the price of the product. The U.S. government does not consider some forms of these payments as illegal.

Use of large intermodal containers discouraged pilferage because many cargo handlers cannot see the specific product they are handling. Full containers are stolen however. However, describing the changes in the problem in the Los Angeles Long Beach area, a policeman said: "hijacking guards and barreling through fences with semis is becoming the preferred technique."[19]

For international shipments, one needs insurance. In a few instances, the firm providing the insurance influences channel decisions, since it will quote higher premiums for what it believes are unsafe alternatives.

Terrorism aimed at airlines is an ongoing problem of great concern. Without belittling the tragedy of losing lives, there are also disruptions in the movement of cargo and mail. Firms shifting personnel will find a reluctance to travel or settle in certain parts of the world.

Summary

The channels approach, which is well developed for analyzing marketing activities, can be used for understanding international logistics. It is possible that the complexity of international logistics activities has discouraged this approach.

The logistical aspects of the international transaction and payments channels differ from domestic practices. First, a decision has to be negotiated concerning the terms of sale. The buying and selling parties look at the steps in the distribution channel and decide where exchanges of goods, payment, and so on should be made. Part of the agreement will also be terms of sale. If the instrument chosen to guarantee payment is an irrevocable letter of credit, then the exact movements through the distribution channel will be specified and agreed upon in a contractual arrangement.

---

[18]*The Journal of Commerce* (December 31, 1997), p. 2B.

[19]*Daily Commercial News and Shipping Guide,* July 2, 1990, p. 1.

End-of-Chapter Questions

1. What are the steps in the order cycle?

2. How, if at all, would the order cycle in a purely domestic transaction differ from one where the order is received from another country?

3. What are some of the choices one needs to make regarding the choice of language to be printed on the product, its accompanying instructions, and its packaging?

4. What are preshipment inspections? Why are they used?

5. What is commercial diversion? Why do exporters consider it to be a problem?

6. What are the factors that influence the transportation manager's choice of seaport to be used for exports?

7. What factors influence the transportation manager's choice of carrier?

8. What are hazardous materials? Why do they require special attention?

9. What kind of threats of terrorism or theft should be of concern to international logistics managers?

10. How does one coordinate and integrate the international transaction channel and the international distribution channel?

CASE • *Manwell Toy Importers*

Headquartered in Winnipeg, Manitoba, Manwell Toy Company operated a large toy store on Portage Avenue, near the location where the company had been founded nearly seventy years ago. Above the toy store were offices from which the firm managed its chain of fifteen retail stores spread through nearly all the Canadian provinces. Very few of their toys were made in Canada; most came from Asia, moving through the Port of Vancouver, BC. Toys containing electronic components came from Taiwan, Japan, and Korea; toys without electronic components came mainly from China and Vietnam. About ten percent of their toys came through the United States; two of the large retail toy chains in the United States would act as wholesalers and sell some of their toys (also originating in Asia) to Manwell.

Toys purchased in Asia were all delivered to a consolidator in Hong Kong, who would load them into containers and ship each container as it was filled. Once or twice a week the filled containers would be loaded aboard a containership and taken to Vancouver, where they would be delivered to a warehouse that Manwell used. Aside from those sold in the Vancouver retail store, all the rest would move eastward by containers on railcars, trucks, and parcel services. Toys moved in a

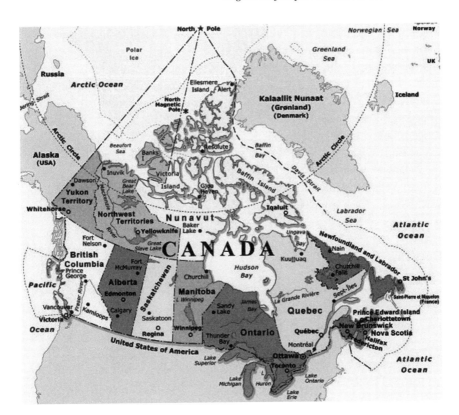

Case Figure 13–1

fairly even flow, leaving Asia from about March through September. Manwell's
Vancouver warehouse stored the toys for their stores between Vancouver and
Regina. A warehouse in Winnipeg served that area and all of Eastern Canada.

Eastern Canada contained most of the nation's population but had some drawbacks as a market; the Maritime Provinces were poor and had little buying
power. In Quebec, the French preferred not to buy toys that featured any English writing. (A decade ago, Manwell was ready to buy a warehouse in Montreal,
Quebec to serve its eastern Canadian markets but decided not to when it was
feared that the Separatist movement would declare Quebec's independence from
Canada.) Despite these drawbacks, eastern Canada was the only geographic area
where Manwell's sales were increasing. In western Canada the market was sat-
urated; large stores and e-merchants were making some inroads.

Toy stores in the United States that imported toys from Asia at one time had
all their cargo move though West Coast U.S. ports. In the late 1990s, there was
considerable port congestion in Los Angeles/Long Beach and a few toy importers began having their imports come in through U.S. Atlantic ports. This

would mean that the toys would be consolidated in Singapore, rather than Hong Kong, and from Singapore would be shipped westward through the Suez Canal and, eventually, to the United States. The time between the Asia toy manufacturer's dock and the U.S. port was about three weeks for goods moving from Hong Kong to West Coast U.S. ports, and four to five weeks for goods moving from Singapore to East Coast U.S. ports. Increased transit times were of little concern in this instance because the majority of toys would be sold at the holiday season.

If Manwell were to receive goods from the east, the most likely port to use would be Halifax. However, Halifax was some distance to the east of most markets. Nonetheless, Manwell's management decided that they must explore the possibilities of having Asian toys move through Singapore to Halifax.

Questions for *Manwell Toy Importers*

1. What are the cost elements included in the costs of having the toys leave the leave manufacturer and reach a consolidator in either Hong Kong or Singapore?

2. At present the consolidator loads toys as received, and every time a container is full he sends it to Manwell in Canada. What if the consolidator, in either Hong Kong or Singapore, had a container destined for each major Manwell outlet and filled each container with toys for that outlet only? What would the costs be of that system?

3. What are the comparable cost elements of their present system?

4. Taking your answers to questions two and three, construct a chart showing costs of each and how they should be compared to show both similarities and differences.

5. If Manwell wished to sell more toys in French-speaking Quebec, how can it cater to this market's desire for seeing everything printed in French? Will this place additional strains on Manwell's logistics system? How?

6. Assume Manwell is interested in comparing the frequency of sailings by containerships from Hong Kong to Vancouver and Singapore to Halifax. Using shipping journals, the Web, or other sources, see whether you can find the answer.

7. Assume that Manwell also wishes to sell toys to Canadian customers over the Web. Does this make a difference as to where Manwell warehouses should be? Why?

14

International Sourcing

Introduction

To this point, the book has usually taken the view of movements along the supply chain toward one's customers and their customers. This chapter looks at the inbound movement from sources located in other nations. This chapter will consider the challenges in coordinating sourcing decisions globally, as well as managing the inputs to production on a global basis. First, the chapter will explore the reasons that companies engage in international sourcing for materials and manufacturing. Then it will examine the international sourcing process, giving particular attention to the coordination necessary among the various procurement and logistics functions. Next, it will consider different import and export options that can enhance system operation. Finally, it will look at opportunities for global sourcing through counter trade arrangements.

For the purposes of this chapter, consider the international sourcing arrangements and system design independent of the ownership of buyer and seller. Most of the factors to be considered in designing international sourcing systems are the same whether one considers interfirm arrangements or interplant situations within the same company. Sometimes international interplant sourcing decisions within a single company must also pay deference to corporate strategic objectives and may seemingly not conform to overall sourcing objectives to be described below. The key to reconciling these differences is to consider the global sourcing system design as one that meets overall system objectives. Those objectives may be held by a single company (as in the case of international interplant sourcing) or by the sourcing partnership as a single unit. Most often, the superordinate goals are improved product quality, lower prices, and better service to end users of the product.

Why Source Globally?

Two competitive forces pushed manufacturing companies around the world toward sourcing internationally. These two strategic forces have been named the *factor-input strategy* and the *market-access strategy*.[1]

The Factor-Input Strategy

The factor-input strategy seeks to create a competitive advantage for a domestic manufacturing company by using the lowest cost or highest quality mix of manufacturing inputs available anywhere in the world. This concept is not new in the economic sense. In 1776, economist Adam Smith posited that the division of labor is limited only by the extent of the market.[2] What Smith meant by this was that increased specialization of both labor and machine technology develops increasing returns to scale. Firms thus tend to evolve that are highly specialized and can perform very specific manufacturing or other business functions at very low cost, and/or to very high quality specifications. The factor-input strategy recognizes the development of such specialized strengths and argues that firms should seek out such specialized sources of inputs rather than create the inputs themselves. In other words, why reinvent the wheel when one can just go buy the wheel from some one else?

Those readers thinking ahead might realize that carrying this strategy to the extreme might lead to markets dominated by a single monopoly producer of a given item. For example: why should RCA outsource the manufacture of its VHS video decks to Matsushita in Japan? Because Matsushita's volume of production has dictated huge economies of scope and scale. Shouldn't Matsushita simply take over RCA's place in the VHS marketplace? Why does Matsushita continue to make decks for RCA when their own Panasonic brand competes in the same retail environments?

This question had been addressed in 1951 by economist George Stigler, who reconciled the notion of increasing returns on labor and technology with the reality of competitive markets:

> Certain processes are subject to increasing returns; why does the firm not exploit them further and in the process become a monopoly? Because there are

---

[1] Stanley E. Fawcett and David J. Closs, "Coordinated Global Manufacturing, The Logistics-Manufacturing Interaction, and Firm Performance," *Journal of Business Logistics,* (1993) 14 (1), pp. 1–24.

[2] Adam Smith, *The Wealth of Nations,* 1776, (London, Penguin Books, 1986 reprint), p. 121.

other functions subject to diminishing returns, and these are, on balance, at least so costly that average cost of the final product does not diminish with output. Then why does the firm not abandon the functions subject to increasing returns, allowing another firm to specialize in them to take advantage of increasing returns? At a given time, these functions may be too small to support a specialized firm or firms. The firm must then perform these functions for itself. But, with the expansion of the industry, the magnitude of the function subject to increasing returns may become sufficient to permit a firm to specialize in performing it. The firms will then abandon the [function], and a new firm will take it over. This new firm will be a monopoly, but it will be confronted by elastic demands: it cannot charge a price for the (function) higher than the average cost of the (function) to the firms which are abandoning it. With the continued expansion of the industry, the number of firms supplying (the function) will increase, so that the new industry becomes competitive and the new industry may, in turn, abandon parts of the (function) to a new set of specialists.[3]

Thus, functions performed by a single firm or firms within an industry may be outsourced when a critical mass of such a function exists that permits a specialized firm to undertake them profitably. As an industry expands, additional firms will enter the market for the outsourced function. Subspecialty firms may subsequently emerge as further specialization occurs. In the RCA/Matsushita example above, Matsushita itself may outsource the raw materials and subassemblies and components of its VHS video decks. This is the case in fact, as Matsushita chooses to purchase raw materials, components, and actually manufacture its decks through outsourcing to firms in Korea, Malaysia, Singapore, Taiwan, and Hong Kong.

How does a firm decide when to take advantage of a global factor-input strategy and outsource? Why do some firms choose to outsource and others not? Stigler also offers insight as to the reasons why selected functions of one firm may be outsourced, and those of a rival may be kept internal.[4] While functions typically outsourced are those with increasing cost structures, firms face different cost structures. Thus, firms need not abandon the entire function, but rather only the subcomponents of the function that are subject to the increasing cost structure. The subcomponents without increasing marginal costs will be retained; those with increasing marginal costs will be spun off to a specialized provider firm.

---

[3]George F. Stigler, "The Division of Labor Is Limited By The Extent of the Market," (1951) *Journal of Political Economy,* 59 (3), reprinted in *The Essence of Stigler,* Kurt R. Leube and Thomas Gale Moore, eds, (Stanford, CA: Hoover Institution Press, 1986), pp. 13–14.

[4]Stigler, pp. 16–17.

So the use of a factor-input strategy in manufacturing really gets down to understanding the marginal cost structures of one's business functions. Each manufacturing process or other business procedure can be analyzed to determine whether the firm faces increasing or decreasing returns on that process. If the returns are increasing, the function may stay inside. If returns are decreasing with additional units of production, it's time to consider outsourcing.

The Market-Access Strategy

The market-access strategy focuses on the firm attaining a local market presence in markets in which they plan to do significant business. This strategy is designed to help a firm gain or maintain access to markets rather than create a strict economic advantage as in the factor-input strategy. Many firms desire to create a manufacturing presence in a foreign market in which they currently sell their goods, or in a market the firm might wish to enter. For example, one sees Japanese automobile manufacturers building cars and trucks in the United States, Canada, and the United Kingdom. Couldn't Toyota, Nissan, Honda, Mitsubishi and other Japanese manufacturers have greater economies of scope and scale (and thus increasing returns) by manufacturing in countries with lower labor costs than the United States, Canada, and the United Kingdom?

The answer is "yes," all other considerations being equal. But the other considerations here are not at all equal. Consider the possibility of negative market perceptions. During the late 1970s and early 1980s, many American consumers began to view the Japanese automobile manufacturers as a drain on the American economy. To the casual observer, it appeared that these huge nondomestic car companies were simply taking sales and profits outside the United States and leaving little behind except very well made automobiles. The consumer's bundle of purchase satisfactions had a social and political component that was not being addressed by Japanese automobile manufacturers. Honda led the way with the opening of its Marysville, Ohio assembly plant in the early 1980s, and very quickly the other major Japanese manufacturers opened their own plants or joint-venture plants with American manufacturers. Today, there is far less negative market perception of Japanese cars due to their country of origin: most American consumers know that many cars that are called "Japanese" are made in the United States.

There are other reasons in addition to negative market perceptions for one to use a market-access sourcing strategy. Some countries use protectionist tactics such as quotas, tariffs, and domestic content rules. Quotas, such as those limiting finished cotton goods imported to the United States, simply set limits on how many of a particular good may be imported in a given time period. The quota is set below the market demand, forcing some of the good's production to be completed inside the country. A tariff is a tax placed on a class of imported goods, with the intention of making the imported goods higher priced in the marketplace. A tariff helps to equalize the cost structures between two national marketplaces, in effect countering some of the advantages of the factor-input strategy. *Domestic content rules* are laws which require that a certain percentage of a good's material content must be made inside the destination country.

Many global firms have been clever in eluding these protectionist barriers without using market-access strategies. For example, in the early 1970s there were high tariffs on imported trucks. Toyota's small pickups had difficulty penetrating the U.S. market due to perceived higher prices. Toyota surmounted the tariff barrier by importing its truck chassis separately from the pick-up box that sat on the back. The boxes were exported to the United States as parts and the chassis as unfinished vehicles, both of which had lower tariffs than those for finished trucks. The boxes were simply welded to the chassis at the West Coast port in a final assembly step. In a similar way, when the Canadian government implemented domestic content rules for its television broadcast stations in the 1960s, U.S. program producers responded by employing Canadian actors in minor roles or by shooting a portion of a program in Canada. Such programs fulfilled the technical requirement for domestic content while not altering the uniquely American program content.

Supposedly, quotas are being phased out. However, they still pose a challenge to the logistics manager concerned with inbound movements because behind each of those quotas lies a logistics decision. Every day the U.S. customs clears cargo that is added to the tally of imports that count against annual quotas that restrict imports of specific merchandise. Once a commodity's quota is filled, no more can be imported from that country. Textile and apparel importers watch fill rates closely. It also behooves carriers and intermediaries to pay attention. Faced with a pending embargo, shippers may call on carriers and intermediaries to jostle the supply chain. Raw materials bound for a country facing embargo may be diverted to a factory in a lower-quota country. Or goods that may have moved by sea may be shipped by air instead.[5]

In 1999 an importer of Chinese-made shirts and trousers said, "If you're worried about the quota, it's easier to produce the goods earlier, bring them in and sit on inventory."[6] In 2001, a Liz Claiborne official indicated that 40 percent of his firm's production was quota-sensitive and that the firm looks as far forward

[5]*JoCWeek,* July 9–15, 2001, p. 17.

[6]*The Journal of Commerce,* July 12, 1999, p. 1.

as they can at fill rates to avoid putting future orders in jeopardy. Production can be distributed to maximize quota advantage and price, or shifted if a country's quota nears its limit. In 1995 Liz Claiborne's manufacturing base of 500 operations in 38 countries produced 65 million garments. In 2000 their base was 280 operations in 32 countries, producing 145 million garments.[7]

Other times, whole industries have agreed to the imposition of a quota system as a lesser evil than high tariffs or banishment from a marketplace. The most notable example was the voluntary export quotas of the Japanese automobile manufacturers that were in place for much of the 1980s. American automobile manufacturers argued that they needed time to retrain workers, upgrade manufacturing facilities, and improve product lines to compete with Japanese manufacturers. The U.S. Congress was favorably disposed to implement restrictive barriers, and the Japanese manufacturers quickly suggested a temporary quota system to preserve their access to the important U.S. marketplace. It was during this period of temporary voluntary quotas that the Japanese automobile manufacturers opened a number of U.S. manufacturing plants for parts and final assembly.

Quotas, tariffs, and domestic content rules are subject to the prevailing geopolitical winds. At the time of this book's writing, the global trend was toward reducing protectionist barriers and opening up markets. During less economically sophisticated times in the past, nations tended to raise protective barriers during periods of economic downturn to preserve domestic employment and thus domestic economies. In today's global economy, it is not so easy to say that protectionism necessarily preserves a nation's economy when the firms operating in that economy are intertwined with operations and markets in many other nations. Both quotas and domestic content rules have many implications when it comes to designing the global supply chain.

Designing a Global Sourcing System

According to strategist Michael Porter, there are two aspects to be considered when designing any firm's manufacturing network, including relationships with suppliers for outsourcing.[8] The first is configuration. Configuration refers to the physical location of manufacturing and value-added facilities and to the allocation of different production activities. Configuration speaks to the who, where, and what questions of system design. It is important to specify in advance which functions will be performed at which facilities and for what reason. Often an-

---

[7]*JoCWeek,* July 9–15, 2001, p. 17

[8]Michael Porter, "Changing Patterns of International Competition," *California Management Review,* (1986) 28, pp. 9–40.

swering these questions requires an analysis of the cost structures under a factor-input approach, and of political and market considerations under a market-access approach.

The second aspect to be considered is coordination. Coordination refers to the integration of the system. Remember that one is designing a system that is governed by some process. Coordination speaks to the why and how questions of system design. While cost rationales have been covered under the configuration aspect, coordination takes on a dynamic perspective, acknowledging that market factors change the requirements of manufacturing systems over time. Coordination considers the continued operation of the system in light of its changing environment and the coordination mechanism responds to help the firm maintain a global competitive advantage.

Both configuration and coordination are implicit in a systems approach to designing a global manufacturing enterprise. Remember that the goals in designing any system are optimizing the output of the system, rather than optimizing any subcomponent of that system. In fact, experience has shown that a focus on optimizing any single aspect of a global manufacturing enterprise usually leads to a sub-optimal system performance.

Sometimes the implications of this systems approach are not entirely obvious. If one decides to locate manufacturing operations in Port Moresby, New Guinea, due to the easy availability of unskilled low-cost labor that suits one's needs, that person must also consider the logistics and transportation issues involved with sourcing goods at a port with less-than-adequate containerization facilities and in a city with an outmoded telecommunications system. While the labor-cost manufacturing subcomponent may be optimized, other aspects of the sourcing system will operate sub-optimally. Often the "pad" in such a system will be the creation of additional inventory to cover the logistics sub-optimizations. Thus the additional overhead and problems associated with excess inventory are added to a sub-optimal system, further degrading overall system performance and helping to disguise the real problem.

With configuration and coordination in mind as the keys to designing a global sourcing system for manufacturing, the book will now examine a number of issues important to the design of a global sourcing system.

Global Sourcing and Procurement

This section will describe an international sourcing/procurement development model that includes the following components: planning, specification, evaluation, relationship management, transportation and holding costs, implementation, and monitoring and improving.

Each of these component sections includes a number of considerations for managers to work into an overall system design. It is important to keep configuration and coordination aspects in mind as each component is discussed.

Planning

Planning is an essential first step in designing any global sourcing system. Number one on the planning list is an honest assessment of international sourcing opportunities. There are many questions to be answered when considering the current feasibility of global sourcing. For example, does the firm have the expertise to manage global sourcing in house, or should its managers consider the use of a trading company partner? How important is the certainty of materials supply? A frank answer to this question may limit sourcing to partners only in the most stable economies of the world. How will one manage the lengthened and sometimes more variable lead times that global sourcing implies? What financial and other criteria will be applied in making the "make or buy" decision?

Synergies are also important when planning a global sourcing and procurement system. They fall into three categories:

> First, economies of information and learning: sharing all available purchasing knowledge on suppliers, new technologies, markets, internal users, applications, the prevention of mutually incompatible negotiating strategies, and the prevention of affiliates from depriving one another of limited available resources.

> Second, economies of process: establishing a common way of working thereby showing worldwide one line of conduct to suppliers, benchmarking procedures and results, joint training and development.

> Third, economies of scale: pooling volumes to enforce purchasing power, reducing the number of global suppliers, standardization and synchronizing requirements.[9]

One area deserving special consideration is the way in which international sourcing could change existing materials resource planning and distribution resource planning procedures. As the firm attempts to operate as an integrated whole, current arrangements with existing suppliers may be changed by the addition of an international sourcing effort. Existing contracts and relationships with suppliers should be evaluated in the context of the new move into international sourcing. Two large restaurant chains in the United States, McDonald's and KFC, rely on outside firms to supply all their individual restaurants' needs.

---

[9]Wouter Faes, Paul Matthyssens, and Koen Vandenbempt, "The Pursuit of Global Purchasing Synergy," *Industrial Marketing Management*, Vol. 29 (2000) p. 541.

When these two chains expanded overseas, they had these same outside firms expand overseas along with them. These suppliers' expanded operations serve the needs of the restaurant chains overseas. Both the restaurant chains and their suppliers are growing overseas, together.

Implicit in the above questions is the development of sourcing alternatives. In designing systems, the prudent manager has an alternative in mind, albeit an alternative that may not be a first choice, but one that will functionally substitute should a given procedure, supplier, or nation become temporarily unavailable. For example, in 1993 a fire devastated a chemical plant in Japan. This plant manufactured over 40 percent of the chemical resin that was used to package microchips in their familiar black plastic form. The plant was expected to be offline for twelve to eighteen months, during which time the world's manufacturers of chips had to seek alternative sources. The Japanese plant was well located for western Pacific Rim manufacturers. Alternative sources included a duPont plant in the United States, and a BASF plant in Germany. The locations of these two alternative suppliers, plus their difficulties in ramping up supply of the resin, quickly caused sourcing headaches for companies like Texas Instruments, Matsushita, Mitsubishi, and Daewoo, all of who manufactured chips in the western Pacific Rim.

The outcome of the planning stage should be a set of policies and procedures to guide international sourcing managers. These policies and procedures should be consistent with the firm's overall philosophy and mission, and should be understood and endorsed by top management. Ace Hardware had been importing about 3 percent of its needs and wanted to increase this to 10 percent. As it instructed its buyers to purchase more overseas, it also made arrangements with overseas consolidators to handle the consolidation and movement of purchases, freeing buyers from that task.[10]

Specification

Specification involves the application of the firm's knowledge about its markets, products, and procedures to procurement in an international context. Specification refers to quantifying and qualifying the firm's present production inputs in terms of quality, reliability, standardization, substitutability, timing, costs, capacity, and compatible technologies. In a sense, one is defining in very precise language all of the ingredients in one's production mix. Specifications can be handled in several manners. First, the buyer may design the item and then

---

[10]*American Shipper,* October 1993, pp. 44–46.

potential sources bid for a contract to supply the item. Secondly, the buyer designs the item and attempts to sell it. The third type "is based on open-ended dialogue based on how the buyer and supplier can join their knowledge of user and producer contexts and develop the specifications together."[11] Figure 14–1 shows how two varieties of coal, each arriving on a Great Lakes vessel, are "blended" as they are loaded on a vessel that will carry them across the ocean.

The ingredients of the production mix include not only specifications for each of one's products, but also for each of one's technologies and procedures, both

Figure 14–1 Three vessels, lashed together, at Seven Islands, Quebec, at the mouth of the St. Lawrence River. (The two closest vessels are "lakers" that can operate on the Great Lakes only. Both are self-unloaders with a boom that reaches to either side and carries a conveyor belt. The distant vessel is an oceangoing bulk carrier. The two lakers are unloading and "blending" coal as they load the ocean carrier that will carry the coal to European markets.) Courtesy Canada Steamship Lines.

---

[11]Luis Araujo, Anna Dubois, and Lars-Erik Gadde, "Managing Interfaces with Suppliers," *Industrial Marketing Management,* Vol. 28, (1999), p. 499.

existent and those anticipated by future changes in product/market demands. Specification should thus include the nature of relationships between the company and its suppliers, appropriate communication styles and linkages, and a clear statement of company philosophy and expectations for dealing with its own customers. This broadened view of production inputs serves two purposes. First, it discloses to potential sourcing partners the exact nature of one's business and how one views his or her relationship to technology and the marketplace. For one's sourcing partner, this information is vital to the development of a coherent response and the creation of a seamless supply system to serve one's needs. The second purpose of this broadened view is to assist the manager in developing a thorough understanding of her or his own expectations and requirements. This understanding will help in choosing sourcing partners that have a greater likelihood of success. As was mentioned in Chapter 3, it is essential in cross-cultural business dealings for clear communication to occur among all parties to a partnership. The creation of successful partnerships is an important aspect of international sourcing.

At about this point in the process, the buyer will have to determine the terms of sale that he or she wishes to use. If they buy and take possession at the source, there is a long string of intermediaries who must also be arranged for and paid, and all their charges must be factored into the delivered or "landed" price of the input being purchased. All these intermediary services must also be purchased and negotiating contracts for these services will also involve either the procurement or the inbound logistics staff. Some large U.S. retailers are now engaged in *self-importing,* which means: "instead of buying a product from a name-brand manufacturer, a retailer will go directly to manufacturing plants in Asia, have them made to its specifications, and then market the product under its own label. . . . Home Depot sends buyers directly to overseas factories, which are provided with product specifications, sales forecasts, and delivery requirements. Home Depot also arranges for transportation from the foreign port to its five distribution centers in North America."[12]

Evaluation

Next comes a process of evaluating potential international sources. In addition to the usual criteria that one may use with a domestic supplier, such as unit cost information and quality specifications, a whole range of new questions with serious implications arises in international sourcing. For example, often

---

[12]*The Journal of Commerce,* Dec. 7, 1999, p. 4.

transportation costs are higher when dealing with shipping materials over long distances in international trade. Does the cost or quality saving offset these costs? If not, what competitive advantage is to be gained by the arrangement? If the offshore supplier has demonstrated higher quality goods at a lower price, but is unreliable in meeting shipping dates, is the added cost of additional safety stock offset by the cost savings or quality improvements? Who will take the financial responsibility for currency shifts? How will quality related costs be shared?

Evaluation also begs the question of performance standards. Should the firm use the same quality and operational standards in evaluating foreign suppliers as it does with domestic suppliers? Does it impose additional standards on the foreign supplier due to the geographic remoteness of a solution to potential problems? While these questions may seem to have obvious answers, managers involved in international sourcing often find themselves comparing apples and oranges when looking at domestic and foreign suppliers with the same performance criteria.

In 1987 a quality process registration system was developed. That today is called the ISO 9000 program, with ISO standing for International Standards Organization, and 9000 standing for one or more areas of achievement. The emphasis is on the quality of the process. ISO 9003 is the least restrictive and relates to standards for final inspection and testing. ISO 9002 includes ISO 9001 and requirements for the purchasing, production, and installation capabilities. ISO 9001 includes the ISO 9003 and 9002 and covers manufacturing and support activities.[13] A number of large buyers require potential suppliers to be ISO certified. Certification is usually achieved with the assistance of outside consultants who help the firm develop, monitor, and maintain quality processes. In an ideal situation, both the vendor and the buyer would be ISO-9000 certified. A more recent ISO certification program, ISO 14000, deals with dedication to standards covering environmental protection. Interest in implementing this standard is not uniform, although Scandinavian and Japanese firms are taking the lead. ISO 14000 is related to some supply chain concepts that require one to be concerned about the recycling issues associated with the products they are making and purchasing. General Motors, for example, has a WECARE (waste elimination and cost awareness reward everyone) program that seeks to reduce inbound packaging materials and encourages recycling and reuse.[14]

---

[13]Robert Monczka, Robert Trent, and Robert Handfield, *Purchasing and Supply Chain Management,* 2d ed. (Cincinnati: South-Western, 2002), pp. 281–288.

[14]R. Anthony Inman, "Environmental Management: New Challenges for Production and Inventory Managers," *Production and Inventory Management Journal,* third quarter, 1999, p. 48.

Relationship Management

Managing a continuing relationship with an international source requires clear and consistent communications. Continuing relationships with suppliers are similar in many respects to marriages. Expectations need to be exchanged, negotiated, and agreed on. Both firms in the partnership must agree to a set of superordinate goals so that each feels a sense of success when the goals are met and share in the downside when goals are not. The creation of such win-win combinations comes about through sharing a common strategic vision. The sharing of that vision is often facilitated by some sort of human exchange. One should consider sending corporate staffers familiar with the outsourced project to the source's location to work with their peers in the source's organization and bringing members of the source's team to the buyer's locations.

Sometimes this extensive sharing can be problematic across cultural lines or when proprietary information is at stake. Cross-cultural communication is often not easy, and visions of shared goals do change over time. The solution is continuous communication by both partners to maintain as open and productive a relationship as possible. When proprietary information is a concern, remember that nondisclosure agreements may be a part of one's specifications, and that firms may be evaluated based on their compliance. While vital technologies and product development plans must be protected, foreign sourcing partners must have adequate information to enable them to perform to specifications. If the information is simply too sensitive to share, that may be an argument for making the "make" decision rather than "buy" in considering outsourcing at the outset.

Current supply chain thinking also requires one to have some concerns involving the source's sources. This would include offering to work with the source as it tries to develop better relationships with its own sources. This might also include monitoring some of the outside factors, such as climate, weather, or politics, that impact any of the supplying parties.

Transportation and Inventory Holding Costs

Even with certainty of supply and a shared strategic vision, one should anticipate that service and costs would be irregular at the outset of any new international sourcing arrangement.

Transporting shoes from Chinese factories to ports used to be an adventure. Ancient trucks would haul the cargo over woefully inadequate roads, then sit in long lines at the border, occasionally inching forward. Cargo frequently was lost or damaged. Poor communications made tracking difficult. But during the last several years, there have been dramatic improvements, U.S. footwear importers say. Highways have been built or improved, particularly in the coastal regions of South China, and the quality of trucks and chassis has improved. Many factories now have computers, and Internet tracking is spreading quickly.[15]

Carter, Pearson and Peng surveyed about 800 U.S. firms that had production operations in China to rank the severity of over 30 different potential logistics barriers to their China operations. The two most severe barriers found were "inadequate transportation infrastructure" and "suppliers' lack of responsiveness to your needs."[16]

Despite the vast improvements in the last decade in the management of on-time transportation modes and the worldwide implementation of just-in-time manufacturing, the simple fact of the matter is that the distances involved in global sourcing are enormous. Greater distances mean some combination of higher transportation costs and/or greater inventory holding costs. Figure 14–2

Figure 14–2 Airplane wing being loaded for delivery. (Photo courtesy of Heavylift Cargo Airlines.)

---

[15]*JoCWeek,* May 21–27, 2001, p. 28.

[16]Joseph R. Carter, John N. Pearson, and Li Peng, "Logistics Barriers to International Operations: The case of the People's Republic of China," *Journal of Business Logistics,* Vol. 18, No. 7, 1997, pp. 129–144.

shows a new airplane wing being loaded in Belfast for delivery to a Fokker plant in Holland, an example of high-cost transportation for an expensive component.

The true impact of these additional costs of transport and of holding can be difficult to estimate in the system design phases. The best advice here is accepting a shakeout phase during the early stages of the sourcing partnership, during which the true transportation and inventory holding costs will be revealed. Building a degree of transportation and inventory cost ambiguity into the system design will allow one to estimate high and low values for these costs, with the comfort that costs will come in between these worst and best cases.

Some attention also needs to be made to the mechanics of moving imported goods through customs and various other inspections. This is the point where all documentation must be available and in order. If import duties are assessed, they must be paid, adding to one's investment in inventory.

Implementation: A Critical Juncture

As the best-laid plans of mice and men frequently go awry, so do the best-designed international sourcing arrangements. The weakness in most plans is in implementation. Implementation failure is due to some error in the execution of the plan. Implementation failure can stem from a variety of sources. First is the failure to have an implementation plan! Believe it or not, many firms rush into sourcing arrangements without a clear understanding of what each partner's responsibilities are in executing the plan. This failure of omission is serious, as roles will be confused, miscommunication likely, and duplication of effort the outcome.

Second, a lack of a comprehensive implementation plan often results in a poor implementation, despite the quality of the original plan. Operational details must be specified down to the line-management level so that field operations employees understand the plan's vital linkages and their roles in insuring total system performance. Implementation plans must contain sufficient detail for the manager to take action.

Third, the line-level manager must be empowered to implement the plan. This involves matching responsibilities and reward systems to the successful implementation of the sourcing plan, and giving the manager the authority to carry out those responsibilities. Fawcett and Scully say that, "initial success in worldwide sourcing is needed to gain the top management support required to obtain the resources needed to build the skills for long-term global sourcing success."[17]

---

[17]Stanley E. Fawcett and Joseph I. Scully, "Worldwide Sourcing: Facilitating Continued Success," *Production and Inventory Management Journal,* first quarter, 1998, p. 7.

Fourth, and related to the last issue, is designing an implementation plan that contains enough flexibility to be implemented. International sourcing is a dynamic arena where any number of environmental factors may come into play with no notice. Implementation plans should contain alternative courses of action, which can be carried out by line-level managers in the event of disruption of the original sourcing plan. Such flexibility doesn't necessarily call for overly detailed plans, which can themselves be difficult to implement. Rather, flexible plans explore contingencies and give guidance to the partners in making decisions under differing circumstances. Flexibility in implementation also relies heavily on good communication between the firm and its sourcing partners.

Monitoring and Improving

Global sourcing systems are also dynamic creatures, subject to change and improvement over time. It is essential that the performance of the sourcing system be monitored by all parties to the partnership to maintain its common focus. Measures of both quantity and quality of performance often used in monitoring global sourcing systems include on-time measures, early/late percentages, completeness of orders, adherence to order cycle parameters as specified, percentages of units accepted on delivery or rejected, and a supplier quality index that considers both the severity of potential defects as well as their frequency and their impact on manufacturing. Global sourcing systems lend themselves well to the application of continuous improvement techniques such as Total Quality Management. Whatever the measures or techniques used, the important factor is the continuous nurturing of the sourcing relationship by both buyer and seller.

Esprit, a well-known U.S. chain that sells ladies' clothing, purchases clothing in over 40 nations. They buy matched fashion coordinates from many sources and must have them all ready at the same time to place into their retail stores. To better manage their inbound flows they employed a third-party provider who linked all the nodes in their supply chain by computer. In the service's model,

> A shipment had a set amount of time to transit the supply chain, with a clear ETA [estimated time of arrival] for delivery. As the . . . network received information from each supply chain participant, the system would automatically update the shipment itinerary, and the ETA. If the ETA fell outside of the primary delivery window, proactive alerts were issued to each party so action could be taken before the issue became a problem. All alerts, in essence . . . "out of tolerance" notifications, were driven by the actual progress of the freight through the supply chain, as measured against the ETA itinerary, and the real-time up-

dates of each participant as they completed their specific task in the delivery cycle.[18]

Issues in Importing and Exporting

Several additional items should be considered whenever international sourcing is an alternative for a firm: possible use of child labor, changing tariff structures, foreign trade zones, exporting for assembly in bond, and counter trade. Each of these issues merits additional discussion.

Child Labor

A number of U.S. retailers, and some of their associated celebrities, have been embarrassed after it has been disclosed that the products they sell were produced by children or by convicts. In 2001, there were news items about large numbers of teen-age boys held in slave-like conditions on some central African cocoa plantations. Sources must continually be monitored to insure that they are not supplying materials produced under inhumane conditions. UNICEF buys relief supplies and, for procurement, it "does not buy from companies involved directly or indirectly in the use of child labor or the production of anti-personnel mines or their components."[19]

Reduced Tariffs

Over time, managers should expect to see lowered tariffs in trade making global sourcing more economically attractive. Supply chain managers should expect continuing fluctuations as nations continue to do battle in the trade wars. In 1993, for example, the United States threatened to raise tariffs on French wines to a level that would have tripled the price to American consumers. This threat was issued in response to French imposition of higher tariffs on some American agricultural commodity goods. Such threats, if implemented, would have dramatically changed the consumer market for French wines in the United States, not to mention the international sourcing plans of a good number of wine importers. Another dispute has involved bananas. The European community has

---

[18]Dan Allison and Elizabeth Peterson, "An Agile Supply Chain for Manufacturers and a Case for e-Business," CLM *Annual Conference Proceedings, 2000,* p. 34.

[19]Philip Damas, "Emergency Supply Chain," *American Shipper* (May, 1997), p. 44.

placed restrictions on bananas grown in the Western Hemisphere in order to protect growers in southern Europe.

As tariff structures remain complex, it is often advisable to seek the assistance of an international trade lawyer, trade broker, or import/export agent during international sourcing negotiations. With the current situation subject to constant change, such issues are sometimes too complex to be managed within the firm.

Foreign Trade Zones

Foreign or free-trade zones were discussed in chapters 8 and 9. The strategic implications of a foreign trade zone to sourcing are considerable. FTZ's provide ready access to convenient transshipping points between markets where goods can be stored, with or without value being added, without the imposition of an onerous third layer of tariffs. They also often provide a pool of lower cost labor when it is desirable to use the zones for adding value to a product through a labor-intensive process. The zones offer alternatives to the individuals making procurement decisions.

Exporting for Assembly In Bond

Macquiladors were discussed in chapter 8. They will be mentioned here as well because of their significance to the procurement process. They offer alternatives that take advantage on the lower wage rates in Mexico. Essentially, the maquiladora is a form of assembly in bond. Raw materials and partially finished goods are sent to special border zone factories inside Mexico where additional assembly work is completed on the goods, which are then transferred back to the United States. All duties are waved by both governments, except on the value added by the additional manufacturing processes taking place in Mexico. All raw materials and partially finished goods must leave Mexico after additional assembly is completed. They may not leave the maquiladora zone under penalty of the payment of full import duty.

As an example of how a maquiladora operates, TDK, a Japanese manufacturer of audio and videotape, ships large reels of bulk-manufactured tape to the United States. Such bulk tape is not in a finished form that is usable by end users, so the import tariffs in the U.S. are quite low. TDK then transports the bulk tape to a maquiladora in Mexico for slitting and respooling into audio and video cassettes. The cassette housings are made of cast plastic in the United States and are similarly shipped to Mexico. Mexican workers perform the labor-intensive operations of slitting, winding, and packaging the tapes. Cases of finished tapes are "exported" to the United States for sale to consumers. TDK pays U.S. duty only on the value added by the Mexican workers, whose wages are considerably lower than a Japanese or U.S. counterpart. Thus TDK manufactures in bond, assuring the Mexican government that no value-added products remain in Mexico, yet at the same time providing jobs to Mexican workers.

Countertrade

Barter has grown in popularity as developing nations have come to see it as a means to economic development. Less-developed countries often have goods or services that can be traded, in the absence of foreign exchange, for goods and services from more advanced countries. Barter deals have increased dramatically since the fall of the former Eastern Bloc nations, as former trading partners of the Soviet Union (and the new CIS states themselves) have increasingly looked to the West for trade opportunities.

Countertrade can take one of four forms, though the increase in countertrade activities has made for several combinations and variations on these. The four forms are: barter, buyback, switch trading, and counter purchasing.[20] *Barter* is a one-for-one exchange of goods with no money exchanged in the transaction. It is the most straightforward, simplest form of counter trade. In a *buyback* arrangement, the seller provides the means of production in return for manufactured goods to be delivered at a later date.

Switch trading is more complex, and involves a third party to the counter trade arrangement. In switch trading, an exporting nation takes payment from an importing nation in the form of goods from a third country. That third country is generally in exchange deficit with the importing nation and accepts the importing nation's currency to reduce its exchange deficit. *Counter purchases* have become increasingly popular. In a counter purchase, a firm exporting its goods agrees to accept payment in some other good. It was through counter purchase that Pepsi first exported Pepsi-Cola to the Soviet Union. Pepsi agreed to purchase Stolichnaya vodka from the Soviet Union, which it then sold in the United States through its Monsieur Henri Wines division.

Countertrade arrangements make it possible for a firm to earn a profit selling to countries that have little or no foreign exchange available to them and to repatriate those profits to the firm's home country. Countertrade often falls within the purview of the international sourcing manager. Why so? It is generally the sourcing manager who needs to be the expert in determining the value of the exchange

---

[20]Warren E. Norquist, (1987), "Countertrade: Another Horizon for Purchasing," *Journal of Purchasing and Materials Management,* Summer 1987, pp. 2–6.

in barter negotiations, and also knows the company's own sourcing needs. Obviously, the most desirable barter would be for goods the firm would otherwise have to purchase on the open market. Second most desirable would be goods that the global sourcing manager sees a ready market for where hard currency can be earned from their sale. For firms lacking in countertrade expertise, it is possible to outsource countertrade activities through third-party experts.

Joseph Carter and James Gagne offer some suggestions for managers in firms considering the use of counter trade:

> For the obvious reason that profit is necessary to finance business growth, restrict counter trading to no more than 15 percent of gross revenues.

> Sell materials only after the firm has something for which to counter trade.

> Standardize counter trade procedures.

> Counter trade wisely. Few, if any, counter trade partners guarantee the quality, the on-time delivery, or warranty the goods or services.

> Coordinate important counter trade functions such as purchasing, marketing, and financing.

> Use imagination . . . remember that everything is negotiable.

> Temper expectations. Few counter trade partners will barter goods or services they can sell for cash.

> Report all income gained through counter trade to the Internal Revenue Service.[21]

Summary

In this chapter were examined two driving factors that have pushed firms to source globally: the factor-input strategy and the market-access strategy. Also detailed in this chapter was a model for the development of an international sourcing program to assist managers in the design of a global sourcing effort. A discussion of issues related to importing and exporting followed, including import tariff and duty structures, foreign or free trade zones, exporting for assembly, and counter trade.

---

[21]Joseph R. Carter and James Gagne, "The Dos and Don'ts of International Countertrade," *Sloan Management Review,* Spring 1984, pp. 31–37.

End-of-Chapter Questions

1. Examine the garments you are wearing. In which countries were they manufactured?

2. Why do some firms source globally?

3. What is the market access strategy? When is it used?

4. What are import quotas? What challenges do they present to managers of inbound logistics?

5. What are some of the synergies involved when a firm sets up its global procurement system?

6. What is the ISO 9000 program?

7. What is the ISO 14000 program?

8. Why is it necessary to monitor the functioning of one's global procurement system?

9. Why must one be concerned about working conditions in their sources' factories and plantations?

10. What is countertrade? Why is it used?

CASE • *Barbara's Blouses*

Barbara Linse buys blouses for a chain of ladies' wear stores in major U.S. cities west of the Mississippi River. They sell clothing made in both the United States and Asia. Asia supplies an increasing amount and percentage of blouses that the chain sells. Twice yearly Barbara travels to Asia, mainly to Korea, Vietnam, and China. On each trip, she has the authority to place orders totaling up to 15,000 blouses. Prior to her trip, she and the chain's other buyers agree on color themes they wish to promote; all items the chain's buyers buy will be in the same, or harmonizing, patterns and colors. If individual buyers are uncertain, samples will be sent to the chain's home office where Barbara's boss makes the final decision. Barbara's boss communicates with all buyers on a near-daily basis when they are on buying trips. Also, since nearly all the offshore buying is done in Asia, the individual buyers try to schedule their trips so they are in the same areas at about the same time.

Questions for *Barbara's Blouses*

1. What are some of the risks of buying overseas that one can avoid by buying from domestic sources?

2. Purchase contracts issued by Barbara's firm provide for the goods to be produced, shipped, and received within five months of the date the contract is issued. Should the monetary amounts specified in the contract be in U.S. dollars or in the currency of the nation where the manufacturer is located? Why?

3. Title to the goods can pass from seller to buyer at any point between the seller's shipping dock and the buyer's receiving dock. Which point should be used for the blouses Barbara's firm is buying? Why?

4. One of the concerns of U.S. retail chains is the possibility that goods they import have been made by child or prison labor. How can Barbara prevent this from happening with products that she buys for her chain?

5. Barbara's firm makes many purchases in Asia. How should they manage, or handle, the physical movement of the goods from Asia to their individual stores in the U.S.?

6. The initial prices that potential sources in Asia quote to Barbara are for the blouses at their (the manufacturers') shipping dock. What are all the additional costs between that point and the sales rack in one of the chain's retail stores?

7. You are Barbara's boss. What criteria would you use to evaluate her work and the work of other buyers under your supervision?

15

Logistics of Famine Relief

Introduction

In famine relief efforts, first- and third-world logistics meet. We have a situation where nations with advanced logistics techniques operate in areas at the other end of the spectrum. Famine relief efforts also provide a view of public sector, or not-for-profit, international logistics efforts. The chapter will also go into detail concerning specific logistics activities related to famine and disaster relief. This should remind readers that logistics does, in fact, consist of many details that the logistics manager must successfully orchestrate.

Famine Relief Logistics

Great interest has been shown in the famine relief efforts in Kosovo and Pakistan that follow, by only a few years, major relief efforts in Somalia and Ethiopia. These efforts consist of combining logistical efforts with an understanding of the political, social, and economic structure of the areas needing help.[1] In many years, deaths from starvation number in the tens of thousands. (As this book is being revised, there are estimates in the press of starvation in both North Korea and Afghanistan with potential deaths exceeding one million in each place. "Aid groups estimate that one million to two million people have died in the famines

---

[1]Much of this chapter is based on the work of Douglas C. Long. See also Douglas C. Long and Donald F. Wood, "The Logistics of Famine Relief" *Journal of Business Logistics,* Vol. 16, No. 1, (1995) pp. 213–229.

that have afflicted North Korea for six years."[2]) In early 2002, news stories appeared almost daily that described the plight of refugees in Afghanistan.)

Famines occur not because there is not enough food in the world, but because the food is not where it is needed. Effective logistics is the essence of famine relief because the greatest task in providing aid is getting the food to the people who are starving. The logistics of famine relief is unique for three reasons. First, while such operations can occur anywhere in the world, they often occur in less developed regions that usually have inadequate infrastructures and are some distance from major traffic lanes. Second, the consumer of the final product is not the customer of either the supplier or the carrier. Finally, the political environment may play a pivotal role in the entire operation. The political and economic (and, sometimes, military) strength of the government in the area where the famine or other disaster occurred is also very significant.

Relief is foreign intervention into a society with the intention of helping local citizens. How this is conducted can either help or hurt that society. The distribution of "free" food can disrupt existing local agriculture and logistics systems, delaying their development and postponing the area's ability to become self-sufficient.

Food relief is a huge institution that moves billions of dollars worth of food every year. There are over 100 major relief agencies worldwide, each with annual budgets over $1 million, and almost every government in the world is involved either as a donor, recipient, or participant. In 2001, the operating budget of the U.N. World Food Program was just under two billion dollars.[3]

The logistics managers handling relief efforts must identify what sort of environment they will be working in, because that will determine the strategic planning required and appropriate operating methods. There are two basic types of famine, environmental and political.

Environmental famines are caused by natural phenomena that result in a lack of food grown or available. Drought is the most obvious cause. There are three specific causes of drought: precipitation drought, resulting from lack of rainfall; runoff drought, resulting from low levels of river flow; and aquifer drought, resulting from lack of groundwater. Logistical requirements vary depending on where the water can be located. If aquifers are adequate, drilling machinery can access well water. When local sources of water are exhausted, the logistical task of carrying in water becomes enormous. The alternative would be to move the

---

[2]*Chicago Tribune,* June 27, 2001, p. 1.

[3]*Time,* February 19, 2001, p. B14.

people to the water, which is extremely disruptive.[4] Sudden disasters such as floods can also result in severely reduced crop yields or loss of water supplies or of roads. Even if food is not a concern in disasters, clean water supplies are.

Political famines are more complex. In the most common scenario, an environmental famine is exacerbated by war. Famine can occur when armed conflict becomes so severe that the population is prevented from growing or importing food. Refugees have left, often fled, their homes and risk famine because they are thrown into their situation with little warning, without a place to settle or a means to support themselves. When large populations are moving about, without any direction, relief workers must either get them to the food, or stop them and bring food to them.

Sometimes even nations at peace force segments of their population into exile from the country (or they just push them around within national borders, as occurred with the areas around Kosovo). Internal refugees, populations uprooted but still within the country, create special political problems for the relief effort. These groups became refugees because they are in political disfavor, and attempts to help them are discouraged. Food can be viewed as a weapon. An army capable of feeding itself is much stronger than an army that cannot. A government that can feed its people has legitimacy, while a government with starving people may encounter food riots and other civil strife. In the extreme, starving people are docile and thus pose no threat to the government. As soon as people are well fed and strong, they pose a threat. Governments will often decide whether they want the starving in their country to receive aid. In the case of Somalia, there was no government and large portions of the relief food had to be used as bribes to local warlords in order to get food to the starving.

Logistical requirements for refugees are complex. Famine victims who are still in their homes have the benefit of local supplies, shelter, and their community. But refugees in camps require food, shelter, medicine, clothing, cooking facilities, water, fuel, sanitation, and security. They are also more vulnerable to communicable diseases.

In addition, famine relief workers must find ways to operate within the war zone to help victims and protect themselves. Operation Lifeline Sudan was a good example of diplomacy used to justify the need for relief workers in the midst of Sudan's civil war. The United Nations used high-level diplomats to convince both sides to negotiate a system whereby relief efforts could operate in both sectors without bias or preference. The relief agencies informed everyone of what they were doing.

---

[4]*The Challenges of Drought,* (Addis Ababa: The Relief and Rehabilitation Commission, 1985.)

In the discussion that follows, many references are made to three specific relief operations. Operation Lifeline Sudan (1989–1990) was a consortium of relief agencies, under the leadership of the United Nations International Children's Fund (UNICEF), which sought to address Sudan's famine in the midst of a drought and a war.[5] Operation Provide Comfort was led by the U.S. Army's 353rd Civil Affairs (CA) command to assist Kurdish refugees in the hills of Northern Iraq/Turkey after the Persian Gulf War. Finally, Operation Sea Angel, led by the U.S. military, helped Bangladesh after a typhoon that killed several hundred thousand people. This was a natural disaster aggravated by human development in the flood plains of Bangladesh, and the main task was the distribution of food that was already in the country. The discussion is based on common categories of logistical activities and describes those aspects that are unique to famine relief.

Nearly all the discussion involves logistics associated with movement of food. Relief efforts also involve medicines and medical supplies. Their volume is considerably less but they often move with higher priority and are handled under closer supervision.

Command and Control

A multitude of organizations participate in different aspects of humanitarian aid. Some are massive operations, such as the United Nation's World Food Program. The United Nations has different components that deal with problems of famines and refugees. They collect food pledges from governments and provide these foodstuffs for development and relief operations. Other, small organizations may deliver one shipment of supplies and then disappear. These institutions are either governments or private voluntary organizations (PVOs).

United States government agencies include the Agency for International Development (AID) that uses food from the Department of Agriculture's Public Law 480 (PL 480) program for relief operations. Within AID is the Office of Foreign Disaster Assistance (OFDA), which conducts the emergency operations. The Department of Defense has Civil Affairs (CA) units that provide leadership whenever the US military becomes involved in humanitarian projects.[6]

Every organization has its unique motivation for providing relief. Govern-

---

[5]Larry Minear, *Humanitarianism Under Siege: A Critical Review of Operation Lifeline Sudan,* (Trenton, NJ: Red Sea Press, 1991).

[6]Interview with Robert Keesecker, Logistics Officer, OFDA, Washington D.C, November 26, 1992.

ments provide food relief primarily to support diplomatic goals and to dispose of excess food resulting from subsidized farming. PVOs are motivated primarily by humanitarian concern. Most PVOs are also working for economic development of distressed countries and find themselves managing emergency food relief when disaster strikes. "Both the International Red Cross and the Catholic Relief Services (CRS) were working in Albania when the Kosovo crisis began . . . and have now received the majority of the international distribution task. The Red Cross is handling supplies for refugees remaining with relatives or in individual Albanian homes, while CRS handles the job of distribution to refugee encampments."[7]

However, and especially when more than one relief agency is working in an area, they compete with each other to lease trucks and trailers or buildings to use as warehouses. This drives up the prices and increases the costs of the specific relief effort.[8]

Smaller organizations can serve vital roles if they fill a particular niche. They become specialists in certain regions, and they save by not having a lot of overhead. Americares, a PVO based in Connecticut, reacts to a disaster by filling a large airplane and flying to the area, all within a matter of hours of perceiving the need. They don't assess the needs of the recipients well, but they make a difference when timeliness counts.

Relief agencies attract certain types of people, which further serve to distinguish their organizations. Working for a PVO, young, predominantly single people are sent to isolated, undeveloped corners of the world for a couple years to work on a development project. The personnel makeup of the relief agencies can serve to protect the workers. If the staff come from a multitude of different countries, the political risk of any harm that comes their way will be mitigated since outside governments will have an interest in the safety of their citizens.

Demand Forecasting

Some famines can be predicted. Pictures taken from satellites allow one to predict harvests from crops that are ripening. Locally, one might observe consumption of wild foods, unusual migration, selling livestock for food, and high food prices.

---

[7]David Maloney, "A supply chain of hope, caring for the Kosovo refugees," *Modern Materials Handling*, June, 1999, pp. 16–17.

[8]Andrew McClintock, "The Goat into the Python," *Purchasing & Supply Chain Management* (September, 1995) pp. 18–23.

Forecasts allow regions at risk to prepare themselves and for relief agencies to prepare their efforts. "Among famine-vulnerable countries, post-Independence India has provided the most well documented examples of effective early warning and public response. . . . The administrative integration of warning and response functions, combined with political will and a free press, have undoubtedly been important to India's success at avoiding famines since Independence, despite numerous droughts."[9]

The management of information during a crisis is the single greatest determinant of success. The needs of disaster victims are presumed initially by people far away, based on limited information. Assumptions are made regarding the kind and quantity of supplies needed, where they are needed, and how they will be distributed. Initially supplies are "pushed." Once relief personnel are in the disaster area, they reassess the situation and try to correct the mistakes. Once better assessments have been made and communicated to the origin of supplies, a "pull" system is put into effect and the process becomes much more effective.

When Americares flew a planeload of supplies into the ex-Soviet Union, they had no contact with their intended recipients and could only guess what they needed. As it turned out, they had packed medical supplies, which proved useful.[10] During the first ten days of Operation Provide Comfort, supplies were coming from an airfield in Europe, without communicating with the personnel on the ground who were with the Kurds. The food was dropped randomly and included every sort of consumable that could be mustered. Only after communicating the needs back to Europe and conferring with PVOs familiar with the dietary needs of Kurds did the relief effort become more focused.

Language and terminology vary with each organization, making coordination more difficult. For example, when the Ethiopian Relief and Rehabilitation Commission published their analysis of relief supplies needed, their statistical measurement was numbers of families, not individuals. This made their analysis difficult for Western relief agencies to translate and led to confusion.

Forecasts must also include allowances for shrinkage in the pipeline between the source and the recipients. For example, having supplies stolen by armed forces cannot be prevented, but the food is still accounted for. Logistical planning can only estimate how much food will be lost before it gets to the recipients, and plan accordingly.[11]

---

[9]Martin Ravallion, "Famines and Economics," *Journal of Economic Literature,* September 1997, p. 1228. See also: William G. Moseley, "Computer Assisted Comprehension of Distant Worlds: Understanding Hunger Dynamics in Africa," *Journal of Geography,* January/February, 2001, pp. 32–45.

[10]Gerald Seib, "A Private US Group Finds Aiding Hospitals in Ukraine Isn't Easy," *The Wall Street Journal,* March 31, 1992, p. 1.

[11]"Death by Looting," *The Economist,* July 18, 1992, p. 41.

Sourcing

The needs of the victims have little correspondence to the level of support received. Some disasters are more popular than others, such as in 1983 when the International Committee of the Red Cross (ICRC) issued separate appeals for Poland and Brazil. The Polish crises received four times more than what was needed, and Brazil received 2.4 percent of its expressed needs.

In operations that require food to be brought in from the outside, food should be obtained as close as possible to the disaster zone in order to minimize transportation requirements. The drought in the Horn of Africa did not affect the rest of the continent to any great extent, so many of the relief supplies were available for purchase in Kenya and other African nations. Sourcing locally also contributes to the quality of the relief effort since unfamiliar foods sometimes disrupt local cultures and lifestyles.

Most relief agencies must work with what they are given. The Red Cross often finds itself being offered food that is unsuited for relief work. They have a list of food that is recommended such as whole grains, salt, and sugar. Then there are restricted foods, such as milk products, precooked, and instant food. Finally, there are foods that are not recommended, such as liquids, frozen and refrigerated food, and canned baby food.[12] The logistics pipeline therefore needs to have at the origin some mechanism to discriminate among donations.

Relief operations also involve a myriad of nonfood commodities such as tools, fuel, shelters, sanitation equipment, and medical supplies. Sourcing these supplies is a matter of determining what contingency stocks are available or where they can be purchased quickly.

Packaging

Packaging determines the survivability of supplies, ease of handling, and transportation requirements. Improper packaging results in large amounts of wasted food. When Americans think of relief food, the first thing they think of is the polypropylene, 50-kilo bags with the handclasp logo stating "From the People of the United States of America." That bag is the result of a 16-page specification that even mandates the color of the threads used.[13] The most common unit

---

[12]"ICRC/League Policies in Emergency Situations," (Geneva: International Committee of the Red Cross, November 2, 1992), pp. 9–11.

[13]"Packaging and Marking Specifications, Announcement M-14, for Purchase of Milled Rice for use in Export Programs," Agricultural Stabilization and Conservation Service, USDA, Washington D.C, July 23,1991. (During famine relief efforts in North Korea in the late 1990s, the North Korean government would not allow food to be distributed in parcels indicating that it had come from outside North Korea.)

of food used by relief agencies are these 50-kilo bags. They are as large as possible while still capable of being carried by an individual. The bags are not waterproof, which means they must be kept under some form of protection. Cans are used for butter, butter-oil or other liquid foodstuffs. Such cargo is more difficult to handle because cans are prone to denting and rupture and cannot be carried as conveniently as bags. Although they won't be destroyed in the rain, they rust over time.

The bagging of grain can take place either at the origin or in the recipient country. Public Law 480 requires that the cargo be bagged in the United States. Bagging facilities are present at ports in most countries. When a ship of bulk grain arrives, the cargo must be transported at once to the bagging station, bagged, and then sent on to its final destination. (Transporting bulk grain to the point of consumption is rarely feasible. Unless that point of consumption is a huge relief facility, such as a refugee camp or a public kitchen, it would not be feasible to build the sort of storage facility required for a truckload of grain. Bags of grain are also easier to account for than tons of loose grain.)

In the Kosovo relief effort, most cargo was palletized and relief agencies used lift trucks in their own facilities, and relied on refugees to unload the pallets that had been hauled by truck to the camps. Containerized cargo has a small role in relief operations, but its use has been restricted because containers have special infrastructure requirements that are not present in underdeveloped countries. Relief efforts in the Balkans made more use of containers.

Managing Inventories

Shrinkage, the amount of supplies lost somewhere in the logistics pipeline between origin and destination, is much greater in an environment of civil strife. Needs assessment must make difficult estimations of shrinkage in order to determine the quantity of supplies needed to be put in the pipeline. In Somalia, relief agencies attempted to flood the country with food so that it lost its value. Only when there is so much food that there is no need to attack relief workers would the starving be fed.[14]

The handling of nonfood items must also be considered because a famine relief operation handles more than food and water. Relief supplies include service support requirements such as fuel and spare parts for maintenance, hand tools, medicines, and water purification equipment. Supplies come from many differ-

---

[14]Interview with Ann Stingle, international spokesperson, American Red Cross, San Francisco, CA, October 28, 1992.

ent locations. Many of these supply items are more tempting targets for theft than is food.

Medicine poses unique logistical problems. Many medicines can only tolerate a certain range of temperature, which complicates matters immensely. Refrigerated vaccines must be flown in and kept refrigerated with the use of portable generators. Even cargo that normally doesn't require refrigeration would require such special treatment in the heat of the Sahara.

Site (or Route) Selection

Routes are selected after having to take into account political or security concerns. In 1997 UNICEF participated in the food distribution program following a "food for oil" agreement reached between Iraq and the allied nations. Iraq was allowed to sell oil (previously embargoed) and the money could be used to buy food. UNICEF was asked to procure and deliver $35 million of food to the population in northern Iraq. The shipments amounted to 2,000 TEUs over six months. The route selected by UNICEF was to ship full container loads by sea from western Europe to Mersin, Turkey, and haul them overland to three cities in northern Iraq.[15]

Distribution of food in a famine becomes a complex operation when the development needs and personal safety of the victims are taken into consideration. Logistical planning should give first priority to information coming from local personnel and should use local labor as much as possible. Local leaders are more likely to take personal interest in the success of the operation, and local knowledge of the area should insure that relief is conducted effectively. This also increases local pride and the motivation to rebuild after a disaster.[16]

Cost efficiency dictates that food be distributed at centralized facilities, where the hungry come to the food. However, this method of food distribution can cause people to become refugees when they must leave their homes behind and travel long distances to get the relief food. This means starving people are traveling, which can be life-threatening for the weak; or it means that only the strong will get the food. "The Kosovo crisis was marked by the reluctance of the refugees to leave the immediate region, motivated by their concerns for missing family members, their hopes that NATO would secure their rapid return, and their willingness to be repatriated into unsettled conditions. The costs of and

---

[15]Philip Damas, "Emergency Supply Chain," *American Shipper,* May, 1997, p. 46.

[16]Mary B. Anderson and Peter J. Woodrow, *Rising From the Ashes: Development Strategies in Times of Disaster,* (San Francisco: Westview Press, 1989), p. 64.

barriers to return are naturally lessened if refugees can simply walk back to their homes or rely on low-cost means of transport."[17] Once people are uprooted, refugee camps become necessary, creating still more logistical problems. Hence, distribution of food should be as decentralized as possible. At the point of final distribution to the intended recipients, care must be taken that they are not victimized because they possess food. This happens in areas of civil strife. Wet rations are sometimes offered to prevent such occurrences, because there is little reason to steal prepared meals.

Warehousing and Storage

Storage of goods provides several logistical purposes. First, inventory is protected from physical harm caused by rain, sun, and vermin. Many undeveloped countries lose more food to rodents than any other cause of shrinkage. Spoiled food creates special concerns because starving people will still want to eat it, resulting in medical problems. Spoilage is normally used as animal feed, but until so, it must be guarded to prevent human consumption.[18] Storage facilities should also be guarded against theft.

In Kosovo, "each refugee center creates two mini-warehouses to handle incoming supplies—one for food and the other for nonfood items such as blankets, beds, shampoos, toothpaste, detergent, and toiletry items. Usually these warehouses are nothing more than tents."[19]

When transportation is unreliable, storage should be as close to the point of consumption as possible. This obviously presents difficulties when infrastructure as a whole is lacking. In a logistical network, storage facilities are needed anywhere the cargo changes from one mode of transport to another, such as the port or airport, even if the cargo is going to move out soon. These storage facilities areas are also used to reconfigure the cargo. In Ethiopia, bulk grain would be unloaded into temporary storage structures and bagged immediately, with each bag being secured by two or three stitches.

Contingency stocks of food are rarely maintained anywhere by relief agencies because they can be purchased at any time. As for nonfood items, OFDA, for example, maintains seven contingency warehouses worldwide, close to air and seaport facilities. They contain basic disaster commodities such as blankets, plastic

---

[17]*The American Journal of International Law,* April, 2000, p. 297.

[18]Interview with Jack Godwin, Food for Peace—Burundi, San Francisco, CA, September 10, 1991.

[19]Maloney, p. 17.

sheeting, water containers, tents, gloves, hard hats, dust masks and body bags. UNICEF maintains a warehouse in Copenhagen that has prearranged kits of staple and emergency items. "Staple supplies are doctors' kits, midwife kits and school kits, emergency goods are first-aid items and shelter equipment such as tents and blankets."[20]

Transport

Ocean transportation is commonly used in relief efforts. Ships have the capacity to move immense quantities of cargo at low cost. The port of importation must be chosen. Important pieces of information in assessing a port are: location; connections to roads leading to where food is needed; water depth; cargo-handling and storage facilities; security; and availability of customs and other governmental agencies. When Oxfam delivered a barge-load of food in Cambodia, the port had no equipment whatsoever—no forklifts, cranes, or conveyors. Using workers who were themselves starving, it took nearly five days for 1,500 tons to be unloaded, even though the organization was being personally directed by the third most important minister in the government.

Air transport can move cargo quickly into remote areas that lack roads, though at much greater cost. Some nations allow their military aircraft to be used. Often the pilots need their flying hours so there is relatively little additional cost. This mode of transport is most valuable in emergency situations, when time is more important than cost, or when civil strife makes overland transport unsafe, which was the situation in Ethiopia. Medicines and medical supplies tend to move by air. Figure 15–1 shows a load of Land Rovers and other supplies destined for the U.N.'s Kurdish relief efforts being loaded aboard a chartered aircraft.

Air transport includes airplanes, helicopters, airdropped cargo that may or may not use parachutes, and helicopter slingloads. Airports and airstrips vary widely in the facilities they offer. Modern airports are often used at origin, but it must be assumed that the delivery point will not be as modern. Airstrips (which can be an open road or field) are indispensable. A dirt strip may be acceptable to a small aircraft such as the Twin Otter, but only during the dry season. Tundra tires are used; they are large tires used by aircraft to prevent them from bogging down in a soft surface. In Operation Lifeline Sudan, logistical planning was simplified by classifying airstrips as either Hercules-compatible or smaller, because the plane in common use was the Hercules.[21]

---

[20]Philip Damas, "Emergency Supply Chain," *American Shipper* (May, 1997), p. 44.

[21]Minear, p. 30.

Figure 15–1 Vehicles and supplies being loaded aboard a chartered aircraft. Courtesy Heavylift Cargo Airlines.

Air-cargo drops are a military technique that has been applied in particularly large and urgent situations such as the Operation Lifeline Sudan or Operation Provide Comfort. Certain planes, such as the U.S. military's C-130 or C-141, can open the cargo door in the tail and palletized cargo is pushed out. This cargo may have parachutes, which is called a Cargo Delivery System (CDS) drop, or it may simply drop to the ground (food bombing). In Afghanistan in late 2001, persons on the ground, trying to be under the "food bombing" aircraft, sometimes ran into old minefields.

Rigging cargo for a parachute drop is a special technique that protects the cargo from major damage and loss. Operation Provide Comfort found that the bottled water burst when the parachutes opened and the rigging tightened around the load. As the riggers gained experience, this and other problems were resolved and the drops made significant contributions to the relief. Nonparachute cargo drops have been well developed by Southern Air Transport in Africa, using Hercules aircraft. They developed a system that minimizes cargo loss by dropping from 700 feet elevation with a rigging system that lets the bags of food fall apart and land individually.[22] Even with parachutes, the pallets of supplies hit the ground at a high velocity, so this method can only be used for very insensitive foodstuffs such as sacks of grain. There is danger to people on the ground because people will often run toward a plane dropping supplies. In 1999, after severe flooding, Bhadani, India was one of the desperate villages that received airdrops of emergency food. "But villagers said the operation was poorly planned. Helicopters dropped heavy sacks containing plastic food packets in the area, but residents said Bhadani got only a few. Many sacks fell into inaccessible waterlogged fields."[23]

Helicopters can take off or land almost anywhere on earth, and move relatively fast, but their cost is several-fold more than plane transport. Slung cargo is placed in nets that are hooked to the bottom of helicopters. The only times helicopters are used are during highly publicized disasters when governments, and particularly their armed forces, get involved. Operation Sea Angel had the benefit of forty Blackhawk helicopters, which cost about $5 million each. They were able to move food anywhere in Bangladesh's flooded lowlands in a matter of minutes, delivered literally to the doorstep of its recipients. However, helicopters require much more maintenance than fixed-wing aircraft.

In many relief operations, the land transportation segment is the most challenging. When the roads are controlled by warring armies, relief workers must find what other roads are available. In Operation Lifeline the rebels insisted that no supplies come into their area from Khartoum, which was the hub of the nation's road system. That forced most of the supplies onto barges and planes, which were very expensive and far from most population centers.[24]

The land transportation segment is where most of the costs are incurred, where the political and environmental risks are the greatest, and where most of the food is lost. Ships occasionally sink or planes sometimes crash, but trucks of food are always being stolen or shot at or sinking into the mud. Even when war isn't a factor, a truck driver carrying food in an area of famine must be very careful. Some very simple equipment or practices can be used to extend the useful capacity of vehicles. Extra gas cans extend the range of the vehicle. Sand ladders are metal planks that can help trucks over particularly sandy or muddy spots. Convoys of vehicles allow one to assist the other in rough spots, where a single vehicle would be rendered helpless and vulnerable.

---

[22]Shahe Ouzounian, "Southern Air Transport Expands Role in Africa," *African Airlines,* September/October 1992, p. 33.

[23]*San Francisco Examiner,* Nov. 7, 1999, p. A-26.

[24]Ouzounian, loc. cit.

Trucks are the most common mode of land transport. Only a few agencies own their own trucks because of the large amount of capital they tie up and the fact that nobody knows whether or where they will need the vehicles after one or two years. Since famines rarely strike in regions with well-developed roads, the trucks used must be able to handle rougher roads with higher clearance requirements and fewer refueling facilities. The commercial trucks used in developed countries do not hold up well in famine relief areas. Rugged terrain increases service requirements to the extent that Catholic Relief Service (CRS) assumed in their planning that only 75 percent of their fleet would be available at any one time.[25] Drivers also need to be skilled. Oxfam Canada reported from Ethiopia that it was "hiring local trucks (with drivers well experienced in driving on desert tracks)" to move grain.[26]

Accurate assessment of the road infrastructure is critical to the operation. A road in Thailand may be a five-foot wide strip of mud only inches above the water line, which can accommodate only scooters and livestock. Bridges have weight limitations, which are invariably less than the loaded weight of the trucks.

In situations where trucks cannot be used, pack animals are employed. During the Sahelian drought of 1983, monsoon rains rendered all roads impassable, as expected, so camels were used to move the relief supplies into the country's interior.

Local communications nearer to the delivery effort, are also important. Unfortunately, the rule for emergency relief operations is that there won't be reliable communication at the local level, so every individual or unit must be self sufficient. Relief organizations operating in Ethiopia improved the effectiveness of their truck deliveries by installing a two-way radio in each truck.

Documentation

Relief supplies face the same paperwork requirements as commercial shipments. Relief agencies use freight forwarders to fulfill documentation requirements and arrange for transportation. Documentation insures that the cargo is identified properly and is in the quantity promised, but is also a bureaucratic routine that often slows a shipment that is urgently needed. Food shipments also entail various hygienic certifications, mostly to comply with the more stringent requirements of the donor nations. In 1998, after Hurricane Mitch battered much of

---

[25]Interview with David Palasites, Logistical Operations Manager, Catholic Relief Service, Baltimore, September 12, 1991.

[26]Oxfam Canada Update on Ethiopian Famine Relief, May 25, 2000 on website *Oxfam.ca/Ethiopia.*

Central America, killing over 10,000, more than one thousand tons of relief supplies were collected in the San Francisco Bay Area. After long negotiations, the U.S. Department of Defense agreed to pay the transportation charges for carrying the goods to Nicaragua, El Salvador, Guatemala, and Honduras. However, they insisted that all the donated goods be sorted, counted, and labeled according to military specifications. Large numbers of volunteers were required to perform this task, and some traffic scofflaws were able to have these inventorying efforts count toward satisfying the community service part of their sentence.[27]

Recipient nations, especially third world countries, have their own documentation requirements, some of which can be very particular. Ethiopia required a certificate of nonradioactivity after the Chernobyl incident. Moslem nations sometimes require proof that cargo meets their religious standards: no pork or alcohol in the shipment.

Documents accompany the shipment from port to distribution point. The system used by CRS in Ethiopia serves as a good example. A truck is loaded at the port with the bagged food and assigned a waybill specifying the following information: driver name, license plate, destination, type of food, operation number, and time of departure from warehouse. Warehouse managers sign the waybill whenever the truck leaves or arrives, noting the amount of cargo on board. Once at the final destination, where the food is consumed, the waybill is returned to CRS's office. This waybill also fulfills US AID's accountability requirements since they are supplying the food. Donors are often insistent on proof that food has reached the needy.

Parts and Service Support

Vehicles and shelters used by the relief agencies need to be marked, because in so doing, they are identified as noncombatants, which makes an attack on them a violation of the Geneva Convention. This may create a minor logistical problem of marking these assets, which may or may not belong to the relief agency.

Logistical requirements increase dramatically when a relief agency assumes responsibility for maintaining the parts and service support for a truck fleet. Mechanics and garages must be available near to the area of operations, and an inventory of parts maintained. As if protecting the food weren't difficult enough, spare truck parts are valuable and much more lucrative to steal. Most PVOs either contract for locally owned trucks or charter trucks from other relief agencies. In Ethiopia, the supply roads soon became littered with abandoned trucks

---

[27]*San Francisco Chronicle,* December 30, 1998, p. 1.

that had broken down and could not be repaired because of lack of parts. Some were surplus military trucks that had been donated by various nations. Mercedes became the preferred truck for relief agencies because Mercedes dealerships already existed in Ethiopia and repair parts could be ordered.

If aircraft are used, service support includes a professional mechanic, spare parts, and aviation gas or jet fuel. During the Ethiopian relief effort, Trans-American Airlines, which had the contract to fly cargo, was using up expensive aircraft tires at the rate of one per day.

"Customer" Service

In humanitarian relief, the sponsor is the constituent, and the victim is a third party, with very little voice in the process. Relief workers must first answer to their sponsor before they can serve the victims, and if the needs of the victims and the sponsors don't correspond, relief workers will have a very difficult time serving both.

There is competition among the agencies for financial support, prestige, and authority in managing projects. In competing for donations, they use publicity associated with the delivery of their food to the needy. This influences how they operate, because certain relief operations provide valuable high-visibility advertising, while others are mundane, expensive but necessary. TV pictures of starving babies receiving food will raise more funds than will an appeal for funds to help a nation improve its farming methods. Interestingly, once a high-profile agency has established itself in a region, other agency participation is discouraged because these others are perceived as subordinate to the established agency.

The lack of understanding of or focus on the "customer" makes the task more difficult. As mentioned earlier, in developed nations logistics systems are customer-driven. This is not a useful criterion for third world logistics practices, and the same conclusion holds for evaluating the effectiveness of relief efforts.

Summary

The chapter contained a discussion of the logistical aspects of famine relief efforts, as currently practiced. Many are military-like in nature. However, the "customer" is hard to define, since it may be the recipient of the aid, the charity managing the operation, or those who donate to support the charity's efforts.

End-of-Chapter Questions

1. What are some of the causes of famines?
2. Which famines are predictable?

3. In famine relief efforts, in which ways do first- and third-world logistics practices meet?

4. What are the advantages and disadvantages of moving refugees into centralized camps where they can be more easily fed?

5. What are some of the hazards in handling relief shipments of food that one does not normally associate with moving food in developed economies?

6. What items, in addition to food, are moved by relief agencies? Do they have special handling requirements?

7. What are some of the challenges associated with the transport of relief supplies in third-world countries?

8. What types of agencies are involved in providing relief to areas suffering from famines?

9. Who is the customer that is being served by these famine relief efforts?

10. In what ways, if any, would the characteristics of an "ideal" logistics manager for a famine relief agency differ from the characteristics of an "ideal" logistics manager of a firm that built automobile mufflers?

CASE • *Famine Relief in East Africa*

Although not especially talented in music, when she was in high school Ellen Scott owned the largest collection of current musical CDs and tapes of any student. Certain popular music could be traced to other parts of the world, and while at Babson College, Ellen took a number of courses dealing with music and with the culture of African nations, which she enjoyed very much. At the end of her sophomore year, she announced to her parents that she intended to major in African studies. Her father asked her some pointed questions about what one does with a degree in that area of study, and Ellen conceded that job opportunities were not promising. Further discussion—some of it heated—led to her father's statement that if she wanted him to continue financing her college education, she'd better find something "practical." Ellen complied and reluctantly switched her major to business administration.

Two years later, Ellen completed college and got a job working for an international freight forwarder in Baltimore. She developed the forwarder's computerized system for handling export documentation, which was soon copied by many other forwarders. Within three years, Ellen was an independent consultant, operating a small firm out of an office in lower Manhattan. She had developed an excellent reputation as a troubleshooter who could unsnarl both paperwork and cargo-flow problems confronting forwarders and their clients. However, she was more interested in troubleshooting than in managing a small firm. She took advantage of an opportunity to merge her firm with that of a one-time competitor. The merger did not go smoothly, and Ellen sold her interest in the new firm. She was unemployed, although by no means out of funds.

She did little more than relax for about six weeks and then decided to reenter the job market. She went to a human resources placement firm that specialized in transportation, supply chain, and international business management. It happened that the firm's interview form had a number of questions concerning interests in overseas areas, and Ellen, remembering her one-time interest in Africa, indicated that interest. Later that same day, after returning to her apartment, she was surprised to hear a message on her answering machine tape asking if she would make an appointment for a job interview. Ellen had trouble understanding the name of the firm; it appeared to be in the entertainment business. Nonetheless, she made an appointment for the next day.

The firm was, indeed, in the entertainment business. Its offices were much fancier than the Spartan-like quarters Ellen was accustomed to in the freight forwarding industry. It turned out that the person with whom Ellen thought she had the appointment was a secretary. Ellen discovered that, in reality, her interview was to be with Donald Saxon.

Donald Saxon was a well-known (famous, actually) promoter of rock stars and concerts. His name appeared in the entertainment sections of newspapers every week, and he had been the subject of a recent cover story in *Rolling Stone*. The walls in his large office were covered with gold records and autographed photos showing Saxon with virtually every rock star and rock group since the Beatles. Ellen was overwhelmed when she was ushered into his office. Was it her destiny to handle the logistics of rock groups?

Saxon spent a few minutes making small talk and then got to the point, saying, "Later today, I'm off to London, but I wanted to chat with you before I left. We moved quickly when the placement agency said you were looking. Actually, your name had surfaced several times in our search, which has been going on for the past several weeks."

"I'm flattered," responded Ellen, "but you must know that my specialty is in moving freight, not rock groups."

"Goodness," grinned Saxon, "I wasn't looking for another roadie. What I have in mind is more important."

"Oh," puzzled Ellen. "What, then?"

Saxon offered her a cup of coffee, which she accepted, and motioned for her to sit in a comfortable chair in a sitting area of his office overlooking much of Manhattan. He said, "As you know, the rock stars have been doing a number of widely publicized shows for a number of worthy causes—famine relief in Africa, aiding U.S. farmers, and so on. This industry has a potential for doing great good. These aid concerts both focus worldwide attention and raise large amounts of money. As an industry, we also benefit because we can demonstrate a sense of social responsibility and offset many of the image problems we sometimes have. Our problem now is, believe it or not, how to spend the African famine-relief money. Real questions are surfacing about how much aid is actually reaching those who are starving. We run the risk that some newspaper reporter will discover that most of the money is being wasted, so not only are the starving left starving, but we, the entertainment industry, get a black eye for misleading tens of thousands of donors."

Saxon stopped to sip his coffee, and Ellen asked, "Where do you think I might fit in?"

"I'm not sure yet," was his response. "I'll know better when I get back from England, in about a week. Indeed, and off the record, one reason I'm going is to discuss arrangements for a concert focusing on Rwanda, and I'm in the position of not wanting to appear reluctant to participate. But I'm also worried that any day, the press will be asking pointed questions about what's happening to the money we've already collected for other causes."

At that moment, Saxon's secretary interrupted to say that the limo was waiting. Saxon asked Ellen, "Do you mind if we continue this discussion on the way to the airport? My driver will drive you back here, home, or wherever."

"No problem," answered Ellen, and soon they were both riding to JFK International.

"Here's what I propose," said Saxon, reaching in his pocket for an envelope, which he offered to Ellen. "I understand you charge $1500 a day for consulting. This check is for $20,000. I don't have time to haggle. If necessary, I'm good for more. What I want is for you to get started. When I come back, I want your advice about what you think the problems are regarding the distribution of aid in East Africa, and I want recommendations about how we should spend the money so that it reaches those who are starving, and how we minimize our exposure to criticisms of waste and mismanagement."

Ellen accepted the envelope, placing it in her purse. Her mind was racing. Here was her chance to combine her business experience with her longtime interest in Africa. She asked a few questions of Saxon, and he started to reply. Just then, the limo drove up to the British Airways VIP entrance. Saxon hopped out as the driver handled his luggage. He said, "Phone my office for an appointment one week from today; they know I want to see you. I'm glad you're helping us."

The driver asked where Ellen wished to be driven. She gave her home address. There were no messages on her answering machine, and she called the placement service and told them that she had been placed. She was pleased to discover that Saxon had paid the service's fees, and she couldn't wait to get started.

During the week that followed, Ellen was extremely busy. She hired a student she knew to do some library research; she called on several acquaintances who had entered this country from Africa; she visited with officials from several African delegations to the United Nations; and she talked to some old contacts in the international transportation industry. In addition, Saxon's secretary gave her a list of contacts with international relief organizations that had experience distributing food and medicine in Africa. Many of the facts she uncovered were contradictory; some were unfavorable to the U.S. government, and many were discouraging. As the week drew to a close, she established a number of different files, each covering what she thought was a different issue or problem area. There was no ranking in terms of importance. However, many of the issues and problems seemed to Ellen to be hopelessly intertwined with each other.

On the cover of each file, Ellen wrote a sentence or two about each issue. Here's what she wrote on the various file covers:

- One U.S. relief organization estimated that 800,000 Africans perished as a result of that area's most recent famines.

- In our world today, we cannot prevent crop failures in various parts of the world; however, elsewhere in the world are huge food surpluses, and we have the resources to move them to where people are starving.

- There's an adage that if you feed a man a fish, you've fed him for a day, but if you teach him how to fish, you've fed him for a lifetime.

- Africa is not a single political area; instead, it is a collection of many nations, most of which are controlled by relatively weak governments. Often the nations are hostile to each other. Within each nation, there are often factions that are hostile to each other; sometimes these hostilities date back over 400 years!

- Relief organizations find that showing pictures of starving people helps to generate contributions, whereas success stories showing how hunger has been reduced tend to dampen contributions.

- A real need for moving relief cargoes is maintenance depots and parts for trucks and aircraft. In Africa commercial dealers stock parts for only one or two makes of trucks. One U.S. charter airline, flying relief cargoes in Ethiopia, wore out, on the average, one tire per day per plane (and each tire cost over $1,000).

- It is alleged that some trucks, donated to carry relief supplies, have been seized for use by the military.

- It is necessary to establish fuel supplies along truck routes. If this is not done, the carriage of fuel supplies cuts into each truck's payload.

- It's difficult to develop local entrepreneurs for hauling relief supplies. The reasons are many, including a lack of backhaul to the port.

- Sometimes governments are too proud to ask for help and tend to play down the extent of any problems.

- In Ethiopia it was necessary to send relief cargoes by air—which is very expensive—because truck convoys were blocked by groups unfriendly to the government or else were attacked by bandits.

- News accounts often indicate that many relief shipments were not reaching the intended recipients.

- A quote from John Donne, an English poet of several centuries ago (in updated English): "No man is an island, entire of itself; every man is a piece of the continent . . . any man's death diminishes me, because I am involved in mankind. And therefore never send to know for whom the bell tolls; it tolls for thee."

- Relief organizations can move faster than governments when it comes to cutting through red tape in order to get a job done.

- Many of the starving Ethiopians are in resettlement camps where the minimal care they receive is actually better than that enjoyed by the surrounding inhabitants. It is alleged that in some areas it is necessary to keep local Ethiopians out of the refugee camps. A news item in the March 2, 2001, *San Francisco Chronicle* described refugee camps being established in Afghanistan. "The amount of aid remains modest. But spare as the camps are, relief workers are concerned about the 'pull factor,' worried that if too much aid is given, this will lure people who are less needy."

- If immediate relief of starvation is the major goal, then military-like relief efforts, staffed by Westerners and using expensive equipment, are the most efficient. However, this approach does nothing to develop the local economy or to reduce its dependence on outsiders.

- Some African governments have many paperwork requirements that delay the inflow of relief goods. Conversely, individuals working for relief organizations feel that they should get to stand at the front of lines because they and their work are more important.

- Communications systems—a necessity for modern logistics operations—are very poor.
- When the U.S. government does give aid, it acts without knowledge of the local conditions. Grain ships are sent to ports that cannot handle such large quantities of cargo, or deliveries are made during the rainy season, when grain is difficult to store and impossible to move to where it's needed.
- Donated relief supplies are often spotted for sale in port city markets.
- Amnesty International has been extremely critical of human rights violations caused by one of the African governments. It was alleged that the government used starvation as a weapon in combating rebel groups.
- It is alleged that some relief organizations make a career out of solving the African famine problem; that is, they perpetuate rather than solve it.
- Very few Africans have training in logistics or supply chain management.
- Once famine has struck, it is too late to save some people. We need a better early-warning system, using devices such as satellites to determine crop yields before harvest. From this information, one would know in advance the areas where there will be shortfalls of food.
- In many of the existing relief food-distribution systems, there is considerable shrinkage due to inefficiencies and graft. However, if these facts become public, the publicity causes donors to reduce or terminate their contributions.
- In February 2002, stories appeared in the press, claiming that aid workers in Sierra Leone, Guinea, and Liberia were exploiting refugee children by forcing them to exchange sex for food.

Questions for *Famine Relief in East Africa*

1. Assuming that Ellen Scott makes some recommendations to Saxon, what are some short range actions (that is, to be undertaken in the next few months) that she should recommend? Why?

2. What longer-range actions should she recommend? Why?

3. In the case is the statement "It is alleged that some relief organizations make a career out of solving the African famine problem; that is, they perpetuate rather than solve it." If Ellen agrees with this, what should she recommend?

4. Saxon asked for Ellen's "recommendations about how we should spend the money so that it reaches those who are starving, and how we minimize our exposure to criticisms of waste and mismanagement." What steps should she recommend with respect to having the food reach those who are starving?

5. What steps should she recommend to minimize the possibilities of waste?

6. What steps should she recommend to minimize the possibilities of mismanagement?

7. Is the overall situation discussed in the case a logistics problem? Why or why not?

8. Is the overall situation discussed in the case a supply chain problem? Why or why not?

16

The Role of Logistics in International Supply Chain Management

Introduction

As the global marketplace continues to expand with advances in technology, the development of sophisticated trade blocs, and the opening of new markets in the emerging nations, international logistics has risen in the minds of leading business executives as a means for strategically integrating global supply chains. It is logistics, after all, that is concerned with the creation of time and place utility—core considerations to doing business in markets that are geographically or temporally separate. Increasingly sophisticated global market demands have forced smart companies to respond with increasingly sophisticated strategies, including the use of international logistics tactics for strategic advantage in managing supply chains with their channel partners.

The drive toward high-performance international logistics seems inevitable for companies operating in the first world of logistics. The presence in these markets of competitors who are already using sophisticated logistics practices to create strategic advantages for their supply chain is reason enough for companies to develop such expertise. Furthermore, the state of the art in advanced consumer economies dictates supply chain performance at very high levels. Consumers and companies now take for granted standards of supply chain performance that were unheard of just ten years ago.

This chapter deals with the creation and integration of international logistics systems into global supply chain strategies. First, we consider the global business climate and factors that influence international logistics and supply chain management. Second, we offer two generic strategies for global supply chain management; and third, we examine the coordinating role of international logistics in global supply chain management.

The Global Business Climate and International Logistics and Supply Chain Management

Why global logistics and supply chain management? And why now? McKinsey & Company consultant Graham Sharman[1] cites three global trends that are affecting the way international logistics managers respond to the strategic demands of their business environments: increasing market concentration; increasing dispersion of production; and increasing product line diversity.

Increasing Market Concentration

Through increased market concentration, so-called "power retailers" have come to rule the marketplaces in first-world economies. In the United States, for example, discount retailers such as Wal-Mart, Kmart, and Target have become dominant chains in general merchandising. "Category killer" retail chains such as Toys 'R' Us, Home Depot, and Circuit City now control substantial shares of the retail market for their specialty goods. These retailers generate tremendous sales volumes: the general merchandise discount trio mentioned above had 2000 sales of approximately $239 billion, with a weighted annual sales growth rate of 15 percent. Home Depot alone had a 19 percent sales increase in 2000, bringing annual sales to $45.7 billion.[2]

Representing a substantial portion of national retail sales, these power retailers have tipped the balance of channel power. A substantial portion of toy manufacturer Mattel's sales are to Toys 'R' Us; a similar relationship exists between Procter & Gamble and Wal-Mart. Remember the joke "where does a nine-hundred-pound gorilla sleep?" With the base of retailers shrinking to a few giant firms, manufacturers and wholesalers now respond eagerly to the demands of these power retailers. Thus the retailers, like nine-hundred-pound gorillas, are able to "sleep" wherever they wish!

According to Sharman,[3] one profit-enhancing strategy commonly used by power retailers is the refusal to hold large inventories. The power retailers have learned the lessons of just-in-time inventory management, and firms such as Wal-Mart focus on zero inventory as a desirable goal. In essence, the power retailers want delivery of goods in precisely defined lots, to dispersed retail locations,

---

[1]Sharman, Graham (1991), "Global Integrated Logistics," *Integrated Logistics: Perspectives for the 1990s,* Dallas, TX: McKinsey & Company, pp. 34–37.

[2]Annual reports of Kmart *(http://www.kmart.com),* Wal-Mart *(http://www.walmart.com),* Target *(http://www.target.com),* and Home Depot *(http://www.homedepot.com).*

[3]Sharman, Graham, op. cit.

at exactly the time they are needed on retail shelves. The retailers have strategically applied inventory technologies such as point-of-sale scanning and electronic automatic reordering to make such split-second logistics performance possible.

When such retailers are paired with responsive and logistically sophisticated manufacturers, retail inventory turnover rates skyrocket. For some categories of fast-selling goods such as toiletries and cosmetics, power retailers achieve thirty-five or more inventory turns per year. This allows the retailer to sell the goods before it even pays its suppliers, lending real-world proof to the concept of zero-inventory retailing. In 2000, almost two-thirds of Wal-Mart's sales were of this type. As this goal is reached, power retailers seek additional higher levels of logistics capabilities from their suppliers and increasingly choose to deal only with suppliers who can guarantee their logistics performance. Logistics performance guarantees are common today. Suppliers who ship with errors in quantity, SKU, packaging requirements, or delivery requirements are today often heavily penalized by their retailer customers through invoice charge-backs. When channel power is exercised in this way, leading-edge logistics performance becomes a norm, not an aspirational goal. As such, firms that cannot provide logistics excellence are left behind their competition. The power of the logistics-linked vertical marketing system is undeniable.

Increased Dispersion of Production

Sharman also cites a trend toward the global dispersion of production. Firms have pursued two distinctly different strategies in locating production facilities. Some have chosen to go where the cost of economic inputs (land, labor, and capital) are lowest. Others, facing unwieldy transportation problems or local trade barriers, have chosen to locate their manufacturing facilities near or in the markets where their goods are sold. In a global marketplace, both of these production location approaches can greatly complicate supply chain management and bring to the forefront excellence in international logistics performance. Adding to this complexity is the continuing trend toward more sophisticated automated manufacturing to increase quality and decrease labor costs.

For global logistics managers, these trends dictate increasingly complex logistics system design. Demand and supply pipelines must now circle the globe, and factory outputs must be directed (and often redirected) with increased precision in timing. In particular, the management of transportation and inventory functions have become quite complicated. Multimodal transportation coupled with improved information management has helped logistics professionals cope with the demands of global sourcing and manufacturing. It is now possible for logistics managers to creatively manage the inbound and outbound inventories

while still in transit to and from manufacturing plants. Supporting such sophisticated management practices are continuing advances in logistics infrastructure
in the first-world nations.

The situation in the emerging countries and the third world is much more tentative. As logistics management consultant Stephen Gould points out:

> [M]ost non-Chinese companies operating or sourcing in China still communi-
> cate with their Chinese partners and vendors almost entirely by telephone, fax,
> and e-mail. And although most shippers—both Chinese and non-Chinese—are
> electronically linked to their logistics services providers, they typically receive
> information from their providers only through one-way data transmissions.
> Most shippers do not have their own advanced technology-enabled tracking sys-
> tems, nor are they comfortable with sharing information online with service
> providers.[4]

Gould goes on to cite a litany of poor supply chain management practices in
China, including vendors' unreliable production schedules, delays in inland
transportation, and errors in customs documentation. Cumulatively, these practices result in significantly higher logistics and inventory-carrying costs in China
(24 percent to 34 percent of the U.S. landed cost of hard goods such as toys, ap-
pliances, and tools) versus 10 percent with U.S. and European vendors.[5]

What, then, is the contribution of international logistics to this global corporate strategy of dispersion of production? Again, as the business function dealing with the creation of time, place, and form utility, leading-edge logistics allows firms to increase profitability, quality, and responsiveness to their fellow
channel members and to consumers. And because such complex systems with
high performance standards are so difficult to duplicate, logistics can give a
tremendous competitive advantage to the entire global supply chain.

Increasing Product Line Diversity

Manufacturers worldwide have responded to the increasingly sophisticated needs
of consumers in first-world nations by lengthening and broadening their product
lines. As marketers have gotten more in tune with the needs and wants of consumers, they have expanded the variety of products offered. A related phenomenon is the general shortening of product life cycles observed in the 1990s, most
exaggeratedly in technology products. Consumers demand goods that meet their

---

[4]Gould, Stephen (2001), "Sourcing Successfully in China," *Supply Chain Management Review,*
July/August 2001, pp. 44–54.

[5]Gould, Stephen, op. cit.

.y, and are willing and eager to change brands to achieve in-
.n. This fickleness and volatility in the consumer marketplace
gistics implications.

change so rapidly, logistics system throughput time becomes crit-
.ust arrive where and when they are demanded, else they risk market ~ .ence. While this may seem obvious and simplistic, the challenge
faced by a firm managing a global supply chain is quite complex. Trends and resulting changes in one market may not parallel those in other first-world markets. Take, for example, the case of Sony's "Minidisc" technology. This home
audio-recording format was intended as a near-CD quality replacement for the
audio cassette. Minidiscs are small, so are easily amenable to both home and
portable use. Minidisc technology has been very successfully adopted by Japanese consumers, and Sony has licensed it to a number of Japanese manufacturers
including JVC and Sharp. However, Minidisc technology did not catch on nearly
as well with North American and European consumers, with market penetrations
standing at just a few percent. In contrast, American consumers rapidly adopted
the MP3 standard for web-shared audio files in comparison with Japanese consumers. Thus Sony finds itself a market leader in Minidisc products in Japan, but
a market follower in MP3 products in the United States.

These market-driven trends have implications for international logistics managers. There are more products in the global supply chain, with shorter life cycles, and with more divergent sourcing requirements. These developments inherently raise the complexity of the logistics task. Dominant power retailers raise
the ante for excellence in logistics by demanding leading-edge performance, and
they increasingly are willing to do business only with partners who can provide
such service. And as manufacturing costs have declined worldwide, increased focus is put on logistics costs. Corporate management will expect logistics costs
to fall with increased logistics system efficiency in the same way they have seen
manufacturing costs fall with increases in manufacturing efficiency. The old
adage "do more with less" seems applicable.

Logistics has become the glue which holds the global supply chain together,
and managing the global supply chain has largely become the management of
sophisticated international logistics.

Two Strategic Approaches for Global Supply Chain Management

Chopra and Meindl[6] propose two generic strategies for managing supply chains.
Each of these strategies begins with a thorough understanding of end customer

---

[6]Chopra, Sunil and Peter Meindl (2001), *Supply Chain Management: Strategy, Planning, and Operations,* Upper Saddle River, NJ: Prentice-Hall, pp. 28–34.

needs and requirements. Today's sophisticated market segmentation strategies result in groupings of consumers with different demand characteristics. Consider, for example, your own differences in need when purchasing gasoline under two different conditions: close to home and while traveling on vacation. When you're buying gasoline in your home town, you likely will know a number of gas stations' locations, as well as which ones generally have the best prices. You may also routinely purchase all your gasoline at the same station out of habit. Thus your demand for gasoline in your home town is likely to be strongly influenced by price and perhaps by habit. When travelling on vacation, however, price and habit may be less significant influences compared to ease of station access to the highway, a single stop with restaurant and fuel, or other issues of convenience associated with your lack of knowledge of the gas stations in a strange area. Your need for gasoline is different in those two shopping occasions, and thus you display different demand characteristics.

Six such common differences in demand attributes are cited by Chopra and Meindl:

1. Quantity of the product needed in each lot.
2. Response times customers are willing to tolerate.
3. Variety of products required by customers.
4. Service level required by customers.
5. Price sensitivity of the customer.
6. Desired rate of innovation in the product by customers.[7]

Consider two extremes in demand: planned and emergency. Under conditions where demand is anticipated, customers may plan to purchase large quantities, be more tolerant of delayed response times, accept limited variety from a single vendor (when using other vendors may also be planned), tolerate vagueness in service level but with expectations for reduced price, and await innovations. When demand is urgent as in an emergency, customers purchase only quantities immediately needed, require urgent response time, may require a large variety of complementary goods from the same vendor, demand precise and prompt service but with reduced sensitivity to price, and demand proven technologies.

Given differences in demand characteristics, Chopra and Meindl characterize supply chains as necessarily either more efficient or more responsive.[8] In most aspects of supply chain management, there are significant cost tradeoffs between

---

[7]ibid., p. 29.

[8]ibid., pp. 32–34.

efficiency and responsiveness. For example, a supply chain with an overall efficiency strategy may have as hallmarks long-term partnership arrangements, highly specified roles, focused manufacturing approaches, a relatively narrow assortment of products, and long lead times. These hallmarks are both causes and effects: long lead times permit optimized distribution systems, thus driving down costs. Conversely, cost-efficient systems typically have long lead times due to a designed-in lack of tolerance for variance in short-term demand.

Responsive supply chains, on the other hand, are flexible in terms of handling variance in customer demand, have short lead times, often use flexible manufacturing strategies, may handle a fast-changing and wide array of products, and do so with high service specifications. Thus two generic supply chain management strategies emerge: the efficient supply chain and the responsive supply chain. Between those two generic end points lies a vast frontier of cost tradeoffs that should be undertaken in direct response to different customer needs as determined by market segmentation. Thus, as Chopra and Meindl state, "there is no right supply chain strategy independent of the (overall) competitive strategy, (and) there is a right supply chain strategy for a given competitive strategy."[9]

Former Xerox executive Fred Hewitt says today's supply chain managers need to transcend the limitations of the supply chain management metaphor by considering the source of demand, the customer, as the prime determinant of strategy. He calls for a conceptual shift from supply chain management to "demand pipeline management."[10] Many firms are now engaged in strategies involving efficient customer response (ECR) tactics. Prompt demand realization and aggregation are combined with flexible procurement, manufacturing, and distribution to provide customers with products which are "mass customized." Such strategies are common in the computer industry, with leaders such as Dell Computer able to offer customized PCs with very short delivery times to customers through their website *(http://www.dell.com)*. Dell's ECR strategy involves sharing of customer order information through a corporate intranet with its supply chain partners.

ECR-based demand pipeline strategies seem appropriate to other industries beyond computers. Automobile companies are taking their first tentative steps in this direction, with programs such as General Motors' "GM BuyPower" website *(http://www.gmbuypower.com)*, which seeks to extend the customer information flow backward in the supply chain all the way to GM's suppliers and OEMs.[11]

---

[9]ibid., p. 37.

[10]Hewitt, Fred (2001), "After Supply Chains, Think Demand Pipelines," *Supply Chain Management Review,* May/June 2001, pp. 28–38.

[11]Becker, Torsten and Bob Pethick (2001), "Automotive's Build-to-Order Crusade," *Supply Chain Management Review,* March/April 2001, Special Supplement.

By doing so, GM will eventually be able to provide assembled-to-order vehicles for its customers within acceptable consumer demand lead times. Such a system would undoubtably result in a higher cost-per-vehicle than the current focused manufacturing and distribution strategy, but may also result in less inventory in the distribution and dealer network as well as higher profit margins-per-vehicle as consumers are often willing to pay a higher price for a perfect match to their needs. Thus GM appears to be shifting its supply chain management strategy from efficiency to responsiveness.

Note that neither the efficient nor the responsive supply chain model is necessarily better than the other. These represent two extremes of a continuum, and decisions on supply chain strategy must fit with those on the firm's marketing and customer service strategy. Most supply chain models have elements of both efficiency and responsiveness.

The Coordinating Role of International Logistics in Supply Chain Management

When one speaks of an integrated global logistics strategy, she or he extends the idea of integrated logistics systems across national boundaries. Multinational companies increasingly manage their diverse functions without regard to nation-states or location. This type of global supply chain seeks to take differential advantage of the strengths and weaknesses provided in locations throughout the world, regardless of whether the corporation actually sells its goods in any given country. Toyota, for example, maintains design bureaus in the United States and Japan, sources parts and components for its automobiles from many nations, assembles cars in the United States, Japan, and the European Community, and sells them in virtually every country in the world. Toyota also maintains an extensive parts and support network to enhance its presence in end-consumer markets. Operationally, Toyota loses its identity as a Japanese company and its logistics management challenges involve the global coordination of numerous and diverse activities.

Logistics in the Context of the Global Supply Chain

It is important to remember that logistics functions are only one part of managing the supply chain. The supply chain typically refers to the linkages among firms engaged in offering a good or service to end users, and to the articulation or coordination tasks required to manage these flows of goods and services as efficiently as possible. In addition to logistics, a number of functions must be carried out to bring goods from the sources to end consumers.

The Global Logistics Research Team at Michigan State University conceptualizes four distinct flows in any supply chain between the resource base and the end customer.[12] The *product-service flow* represents the value-added nature of manufacturing in the supply chain. The *market-accommodation flow* recognizes the time and place utility created by logistics and distribution functions in the supply chain. The *information flow* is multi-directional, and is a coordinating mechanism in a supply chain where forecasts, inventory data, and transactional data are shared among supply chain participants. Finally, the *cash flow* tends to move in a reverse direction from the product-service flow, though there may be exceptions to this backward flow in the case of marketing strategies involving discounts, coupons, or rebates.

This discussion will focus on the market-accommodation flow, which is the flow in which most logistics activities take place. The market-accommodation flow can be viewed in three contexts: operational, planning and control, and behavioral.

The Market-Accommodation Flow in the Operational Context

The operational context involves the coordinating activities necessary to achieve both internal and external integration of the supply chain. Internal integration comprises those logistics activities within the firm that coordinate procurement, production, and distribution. A firm must successfully transcend internal barriers to have a smooth-functioning supply chain. Many companies have a great deal of difficulty coordinating marketing activities, sales forecasts, procurement activities, and manufacturing scheduling. Three strategies for improving internal integration of the supply chain are simplification, consolidation, and internal buy-in. Reducing complexity facilitates the supply chain in its ordinary operations. Companies commonly do this by reducing the number of stock-keeping

---

[12]Discussion of these channel flows is based on the following work by the Global Logistics Research Team at Michigan State University:

World Class Logistics (1995), Oak Brook, IL: Council of Logistics Management.

Bowersox, Donald J., David J. Closs, and Theodore P. Stank (1999), "21st Century Logistics: Making Supply Chain Integration a Reality, *Supply Chain Management Review,* Fall, pp. 24–32.

Bowersox, Donald J., David J. Closs, Theodore P. Stank, and Scott B. Keller (2000), "How Supply Chain Competency Leads to Business Success," *Supply Chain Management Review,* Sept/Oct, pp. 44–53.

Stank, Theodore P., Robert Frankel, David J. Frayer, Thomas J. Goldsby, Scott B. Keller, and Judith M. Whipple (2001), "Supply Chain Integration: Tales From the Trenches," *Supply Chain Management Review,* May/June, pp. 63–70.

units (SKU: each single product variation) they produce, and by taming managerial information overload by managing on an exception basis (management focus is directed on exceptions to normal outcomes rather than on expected outcomes). Consolidation also assists in reducing complexity by improving economies of scale and thus reducing costs. Typical logistics consolidation opportunities could include redundant facilities, duplicate safety stocks, and slow moving inventory items. Managerial and line-level employees must also buy-in to the idea of internal integration, shifting from a focus on functional excellence to organizational excellence. Obviously, managerial incentives must also make this shift. A renewed emphasis on cross-functional improvements must be matched with cross-functional rewards for all participants.

The Market-Accommodation Flow in the Planning and Control Context

The planning and control context involves technology and planning integration, and measurement integration. Technology and planning integration deal with the sharing of strategies, information, and systems within a supply chain. Smooth-functioning supply chains share common technologies among their members and eliminate duplicate activities and functions. Information moves easily among the supply chain participants, enabling all to both jointly plan and monitor performance. One example of technology and planning integration has been termed *scan-based trading*. In scan-based trading, a manufacturer (or distributor or third-party logistics provider) takes the responsibility for retail store-shelf replenishment and consigns the inventory to the retailer. The retailer does not pay for the inventory on its shelves until a consumer buys an item, confirmed by the retailer's point-of-sale scanning information. Wal-Mart has extensively used this approach to lower inventory costs, speed inventory turnover rates, and improve shelf-merchandising. Note that for scan-based trading to be successful, the retailer must surrender control of valuable shelf space and scanner data to other supply chain participants.

Measurement integration deals with the use of common performance measurements throughout the supply chain, and the rapid sharing of information necessary to enable accurate and timely performance measurement. Typically, most of the performance measures in a supply chain will be tied to improvements in end-customer value.

The Market-Accommodation Flow in the Behavioral Context

The behavioral context involves a long-term perspective on how the supply chain partners will interact with each other, criteria for firms' inclusion in the supply chain, which firms will direct the efforts of the supply chain, which firms shall provide which functions within the supply chain, and the design and provision of necessary communication and reconciliation frameworks. Achieving such relationship integration differentiates excellent supply chains and provides a strategic advantage to the firms involved.

How does one create such relationship integration? Six characteristics have been shown to mark successful supply chain alliances.[13] First, the partners must share a common perspective. All must share superordinate goals and keep their eyes on the big picture, rather than getting bogged down in operational detail. The relevant issue is adding value throughout the chain to create a strategic differential advantage. Second, partners should match up selectively. It is essential that the operational strengths of one partner in the supply chain be matched to the weaknesses of the other. All members of the supply chain need be financially and managerially strong to ensure that the alliance has longevity. Third, information must be shared freely among members of the supply chain. Firms working together toward superordinate goals must have a common vision and a common strategy. To enable this vision and successfully carry out strategy, the partners must freely exchange information.

The fourth key to success is a clear specification of role. It is essential to the success of the supply chain for members to clearly understand their own and others' operating objectives. Ambiguity in roles can be disastrous. Well-established ground rules contribute to this role specification, and form the fifth key to success. While the dominant operating mode in a supply chain is cooperation, a clear statement of basic ground rules helps to mitigate disagreements when they do occur. And a thorough understanding of the ground rules helps to head off dysfunctional conflict and prevent premature dissolution. Sixth and finally, a commonly understood freedom to exit is essential to any supply chain. Partners must understand that sometimes good things do come to an end, and that parties in the supply chain agree in advance under what terms they will end their participation. The termination of participation in a supply chain is less painful when the partners know in advance how it could end. Such a specification also helps partners to retain a sense of independence and self-identity.

---

[13]Bowersox, Donald J., Patricia J. Daugherty, Cornelia L. Dröge, Dale S. Rogers, and Daniel L. Wardlow (1989), *Leading Edge Logistics: Competitive Positioning for the 1990s,* Oak Brook, IL: Council of Logistics Management, pp. 224–228.

Managing Successful Global Supply Chain Collaboration

Creating such integrated supply chains is not the easiest of managerial tasks. In a 2001 survey of 145 U.S. high-tech firms using supply chain management strategies, the top ten barriers to supply chain management collaboration were:

1. The cost and complexity of technology integration
2. Lack of trading partner technology sophistication
3. Lack of clear benefits and/or ROI
4. Cultural resistance to new trading partner paradigms
5. Until recently, few native Web-centric applications designed for this collaboration
6. Lack of technical standards
7. Fear of divulging proprietary information to business partners
8. Lack of awareness of solutions
9. Lack of commitment by top management
10. Lack of vendor support for collaborative processes.[14]

Obviously, the key to successful global supply chain management is collaboration among all parties to the supply chain. Professor Karl Manrodt and logistics executive Mike Fitzgerald offer seven suggestions for successful supply chain collaboration.[15]

Proposition 1: As companies move toward collaborative strategies, logistics and supply chain executives must increasingly apply a process view of their organizations.

By *process view,* Manrodt and Fitzgerald mean that managers should view their company's activities as linked and continuous, contributing to a single outcome. When managers take such a view, they come to realize the interdependent nature of the firms in the supply chain, since many business processes both extend outside the firm and transcend any single functional area in the firm. This process view represents a conceptual leap in the experience of many managers,

---

[14]*Marketing News* (2001), "Up the Down Supply Chain," September 10, 2001, p. 3.

[15]Manrodt, Karl B. and Mike Fitzgerald (2001), "Seven Propositions for Successful Collaboration," *Supply Chain Management Review,* July/August 2001, pp. 66–72.

but is essential for understanding how collaboration in the supply chain can be achieved with both efficiency and strategic intent.

> Proposition 2: Not all processes are created equal. The importance of each process should be based on a company's corporate strategy.

The two generic supply chain management strategies presented earlier in this chapter provide an excellent example of this second proposition. A firm having customer responsiveness as its overall corporate strategy is likely to create a far different supply chain than a firm whose goal is efficiency. Customer service, manufacturing, transportation, inventory management, and a whole host of business processes would rise and drop in prominence depending on the firm's overall strategy. It is important to insure that supply chain management strategy is consistent with corporate strategy.

> Proposition 3: Before collaborative logistics can be effective, coordination must be improved.

Manrodt and Fitzgerald coin the term *intragration* to describe the movement of information within a single organization, and such intragration is an important first consideration that each participant in a supply chain must make for a successful collaboration. They discuss four steps toward intragration: awareness, measurement, coordination, and integration. Firms must first be aware of the potential benefits of coordination, and then must develop appropriate process-based measurements to meter improvements and problems in coordination. Coordination speaks to the implementation of process-based improvements, with integration achieved as a firm transcends functional boundaries within the organization and successfully adopts the process view in business practice.

> Proposition 4: Collaborative logistics, currently at an immature level, is moving toward more intelligent communities.

Firms can extend their notion of a supply chain by adding entities not directly related to the market-accommodation flow, and thus leverage the assets of firms not traditionally considered to be a part of a supply chain. Such firms then become part of an intelligent community. Manrodt and Fitzgerald give several examples in transportation consolidation, where firms from different industries gain truckload (TL) rates by consolidating less-than-truckload (LTL) shipments. Similar collaborations are possible in warehousing, container consolidation, and in conducting joint negotiations or "bulk buys" across the supply chain. Such collaborative intelligent communities of firms can be facilitated by Web-based information exchanges (for example, ShipChem in the chemicals industry, *http://www.shipchem.com*).

> Proposition 5: New tools will enable and facilitate increased levels of "intragration," coordination, and collaboration.

In the late 1990s, the Internet demonstrated its value as an efficient communications medium that allowed real-time sharing of information in supply chains. One study of information systems in supply chain management defines four distinct types of collaborative management tools: 1) enterprise resource planning (ERP), linking functions within an organization through an integrated database; 2) advanced planning and decision support systems, allowing dynamic and continuous planning; 3) logistics execution systems, including order management, manufacturing execution, warehouse management, and transportation management; and 4) electronic data interchange (EDI), permitting the transmission of standardized information among partners in the supply chain.[16] Further development and integration of Web-based technologies will enhance global supply chain collaboration.

> Proposition 6: The key to "intragration," coordination, and collaboration is visibility of key supply chain activities.

Visibility speaks to the transparency and availability of information throughout the supply chain. Barriers to information sharing must be broken down. The key to success is "the right information, at the right time, in the right quantity, to the right people."[17]

> Proposition 7: The future lies beyond collaboration—in synchronization.

While few supply chains have achieved the level of collaboration envisioned by Manrodt and Fitzgerald, they see a higher level still: synchronization. Synchronization is collaboration among intelligent communities, linking disparate supply chains for additional efficiencies. They call for collaboration efforts to be inclusive and open to develop such cross-community synergies.

---

[16]Erdmann, Till (1998), *Supply Chain Management Through Corporate Intranets, Extranets, and the Internet,*" unpublished master's thesis, San Francisco State University, pp. 22–40.

[17]Manrodt, Karl B. and Mike Fitzgerald, op. cit., p. 71.

Summary

This chapter dealt with the role of international logistics in managing the global supply chain. The global business climate and factors that influence international logistics and supply chain management were discussed. Two generic strategies for global supply chain management were described as prototypical strategic designs. Finally, the coordinating role of international logistics in global supply chain management was explored, and suggestions for enhancing the success of global supply chains through collaboration was discussed.

End-of-Chapter Questions

1. Discuss the ways in which increased market concentration at the retail level changes the management of the supply chain.
2. In what ways does increasing dispersion of production make supply chain management more complex?
3. What are the international supply chain management implications for suppliers, manufacturers, wholesalers, and retailers of the trend toward increasing diversity in product lines?
4. What are the unique characteristics of efficient supply chains?
5. What are the unique characteristics of responsive supply chains?
6. Explain the differences in inventory management strategies at manufacturer and retailer levels between efficient and responsive international supply chain strategies.
7. Describe the market-accommodation flow in a supply chain. Be sure to include characteristics from three different perspectives: operational, planning and control, and behavioral.
8. What advice would you give to the managers of a firm about to shift to a supply chain management philosophy?
9. What is meant by collaborative logistics?
10. What are the characteristics of an "intelligent community" in business?

CASE • *Fedco Fasteners*

Paul Abraham was near completing his MBA studies in logistics at the University of Tennessee. His mother, Mary Abraham, had long managed Fedco Fasteners, the family business begun by his grandfather. Fedco was a decidedly low-tech business. They made screws, rivets, and other metal fasteners for the automotive and electronics industries from a plant in Holland, Michigan.

Mary had suddenly taken ill, and it quickly became apparent that she would no longer be able to maintain her operational role in the firm. Paul was encouraged by his mother and other family members to return to Holland and take up her role as the firm's general manager. Paul was depressed by his mother's illness, excited about carrying on in her footsteps, but quite unsure as to whether or not he was up to the task.

On his first day on the job, Paul called together the sales manager, production manager, heads of purchasing and engineering, and the accounting manager for a meeting to learn about the problems facing the firm. Carol Barbera, the sales manager, dominated the meeting with a discussion of a new set of "vendor performance standards" they'd received from General Motors. Almost one-third of Fedco's business was with GM's 14 assembly plants in Michigan, Ohio, Kentucky, and Ontario (Canada). Currently, Fedco provided 155 unique fasteners to GM, a number that GM wished to reduce to 40 with engineering assistance from Fedco.

"I don't see a way around complying with these new standards. They're going to do nothing but raise our costs to do business with GM. It's like GM is trying to take over and run our business without taking any of the risks of our business. But if we don't go along with this, I'm sure they'll find another fastener supplier for those 14 plants." Carol was clearly upset at the prospects.

Paul flipped through the GM guidelines and looked at the major headings: e-procurement, e-fulfillment, systems integration, concurrent design and engineering, JIT, and consistent references to the vendors as "supply chain partners." The task at hand was obvious to Paul. He needed to change Fedco's business practices and internal culture to fit into GM's supply chain, or Fedco would lose one-third of its business, a prospect which would be disastrous. Paul wondered: how would Fedco ever make this important transition and keep GM as a customer?

Questions for *Fedco Fasteners*

1. Consider the nature of the automobile industry and its relationships with low-tech suppliers of products like metal fasteners. Are you more apt to find efficient or responsive supply chain management philosophies? Why?

2. Assume that GM is asking Fedco to change from an efficient vendor to a responsive vendor. What kinds of changes might be necessary for Fedco to implement?

3. Consider the market-accommodation flow between Fedco and GM from the following perspectives: operational, planning and control, and behavioral. What kinds of changes might you anticipate for Fedco from each of those perspectives?

4. Paul's aunt, Katie Abraham, is Fedco's accounting manager. During the meeting, she flew off in a tirade against GM's JIT strategy, saying "GM's JIT is Fedco's excess inventory!" What does that tell you about Fedco's current inventory management processes? What kinds of cultural changes might be necessary to implement GM's new vendor standards with regard to inventory?

5. Consider Carol Barbera's role as sales manager and her comments in the meeting. What kinds of suggestions would you have for Paul for changing her role in the firm to fit GM's desire for closer collaboration with vendors?

6. On returning to work the following day, Paul decides to conduct a cost/benefit analysis for implementing GM's new vendor standards. What factors would you encourage Paul to consider in this analysis? What types of additional investment might Fedco have to make to fulfill GM's vendor requirements? Could there be strategic benefits beyond the GM relationship which should interest Fedco in making those investments? Under what conditions might Fedco be better off to drop GM as a customer?

17

Future Issues in International Logistics

Introduction

This chapter is brief; rather than summarizing what has been written so far, it attempts to look forward into the early part of the 21st century and envision key supply chain "happenings." There is little question that political considerations have influenced, and will continue to influence, international logistics strategies and tactics. Political considerations are relevant to logistics in the sense that improved political relationships between countries can generate improved trade relationships between countries. How will the shifting political landscape influence the design and operation of logistics systems?

While the United States remains a global economic and military superpower, other countries, particularly in Asia, have tremendous economic potential. Indeed, there are estimates that China's Gross Domestic Product (GDP) will surpass U.S. GDP sometime in the first part of the 21st century, perhaps by as early as 2015. How will logistics systems be designed to reflect the growing economic clout of China and other nations?

It's not possible (or practical) to discuss every issue that might impact international logistics in the early part of the 21st century. We will focus on a few of the more prominent issues in this chapter.

Increased Use of World-Class Logistics Practices

Ongoing research has demonstrated that world class logistics—how the world's best firms achieve and maintain logistical excellence—is delineated by four distinct competencies: *positioning,* or the selection of structural and strategic approaches to guide operations; *integration,* or what to do and how to do it creatively; *agility,* or the achievement and retention of competitiveness and customer success; *measurement,* or the internal and external monitoring of operations.[1] While world-class organizations tend to be most prominent in North America and Western Europe, they can be found worldwide.

Distinguishing attributes of world-class logistics firms include, but are not limited to, a strong commitment to their customers, sophisticated information technology, commitment to the development of long-term relationships with suppliers and customers, and comprehensive performance measurement. Moreover, world-class firms tend to exhibit superior competitive performance in fundamental areas such as low logistics cost, delivery dependability, and order fill capacity, among others.[2]

Multi-Country Trade Alliances

The European Union (EU) and the North American Free Trade Agreement (NAFTA) represent two of the most prominent multi-country trade alliances from the 1990s. While these two alliances have unquestionably facilitated trade among the participating countries, they have also had important logistical consequences as well, particularly with respect to the design of logistical systems. For example, the EU has allowed many companies to reduce the number of warehouses/distribution centers needed to serve EU member nations.

New multi-country trade alliances are being discussed as this book is being prepared. Moreover, in the early years of the 21st century, existing multi-country trade alliances may be modified to include new countries. Chile, for example, has lobbied to become the next nation in NAFTA, and several nations are lobbying to be added to the EU. Regardless of what new multi-country trade alliances are formed, or what countries are added to existing alliances, logisticians need to keep in mind that freer trade impacts distribution patterns; distribution patterns, in turn, affect the design of supply chains.

One-Stop Shopping Concept

The "one-stop shopping" concept refers to the ability of one provider to offer potential customers multiple logistics services under one umbrella, rather than cus-

---

[1]The Global Logistics Research Team at Michigan State University, *World Class Logistics: The Challenge of Managing Continuous Change.* Oak Brook, IL: Council of Logistics Management, 1995.

[2]The Global Logistics Research Team at Michigan State University, 1995.

tomers having to use several different companies for their global logistics needs. There are several ways that one-stop shopping has been implemented with respect to global logistics. One involves horizontal diversification in the sense that global logistics intermediaries, such as international freight forwarders, add (or acquire) other value-adding intermediaries, such as customshouse brokerages, that provide somewhat complementary services.[3]

Another involves vertical diversification in the sense that one company attempts to control several levels of global logistics service providers. During the past few years, for example, the German Post Office (Deutsche Post) has purchased an airfreight company (DHL) as well as several international freight forwarders (for example, Danzas and AEI). Regardless of how it is implemented, the one-stop shopping concept offers the potential for abuses in that the service provider may seek to maximize their interests rather than those of the customer.

Amodalism

Some shippers, as well as a few carriers, are becoming increasingly "amodal." That is, some shippers are more interested in the end result from transportation (for example, claim-free service, on-time pickup and delivery, among other service metrics) than with using a specific mode of transportation. So long as the shippers' service requirements are met, they are essentially indifferent as to the mode used to provide the transportation.

The shippers' amodalism is reflected by carriers in the sense that several may be losing their identification as being associated with a specific transport mode. For example, FedEx has long been regarded as an international air express company. Although FedEx Express is still a preeminent air express company, the FedEx corporate umbrella includes regional LTL motor carriers (Viking, American Freightways), a small package ground carrier (FedEx Ground), and an expedited carrier (FedEx Custom Critical).

Environmental Concerns

The latter decades of the 20th century witnessed increasing concern about the environmental consequences of business practices, with particular emphasis on various types of pollution and resource conservation. While the environmental protection movement has largely been concentrated in highly industrialized

---

[3]P.R. Murphy and J.M. Daley, Profiling International Freight Forwarders: An Update. *International Journal of Physical Distribution & Logistics Management,* Vol. 31 No. 3, 2001, pp. 152–168.

countries, especially in Western Europe, there are indications that environmental concerns are becoming more important in developing countries as well.[4]

International logistics managers in the 21st century will have to make numerous adjustments to their strategies, tactics, activities, and practices in order to accommodate the concerns of environmental stakeholders such as activist groups, governments, and the general public. Indeed, environmentally responsible logistics (ERL) has potential implications for the sourcing of raw materials, inbound and outbound logistics, logistics system design, and reverse logistics.[5]

Space Transport and Exploration

An exciting development that can be anticipated to increase in the 21st century involves space transport and exploration, which creates some interesting and unique logistical challenges. For example, the International Space Station (ISS), which was launched in 1998, must be supplied with construction payloads, products for its inhabitants, and fresh personnel from time to time. While moving a shipment from Shanghai to Los Angeles can be challenging, imagine the challenges in attempting to supply and re-supply a site located approximately 250 miles above Earth and traveling more than 17,500 miles per hour![6]

Another important issue associated with space transport and exploration involves the management of "space junk," or "orbital debris," or objects such as discarded parts of space vehicles, space vehicles at the end of their useful lives, and paint fragments from orbiting satellites, among others.[7] There is concern that this space junk presents safety risks to other objects in space; in some cases, the space junk can pose safety risks to Earth as well. Indeed, some experts have suggested that an agency needs to be created with primary responsibility for managing space junk.[8]

The Internet

When the first edition of this book appeared in the mid-1990s, the Internet was virtually unknown—an interesting tool used primarily by academicians. Since

---

[4]R.Y.K. Chan, Environmental Attitudes and Behavior of Consumers in China: Survey Findings and Implications. *Journal of International Consumer Marketing*, Vol. 11 No. 4, 1999, pp. 25–52.

[5]H-J Wu and S.C. Dunn, Environmentally Responsible Logistics Systems. *International Journal of Physical Distribution and Logistics Management*, Vol. 25 No. 2, 1995, pp. 20–38.

[6]D.S. Goldin, Human Quest: The International Space Station and Mars Exploration. *Harvard International Review*, Vol. 25 No. 2, 1999, pp. 26–28.

[7]F. Espirito, Space Junk Danger. *Reactions*, Vol. 17 No. 6, 1997, p. 11.

[8]J.R. Asker, Space Traffic Management. *Aviation Week & Space Technology*, Vol. 154 No. 14, p. 31.

that time, Internet usage by organizations and consumers has exploded. While Internet connectivity and usage has been highest among Western industrialized nations, connectivity and usage in other parts of the world can be expected to grow during the early years of the 21st century.

From a supply chain perspective, the Internet offers potential opportunities for companies to reduce their supply chain costs *and* improve customer service. While these opportunities span most, if not all, logistics activities, the opportunities that have received the most attention to date include procurement, transportation scheduling, vehicle tracking, and customer service.[9] Of particular interest to international logistics is the possible impact of the Internet in terms of *disintermediation* (the removal of intermediaries from distribution channels) and *reintermediation* (the addition of intermediaries to distribution channels).

Summary

This chapter has discussed some of the key issues that are likely to influence international logistics and international supply chains during the first part of the 21st century. There is little question these, and other, issues offer both opportunities and challenges to contemporary logisticians.

End-of-Chapter Questions

1. Which of the future issues discussed in this chapter do you believe is most important for international logistics? Why?

2. What are world-class logistics practices?

3. How might multi-country trade alliances influence logistics strategies and tactics?

4. What is the one-stop shopping concept?

5. Discuss the concept of amodalism.

6. Choose one logistics activity (for example, transportation) and discuss possible environmentally responsible logistics practices associated with this activity.

7. During 2001, a U.S. civilian paid a substantial fee (in the millions of dollars) to the Russian government in order to be able to travel with a Russian space crew for about one week. What are some potential risks associated with allowing civilians to travel in space?

---

[9]R.A. Lancioni, M.F. Smith, and T.A. Oliva, The Role of the Internet in Supply Chain Management. *Industrial Marketing Management,* Vol. 29, 2000, pp. 45–56.

8. What is the biggest advantage (disadvantage) that the Internet offers international logistics? Support your answer.

CASE • *Global Trust Company*

Betsy Bertram had worked in the commercial loan office of the Farmers and Merchants' Bank in Chicago, which recently had become part of an international banking conglomerate headquartered in Amsterdam. She supervised the section that handled loans to carriers, firms that were involved in supply chain activities, and to manufacturers of transportation equipment. Her new boss had just been transferred in from the bank's computer department, and she asked Betsy to help her understand some of the issues the bank might confront when evaluating loan applications.

Questions for *Global Trust Company*

1. If a potential investor in a large dry bulk carrier that would be chartered out to various users over the next 20 years were trying to determine the size of the vessel, what factors should be considered? Discuss.

2. In the late 1990s, there was great interest in the FastShip that would cut the transit time between the U.S. East Coast and Western Europe from 14 to 7 days because of less time in port and at sea. How would one determine the potential market for containerized cargo that would use this faster service? Discuss.

3. There is a "green" political movement throughout much of the world that is interested in preserving and/or improving our environment. What sorts of impacts might the greens have on the operation of global supply chains? How, if at all, should this impact upon investors? Discuss.

4. Should the bank be considering investing in Eastern Europe's transportation and communication infrastructure? Why or why not?

5. What impacts, if any, will the growth in the Internet have on the design and operation of supply chains throughout the world? Why should this be of interest to investors?

6. Should the bank be considering loans to companies that want to engage in space transportation or exploration? Why or why not?